THE TRANSITION FROM PRELINGUISTIC TO LINGUISTIC COMMUNICATION

List of Contributors

LOIS BLOOM
Developmental Psychology
Teachers College
Columbia University
New York, NY 10027

SUSAN R. BRAUNWALD
Department of Psychology
California State University, Northridge
1811 Nordhoff Street
Northridge, CA 91330

JEROME BRUNER
Department of Psychology
New School for Social Research
65 Fifth Avenue
New York, NY 10003

ROBIN S. CHAPMAN
Department of Communicative Disorders
University of Wisconsin
Madison, WI 53706

JOHN DORE
Department of English
Baruch College and Graduate Center
City University of New York
42nd Street
New York, NY 10036

CATHERINE GARVEY
Department of Psychology
Johns Hopkins University
Baltimore, MD 21218

ROCHEL GELMAN
Department of Psychology
Faculty of Arts and Sciences
University of Pennsylvania
3815 Walnut Street
Philadelphia, PA 19104

BETTY J. GILBREATH
Graduate School of Education
Roy Larsen Hall
Harvard University
Laboratory of Human Development
Cambridge, MA 02138

ROBERTA MICHNICK GOLINKOFF
Department of Educational Studies
University of Delaware
Newark, DE 19711

LAURA GORDON
Department of Educational Studies
University of Delaware
Newark, DE 19711

CAROL GIBB HARDING
Department of Foundations of Education
Loyola University
Lewis Towers
820 N. Michigan Avenue
Room 811
Chicago, IL 60611

JUDITH R. JOHNSTON
Department of Speech and Hearing Sciences
Indiana University
Bloomington, IN 47402

PHYLLIS LEVENSTEIN
Verbal Interaction Project, Inc.
Adelphi University
Executive Office
3268 Island Road
Wantagh, NY 11793

DAVID J. MESSER
Department of Psychology
The Hatfield Polytechnic
College Lane
Hatfield, Herts AL10 9AB
England

JON F. MILLER
Waisman Center on Mental Retardation
  and Human Development
University of Wisconsin
Madison, WI 53706

ELINOR OCHS
Department of Linguistics
University of Southern California
Los Angeles, CA 90007

BAMBI B. SCHEIFFELIN
Graduate School of Education
Education, Society and Culture Program
University of Pennsylvania
Philadelphia, PA 19104

MARILYN SHATZ
Department of Psychology
Human Performance Center
University of Michigan
Ann Arbor, MI 48104

CATHERINE E. SNOW
Graduate School of Education
Roy Larsen Hall
Laboratory of Human Development
Harvard University
Cambridge, MA 02138

SUSAN SUGARMAN
Department of Psychology
Princeton University
Princeton, NJ 08544

THE TRANSITION FROM PRELINGUISTIC TO LINGUISTIC COMMUNICATION

Edited by
Roberta Michnick Golinkoff
University of Delaware

LEA
LAWRENCE ERLBAUM ASSOCIATES, PUBLISHERS
1983   Hillsdale, New Jersey   London

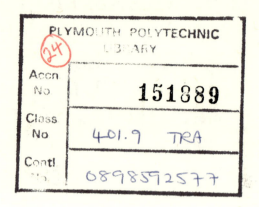
Lawrence Erlbaum Associates, Inc., Publishers
365 Broadway
Hillsdale, New Jersey 07642

Library of Congress Cataloging in Publication Data
Main entry under title:

The Transition from prelinguistic to linguistic communication.

  "Proceedings of the sixth in a series of annual
College of Education symposia at the University of
Delaware"—Foreword.
  Bibliography: p.
  Includes index.
  1. Language acquisition—Congresses. 2. Nonverbal
communication in children—Congresses. I. Golinkoff,
Roberta M. II. University of Delaware. College of
Education.
P118.T7 1983   401'.9   83-5494
ISBN 0-89859-257-7

Printed in the United States of America
10 9 8 7 6 5 4 3 2 1

To Jordan Seth and Allison Ruth,
delightful sources of fatigue and
inspiration.

Contents

Foreword

This volume is the proceedings of the sixth in a series of annual College of Education symposia at the University of Delaware. The first was devoted to the "contributions of learning theory to educational practice," a very slim proceedings when all was said and done in which we concluded, I think, that if a difference didn't make a difference, it didn't make any difference. In other years, we examined the cognitive prerequisites for reading, school desegregation in Delaware, some new models of measurement and evaluation, and ethnographic methods in educational research.

The sixth symposium was focused upon how preverbal communication is functionally related to the initial acquisition of language, not so much because anyone really has much trouble acquiring language, but because these links between preverbal communication and verbal communication may be prototypical of all developmental links. They may, consequently, provide clues for our understanding of other developmental precursors and links across the lifespan, particularly those that figure in the acquisition of school-related knowledge and especially those that can be manipulated in the service of subject matter sophistication.

We are, after all, dealing with the most troublesome theoretical issue in developmental psychology and education—the issue of emergence—the emergence or spontaneous appearance of what seem to be new behaviors, qualitatively distinct from their predecessors, not reducible to them, so that the new event, in this case speech, is somehow greater than the sum or product of its preceding constituent parts.

The issue and inevitable problems of the symposium are crystallized in Piaget's account of the transition from the fifth to the sixth substage in the sensorimotor period in which, according to him, the ability to imitate events no longer present is taken as the developmental cause of representation, upon which language undoubtedly depends; but it has always seemed equally plausible that it is the other way around, that is, delayed imitation is conditioned and dependent upon some representational competence.

In a larger context, the careful delineation of the transition from prelinguistic to linguistic communication may illuminate how the *act* of communication, whether preverbal or otherwise, contributes to the formation of a human mind. This is, in a sense, a re-examination of Aristotle's assertion that man *qua* man was *by nature* a political animal. The question is whether the pure or complete hermit, who communicated with no one, would have so violated his nature that he would have a mind qualitatively distinct from the rest of us.

Our own research has led us to examine the cognitive benefits which accrue from the act of teaching, not to the pupil but to the teacher. We have been struck by the cognitive reorganizations, even in young children, when they attempt to communicate or teach someone something. We have seen that information embedded in a social interaction setting, which demands communication, promotes cognitive growth to a greater extent than the very same information presented in other ways. This growth may occur even when children are presented with incorrect information provided it occurs in a social interaction format. In this latter case, we had two children, both nonconservers and wrong in their solutions to conservation tasks but for different reasons, confront one another with the remarkable outcome that significant numbers of them adopted conservation solutions to the tasks thereafter (Ames & Murray, 1982). What was there about the communication, even with faulty data, which promoted cognitive development? The role of our acts of communication in the formation of our minds is a question just beneath the surface in the succeeding chapters of this volume.

At the same time, there is the caution that preverbal communication need not have any functional or interesting link to verbal communication. Is there, at present, any more reason to suppose a connection between preverbal and verbal communication than there is to suppose a connection, which is known to be nonexistent, between babbling, which looks so much like speech, and language? This question, too, underlies the following chapters in which plausible speculations, some more so than others, are made about the preverbal-verbal communication connection. Although events like babbling may have no interesting connection to speech and communication, it is clear that other not-so-well specified preverbal events are functionally connected linguistic communication. We know, for example, that language aberrations occur in children who are abused and isolated during the preverbal stages of development.

Finally, apart from the fact mentioned at the outset, that the preverbal-verbal transition in communication may be prototypical of other developmental transitions, there is the possibility that the close scrutiny of the transition may illumi-

nate our understanding of those tragic instances where communication competence fails to develop altogether.

Frank B. Murray
Dean, College of Education
University of Delaware

REFERENCE

Ames, G. J., & Murray, F. B. When two wrongs make a right: Promoting cognitive change by social
conflict. *Developmental Psychology,* 1982, *18,* 894–897.

Preface

Much research in the area of language acquisition, as in most areas of developmental psychology, begins with cross-sectional descriptions of phenomena. Be it metamemory, conservation, or the use of plural forms, the phenomenon and its apparent developmental course is charted and a complex of related skills is identified through correlations with performance on other tasks. At this point, developmental researchers begin to ask about transitions. Although the first round of research established that skill levels A, B, and C of the phenomenon exist, subsequent research focuses on how the child moves from A to B and then to C. In other words, developmental psychologists begin to ask "how" questions? How is it that B emerged from A? What processes mediate such transitions? How do various environments facilitate or impede the appearance of B? "How" questions are obviously among the more difficult ones to answer because they focus on dynamic interpretations of *developmental change* and not on "snapshot" descriptions of some capability at different points in time. Developmental change cannot be directly observed but only inferred when the child reveals new competencies.

The last 20 years, the Chomskyan era, has witnessed tremendous growth in the study of the phenomenon of early language production and comprehension (see Golinkoff & Gordon, this volume). Subsequently researchers turned to the prelanguage period of the first year of life, probing the communicative precursors of language acquisition. What is missing in the literature is a focus on *how* the child moves from prelanguage communication to language. How are prelinguistic gestural and vocal means of communication gradually transformed into linguistic means of communication? How do species-specific capabilities interact with the environment to assist the child in making this critical shift? Transition questions such as these are what motivated this volume.

The chapters of this volume were originally prepared for a conference funded by and held at the University of Delaware on September 11 and 12, 1981. At that time in the field of language acquisition many assertions were put forward about how communication development in the first year of life was sufficient to explain subsequent language development. One of the express purposes of this conference was to force a critical re-appraisal of the relationship between early communication development and language development (see Golinkoff & Gordon).

Contributors to this volume were asked to consider a common set of questions: First, what constitutes communication in the prelinguistic child? What features does this account share with communication in a child who has language? Second, how, if at all, does our recently obtained knowledge about the course of preverbal communication illuminate our understanding of the acquisition of language? For example, to what extent are social-interactional achievements of the preverbal period important in accounting for language acquisition? Third, is the development of language a continuous or discontinuous process with prior nonverbal communication development? Fourth, what theoretical accounts of this transition period are plausible? Fifth, are there ways in which the nonverbal communicative relationship between caregivers and infants in the transition period supports the infant's linguistic development? That is, beyond the use of the special language register addressed to children and often referred to as "motherese," do caregivers use other behaviors (verbal and nonverbal) that assist the child in passing through the transition period? Sixth, how are changes in the child's cognitive, social, and affective capabilities during this transition period related to the development of language and linguistic communication? What assumptions about these capabilities are implicit in the various theoretical accounts of the transition period? Seventh, are there individual differences in how infants make the transition and in what these differences relate to? Are there cultural differences in the environment's handling of the transition period and how do such differences speak to the factors that are necessary and sufficient for a successful outcome to the transition period? Eighth, depending upon the view held of the importance of the transition period and the nature of the implied mechanisms, what are the implications for policy and early intervention? And ninth, will the transition period be useful for understanding phenomena such as delayed language?

These questions also served the function of ensuring a common core of concerns for presentations and discussions at the conference. Treatment of the questions appears in all four sections of this book. Another way in which I attempted to ensure a common framework was by opening the conference with a presentation of a brief historical overview of the field of language acquisition and the way in which the conference logically followed in that progression. Using a metaphorical parallel to the Bible's seven days of creation, an extended version of that history (written with Laura Gordon) is the first chapter of this book.

Keynote addresses at the original conference were delivered by Jerome Bruner and Marilyn Shatz. These became the second and third chapters, respectively. In his paper, Bruner moves away from his earlier view that prelinguistic social interaction is constitutive of the acquisition of linguistic forms. Instead, Bruner develops the position that the adult's "framing" of the interactions between adult and child leads to construction of "formats" by the dyad. These formats provide the routinized substrate into which language is first introduced by the child. Shatz' paper questions the importance many researchers in the field of language acquisition have recently given to prelinguistic social interaction and whether continuities between prelanguage and language behaviors are more apparent than real. She further questions the notion that language acquisition represents the culmination of advances in communicative understandings because she claims that even the preschooler has much social-cognitive knowledge yet to acquire.

The third chapter in this first section is my own, in which I make the case for studying the elaboration and refinement of the child's communicative skills during the transition period by focusing on a phenomenon referred to as the "negotiation of failed messages." When the transition-age child fails to get her meaning across, we are allowed a glimpse of the communicative capabilities she has available as she pursues her goals interactively.

Lois Bloom's discussion of these 3 chapters highlights and critiques a number of the theoretical assumptions that characterize the field and to some extent the papers by Bruner and myself. For example, she considers the issue of the continuity between prelinguistic and linguistic communication development in a historical and biological light, pointing out the parallels with the classic developmental issue of nature versus nurture.

The second section of the volume contains a chapter by Carol Harding, and one by Bambi Schieffelin and Elinor Ochs with a discussion by Susan Sugarman. Harding presents a review of what is known about communication development in the first year of life along with some new longitudinal data on the development of intentional communication. The new data focus on the interplay between the mother's evaluation of her infant's communicative skills, mother–infant communicative interaction, and cognitive development in determining the child's ability to use preverbal signals intentionally to attain material ends. Although, as Harding points out, we do not know whether such prelinguistic achievements are either necessary or sufficient for the transition to language, her evidence indicates that mothers' beliefs and responses to their children's communicative efforts may facilitate communicative development. Schieffelin and Ochs question the universality of our descriptions of early communication development in that these achievements may differ by culture. They point out that the assumptions Western researchers make about mother–infant communicative interaction at the beginning of the first year of life and in the transition period may be ethnocentrically embedded in their own cultural frame. In non-Western cultures, early communicative interactions between mother and infant may lack many of the affective and interpretive properties found in Western societies. Schieffelin and Ochs' chapter suggests a re-examination of the nature of environmental supports for communication and language development. Sugarman's discussion of this section has relevance not only to these particular papers but to the field as a whole. Sugarman takes on the issues of continuity versus discontinuity, the role of preverbal communication development for language development, and the causal implications for language development of differing cross-cultural practices.

The next section of the volume considers the role of the relationship between caregiver and infant in promoting language development during the transition period. While Dore develops a much neglected affective perspective on this issue, Messer treats the relationship between properties of caregiver speech and nonverbal behavior. Dore is concerned with what might be called the "why" question of language development, viz, why does the child go on to acquire the forms of language? He locates the answer in the "immediate context of the affective conflict" which takes place between infant and caregiver as they "maintain and negotiate their relationship through dialogue." With his emphasis on resolution of conflict, his chapter resembles my own. However, his emphasis on the affective base for intentionality and reference is unique.

Messer is concerned with reference too, but from the perspective of how nonverbal information supplied by adults helps children understand the relationship between words and objects. He reviews many empirical studies, including his own work, which reveal the way in which social interaction in the transition period may facilitate the acquisition of words. For example, several studies report that mothers are more likely to refer to objects they or their children are holding than objects previously manipulated. Garvey's discussion makes the point that more attention should be paid to the paralinguistic features of communication such as gesture, prosody and stress and the way in which such features are used to indicate to the child that a "naming game" is occurring. These paralinguistic features are also certainly implicated in Dore's affective account of the transition period.

The last section of the volume focuses on children who fail to make an optimal transition to language for either environmental or biological reasons. Braunwald's chapter describes abused and neglected toddlers and considers whether the form, content and use of language are differentially sensitive to environmental variation. She develops a case for the necessity of an experiential framework reminiscent of Bruner's formats for the transition into language. Chapman and Miller's chapter deals with children who apparently have the rudiments of this experiential matrix but still fail to move readily into linguistic communication. Chapman and Miller discuss how descriptions of the process of language acquisition in normal children can provide strategies for intervention in the transition period for certain types of language disorder. Levenstein's chapter is about her 12–year–old home based program designed to promote the development of verbal skills in populations of low socio-economic status children. Levenstein's current goal is to see if the enriched verbal interactions of the program-trained mothers with their children facilitates school performance some years later. Johnston's discussion of this section contains a number of caveats about the role of the environment in causing language problems. She consludes that the social context in combination with biological variables must continue to enter into our explanations of disorder or delay.

Gelman and Snow and Gilbreath close the volume by commenting on it as a whole. Their charge was to integrate the chapters and highlight recurring themes. Gelman's remarks remind us of the enormous complexity of the language acquisition process. Assumptions made by researchers about the link between prelinguistic communication and linguistic communication may indeed have been too simple in the recent past. Snow and Gilbreath observe that the chapters may overemphasize social-interactive explanations for language development. They, in turn, address the importance of cognitive factors and argue that a balance be struck between these poles. The reader may wish to read their paper before reading the volume because it explicates many recurring threads in the book.

The support staff who attended to the details surrounding the conference made it possible for the participants and the people in the audience to concentrate on these threads. Specifically, Laura Gordon is to be commended for her heroic performance as my administrative assistant and for her preparation of the subject index. In addition, I wish to thank the following graduate students for giving so freely of their time and effort to the conference: Roberta Murphy, Timothy Smith, James Frey, Helen Gauntt, Deborah Smith, Kathleen Cauley, and Martha Boston.

Another group of individuals contributed their time to improve the written versions of the original presentations. Most of the major chapters in this volume have profited from one or more anonymous critiques, in addition to my own critique. For having assisted in this way I wish to thank Roger Bakeman, Lois Bloom, Courtney Cazden, Celia Genishi, Kathryn Hirsh-Pasek, Leslie Rescorla, Marilyn Shatz, and Catherine Snow. In addition, Bambi Schieffelin of the University of Pennsylvania, where this conference was conceived while I was on my sabbatical in the Department of Psychology, provided me with much intellectual support throughout the initial stages.

Lastly, Frank B. Murray, Dean of the College of Education at the University of Delaware, provided the funds to conduct this conference. His unflagging support of my research efforts during my tenure at the University of Delaware is greatly appreciated.

To conclude, this volume is concerned with an examination of the transition between prelinguistic and linguistic communication development. However, as with all scientific phenomena, the prospect of this transition seems formidable only to researchers and theoreticians; the great majority of children intrepidly cross the bridge in a matter of months, not waiting (fortunately) for our explanations and descriptions. Their practical success notwithstanding, more rigorous understanding of events during this period is important for explaining the transition into language.

Roberta Michnick Golinkoff
Departments of Educational Studies
and Psychology
University of Delaware

THE TRANSITION FROM PRELINGUISTIC TO LINGUISTIC COMMUNICATION

1 In the Beginning Was the Word: A History of the Study of Language Acquisition

Roberta Michnick Golinkoff
Laura Gordon
University of Delaware

The study of language acquisition has grown disproportionately as compared to other areas of developmental psychology within the last 10 years. Research has proliferated because language acquisition has become incorporated into many different areas within a range of disciplines, sometimes to the point of submerging key issues. A primary goal of this volume is to retrieve language acquisition from these scattered directions and to reflect on the broadening of its concerns.

The purpose of this introductory chapter is to give an account of the expansion and diversity characterizing current research and to evaluate whether the broadened focus of recent years has added anything substantial to our understanding of language acquisition. To accomplish this goal we provide a brief, non-exhaustive historical overview of how the field of language acquisition has evolved in the past 20 years. This leads to a critique of issues that have been either presupposed or ignored, such as the importance of the transition period from pre-linguistic to linguistic communication. We conclude by pointing out future directions that appear promising with respect to critical issues in language acquisition.

Our historical account borrows a novel form; we present a "creation science" view of language acquisition, designed to parallel the seven days of creation. On each day of creation, the theoretical focus of language acquisition changed and as a by-product, the nature of the linguistic (or nonlinguistic) unit considered worthy and appropriate for study also changed. Just as the seven days in the creation of the world, seen metaphorically, encompass events by telescoping them, the field of language acquisition may be understood by segmenting into separate periods the scholarly progression of ideas in the past 20 years.

The First and Second Days of Creation: The Revelation of Generative Transformational Grammar

On the *first day* the deity created Chomsky. On the *second day* Chomsky—without the deity's help—created generative transformational grammar. This event occurred in 1958 with the publication of *Syntactic Structures,* Chomsky's dissertation, which caused a revolution in the field of linguistics (Searle, 1972). Certainly Chomsky did not create the field of child language, any more than Crick and Watson created the field of molecular genetics when they unraveled the genetic code. However, just as Crick and Watson's work reoriented the research of a generation of geneticists, Chomsky's work renewed and invigorated the field of language acquisition. What Chomsky did was to postulate a biologically programmed, species-specific universal model of language that others used as their theoretical base to explain the regularities which seemed to appear in child language. Chomsky's beliefs gained additional power with the publication of Lenneberg's (1967) influential volume which argued for the universality of the order and timing of acquisition across radically different languages, as well as mastery of language essentials among all children regardless of intelligence.

In reviewing the biological bases and evolutionary evidence for language as a species-specific signal system, Lenneberg (1967) began by writing that "reason, discovery, and intelligence are concepts that are as irrelevant for an explanation of the existence of language as for the existence of bird songs or the dance of the bees [p. 1]." Research by Marler (see Marler, Dooling, & Zoloth, 1980, for a review) on how birds learned their song did in fact seem to support this assertion. Marler found that if two types of sparrows are kept in isolation where they can hear no bird song during a critical period of exposure to song between 20 and 50 days of age, they will sing an abnormal, garbled song when they reach maturity. However, if isolated sparrows hear artificially combined elements of bird songs, parts of which do and parts of which do not match their species' song, they will sing a version of their species song when they reach maturity, approximately 300 days after their exposure to the artificial song. This finding suggests the existence of a template for the species song which is activated only under exposure to song—even unnatural, artificially constructed song. Parallels with human language acquisition are tempting to construct; Lenneberg (1967) argued strongly for a critical period of exposure to language, for its species-specificity and for its appearance among virtually all members of the species exposed to language. In other words, the idea that the capacity for language was prewired into the human brain, destined to emerge as the organism matured biologically, seemed to support Chomsky's views and was Lenneberg's contribution to the study of language acquisition.

As a farewell to behaviorist accounts of language acquisition, Lenneberg's book also opened up the possibility of an interdisciplinary approach to language study which could incorporate not only psychology and linguistics, but neurobiology and language pathology as well. "Language" was not equivalent to "speech" since it resided in the unique capacities of the human brain; disruption of speech could still permit language.

The theoretical weight and apparent empirical evidence behind Lenneberg's arguments combined with the paucity of methods available to investigate what Chomsky had called "competence" and "deep structure" often led psychologists to presuppose innateness as a solution to the problem of language acquisition. Although many researchers had interpreted statements by Chomsky (1965) as a blanket endorsement of a radically innatist position, Chomsky had in fact said, "any [evaluation] proposal . . . is an empirical hypothesis about the nature of language . . . we are very far from being able to present a system of formal and substantive linguistic universals that will be sufficiently rich and detailed to account for the facts of language learning [p. 46]." (See Piatelli–Palmerini (1980) for a recent formulation of Chomsky's position on language acquisition.)

The Third Day: Language Acquisition as the Acquisition of Syntax

On the *third day* Miller (1962) appeared and brought down to the psychologists tablets on which were inscribed the highlights of generative grammar. For lack of good theory psychologists had for the most part relegated the study of language and language acquisition to a minor position within their science. Here was Miller interpreting a rich, though elusive, theory to guide psychologists in their inquiry. At the same time, Braine (1963) claimed that children possessed a puerile version of the adult language model which he called "pivot-open grammar." Brown and Bellugi (1964), Miller and Ervin (1964), and McNeill (1966) all posited some version of a grammar in an attempt to account for children's 2– and 3–word utterances. As Fig. 1.1 indicates, at this time language acquisition was synonymous with the acquisition of syntax. The unit of analysis was at minimum the 2–word combination, since the study of syntax presumably could not begin before its appearance.

Although it is easy in retrospect to criticize developments on the third day of creation, that is, why an exclusively syntactic approach failed for both adult sentence comprehension (see Fodor, Bever, & Garrett, 1974) and children's early production (see Brown, 1973), developments on the third day should be seen in the context of the prevailing Zeitgeist. Many psychologists were not ready to abandon behaviorist accounts of cognitive processes, including language. That children under 2-years-of-age had themselves either induced or were endowed with grammatical rules and mysterious "deep structures" seemed to be heretical assertions. Thus, although the exclusively syntactic approach discussed earlier was eventually abandoned, these new ideas on language, in combination with other developments in what was not yet called "cognitive" psychology, were to change the landscape of the science of psychology.

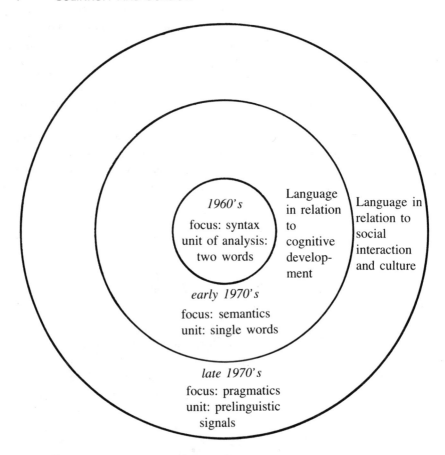

Fig. 1.1.   Concentric circles represent the ever-widening view of language acquisition seen from an historical perspective.

The Fourth Day: The Reincorporation of Semantics into Child Language

On the *fourth day* (see the next larger circle in Fig. 1.1) Bloom (1970), Kernan (1970), Schlesinger (1971), and Slobin (1969) incorporated semantics into the study of language acquisition. Now not only the form but the *content* of children's earliest utterances was scrutinized. Developments in psycholinguistics and linguistics moved independently in this direction as well. For example, the "derivational complexity" issue (Fodor, Bever, & Garrett, 1974), which first appeared on the third day, was sacrificed on the altar of semantics. That is, the notion that the difficulty of comprehending a sentence should be linearly related to the number of transformations that the sentence contained was not true; sentence meanings could override the number of transformations, making some derivationally complex sentences easier to comprehend than some derivationally simpler sentences. In addition, theoretical linguists such as Chafe (1970) and Fillmore (1968), while basically accepting Chomsky's transformational view, seriously questioned whether deep structure contained more world knowledge than Chomsky seemed to grant in his 1965 version or indeed whether the notion of a deep structure was needed at all (McCawley, 1968).

The assertion that children possessed more knowledge of the world than their limited surface structures expressed caused researchers to expand their interpretation of 2– and 3–word utterances, and finally to examine single-word utterances (Greenfield & Smith, 1976) using the method of "rich interpretation." As Bloom (1970) and others astutely noted, the very same surface structure (e.g., the now famous "Mommy sock") could mean completely different things depending on the context in which it was uttered. What was so appealing about this account for many psychologists was that the study of the tacit, often inchoate knowledge of the world encoded by language was just what many psychologists (although not many linguists) called their life's work. Psychologists strongly believed in the power of context and task for determining perception, e.g., the perception of ambiguous figures; memory, e.g., intentional versus incidental learning; and reasoning, e.g., functional fixedness. Why shouldn't young children rely on context to convey meanings which their undeveloped linguistic skills prevented them from completely communicating?

Now children's early verbal productions were taken to reflect considerable world knowledge. Using this argument, early productions could be profitably studied even before two words appeared, since the concepts underlying these early utterances were an outcome of sensorimotor achievements such as object permanence and causal inference. Specifically, children's ability to encode case role concepts which specified such things as who did the action (the agent), who received the action (the patient), and where the action took place (location), received some support from perceptual research (see Golinkoff, 1981a, for a review) as well as from the broad outlines of Piaget's theory.

Instead of Chomsky's (1980) "Cartesian theory of mind" in which the infant's mind is compared to "a function that maps experience onto a steady state [p. 109]", Piaget's constructivist account stressed the infant's activity in selecting from experience and constructing first, conceptual, and then linguistic structures. Piaget (1951) proposed to incorporate language into the semiotic function which included symbolic play, deferred imitation and mental imagery. Thus, the cognitive hypothesis placed language acquisition in a general developmental framework that provided an alternative to earlier innatist views.

While the field turned away from linguistic nativism in that linguistic universals became cognitive universals, e.g., McNeill (1970), Slobin (1973), the linguistic environment available to the child was still seen only as providing information about the child's specific language community. The prevailing view of the child was as an hypothesis tester (Fodor, 1966) and solitary constructor of a language which mapped onto preexisting concepts. The acquisition of syntax was reduced for some to the acquisition of linguistic devices to map onto world knowledge.

Thus, on Day 4 the child's cognitive resources seemed sufficient to account for the acquisition of both the semantic underpinnings and the syntactic structures of language. Disenchantment with this position occurred when cognitive structures were not invariably found to precede linguistic structures or even to be closely linked (e.g., Beilin, 1975; Corrigan, 1979).

The Fifth Day: The Social-Functional Approach to Language Acquisition

On the *fifth day,* "pragmatics," or the "functions of signs in context" (Morris, 1946), represented by another circle in Fig. 1.1, caused language acquisition to be thought of as embedded in a social and cultural context. Children didn't just learn *language,* mysterious as that task alone might be, they learned a social system and how language functioned within it. For example, they learned forms of address, ways of asking, and other sociolinguistic rules that varied by culture and that defined a competent speaker in that culture. At that time Bruner (1974) wrote:

> Neither the syntactic nor the semantic approach to language acquisition take sufficiently into account what the child is trying to do by communicating. As linguistic philosophers remind us, utterances are used for different ends and use is a powerful determinant of rule structures . . . one cannot understand the transition from pre-linguistic to linguistic communication without taking into account the uses of communication as speech acts [p. 282].

Ervin–Tripp and Mitchell–Kernan (1977) also speculated that without attending to the *functions* language served for the young child, we could not account for the acquisition of the *forms* of language.

Thus, on the *fifth day* formal analyses of the information available in the linguistic signal seemed incomplete, and the acquisition of "communicative competence" (Hymes, 1971) was sometimes used synonymously with "language acquisition" (see Berko–Gleason & Weintraub [1978] for a further discussion of this development). Knowing *how* to say something; that is, knowing how to employ the formal linguistic system was important but equally important was knowing *what* to say and knowing *when, where,* and to *whom* to say it. Theoretical linguists such as Austin (1962) and Searle (1969) brought researchers up short with their observations that precise analyses of the abstract form and content of a sentence could never be sufficient for knowing what that sentence actually meant in ordinary discourse. For example, "I love your tie" could mean

"I hate it," if said sarcastically, and "Gee, it's hot in here," uttered by a college president could make untenured faculty rush to open windows as if by royal command. In other words, the illocutionary force or intent of an utterance could contrast with the utterance's locutionary or propositional content. Psycholinguistic research by Clark and Lucy (1975), Jarvella (1974), Schweller, Brewer, and Dahl (1976), and others supported the view that adult speakers do, in fact, make inferences about illocutionary forces and perlocutionary effects from linguistic signals whose literal meanings contrast sharply with their conveyed meanings. Subsequent research using both experimental and naturalistic data indicates that even young children seem to have sophisticated knowledge of the shades of meaning possible in a speech act (see Shatz, in press, for a review).

If language acquisition was motivated by function one could look for the prelinguistic counterparts of such functions. Thus, the unit of analysis shrank even further on this day, moving from 2– and 3–word utterances (Day 3), to single-word utterances (Day 4), to preverbal signals used for intentional communicative ends (Day 5). Language acquisition was now seen by some researchers as the inevitable by-product of 18 or so months of social and communicative interaction where much shared meaning had been constructed between the infant and its caregivers. Schaffer (1977) wrote:

> Conceived initially as a beneath-the-skin system, as a set of behavioral patterns explicable purely in terms of the psychological organization of the individual, it [language] has increasingly been recognized as in fact deriving its significance primarily from its communicative function and is in need consequently of dyadic settings . . . Instead of seeing language arising *de novo* at the beginning of the second year, it is now being related to the preverbal communication patterns that are already established between mother and infant in the early months of life. Language acquisition in other words, has been firmly placed within a social setting [p. 4].

Research on the origins and growth of communication in the first year of life began to appear. Often using terms borrowed from linguistics, researchers began tracing the development of the child's communicative competence. For example, experimenters examined the infant's ability to preverbally establish reference (Bruner, 1974; Bates, Camaioni, & Volterra, 1975), to signal their intentions through illocutionary vocalizations (Harding & Golinkoff, 1979), to engage in turn-taking in protodialogues or protoconversations (Stern, 1977; Bullowa, 1979), and to establish topic-comment structures in social interaction (Bruner, 1974). Such research, while providing much new and important information on the infant as a communicative being, had another unexpected consequence.

Increasingly, as researchers moved back earlier and earlier in the child's life in an attempt to bridge the transition from preverbal to verbal communication, the study of language merged into the study of communication. Bruner (1975) was the most radical and articulate proponent of this merging. He described how "joint action formats," originally initiated by the mother and then by the child during play, helped preverbal children to realize concepts such as agent, action, and object which were later directly translated into language.[1]

Aside from reducing the problem of language acquisition to a problem of understanding communicative social interactions between mother and infant, research on the functions expressed by the infant's preverbal communicative signals was plagued by an old problem: The rich interpretation of the infant's signals was done from the perspective of the adult researcher with little external evidence to support the researcher's fine categorical cuts (see Francis, 1979). For example, just as "Mommy sock" could mean a possessor-possessed relationship or an agent-object relationship (see Day 4), a preverbal vocalization could have either a "regulatory" or an "instrumental" function (Halliday, 1975) depending on context.[2]

Thus, the acquisition of language was seen as occurring in early dyadic social relationships. Given the importance of social interaction, the individuals interacting with the child might be expected to either facilitate or impede the child's language acquisition. Phillips (1973) was the first to falsify the oft-cited Chomsky dictum that the linguistic data available to the language-learning child was "defective," "degenerate," and full of slips of the tongue and grammatical errors. While this was not the only claim Chomsky made about the input language, psychologists chose to establish that parents do modify their speech when interacting with their children (see Snow & Ferguson, 1977). Moreover, children acquiring language seem to be exposed to adjusted speech no matter whom they interacted with: 4-year-olds (Shatz & Gelman, 1973); women without children (Snow, 1972); and fathers (Golinkoff & Ames, 1979).

Despite many studies on parental speech, three discordant notes have been sounded with regard to the impact of adjusted parental speech on the child's language acquisition. First, just documenting that adjusted parental speech is a fairly robust phenomenon, does not prove that it actually influences the child's acquisition of language. Shatz (1982) has referred to this logical error as an "existence proof." In addition, given that there are many possible grammars which can be induced from a limited corpus of utterances, without some "built-in" constraints on induction, it is not clear that the adjusted input language would lead the child to induce the right grammar (Gleitman & Wanner, 1982). Furthermore, results on the effects of parental speech adjustment on child language acquisition (Furrow, Nelson, & Benedict, 1979; Nelson, 1977; Newport, Gleitman, & Gleitman, 1977) have been mixed and controversial (see Snow & Ferguson, 1977).

[1]See Bruner (this volume) for a retraction of the position that concepts of action derived from non-linguistic routines are translated directly into language.

[2]A new phenomenon called the "negotiation of failed messages" (see Golinkoff, this volume) may help circumvent this problem since interpretation of the infant's meaning is done from the infant's perspective.

Bohannon and Hirsh-Pasek (1983) have further suggested that we may be pursuing the wrong model of the effects of parental adjustment. They argue that the field may have been presupposing an uncomplicated linear relationship between child competence and parental adjustment, whereas more sophisticated statistical models which do not presuppose linearity may be needed to evaluate the effects of parental speech. Little is known about which aspects of parental speech adjustment (isolated from the welter of other factors) have an effect on the child's language acquisition (if they do) and at what particular points in the child's language development.

The second discordant note in the parental speech adjustment literature has to do with claims of universality for a baby-talk register when addressing young children. Schieffelin and Ochs (this volume) and Ochs (1982) do not report any parental adjustment of the type reported in Western cultures among the Kaluli of Papua, New Guinea, and the Samoans of Samoa, respectively. If a baby-talk register on the part of parents proves not to be universal, "baby-talk" as presently defined, cannot be necessary for language acquisition. It is of course possible that parents are not the primary providers of the input language in these cultures; researchers must examine the extent to which peers and siblings in these cultures provide linguistic models of reduced complexity.

The third discordant note on the effects of parental speech adjustment comes from cases where linguistic input is unavailable to the young child. In these cases there is evidence that children's proclivity to symbolize their thoughts emerges under the worst of conditions. Linguistically-isolated deaf children (exposed neither to oral language nor to sign) seem to invent their own version of sign language called "home sign" by Feldman, Goldin-Meadow, and Gleitman (1978). Hearing children of deaf parents, who have had neither exposure to sign nor oral language (except television) may acquire the rudiments of linguistic expression, but achieve little conversational facility (Sachs, Bard, & Johnson, 1981).

In sum, on the fifth day the child's environment (both linguistic and social) came to the forefront in the study of language acquisition. The accomplishments of the fifth day will be evaluated on the seventh day, the day of judgment.

The Sixth Day: The Revival of Formal Approaches and Nativism

On the *sixth day* formal and nativistic approaches to language acquisition were revived, partly as a backlash to the myriad directions in which the field of language acquisition had gone. As Slobin (1981) put it, seven popular terms characterized attempts in the late 1960s and 1970s to enrich the field's purely structural approach to language acquisition, namely, "semantics, context, input, pragmatics, discourse, cognition, and strategies [p. 275]." He went on to write, "Although these terms obviously represent important variables, embedding language acquisition within developing processes of social, logical, and physical cognition, the original *linguistics issues of the acquisition of language* as a peculiarly structured system in its own right have often been obscured or even willfully abandoned [p. 275, our underlining].'' Thus, in the late 1970s there appeared a renewed interest in the acquisition of syntax per se and in the unspecified native endowments which may make language acquisition possible. These new developments were partly inspired by research in the field of artificial intelligence and in animal learning.

The field of artificial intelligence, and computational linguistics in particular, has provided new impetus to formal approaches to language and language acquisition. Attempts to simulate language acquisition on the computer have been useful because they force researchers to specify the conditions that an explanatorily-adequate theory must meet in order to account for language acquisition on the basis of limited exposure to linguistic data. Pinker (1979) lists six conditions that must be satisfied by an explanatorily-adequate theory of language acquisition: (1) learnability (the fact that languages can be learned, as children learn them, in the first place); (2) "equipotentiality" (the necessity for positing learning mechanisms that can apply to all natural languages); (3) the "time condition" (the theory must take account of the fact that children learn the rudiments of a language within their first three years; (4) the "input" condition (only input actually available to the child must figure into the theory); (5) the "developmental" condition (the theory must make the putative child go through the same stages of acquisition that the real child goes through; and (6) the "cognitive" condition (the theory must be realistic about cognitive abilities the child actually possesses). The satisfaction of all six of these conditions seems at the present time to be a Herculean task. Pinker (1979) reviews which of the above conditions are successfully addressed by various existing theories, concluding that Anderson's (1977) Language Acquisition System (LAS) and Wexler, Culicover, and Hamburger's (1975) Invariance, Binary, and Freezing Principles look most promising. As explanatorily adequate learning models, the LAS program seems to satisfy the cognitive, input, and time conditions, whereas the Wexler, Culicover, and Hamburger model meets the learnability and equipotentiality conditions.

It has been demonstrated that there are a tremendous number of linguistic rules which could be induced from a limited corpus (Gold, 1967, in Pinker, 1979). Therefore, it appears that unless the computer can be given *a priori* constraints to guide its induction of grammatical rules, learning a language requires more than a human lifetime. Just selecting the right set of rules would require much time since incoming linguistic data must be tested against each successive model which the processor constructs. In reality, only certain categories of rules actually are induced by children. Thus, the processor (be it the computer or the child) must have some built-in predilection to construct certain rules over others.

Such predilections or constraints on learning are also present, Keil (1981) suggests, in the domains of ontological knowledge, number concepts and deductive reasoning. A belief in constraints on learning in humans bears comparison to the new nativism in animal learning (see Seligman & Hager, 1972; Hinde & Stevenson-Hinde, 1973). Learning theorists have documented many cases of learning—or failure to learn—which cannot be explained by traditional learning theories. One example is the Garcia effect in which food-aversion learning occurs after a single food and illness pairing mediated by a long delay. It appears that different species do not associate events in arbitrary ways; rather, they come prepared to acquire certain linkages over others. As Bolles (1975) writes, "if a particular animal can learn a particular thing it is because it is *genetically endowed to do so* [p. 176, our underlining]."

Human beings, whether normal, retarded, or deaf, may be endowed in some way to learn language. Neo-nativist accounts differ, however, from the nativism of the 1960s. While earlier the linguistic structures themselves were given (e.g., McNeill, 1966), now constraints which guide the learner's *search* for the structures are given (e.g., see Wexler, 1978).

Some neo-nativists also continue to endorse the notion of a critical period for language learning. There have been a number of "natural experiments" which take the opportunity to study children after they have been in prolonged social isolation. Genie's case (a child who was locked in a bedroom and not spoken to for her first 13 years) (Curtiss, 1977) suggests that first language learning is even possible after puberty. However, in some ways Genie's speech never developed beyond the basics. It is tempting to draw an analogy between the inadequacies of Genie's speech and the sparrow's "abnormal garbled" song (discussed earlier) when it has not been exposed to its species song during the sparrow's critical period of exposure (Marler, 1980). Exposure to language prior to puberty may be necessary for the appearance of certain syntactic capabilities which Genie continues to lack.

To summarize, scientific thought in the area of first language acquisition seems to have gone in a spiral as opposed to a circle. That is, although some theorists have on Day 6 returned to formal approaches to language acquisition and a form of nativism (earlier seen on Day 2 and Day 3), these recent attempts have been enriched and broadened by intervening developments in language acquisition, cognitive learning theory, and computational linguistics. However, unlike the creation of the world, the creation of the field of language acquisition is not complete. Nor do the concerns of Day 6 supersede earlier concerns. The issues of Day 4 and Day 5 continue to be studied extensively along with the work motivated by developments on Day 6.

The Seventh Day: The Day of Rest and Judgment

On the *seventh day*, worn out from these theoretical struggles, researchers rested and reflected on what they had done in creating the field of language acquisition as they had. What they saw, by way of summarizing the products of Days 1 through 6, was the following: Day 1 witnessed the creation of Chomsky who on

Day 2 created generative transformational grammar, a theoretical breakthrough that transformed psycholinguistics and the study of language acquisition. Day 3 witnessed the first ambitious but mostly unsuccessful attempts to translate Chomsky's theory into psycholinguistic research and to look for grammatical rules behind children's early linguistic productions. An exclusively syntactic approach to language acquisition begun on that day proved too narrow and soon yielded to semantic approaches to language acquisition on Day 4. On that day, the revelation that children could apparently discuss events and relations they perceived in the world became a focus for research, and language acquisition was seen as prompted by prior cognitive developments. On Day 5, researchers discovered the child as a social being in a cultural context and theoretical concerns shifted to the *functions* of language during communication. In fact, language acquisition was often treated as a problem the child solved exclusively through social interaction, apart from collateral cognitive achievements.

On Day 6, partly as a backlash against the diverse directions in which the study of language acquisition had gone, some researchers returned to the study of the acquisition of syntax per se, although now their theories were informed by the emphasis on semantics gained from Day 4. Computer simulations of the language acquisition process clarified for researchers the view that human beings had some innate propensity to learn particular grammars over others. Neo-nativist views on syntax acquisition were indirectly supported by new discoveries of constraints on learning in animals.

Despite the fact that the field of language acquisition had expanded dramatically, touching on new areas of research as well as reinvigorating traditional areas, solutions to a key problem in language acquisition, namely, the acquisition of the formal syntactical system presumably at some level common to all natural languages, eluded explanation. There also lurked the distinct possibility, as Brown (1977) wrote, that the burgeoning and increasingly amorphous area of language acquisition would become one of those areas that psychologists studied intensively but eventually abandoned. Therefore, on this day of judgment, it is timely to consider theoretical and empirical problems which have continued to plague our efforts.

Four problems are discussed: First, and perhaps most fundamental, is the conflation of "communication" and "language." Efforts to understand the latter have been stalled in recent years by overemphasis on the former, while language's unique properties have been played down or ignored. Second, the importance of cognitive development for language acquisition is still controversial. One aspect of this problem is that the metaphor of the child as "active processor," or constructor of her cognitive and social environment, seems to have met its demise in some accounts of language acquisition which emanate from Day 5. Another aspect is the premature abandonment of the semantic relations view of Day 4. The third problem is the overabundance of "universals" found in the literature on communication development and language acquisition.

We continue to disregard culturally shaped variation in communication and language socialization. The fourth major problem is the issue which motivated the organization of the original symposium and of this volume: What occurs in the transition period from prelinguistic to linguistic communication development? This chapter concludes with a brief discussion of how the field of language acquisition may fare in the future, given its recent tumultuous past.

Problem 1: The Conflation of Communication and Language. As researchers endeavor to determine what role, if any, the development of communication plays in the acquisition of language, little progress will occur if communication and language are persistently conflated. Language is only one of the many channels which human beings use to communicate, so that language use falls under the rubric of communication. However, though it is a component of communication, language in itself is *more* than communication. For one thing, all natural languages are describable by a finite set of rules for the infinite recombination of their elements. To our knowledge no aspect of nonverbal communication—although such communication may be systematic and rule-governed—has the complexity, uniqueness, and power afforded by knowledge of the linguistic code. Bierwisch (1980) lists three other distinguishing characteristics between language and communication. First, in many cases language is used outside of any communicative interaction, such as when constructing interior monologues or in making notes to aid memory. Second, much communication is not based on language—that is, nonverbal acts such as a handshake or a salute carry meaning efficiently without language. Third, language and communication, aside from being based on different sets of rules, tap into different systems of knowledge.

Unfortunately, there has been a tendency in some of the literature which focuses on the preverbal aspects of communication development to conflate language and communication. A practice which may inadvertently contribute to this conflation is the fact that much of the terminology in early communication development has been borrowed from linguistics (discussed earlier) with the result that terms describing *communicative* achievements are used interchangeably with terms describing *linguistic* achievements. Trevarthen (1979), for example, has made strong assertions about very young infants' communicative abilities:

> In primary intersubjectivity [communication between the mother and the 3-month-old infant] the infant exhibits a number of preadaptations to language in which speech and gesture express acts of communication in address and reply with another . . . There is no discernible topic contained in these 'messages' apart from their quality of intersubjectivity within the dyad of mutual interests, and the infantile communications must be regarded as very crude in linguistic differentiation. Most are unvocalized. Nevertheless it is not a great act of interpretation to attribute

a presumptive language function to the remarkable associations of movement of head or body, of aims of gestures of hands, of expression of mood on the face, and of lips and tongue in articulations of prespeech [p. 548].

This tendency to credit even young infants with rudimentary aspects of linguistic knowledge is perhaps a natural outgrowth of the continually shrinking unit which is subject to analysis in language acquisition research (see Fig. 1.1). However, statements such as Trevarthen's only serve to confuse the issues. Communicative precursors, impressive as they are, have not solved and cannot solve the problem of language acquisition. Nor apparently does language acquisition guarantee communication (e.g., Blank, Gessner, & Espocito (1979); Braunwald, this volume) since there are cases of children who possess linguistic structures which they cannot harness in service to communication. Communication development and language acquisition are theoretically and empirically divisible processes. This conflation of communication development and language acquisition has contributed to two major problems in this area: (1) the tendency to argue for vague continuities between the two achievements, sometimes to the point of explaining the latter by reference to the former; and (2) the tendency to minimize the cognitive correlates and bases of language acquisition in favor of correlates and causes emerging from social interactional sources in the environment.

Since several chapters in this volume (Bloom, Shatz, Sugarman, and Snow and Gilbreath) consider the meaning of continuity positions in development, this issue will not be discussed here except to cite Kaye's (1979) caveats about apparent continuities:

> To find nothing in early communication but protolanguage and precursors of language would be virtually devoid of explanatory value. It is self-evident that everything one observes in adult language has an origin, and if one defines a phenomenon sufficiently broadly and vaguely one can always see some manifestation of it or analogy to it, in infancy or perhaps in the womb. Taken by itself this tells us nothing about the process by which the early form comes to be the later form. In fact it need not be the case that the formal similarity has any psychological, developmental reality at all [p. 192].

To summarize, achievements on Day 5 during which communicative competence and the functions of language were stressed, have sometimes led to a blurring of the boundaries between language and communication. This has misled researchers into thinking that issues in language acquisition could be resolved by finding precursors to language such as gestures and dialogic structures in communication development. Thus, the literature contains arguments of continuity between communication development and language acquisition which rely heavily on social-interactional mechanisms. As a consequence, the child's cognitive contributions to communication and language development have been underplayed. Problem 2 below focuses on the recent minimization of the infant's cognitive capabilities.

Problem 2: The Failures (Both Actual and Apparent) of Cognitive Accounts of Language Acquisition. Since Day 5 there seems to be a trend toward minimizing the role of the infant as an active processor and constructor of both the linguistic system and the social system in which language is embedded. Extreme statements treat the child's cognitive faculties as though they had become irrelevant to the language learning process. Although Vygotskyan approaches to cognition emphasizing the construction of knowledge as occurring first on the intermental level have increased in popularity, there is clearly some "mental" called for on the part of the child to even collaborate in this knowledge construction. Atkinson (1980) and Shatz (1981) both point out that the communication-based approaches to language development which emerged on Day 5 often neglect to provide explicit characterizations of the mechanisms of development which might account for changes in language skill.

Instead, increasing responsibility for the process of language acquisition is vested in the child's environment. However, even if we could specify the characteristics of environments which are maximally conducive to language acquisition, we would still not possess a sufficient account of how language acquisition occurs. What the child selects from the environment at various points in development and how the child processes what is selected must be known as well. An analogy can be seen in the phenomenon of combustion: It is patently false that the mere existence of oxygen, combustible material, and a matchbook necessarily implies that there must be a fire. Combustion will not occur unless a causal agent (or a bolt of lightning) lights a match to the combustible material. Environmental accounts of language acquisition make an analogous error; such accounts ignore the causal agent in the process (the child) whose function it is to interpret both the linguistic and the non-linguistic environment, guided by what their evolutionary heritage and developmental status make available.

It is an interesting coincidence that the infant's cognitive abilities are being down-played in communication-based approaches to language acquisition at the same time that the optimism of the last decade about how cognitive factors would eventually account for language acquisition has faded. Bates and Snyder (in press), Bloom, Lifter, and Broughton (in preparation), and Corrigan (1979), have discussed the failure to find close correspondences, let alone causal links, between variables such as level of object permanence and lexical or syntactic production. In retrospect the failure of what may be referred to loosely as the "cognitive hypothesis" of language learning is not surprising. Piaget's theory (1951, 1954) was the one most relied on for making the link between, on the one hand, general representational and cognitive abilities, and on the other, language development. Yet this theory has notoriously underplayed the importance of language in development and has failed to provide a consistent and clearly articulated theoretical approach to language development itself (see Beilin, 1980; Piatelli–Palmerini, 1980; Ryan, 1974).

Further disenchantment with the cognitive hypothesis is reflected in the apparent eagerness with which some researchers have abandoned the belief that infant's early utterances encode role relations, the achievements noted on Day 4. Howe (1976) and Macrae (1979) have concluded that it is presumptuous to presuppose, as many theorists of language acquisition have done (e.g., see Brown, 1973, for a review), that children are capable of commenting on relations such as "agent" of the action, "location" of the action, and "recipient" of the action. The end result of such a counterproposal would be a return to the situation which Schlesinger (1971) criticized in accounts of Day 3, during which language was synonymous with the acquisition of syntax; such accounts left the child holding "empty structures which he subsequently stuffs with meanings [p. 85]." The problem of meaning in early language, however conceived, is interconnected with the acquisition of syntax and must be included in any theory of language acquisition. The rejection of semantic relations has been criticized on logical grounds by Bloom, Capatides, and Tackeff (1981) and on logical and empirical grounds by Golinkoff (1981a). The latter paper describes a mounting body of evidence which suggests that infants in their second year are capable of discriminating at least the roles of agent and recipient in the nonlinguistic events they observe.

Problem 2, the minimization of cognition's contribution to the child's communicative and linguistic development, has yielded to an alternative theoretical focus. The social-interactional, environmentally-based explanations of language development, have succeeded no better than exclusively cognitive explanations. An argument has been made that the minimization of the importance of cognition for both communication and language development was spurred by the simultaneous rejection of Piagetian-based cognitive "explanations" of language development as well as a partial rejection of the semantic relations position, both seen first on Day 4. To conclude, explanations of language development which rely exclusively on either social or cognitive mechanisms fail to capture the complexity of learning language.

Problem 3: The Overabundance of Universals.   Only recently has there been some concern about whether statements made about the course of communicative development in our culture are true of other cultures as well (see Field, Sostek, Vietze, & Leiderman, 1981; Schieffelin & Ochs, this volume). In general, the literature is replete with unquestioning assertions about the nature of the mother–infant relationship and how that relationship contributes to communication and language development. For example, Newson (1978) among others has argued:

> The desire to establish a degree of shared understanding with her baby is normally a powerful motive for the mother. She treats him from birth as a person who can be

credited with feelings, desires, intentions, etc., and looks for confirmation that he will relate to her in a person-like way [p. 37].

Such statements, so comprehensible and "natural" when read by Western researchers who hold these views of the infant as well, have led to an uncritical acceptance of the "necessary" environmental influences for communication and subsequent language development. These "necessary" experiences may simply be artifacts of child-rearing in Western culture. At least four specific "universals" are now being challenged from data derived from ethnographic and experimental studies of non-Western cultures (see Schieffelin & Ochs, this volume): (1) the attribution of intentions and feelings to prelinguistic infants; (2) the prevalence of the baby-talk or adjusted speech register when adults address infants and young children; (3) the primacy and importance of the dyadic relationship between mother and infant for communication development; and (4) the necessity for affect-reciprocity in extended face-to-face interactions for language development (see Dixon, Tronick, Keefer, & Brazelton, 1981). Until very recently these four claims were not considered controversial. Despite the fact that cross-cultural differences make our explanatory attempts more difficult, they cannot be swept under the rug.

A further result of the often unquestioning acceptance of Western, middle-class beliefs about infants is our implicit assumption of homogeneity among the middle class mothers whose interactions with their children comprise our data sets. Explorations of how mothers report that they perceive and interpret their infants' communicative behaviors are rare (e.g., Harding, this volume; Hayes, 1982; Ninio & Wheeler, 1983). Rarer still are studies of whether individual differences in such interpretations affect the infant's communication and language development (Harding, 1981).

To summarize, as a result of Day 5 when social-interactional concerns began to be considered as pertinent to the development of communication and language, the experiences of Western investigators and their middle class subjects began to be treated as though they were universal and necessary precursors for the development of language. In addition, perhaps because of the presumption of homogeneity within cultures, the child rearing beliefs which guide Western mothers have rarely been examined. The failure to close these research gaps will greatly limit the generalizability of our theoretical claims and empirical findings.

Problem 4: Understanding the Transition from Prelinguistic to Linguistic Communication. The goal of this volume and of the conference which preceded it[3] has been to examine the period during which children move from using predominantly nonverbal and vocal means to using predominantly linguistic

---

[3]Aside from the discussion of this issue here, the reader may wish to refer to the preface which details the charge given to the contributors to this volume with regard to conceptualizing the transition from prelinguistic to linguistic communication.

means for communication. This transition period occurs between approximately 12 and 18 months. During this time, infants, in collaboration with their communicative partners, augment, refine, and coordinate their nonlinguistic communicative signals enabling them to convey their goals and intentions in extended "conversational" interactions. This development has been little studied. Research done during the transition period focused either on infant communication behaviors or on maternal language input without regard for the infant's response. To trace development in the transition period, studies conducted within an *interactive* perspective are required in which the infant's communicative development is described in the context of everyday conversational interactions. An interactive perspective presupposes that communicative development is a) partially a product of communicative episodes constructed by infant and mother; and b) that the meaning of the infant's evolving communicative signals must be interpreted in their functional context. On the other hand, some have argued that little of communicative or linguistic note occurs during this period (Bates, 1979; Shatz, this volume). However, the interactive examinations of the child's communicative skills during this period are yet to be conducted.

Up to now, research in communication development has focused on exciting discoveries about communicative interaction between mother and infant in the first 6 months of life (see Bullowa, 1979; Lock, 1978; Schaffer, 1977), the period characterized by Adamson and Bakeman (1982) as "affective communication." For example, the early communicative exchanges which occur between young infants and their mothers (aptly described by Stern, 1977) have been argued to possess the dialogic qualities of linguistically constructed conversations (e.g., intersubjectivity and turn-taking). Although these forays into early communication development have been partly in service to learning more about language acquisition (Schaffer, 1977), they have provided relatively meager returns for the study of the transition period or the acquisition of the formal structure of language per se.

Since research on early communication often uses terms borrowed from linguistics, it seems ironic that the use of these linguistic terms may have hampered the study of the transformation of the child's communicative skills during the transition period. Sometimes, use of these labels has persuaded researchers that non-linguistic achievements were actually linguistic ones (see Problem 1). Further, some researchers' optimism about the contribution of early communicative precursors to language acquisition has been deflated by the lack of evidence to support this presumed relationship. Bates, Bretherton, Beeghly–Smith, and McNew (1981) in an extensive review of the effects of early communication development on language acquisition, report few apparent effects between these variables, measured in diverse ways. For example, Kaye's (1979) research included a multifaceted microanalytic analysis of the relationship between many measures of the mother–infant communicative relationship in the first 6 months of life and later language development. Kaye's results (or rather lack of results) led him to conclude:

> We certainly cannot say that our contingent and interactive measures (taken before 6 months) added anything to our ability to predict outcomes in the children's cognitive, language, or social development at 2 1/2 . . . mother and infant do not constitute a dyad or social system *until the infant becomes an intentional and skillful partner in their interaction* [p. 17, our underlining].

The period alluded to in Kaye's statement, roughly dating from the beginning of the second year of life and not the first 6 months, seems a much more likely candidate for helping us understand the role of communicative development in the transition into language use. This is because two very different kinds of communicative interaction are being initiated by the infant in the first 6 months and in the transition period. Golinkoff (1983) has distinguished between intentional communication for *interactional* purposes, appearing in the first months of life and intentional communication for *instrumental* purposes, appearing in the last quarter of the first year. It is this latter type of communication which seems to herald the onset of the transition period. At that time infants begin to use communication for the purpose of manipulating others to attain their goals. Prior research has shown that they have begun to perceive the instrumentality of their communicative signals and the necessity to contact another (see Golinkoff, 1981b, for a review; Harding, this volume). The ways in which infants can reformulate and repair their signals and attempt to gain their mother's attention as a prerequisite to communicating are discussed in Golinkoff (this volume).

Despite the apparent achievements of this period, accounts of communicative development dwindle at this point, only to increase once language, in the form of isolated lexical items, appears. However, the way in which the infant's communicative skills expand and grow in complexity and sophistication during this period is not known. Research available on the transition period has focused on lexical development (e.g., Nelson, 1973) and on language comprehension (e.g., Huttenlocher, 1974). Few investigators have attempted to trace the child's communicative achievements within their everyday communicative contexts. The studies available (e.g., Carter, 1979; Dore, 1974; Dore, Franklin, Miller, & Ramer, 1975; Greenfield & Smith, 1976; Halliday, 1975; Lock, 1979; Scollon, 1976), although informative, provide only a partial account of what occurs during the transition period. One of the most well-known of these studies (Halliday, 1975) followed the author's son as the child's range of preverbal communicative functions (analyzed only in his vocal output) expanded. Halliday's emphasis on the differentiation of communicative functions reflected a new conceptual approach to the transition period, although the approach taken in this study has been criticized by Francis (1979).

Golinkoff and Harding (1980) have argued that communication continues to develop in at least two ways during the transition period before language emerges. First, preverbal signals begin to be combined and coordinated. In this way the goal of the infant's signals becomes clearer. Second, communicative episodes increase in length and complexity as the infants' initial failures are followed by repeated and more varied attempts at communication. Golinkoff (this volume) attempts to capture these developments by studying how infants persevere when their first attempts to establish a particular meaning fail. Research of this nature may provide links to both language onset as well as the child's progress in mastery of the linguistic code. While syntax acquisition may certainly be driven by innate, species-specific constraints, environmental influences on this process should not be underplayed since the child's development of communication skills seems to partly depend on the interactional opportunities the infant experiences with its caregivers. The puzzle of the transition period is two-fold: first, what is the nature of communicative development during this period; and second, how do changes in communicative skill, which occur at this time, relate to the onset and rapidity of language development?

To conclude, the University of Delaware conference and the chapters in this volume are concerned with Problem 4, namely, the transition from the use of prelinguistic to linguistic means of communication. Relative to other periods of communication development this period has not received sufficient attention. Many of the chapters also assess what the field of language development gained from focusing on communication development in the first year of life. Unfortunately it appears that we still do not know what, if any, are the nonverbal communicative achievements that provide the foundation for the transition into language. Thus, Problem 4, understanding the transition period, may be restated as a question: What is the relationship in ontogeny between communication development in the transition period and language development?

Our Fall from Eden and Our Search for Redemption

Researchers in the field of language acquisition are no longer the naive, unknowing individuals we once were. We perceive our naked state in the face of the complexity of the language acquisition process. Simple solutions sought either in the infant's first year of life or during the actual process itself have been cast aside. Since Eden is gone forever, what new directions will the field of language acquisition take? Given that neither author of this chapter has been trained in prophecy, this section will be brief.

First, we predict that there will be more of a theoretical bifurcation between those who study communicative development and those who study language development. Both areas will profit from a clearer demarcation of the uniqueness of language and communication. Nonetheless, researchers in communication development will continue to be enriched by theorizing in linguistics; language researchers will continue to follow research on how linguistic structures are actually deployed. Second, within the field of language acquisition the child will continue to be viewed in a holistic light. Many of the researchers who were present during the seven days of creation would not return to Eden even if given the choice. They could no longer be content to work on isolated syntactic frames devoid of meaning and considered without regard to their function within the extralinguistic context. Once having bitten of the apple of semantics and pragmatics, they will continue to view the acquisition of the formal aspects of language within a social and cultural frame. Although the metaphor of the infant as the isolated hypothesis tester may no longer be useful, we can now recognize the child's critical role as well as the environment's role in contributing to linguistic growth.

Researchers have sometimes studied the impact of the environment by following cases of language acquisition in disabled or disordered populations. Thus, a third trend we see is a proliferation of such studies for the purpose of clarifying and resolving theoretical arguments about the interaction of the environment and innate programming in language acquisition.

In addition, new developments in linguistic theory will continue to influence research in language acquisition. Specifically, a recent lexical interpretive theory of grammar (Bresnan, 1978) which reduces the need for transformations and deep structure by placing additional knowledge in the lexicon is already inspiring some researchers to propose new models of language acquisition (see Pinker, 1982).

To conclude, it is our hope that future researchers may be inspired, rather than burdened, by the problems and pitfalls we have outlined in this paper. Just as the Bible did not end with the seven days of creation, the field of language acquisition has many chapters (some no doubt based on revelations) yet to be written.

REFERENCES

Adamson, L., & Bakeman, R. Affectivity and reference: Concepts, methods, and techniques in the study of communication development of 6 to 18 month old infants. In T. Field, & A. Fogel (Eds.), *Emotion and early interaction*. Hillsdale, N.J.: Lawrence Erlbaum Associates, 1982.

Anderson, J. Induction of augmented transition networks. *Cognitive Science, 1977, 1*, 125–157.

Atkinson, M. Review of A. Lock (Ed.), *Action, gesture and symbol*. London, England: Academic Press, 1978. *Journal of Child Language, 1980, 1*, 579–610.

Austin, J. *How to do things with words*. Cambridge, Mass.: Harvard University Press, 1962.

Bates, E. *The emergence of symbols*. New York: Academic Press, 1979.

Bates, E., Camaioni, L., & Volterra, V. The acquisition of performatives prior to speech. *Merrill-Palmer Quarterly, 1975, 21*, 205–226.

Bates, E., Bretherton, I., Beeghly-Smith, M., & McNew, S. Social bases of language development: A reassessment. In H. W. Reese & L. P. Lipsitt, (Eds.), *Advances in child development and behavior*, Vol. 16. New York: Academic Press, 1982.

Bates, E., & Snyder, L. S. The cognitive hypothesis in language development. In I. Uzgiris, & J. McV. Hunt (Eds.), *Research with scales of psychological development in infancy*. Champaign-Urbana: University of Illinois Press, in press.

Beilin, H. *Studies in the cognitive basis of language development*. New York: Academic Press, 1975.

Beilin, H. Piaget's theory: Refinement, revision, or rejection? In R. H. Kluwe, & H. Spada (Eds.), *Developmental models of thinking*. New York: Academic Press, 1980.

Berko-Gleason, J., & Weintraub, S. Input language and the acquisition of communicative competence. In K. E. Nelson (Ed.), *Children's language, Vol I*, New York: Gardner Press, 1978.

Bierwisch, M. Semantic structure and illocutionary force. In J. R. Searle, F. Keifer, & M. Bierwisch (Eds.), *Speech act theory and pragmatics*. Dordrecht, Holland: D. Reidel, 1980.

Blank, M., Gessner, M., & Espocito, A. Language without communication: A case study. *Journal of Child Language*, 1979, *6*, 329–352.

Bloom, L. *Language development: Form and function in emerging grammars*. Cambridge, Mass.: M.I.T. Press, 1970.

Bloom, L., Lifter, K., & Broughton, J. Early cognition and language: Exploring convergences in the second year of life. Manuscript in preparation.

Bloom, L., Capatides, J. B., & Tackeff, J. Further remarks on interpretive analysis: In response to Christine Howe. *Journal of Child Language*, 1981, *8*, 403–411.

Bohannon, J. N., & Hirsh–Pasek, K. Do children say as they're told? A new perspective on motherese. In L. Feagans, C. Garvey, & R. M. Golinkoff (Eds.), *The origins and growth of communication*. Norwood, N.J.: Ablex, 1983.

Bolles, R. C. *Learning theory*. New York: Holt, Rinehart & Winston, 1975.

Braine, M. D. The ontogeny of English phrase structure: The first phase. *Language*, 1963, *39*, 1–13.

Bresnan, J. A realistic transformational grammar. In M. Halle, J. Bresnan, & G. Miler (Eds.), *Linguistic theory and psychological reality*. Cambridge, Mass.: MIT Press, 1978.

Brown, R. *A first language: The early stages*. Cambridge, Mass.: Harvard University Press, 1973.

Brown, R. Word from the language acquisition front. Invited address at the meeting of the Eastern Psychological Association, Boston, 1977.

Brown, R., & Bellugi, U. Three processes in the child's acquisition of syntax. *Harvard Educational Review*, 1964, *34*, 133–151.

Bruner, J. S. From communication to language—a psychological perspective. *Cognition*, 1974, *3*, 255–287.

Bruner, J. S. The ontogenesis of speech acts. *Journal of Child Language*, 1975, *2*, 1–19.

Bullowa, M. Prelinguistic communication: A field for scientific research. In M. Bullowa (Ed.), *Before speech*. Cambridge: Cambridge University Press, 1979.

Carter, A. L. The disappearance schema: Case study of a second-year communication behavior. In E. Ochs, & B. B. Schieffelin (Eds.), *Developmental pragmatics*. New York: Academic, 1979.

Chafe, W. L. *Meaning and the structure of language*. Chicago, Ill.: University of Chicago Press, 1970.

Chomsky, N. *Syntactic structures*. The Hague: Mouton, 1958.

Chomsky, N. *Aspects of the theory of syntax*. Cambridge, Mass.: M.I.T. Press, 1965.

Chomsky, N. The linguistic approach. In M. Piattelli–Palmarini (Ed.), *Language and learning: The debate between Jean Piaget and Noam Chomsky*. Cambridge, Mass.: Harvard University Press, 1980.

Clark, H. H., & Lucy, P. Understanding what is meant from what is said: A study in conversationally conveyed requests. *Journal of Verbal Learning and Verbal Behavior*, 1975, *14*, 56–72.

Corrigan, R. Cognitive correlates of language: Differential criteria yield differential results. *Child Development*, 1979, *50*, 617–631.

Curtiss, S. *Genie: A psycholinguistic study of a modern day "wild child."* New York: Academic Press, 1977.

Dixon, S., Tronick, E., Keefer, C., & Brazelton, T. Mother–infant interaction among the Gusii of Kenya. In T. M. Field, A. M. Sostek, P. Vietze, & P. H. Leiderman (Eds.), *Culture and early interactions*. Hillsdale, N.J.: Lawrence Erlbaum Associates, 1981.

Dore, J. A pragmatic description of early language development. *Journal of Psycholinguistic Research.* 1974, *4,* 343–350.

Dore, J., Franklin, M., Miller, R., & Ramer, A. Transitional phenomena in early language acquisition. *Journal of Child Language,* 1975, *3,* 13–78.

Ervin–Tripp, S., & Mitchell–Kernan, C., (Eds.), *Child discourse.* New York: Academic Press, 1977.

Feldman, H., Goldin–Meadow, S., & Gleitman, L. Beyond Herodotus: The creation of language by linguistically deprived deaf children. In A. Lock (Ed.), *Action, gesture and symbol.* London, England: Academic Press, 1978.

Field, T. M., Sostek, A. M., Vietze, P., & Leiderman, P. H. (Eds.) *Culture and early interactions.* Hillsdale, N.J.: Lawrence Erlbaum Associates, 1981.

Fillmore, C. J. The case for case. In E. Bach, & R. T. Harmes (Ed.), *Universals in linguistic theory.* New York: Holt, Rinehart and Winston, 1968.

Fodor, J. A. How to learn to talk: Some simple ways. In F. Smith, & G. A. Miller (Eds.), *The genesis of language.* Cambridge, Mass.: M.I.T. Press, 1966.

Fodor, J. A., Bever, T. G., & Garrett, M. F. *The psychology of language.* New York: McGraw–Hill Book Company, 1974.

Francis, H. What does the child mean? A critique of the 'functional' approach to language acquisition. *Journal of Child Language,* 1979, *6,* 201–210.

Furrow, D., Nelson, K., & Benedict, H. Mothers' speech to children and syntactic development: Some simple relationships. *Journal of Child Language,* 1979, *6,* 423–442.

Gleitman, L. R., & Wanner, E. (Eds.). *Language acquisition: The state of the art.* New York: Cambridge University Press, 1982.

Gold, E. Language identification in the limit. *Information and Control,* 1967, *16,* 447–474.

Golinkoff, R. M. The case for semantic relations: Evidence from the verbal and nonverbal domains. *Journal of Child language,* 1981, *78,* 413–438. (a)

Golinkoff, R. M. The influence of Piagetian theory on the study of the development of communication. In I. E. Sigel, D. M. Brodzinsky, & R. M. Golinkoff (Eds.), *New directions in Piagetian theory and practice.* Hillsdale, N.J.: Lawrence Erlbaum Associates, 1981. (b)

Golinkoff, R. M. Infant social cognition: Self, people and objects. In L. Liben (Ed.), *Piaget and the foundations of knowledge.* Hillsdale, N.J.: Lawrence Erlbaum Associates. 1983.

Golinkoff, R. M., & Ames, G. A comparison of fathers' and mothers' speech to their young children. *Child Development,* 1979, *50,* 28–32.

Golinkoff, R. M., & Harding, C. G. *Directives in preverbal communication: Messages mothers can't ignore.* Southeastern Conference on Human Development, Baltimore, Md., April, 1980.

Greenfield, P. M., & Smith, J. H. *The structure of communication in early language development.* New York: Academic Press, 1976.

Halliday, M. A. K. *Learning how to mean.* London, England: Arnold, 1975.

Harding, C. G. *A longitudinal study of the development of the intention to communicate.* Unpublished doctoral dissertation, University of Delaware, 1981.

Harding, C. G., & Golinkoff, R. M. The origins of intentional vocalizations in prelinguistic infants. *Child Development,* 1979, *50,* 33–40.

Hayes, A. *Constructions of infant social behavior by mothers and researchers.* Presented at the International Conference on Infant Studies, Austin, Tx., March, 1982.

Hinde, R. A., & Stevenson–Hinde, J. (Eds.), *Constraints on learning.* New York: Academic Press, 1973.

Howe, C. The meanings of two-word utterances in the speech of young children. *Journal of Child Language,* 1976, *3,* 29–47.

Huttenlocher, J. The origins of language comprehension. In R. L. Solso (Ed.), *Theories in cognitive psychology.* Potomac, Md.: Lawrence Erlbaum Associates, 1974.

Hymes, D. Competence and performance in linguistic theory. In R. Huxley, & E. Ingram (Eds.), *Language acquisition: Models and methods*. London, England: Academic Press, 1971.

Jarvella, R. Memory for the intentions of sentences. *Memory and Cognition*, 1974, *14*, 185–188.

Kaye, K. *The social context of infant development*. Final report to the Spencer Foundation, 1979.

Keil, F. C. Constraints on knowledge and cognitive development. *Psychological Review*, 1981, *88*, 3, 197–227.

Kernan, K. T. Semantic relations and the child's acquisition of language. *Anthropological Linguistics*, 1970, *12*, 171–187.

Lenneberg, E. H. *Biological foundations of language*. New York: Wiley, 1967.

Lock, A. (Ed.), *Action, gesture and symbol*. Cambridge, Mass.: Academic, 1978.

Lock, A. *The guided reinvention of language*. New York: Academic Press, 1979.

Macrae, A. Combining meanings in early language. In P. Fletcher, & M. Garman (Eds.), *Language acquisition*. Cambridge, England: Cambridge University Press, 1979.

Marler, P. R., Dooling, R. J., & Zoloth, S. Comparative perspectives on ethology and behavioral development. In M. H. Bornstein (Ed.), *Comparative methods in psychology*. Hillsdale, N.J.: Lawrence Erlbaum Associates, 1980.

McCawley, J. D. The role of semantics in a grammar. In E. Bach, & R. T. Harmes (Eds.), *Universals in linguistic theory*. New York: Holt, Rinehart, and Winston, 1968.

McNeill, D. Developmental psycholinguistics. In F. Smith, & G. A. Miller (Eds.), *The genesis of language*. Cambridge, Mass.: M.I.T. Press, 1966.

McNeill, D. *The acquisition of language*. New York: Harper & Row, 1970.

Miller, G. A. Some psychological studies of grammar. *American Psychologist*, 1962, *17*, 748–762.

Miller, W., & Ervin, S. The development of grammar in child language. In U. Bellugi, & R. Brown (Eds.), The acquisition of language. *Monographs of the Society for Research in Child Development*, 1964, *29*, (92, Serial No. 149).

Morris, C. *Signs, language and behavior*. Englewood Cliffs, N.J.: Prentice-Hall, 1946.

Nelson, K. E. Structure and strategy in learning how to talk. *Monographs of the Society for Research in Child Development*, 1973, *38*, (1–2, Serial No. 149).

Nelson, K. E. Facilitating children's syntax acquisition. *Developmental Psychology*, 1977, *13*, 101–107.

Newport, E., Gleitman, H., & Gleitman, L. Mother, I'd rather do it myself: Some effects and non-effects of maternal speech style. In C. Snow, & C. Ferguson (Eds.), *Talking to children: Input and acquisition*. New York: Cambridge University Press, 1977.

Newson, J. Dialogue and development. In A. Lock (Ed.), *Action, gesture and symbol: The emergence of language*. London, England: Academic Press, 1978.

Ninio, A., & Wheeler, M. Functions of speech in mother-infant interaction. In L. Feagans, C. Garvey, & R. M. Golinkoff (Eds.), *The origins and growth of communication*. Norwood, N.J.: Ablex, 1983.

Ochs, E. Talking to children in Western Samoa. *Language in Society*, 1982, *11*, 77–104.

Phillips, J. Syntax and vocabulary of mothers' speech to young children: Age and sex comparisons. *Child Development*, 1973, *44*, 182–185.

Piaget, J. *Play, dreams, and imitation in childhood*. New York: Norton Press, 1951.

Piaget, J. *The construction of reality in the child*. New York: Basic Books, 1954.

Piattelli–Palmarini, M. (Ed.), *Language and learning: The debate between Jean Piaget and Noam Chomsky*. Cambridge, Mass.: Harvard University Press, 1980.

Pinker, S. Formal models of language learning. *Cognition*, 1979, *7*, 217–283.

Pinker, S. A theory of the acquisition of lexical-interpretive grammars. In J. Bresnan (Ed.), *The mental representation of grammatical relations*. Cambridge, Mass.: MIT Press, 1982.

Ryan, J. Early language development. Towards a communicative analysis. In M. P. M. Richards (Ed.), *The integration of a child into a social world*. Cambridge, England: Cambridge University Press, 1974.

Sachs, J., Bard, B., & Johnson, M. L. Language learning with restricted input: Case studies of two hearing children of deaf parents. *Applied Psycholinguistics,* 1981, *2,* 33–54.

Schaffer, H. R. *Studies in mother–infant interaction.* London, England: Academic Press, 1977.

Schlesinger, I. M. Production of utterances and language acquisition. In D. I. Slobin (Ed.), *The ontogenesis of grammar.* New York: Academic Press, 1971.

Schweller, K. G., Brewer, W. F., & Dahl, D. A. Memory for illocutionary forces and perlocutionary effects of utterances. *Journal of Verbal Learning and Verbal Behavior,* 1976, *15,* 325–337.

Scollon, R. *Conversations with a one year old.* Honolulu: University of Hawaii Press, 1976.

Searle, J. R. *Speech acts.* London, England: Cambridge University Press, 1969.

Searle, J. R. Chomsky's revolution in linguistics. *New York Review of Books,* June 2, 1972, *7.*

Seligman, M. E. P., & Hager, J. L. (Eds.), *The biological boundaries of learning.* New York: Appleton Press, 1972.

Shatz, M. Learning the rules of the games: Four views of the relation between social interaction and syntax acquisition. In W. Deutsch (Ed.), *The child's construction of language.* London: Academic Press, 1981.

Shatz, M. On mechanisms of language acquisition: Can features of the communicative environment account for development? In L. Gleitman, & E. Wanner (Eds.), *Language acquisition: The state of the art.* New York: Cambridge University Press, 1982.

Shatz, M. Communication. In J. Flavell, & E. Markman (Eds.), *Cognitive development.* P. Mussen (Gen. Ed.), *Carmichael's manual of child psychology.* 4th ed. New York: Wiley, in press.

Shatz, M., & Gelman, R. The development of communication skills: Modifications in the speech of young children as a function of listener. *Monographs of the Society for Research in Child Development,* 1973, *38,* (5, Serial No. 149).

Slobin, D. I. *Universals of grammatical development in children.* Language Behavior Research Laboratory, Working paper 22, 1969.

Slobin, D. I. Cognitive prerequisites for the acquisition of grammar. In C. A. Ferguson, & D. I. Slobin (Eds.), *Studies of child language development.* New York: Holt, Rinehart & Winston, 1973.

Slobin, D. I. Psychology without linguistics = language without grammar. *Cognition,* 1981, *10,* 275–280.

Snow, C. E. Mothers' speech to children learning language. *Child Development,* 1972, *43,* 549–565.

Snow, C. E., & Ferguson, C. A. (Eds), *Talking to children.* Cambridge: Cambridge University Press, 1977.

Stern, D. *The first relationship: Infant and mother.* Cambridge, Mass.: Harvard University Press, 1977.

Trevarthen, C. Instincts for human understanding and for cultural cooperation: Their development in infancy. In M. VonCranach, K. Foppa, W. Lepenies, & D. Ploog (Eds.), *Human ethology: Claims and limits of a new discipline.* Cambridge: Cambridge University Press, 1979.

Wexler, K. Empirical questions about developmental psycholinguistics raised by a theory of language acquisition. In R. N. Campbell, & P. T. Smith (Eds.), *Recent advances in the psychology of language.* New York: Plenum Press, 1978.

Wexler, K., Culicover, P., & Hamburger, H. Learning-theoretic foundations of linguistic universals. *Theoretical Linguistics,* 1975, *2,* 215–253.

2 The Acquisition of Pragmatic Commitments

Jerome Bruner
New School for Social Research

The announced object of our symposium was to explore "The Transition from Prelinguistic to Linguistic Communication," and the participants included many of the investigators who, over the last decade, have been working most mightily on this vexed and ancient topic. The history of our topic has been reviewed so often in recent years that it need not be passed in review yet again. What we know from those reviews is that we shall make little progress if we adhere either to the impossible account of extreme empiricism or the miraculous one of pure nativism. We might well begin by exploring some of these accounts.

"REAL-WORLD-KNOWLEDGE"

One of the middle-ground approaches to the problem has been particularly popular in the last decade. It is an essentially semantic approach and is often called the "real-world-knowledge" approach. Its theme is that if the child knows certain distinctions *conceptually,* learning them *linguistically* would be that much easier. It is not an unreasonable approach on the face of it. This approach has both a strong and a weak form—or rather a continuum from strong to weak. They need separate scrutiny since their assumptions are, I think, quite different.

The strong version holds that there is something intrinsic in the nature and organization of concepts that are formed in commerce with the world that predisposes language to be the way it is—including its grammar. It is a view that appeals implicitly to arguments about "naturalness." A strong version claim would be, for example, that there is something natural about the order SUBJECT-VERB-OBJECT (SVO) by virtue of that order reflecting how we experience the non-linguistic world. That is to say, our order of awareness may follow the sequence "doer of action," "action," and "object acted upon" which in turn makes SVO grammatical sequences "easier." The sort of evidence one might invoke would be Greenberg's (1963) finding that SVO orders are widespread, if not universal. Or, to expand the argument, one would expect to find grammatical categories and procedures that would conform rather than conflict with the shape of ordinary human experience or ordinary ways of processing non-linguistic knowledge. To take two instances, one might claim that the universal linguistic distinction, MARKED-UNMARKED, exists in all languages by virtue of its conformance to something intrinsic in human attention, or that case grammar is easily grasped because we already know in some nonlinguistic way about the arguments of action and that the grammar is some sort of "distillation" of non-linguistic knowledge. Let me call this type of claim the Precursor Hypothesis.

It is a seductive argument—particularly for psychologists who yearn for derivational simplicity and believe that the structure of language must, in some way, derive from general principles of cognition that preceded the onset of language. Indeed no psychologist who would claim kinship with William of Occam would pass up an opportunity to ponder the possibility of such derivational simplicity. I am among them (Bruner, 1975), and I should say now why I find this tempting view no longer satisfactory as an explanation of why children find it "easy" to move from prelinguistic communication to the use of lexico-grammatical speech. I have come to the conclusion that systems of language—and I emphasize the systematicity of language here—are autonomous problem spaces that, however much their conquest may be aided by non-linguistic knowledge or external support from others, must be mastered on their own.

My defection was produced by two lines of reasoning. Well-formedness in language is determined by sets of rules that are internally consistent within language. There is nothing about one's concepts of time, for example, that can lead one derivationally to the consistencies of tense marking, nothing about knowledge of action that could provide a clue as to how to realize case marking or aspect. Grammar requires problem solving of its own, and the progress of that problem solving is not linked to naturalness but to internal consistency. If I were to choose a single study by which I would illustrate the point, it would be Karmiloff-Smith's (1979). The second line of argument inheres in the distinction between "natural" and "non-natural" as made by Grice (1975) and other philosophers of language of the so-called Oxford School. When we speak by the use of lexico-grammatical language, the messages are constructed and comprehended with a view to a shared conventionality in usage. Some of the conventions may have an added support from "naturalness" (i.e., in a resemblance between a linguistic convention and a "natural" way of communicating, as is probably the case with some prosodic marking). But the expectancies of speaker and listener, characterized by something like the Gricean cycle (cf. Denkel, 1977), are conventional. I will come back to this point in more detail.

Having said that much, let me consider now the weaker version of the "real-world-knowledge" approach. In its least adorned form its claim is that if you already know what it is that language is designed to distinguish in the real world, you will presumably be alerted to relevant linguistic distinctions that are uttered in the presence of what you already distinguish non-linguistically. It is a weak claim in the sense that it has nothing to say about the naturalness of certain grammatical forms, indeed nothing to say about grammatical forms altogether. Its claim is only that it is immeasurably valuable, in learning a code, to know already what the code "stands for." This view may be called the Alerting Hypothesis.

This claim is, for all its weakness, decidedly non-trivial. For example, it categorically denies that language can be learned easily or, possibly, at all without *some* prior knowledge of the domain for which the language will serve as a system of descriptors. How much "some" is required must remain obscure for the time being. If "some" were too much, the Alerting Hypothesis would be in the odd position of denying that linguistic distinctions encountered by language learners may lead them to look for and find distinctions in the real world, and to do so cleverly as in the Carey and Bartlett (Miller, 1977) study of color naming. An Alerting Hypothesis need not rule out the possibility that, as Roger Brown (1973) put it, words are invitations to form concepts, or indeed, that grammatical distinctions may do the same.

Nor need this view deny the constitutive role of language—its capacity for creating "social realities" by virtue of its performatives. There are some distinctions in the "real world" that exist only by virtue of language—like promising and other speech acts. Yet, it is true that the Alerting Hypothesis is most convincing when it is assumed to be operating at the indexical level of speech acquisition and use—when words and expressions stand for events, objects, and states in the world of experience. As language use becomes more intralinguistic and performative, the power of the hypothesis declines.

I find no difficulty in adhering to the weaker version of the "real-world-knowledge" position in some such form as that enunciated by Macnamara (1972). I think, as already noted, that its principle power is in the early, indexical period of language learning. It is at best a low-grade aid, but it may be invaluable in getting the child *into* language. In sum, then, the "real-world-knowledge" approach in either of its forms seems to not go very far in explaining how the child moves so easily into proper speech.

SPEECH ACTS AND FINE TUNING

Another, more recently popular middle-ground position rests its case upon the role of social interaction and function as the supports for language acquisition. There are several variants. None of them is centrally concerned with grammar and syntax as such but, rather, with procedures for the realization of communicative functions—linguistic and prelinguistic procedures and how the latter turn into the former.

One approach grows out of the speech act theory and its central argument is that prelinguistic infants already know, say, how to declare and demand (e.g., Clark & Clark, 1977) by means other than language—gestures, vocalizations, etc. Acquiring the more conventional linguistic forms for carrying out these acts is a matter of encountering input of appropriate forms in appropriate contexts in which the child is intending to achieve a communicative result. This happy encountering of appropriate input in appropriate context depends in considerable measure upon interaction with an adult who is finely tuned to both the child's growing linguistic capabilities and to his communicative intentions. Much of the literature on Motherese deals with how this is presumably brought about (e.g., Snow & Ferguson, 1977). I would take two of my own studies as typical of this approach—Ninio and Bruner (1978) and Bruner, Roy, and Ratner (1982). John Dore (1974) is one of the pioneers of this approach. One supplement to this hypothesis is attributable to Joanna Ryan (1974): That the adult's assignment of an interpretation to the child's communicative effort also socializes the child's communicative intentions to the forms that characterize speech acts in the adult language community. Let me use the clumsy name of Functional Substitution Hypothesis for this approach.

It has very little to say about the acquisition of grammar, save that grammar is acquired in the context of fulfilling various communicative intentions and not as a matter of learning or otherwise acquiring autonomous rules in social isolation. Perhaps it has one other point to make about this matter, related to the "fine tunedness" of Motherese. It proposes something like a principle of readiness which is usually illustrated by noting the striking correlation between the grammatical complexity of the mother's speech and the child's. The implicit assumption is that the mother uses grammatical forms that are within reach of the child's changing performance capacity (or, indeed, his changing competence). The two variants—the one centering on the increasing conventionalization of the child's speech acts (e.g., McShane, 1980), the other on Motherese and "fine tunedness"—can presumably operate in unison and can indeed be further supported by some version of the Alerting Hypothesis.

The aggregate of these several views is a long chalk from the very early views of a Language Acquisition Device (LAD) that, with virtually no priming and no support, could recognize the deep structure of language that the child just happened to encounter, however degenerate it might be. In place of early LAD there has emerged a highly context-sensitive view of language acquisition and one that places a great deal of emphasis upon linguistic input being "appropriate." In the end, it requires for completion as a theory of acquisition, some sort of a device that is able to abstract rules from the ongoing, functionally relevant flow of language.

The contemporary view leaves a great deal unexplained about how the child masters well formed linguistic communication. Rather, its emphasis is upon the way such communication is framed functionally and contextually. It may well be that this seeming weakness is a strength, for we may indeed need a season for scrutinizing how communicative functions are developed and how conventionalized and finally, how they are made sensitive to the contexts in which language is to be used. I would like to turn to such matters now—to the pragmatic run-up to language.

THE PRAGMATICS OF ACQUISITION

The first question that I want to raise is whether we can, in studying the transition from prelinguistic to linguistic communication, profitably commit ourselves any longer to the three-branched linguistic tree. May not the tired old distinction between syntax, semantics, and pragmatics obscure their relationship by making them seem so parallel and autonomous?

Let me begin by arguing that pragmatics involves issues that are virtually altogether different from those involved in either semantics or syntax. Semantics and syntax are formulated to deal almost exclusively with the communication of information and with codes whose elements "stand for" something—either the function something is to serve in a sentence or for knowledge of the "real world." The two codes operate together in a fashion to specify the meanings of lexical items, phrases, or sentences. Taken together, they serve as the means, classically, of going from sound to meaning. The meanings with which they deal are classically timeless ones, sensitive to sentential context but insensitive to communicative intent, to conditions of utterance, to presupposition, and so forth.

Pragmatics is not restricted in that way. It is the study of how speech is used to accomplish such social ends as promising, humiliating, deceiving, assuaging, warning, declaring. It takes into account what has gone before and what is intended to follow—and not simply by the use of anaphora or tense and aspect marking, but by the imbedding of presuppositions and the marking of intent through performatives in ways not specifiable either by ordinary sentence grammar or by an ordinary use of the lexicon. Conventional grammars and lexicons are designed to characterize a *language,* not a language *user.* This need not be true—and Fillmore (1977) and Chafe (1970) are notable exceptions. But in the main it is true. There is nothing in conventional grammar about stance (e.g., Feldman, 1974) or about whether an utterance has fulfilled the felicity conditions that a speech community imposes. These are matters that are the "leftovers"— rather like *la parole* after syntax and semantics have exhausted the study of *la langue.* One is led, in the classical accounts, to wonder whether there can ever be a science of pragmatics, so idiosyncratic and use-bound is it made to seem. But as Culler (1978) points out, Saussure (1955) himself was often confused as to where the line should be drawn between the two. He even thought that grammar might be an aspect of *la parole,* so latitudinarian were the choices it left open for the realization of meanings.

The elements of pragmatics do not "stand for" anything in the exclusive sense that elements in syntax and pragmatics do. For they also *are* something. They constitute a social reality in their own right in a manner that neither the rules of syntax nor the codes of a lexicon do. If they are signifiers (in the Sausurrian sense), then what they signify is not "meaning" in any disembodied sense but, rather, "stance." *Stance* is a set of orientations toward social reality. It includes the orientation of the speaker: (1) toward the conventions of speaking, as in Grice's Conversational Maxims (1975); (2) toward the message, as in Feldman's account of modal auxillaries (1974); (3) toward the present context as in Keenan and Schieffelin's description of urgency (1976); (4) toward the past of which the message is a continuity as in Chafe's account of the "given" and the "new" (1970); (5) toward the future to which the message is related as in the intention marking of performatives (Austin, 1962); and (6) toward the interlocutors for whom message is intended as in Esther Goody's discussion of "questions of respect" (1978). Even silence, though it cannot be specified syntactically or semantically, may speak volumes pragmatically for the stance it signals in the context where it occurs. It is certainly not just like a deletion rule where patterned absence implies presence. Language is a vehicle, in this pragmatic perspective, for doing things with and to others, many of which things could not be conceived and/or done but for language. It is the aspect of language that makes it patently false that "sticks and stones will break my bones but names will never hurt me."

Acts of speech "stand for" something in this sense in a manner that is quite specialized. To revert to the Sausurrian perspective, they differ both in their signifiers and in what they signify from either lexical items or grammatical structures. They are on a different level in much the same way that distinctive features are on a different level from phonemes, phonemes from morphemes, morphemes from phrases, and so on. They use the output of the phonological, syntactic, and semantic systems as their elements. But they use this output in a fashion that is discontinuous with the lower level. To take another example from Feldman (1974), the use of terms like *only* and *even* in their pragmatic sense is discontinuous with their semantic scope and their syntactic function, as in the sentence, *Even Carol will find this odd.* What the act of speech stands for is some shared social history and one's attitude toward it.

One other matter. There is much contemporary discussion about the negotiation of "meanings" in more hermaneutical approaches toward communication (e.g., Foucault, 1971; Habermas; Ricoeur, 1970). This is not the place to examine the issues that grow out of these often clouded discussions. One point is plain and relevant. Negotiation is *not* about syntactic rules and it is rarely about such matters as scope, selection restrictions, or other "timeless" semantic issues. It is about problems in the assignment of pragmatic interpretations by parties to a discourse. This fact suggests further that pragmatics is not "what is left after the others are done," but that it is something in its own right. Or as Dell Hymes once put it in conversation, you can be master of the grammar and lexicon and still be a linguistic idiot.

Given this very distinctive role of pragmatics, might it not be wise to examine how its subtle "rules" are acquired and, after doing so, to examine anew what role it might conceivably play in aiding the child master the other aspects of language?

A pragmatic analysis presupposes a reciprocal commitment between speakers sharing a common culture. It is a complex commitment that includes at least three abstract features (to which I have already alluded in an earlier paragraph): (1) a shared set of conventions for establishing speaker intent and listener uptake, including procedural conventions like those proposed by Grice (1975) in his celebrated discussion of Conversational Principles; (2) a shared basis for exploiting the deictic possibilities of spatial, temporal, and interpersonal context, subject to "shifting" in Jakobson's sense (1971) or to role interchangeability in Hockett's (1960); and (3) conventional means jointly for establishing and retrieving presuppositions. These three elements—announcement of intention, regulation of deixis, and control of presupposition—give speech its shared future, present, and past orientations.

These orientations are not simply "interpersonal" in the sense of involving only the participants in a speech exchange. They are part of a culture of which the participants are members. L. Jonathan Cohen (1974) comments, in discussing a taxonomy of speech acts, that it is difficult to know where linguistics lets off and anthropology begins. For in fact, it is not a question of dividing the two disciplines, even by a fuzzy line. The culture must be regarded as a product of language and language as an instrument of the culture—a curious paradox. But it is a useful paradox. What I take this to mean is that one constitutes cultural realities by acts of using the language, performatives, and one then interprets the force of these realities by using language in negotiating pragmatic meanings. It is in this sense that culture can be conceived of as a text that requires interpretation by those who operate under its sway. When one "becomes" a member of a culture, one shoulders a *commitment* to operate in the light of its maxims (I prefer Grice's term to the usual "cultural rules"). The commitment has, at the language level, the force of demanding compliance to the abstract ways of forming past, present, and future—presuppositions, deixis, and intentions.

A great many acts of speaking will be found to be ways of "tuning" reciprocal commitments. Indeed, some linguistic theorists have even proposed that the grammatical categories of language exist, *inter alia,* to assure such pragmatic tuning and calibration as well as to assure reference and meaning. You will recall that Benveniste (1971) long ago raised the question of the function served by personal pronouns, a universal feature of all known languages. Why are they needed, he asked, when in fact we could accomplish the same semantic ends more reliably by using nominals to specify people or objects rather than having to employ tricky, shifter pronominals. His answer, of course, was that shifters like *I* and *you* serve as economical ways of sharing and calibrating the perspectives of two speakers through reciprocal role shift. More recently, Karmiloff–Smith (1979) has shown the manner in which young children, in making up a story about a scene, use pronominalization to indicate which elements they wish to foreground, relegating background by the use of nominals. I have already alluded to Feldman's study (1974) on the use of modal auxilliaries. She found that they too were used to indicate not so much the structural position of characters in a plot, but to indicate the stance of the speaker toward the message and the listener. Thus, modal auxilliaries expressing doubt and uncertainty were much more likely to appear in teachers' talk to fellow teachers than in their talk to their pupils.

It would seem to be the case, as noted, that some grammatical forms (or perhaps it would be better to say some grammatical choices) are strongly determined by pragmatic considerations—like choice of the pronominal system over the nominal, choice of modal auxilliaries for modulating the force of verbs, and so on. Yet pragmatics obviously cannot be based upon ordinary grammatical categories alone. Grammar traditionally is based upon the concept of the isolated sentence and on "sentence parts." But we know that the performative, deictic, and presuppositional uses of language depend upon the placement of expressions in discourse and dialogue, and not just in individual sentences.

This has always bothered pragmatically sensitive linguists. Perhaps you will recall that the Prague School tried to derive sentence grammar constitutively from discourse requirements such that, for example, topic/subject were said to be the "given" in discourse and comment/predicate the "new." And where discourse is "shared" in dialogue, the given-new distinction becomes bound not in discourse but in exchange. Doubtless, the idea is attractive to pragmaticians— that grammar is derived from the pragmatic uses to which language is put. I think that it would be more modest to claim that the grammar and lexicon of a language must have been influenced in some measure by pragmatic requirements—but that could not be the whole story. What also makes the stronger claim unlikely is that the stance marking of pragmatics requires considerably more procedurally, than just the grammar of sentence parts, something else that is trans-sentential and dialogic.

PRAGMATICS AND SYNTAX REVISITED

This brings us back to the question, "Can the child's prelinguistic knowledge of social interaction help him master the syntax of language?" It is a considerably subtler question than it first appeared to be. Can we sensibly reformulate it in the light of what has just been said?

We can now discern both a weak and a strong hypothesis about the putative role of interaction in aiding the child in mastering syntax. The strong form is based on a "Prague-like" hypothesis to the effect that social interaction is constitutive of the rules of grammar themselves—as implied, for example, in Benveniste's (1971) account of the emergence of the pronominal. But the general idea is a curious one. It asserts that *if* grammatical categories in some way historically reflect the social interactive requirements of speaking *then* it should be the case that the young infant (because he already knows how to interact socially *without* speaking) should be better able to figure out how to do it linguistically. Is this a slyly masked variant of the principle of Haeckel that ontogeny recapitulates phylogeny? And is it not subject to the same criticism as the strong version of the "real-world-knowledge" hypothesis? Even if grammar were derived *á la* Prague, how would that help the child figure out the grammatical realization rules by which the originally pragmatic distinctions were expressed? Grammar would still constitute its own problem space.

The weak version becomes more reasonable. If the child has learned many of the conceptual distinctions upon which pragmatics is based, and if he has learned prelinguistic ways of communicating about them, then both the Alerting Hypothesis and the Hypothesis of Functional Substitution would seem like good candidates for supporting language acquisition.

In the light of what has been said, do we now need to reexamine the implication of "Motherese" and "fine tuning" as aids to the child in acquiring grammar? Even if social interaction were not constitutive of grammar, perhaps it *frames* the process of acquisition in a way that make it easier for the child to become an expert grammarian sooner. Consider this for a moment.

If one now grants that grammatical distinctions have both semantic and pragmatic uses, then social interaction can serve a dual role in clueing the child into grammar. An adult in interaction with a child can both clue him with respect to pragmatic functions and at the same time organize the child's immediate surroundings in a fashion to make selected world knowledge more accessible to him in the presence of fine-tuned grammatical modelling. We see something of this order happening in the ubiquitous "give-and-take" games played by adults and children just at the threshold of language learning (e.g., Bruner, 1978). They characteristically involve negotatiations about role and the arguments of action, and contain striking examples of the highlighting of referents while grammatical distinctions are being modelled. In a sense, they seem to be doing everything at once in a highly contextualized and organized fashion.

This adult controlled framing, I would argue, accomplishes by external means a necessary regulation of the child's attention. Fillmore (1977) has, perhaps, written in the most compelling manner about the organization of attention in language use. He proposes that one function of sentence grammars is to establish a *perspective* on the *scene* that the sentence depicts or represents. Perspective setting requires the selective direction of attention and there are many grammatical devices for accomplishing these ends in adult speech like subject placement, passivization, clefting, etc. Early interaction similarly abounds in procedures for regulating attentional perspective on scenes in the form of vocatives, demonstratives, pointing gestures, and intonational contours, employed by both adult and child. The child has his or her own natural means for calling attention selectively to aspects of a scene (cf. Bruner, 1982). Interaction with an adult provides the child with the opportunity to learn the conventional or "non-natural" means for doing so. I shall illustrate this later.

All of this leads me to a consideration of the structuring of adult-child interaction, for there is now every reason to believe that there is a great deal of regularity in ordinary interactions (Bruner, 1981; Snow & Ferguson, 1977). This brings me to a central idea in my argument: the role of the *format*. A format is a rule-bound microcosm in which the adult and child *do* things to and with each other. In its most general sense, it is the instrument of patterned human interaction. It is of particular importance to us at this point since formats are established between infant and caretaker before lexico-grammatical speech begins, and they provide the framing context into which language is introduced. So let us turn to the matter immediately.

RECIPROCAL COMMITMENT AND FORMATS

I spoke earlier of three forms of reciprocal commitment in "pragmatic interaction": (1) relating to the future and to signalling and acknowledging intention; (2) to the present that is deictic; and (3) to the past that is presuppositional. They provide a useful set of rubrics for considering what is meant by a format.

A format formally entails a contingent interaction between at least two acting parties, contingent in the sense that the responses of *each* member can be shown to be dependent upon a prior response of the *other*. Each member of the minimal pair has a goal and a set of means for its attainment such that two conditions are met: first, that a participant's successive responses are instrumental to that goal, and second, that there is a discernible stop order in the sequence indicating that the terminal goal has been reached. The goals of the two participants need not be the same; all that is required is that the conditions of intra-individual and inter-individual response contingency be fulfilled. Formats, defined formally in this sense, represent the simplest instance of what Schank and Abelson (1977) characterize as a "scenario." Formats, however, "grow" and can become as varied as the scenarios described by those authors. Their growth is effected in several ways. They may in time incorporate new means or strategies for the attainment of goals, including symbolic or linguistic ones. They may move toward coordination of the goals of the two partners not only in the sense of "agreement" but also with respect to a division of labor and a division of initiative. And they may become conventionalized or canonical in a fashion that permits others within a symbolic community (e.g., a "speech community") to enter the format without special instruction.

Formats are also modular in the sense that they are amenable as subroutines for incorporation into larger scales, longer term routines. A greeting format, for example, can be incorporated in a larger scale routine involving other forms of joint action. In this sense, any given format may have a hierarchical structure, parts being interpretable in terms of their placement in a larger structure. The creation of higher order formats by incorporation of subroutine formats is one of the principal sources of presupposition. What is incorporated becomes implicit or presupposed.

Formats, except when highly conventionalized, cannot be identified independently of the perceptions of the participants. In this sense, they have the property of contexts generally in being the resultant of definition by the participants. The definition of formats communally is one of the major ways in which a community controls the interaction of its members. Once a format is conventionalized and "socialized" it comes to be seen as having externality and constraint and (in Karl Popper's, 1968, sense) becomes "objective." This is typical of such speech act formats as "promising."

One special property of formats involving an infant and an adult is that they are usually asymmetrical with respect to the "consciousness" of the members, one "knowing what's up," the other not knowing or knowing less. Consciousness in this sense is not intended to imply psychological heavy weather. I hope I can make that clearer later. I intend it in the sense used by Vygotsky (1962), discussing how the adult helps the child achieve realization of the Zone of Proximal Development or, in the sense of metacognition, the child learning by interaction with a tutor how to monitor and correct his own usage.

Now return to the three rubrics with which I introduced the idea of formats: intentions, deixis, and presuppositions. It is the goal-directed aspect of formats that makes the signalling of intention (and the signalling of uptake) so simple. This is greatly aided by the fact that early formats are so overt, as in games like hide-and-seek, give-and-take, peek-a-boo, and where's the X?. As my colleague and I (Ratner & Bruner, 1978) tried to show, overt signalling marks the steps toward the final goals of these games, and such aspectual completives as *all gone* and *dere* are among the first kinds of formulaic speech to appear on the scene. Indeed, Campos (1979) has reported instances where a Brazilian-Portugese speaking child, at 16 months, picked up the post-positional aspectual completive *-bo* as a terminal marker for completed acts, though in no other way was she capable of discriminating the inflectional markings of her native language. She simply tacked it to the end of babble strings. Infants learn early to signal intended action formats and to expect uptake. Indeed, what seems to be going on is a segmentation of the action into constituents, the child then seeking an appropriate way of signalling his intentions to the adult not only at the beginning, but at each segment. This provides the almost ideal-typical case of framing, for it assures that the child knows the referent for which he is signalling and can recognize by immediate context what the mother's utterance, provided as corrective, "means."

Consider what happens in a particular case, reported by Bruner, Roy, and Ratner (1982). Richard, now 20-months-old, has adopted what the authors call a successive guidance strategy for making requests. He begins with a requestive vocative—an intonationally marked object or action word or simply a requestive *Mummy*. This signals the pragmatic function in force. When she signals uptake, he then introduces a second element, usually a locative to indicate place where the object is or the locus of the desired action. By 22 months, the mother will no longer tolerate being dealt with in this robotic way and insists that Richard now fulfill one of the felicity conditions on requesting—full disclosure of intention in advance. *No, Richard, tell me what you want FIRST,* she demands. Richard responds with one of his first three-word sentences, strung together with slight pauses but including *Mummy* as Agent, the required Action, and the sought after Object, the whole marked with what is to be the requestive intonation contour of such utterances on later occasions. When mother failed at uptake, he then provided Locus.

All of this is not to say that there was anything *in* the prior interaction *per se* that could have given Richard any clues about how to handle the linearization of a sentence involving the sequence Agent-Action-Object-Locus. I do not believe, as I commented earlier, that there is any ''natural order'' in experiencing of action that tells you the order of corresponding elements in a sentence. But I do think that the child's search for appropriate order is greatly aided by the kind of framing the mother provides in the format. For, in effect, her successful effort at regularization has the effect of freeing the child's attention to explore linguistic hypotheses rather than spending his effort in negotiating the pragmatics of the situation.

The request format in question was a well established one—one where the child requests aid of the mother in obtaining an object out of sight or out of reach. It was already well constrained in terms of such felicity conditions as *essentiality* (do not ask for what you can accomplish yourself!), *sincerity* (do not ask for things that you really do not want!) and *preparation* (request rather than demand!). While mastering these felicity conditions, he was also mastering the conventional locutions by which requests are made. This is what I meant when I noted that in this early period, children seem to be doing everything at once in an almost indissoluble context.

I would like to touch very lightly on the second feature of formats: their role in providing a base for context sensitivity or deixis. It was Grace de Laguna (1927) who noted in her remarkable book that it was impossible to know what a child meant without knowing what he was doing whilst speaking. Roman Jakobson (1971) has very often commented that the principal vehicle by which the child goes beyond such context dependence is through mastery of the two-part, subject-predicate sentence that permits realization of remote reference, counterfactuality, possibility. I think it can be said that in the regularized formats that we have observed, the child begins to make the passage into greater independence from non-linguistic context by depending increasingly upon mother's speech rather than concrete events. He or she begins to match utterances to mother's utterances rather than to the events and objects involved in the format. In Peirce's sense (1931), the child's speech and symbolic acts become less indexical and more intralinguistic. I think this is well illustrated in another set of observations of Richard and his mother.

In the growth of labeling (cf. Ninio & Bruner, 1978), Richard's mother sets up a routine format for book reading in which she employs four invariant dialogue markers: (1) an initial attentional vocative in the form, *Oh look, Richard;* (2) followed, when his attention is gained, by the query, *What's that, Richard* (pointing), with stress and rising intonation peaking at the second word; (3) which is followed, if Richard should reply by any vocalization even in the form of a babble string initially, by *Yes, that's an X;* and (4) terminated by a general reinforcing remark like, *That's very good.* The result is that by the latter months of his second year, his pointing and labelling and even his gaze direction in the book reading situation can be predicted from his mother's vocalizations more than from the situation. However, it does not stop there.

At the point in progress when Richard reliably can produce the correct label or some phonologically constant form that the mother can imitate herself, her intonation contour changes. For items of this class, she still uses her second discourse marker, *What's that, Richard,* but now with a falling intonation on the second word. It is as if she is signalling that she knows that he knows, and the shift often produces ''knowing smiles'' between the two. Then, shortly after, she introduces an extended routine where after the presuppositionally marked request for a label she asks a second question calling for an answer in the form of a predicate of action or of state related to the child's just provided label—like *What's the X doing?* with stress and rising intonation on the terminal word. The same sorting of given and new can be observed in the development of request, when Richard's mother begins to establish a concept of canonical locus in responding to his request for absent objects: *It's in the ice box, you know,* etc. In both instances, one can observe not only the introduction of anaphoric pronominals as substitutes for nominals (as in the last example), but also a differentiation between definite and indefinite articles to mark anaphora as well. What one observes, in short, is the mother moving from a completely deictic procedure of labelling present and evident objects in the perceptual context, to indicating objects or states intralinguistically.

In this process, the existence of an agreed upon format is crucial. It provides the ''limited world,'' the microcosm of limited degrees of freedom, that makes it possible for the child to recognize what the next steps require linguistically. But what is striking to me is the degree to which these are fitted appropriately into the sequence of the mother's speech rather than tripped off by opportunities provided in the non-linguistic world.

In short, formatted discourse provides crucial framing that helps the child discover (or recognize) how to use language to inform others, to get them to do things for him, to please them, etc. And it does so by disposing the child toward intralinguistic contexts rather than extralinguistic ones.

The foregoing discussion, it seems to me, gives a very considerable role to the adult as an aid to the child in language learning. Indeed, I think the solo model of social learning, however useful it may be in goading us to look for internal structures and processes, has by now become a bit threadbare. One can say that the adult monitors the child's performance and "scaffolds" it by supplying missing supports until the child can monitor his own performance and fit it into the ongoing dialogue (cf. Kaye & Charney, 1980). What is now badly needed is more research, specifically designed to find out the various "pedagogical" procedures by which adults use formatting and other means to aid the child into different forms of language use and their supporting linguistic structures.

SOCIAL INTERACTION OR SYNTAX?

Let me make one final point, this one a reversion to the argument of writers like Peirce (1931), Benveniste (1971), and Jakobson (1971) about the "intersubjective" origin and function of linguistic forms. Peirce commented, particularly in his letters to Lady Welby (1953), on the duality of symbolic forms in natural language in serving both to *represent* concepts and to *communicate* them. He saw this as creating complexities, since one's own perspective often differed from those of an interlocutor. It was Benveniste who, as already noted, commented on the resort to pronominal shifters as a universal means of dealing with interpersonal perspective. To Jakobson, finally, goes the credit for exploring the interconnectedness of pronominal shifters with such contrastive deictic pairs as *this* and *that, here* and *there, to* and *from* and even verb forms like *come* and *go.*

The message that I read into the writings of these towering linguists is that it would be impossible to learn a *language in use* without knowing in advance or learning concurrently the perspectival complexities involved in using a set of symbols both to represent and to communicate—to assure eventual appreciation of intention, contextual constraint, and presupposition. I have no idea whether insights about interaction required of speakers and hearers of a natural language belong in the domain of social interaction or linguistics or, more likely both. What I think I dimly begin to see is that a sharp separation of the two—as in Saussure's distinction of *la langue* and *la parole* or in Charles Morris's three-branched linguistic tree—does little to aid the progress of developmental linguistics.

Early language is performance in pursuit of competence, semantics and syntax gradually entering into *la parole* to make it better fit the conventions and the requirements of pragmatics. I hope that I have succeeded a little bit in convincing you that pragmatics is interesting and important in its own right and not merely as a kind of contextual support for the syntactic and semantic instruments that are used in getting things done with words. I commented early in the paper that pragmatics concerns itself with how we do things to and with other people through the vehicles of language and culture—how one takes a stance toward events and people, past, present, and future. I think that the more specific questions of *language* acquisition in the narrower sense will become clearer when these pragmatic issues are better understood.

REFERENCES

Austin, J. *How to do things with words*. Oxford: Oxford University Press, 1962.

Benveniste, E. *Problems in general linguistics*. Coral Gables, FL: University of Miami Press, 1971.

Brown, R. *A first language*. Cambridge, MA: Harvard University Press, 1973.

Bruner, J. S. The ontogenesis of speech acts. *Journal of Child Language*, 1975, *2*, 1–19.

Bruner, J. S. Learning how to do things with words. In J. S. Bruner & A. Garton (Eds.), *Human growth and development: Wolfson lectures*. Oxford: Oxford University Press, 1978.

Bruner, J. S. The social context of language acquisition. *Language and Communication*, 1981, *1* (#2/3), 155–178.

Bruner, J. S. The formats of language acquisition. *American Journal of Semiotics*, 1982, *1*(3), 1–16.

Bruner, J. S., Roy, C. & Ratner, N. The beginnings of request. In K. Nelson (Ed.), *Children's language* (Vol. 3). Hillsdale, N.J.: Lawrence Erlbaum Associates, 1982.

Campos, F. The emergence of causal relations and the linguistic development of Brazilian children. Ph.D. thesis, University of Campinas, Brazil, 1979.

Carey, S. & Bartlett, E. Study reported in G. A. Miller, *Spontaneous Apprentices: Children and Language*. New York; Seabury Press, 1977.

Chafe, W. *Meaning and the structure of language*. Chicago; Chicago University Press, 1970.

Clark, H. H. & Clark, E. V. *Psychology and language: An introduction to psycholinguistics*. New York; Harcourt Brace Jovanovich, 1977.

Cohen, L. J. Speech acts. In T. Sebeok (Ed.), *Current trends in psycholinguistics* (Vol. 12). The Hague: Mouton, 1974.

Culler, J. *De saussure*. London; Fontana, 1978.

de Laguna, G. *Speech: Its function and development*. New Haven, CN: Yale University Press, 1927.

Denkel, A. Communication and meaning. Unpublished Ph.D. Thesis submitted to the Department of Philosophy, Oxford University, 1977.

Dore, J. A pragmatic description of early language development. *Journal of Psycholinguistics Research*, 174, *3*, 343–350.

Feldman, C. Pragmatic features of natural language. In M. W. La Gally. R. A. Fox, and A. Bruck (eds.). Papers from the Tenth Regional Meeting. Chicago Linguistic Society. Chicago: Chicago Linguistic Society, 1974. pp. 151–160.

Fillmore, C. J. The case for case reopened. In P. Cole & J. M. Sadock (Eds.), *Syntax and semantics, (Vol. 8), Grammatical relations*. New York: Academic Press, 1977.

Foucault, M. *The Archeology of Knowledge*. New York: Pantheon, 1972.

Goody, E. (Ed.), *Questions and politeness: Strategies in social interaction*. Cambridge: Cambridge University Press, 1978.

Greenberg, J. H. Some universals of grammar with particular reference to the order of meaningful elements. In J. H. Greenberg (Ed.), *Universals of language*. Cambridge, MA: M.I.T. Press, 1963.

Grice, H. P. Logic and conversation. In P. Cole & J. L. Morgan (Eds.), *Syntax and semantics, (Vol. 3)*. New York: Academic Press, 1975.

Habermas, J. *Communication and the evolution of society*. Boston: Beacon Press, 1979.

Hockett, C. F. The origins of speech. *Scientific American,* 1960, *203*(3).

Jakobson, R. *Selected Writings*. The Hague: Mouton, 1971.

Karmiloff-Smith, A. *A functional approach to child language*. Cambridge: Cambridge University Press, 1979.

Kaye, K. & Charney, D. How mothers maintain "dialogue" with two-year-olds. In D. Olson (Ed.), *The social foundations of language and thought*. New York: W. W. Norton Co., 1980.

Keenan, E. O. & Schieffelin, B. B. Topic as a discourse notion: A study of topic in the conversations of children and adults. In C. Li (Ed.), *Subject and Topic*. New York: Academic Press, 1976.

MacNamara, J. Cognitive basis of language learning in infants. *Psychological Review,* 1972, *79,* 1–13.

McShane, J. *Learning To Talk*. Cambridge: Cambridge University Press, 1980.

Ninio, A. & Bruner, J. S. The achievement and antecedents of labelling. *Journal of Child Language,* 1978, *5,* 1–15.

Peirce, C. S. *Collected papers*. Cambridge, MA: Harvard University Press, 1931.

Peirce, C. S. *Charles S. Peirce's Letters to Lady Welby*. (I. Lieb, Ed.) New Haven: Whitlock Inc., 1953.

Popper, K. *The Logic of scientific discovery*. New York: Harper & Row, 1968.

Ratner, N. & Bruner, J. S. Games, social exchange and the acquisition of language. *Journal of Child Language,* 1978, *5,* 391–401.

Ricoeur, P. *Freud and philosophy: An essay on interpretation*. New Haven, CT: Yale University Press, 1970.

Ryan, J. Early language development. In M. P. M. Richards (Ed.), *The integration of a child into a social world*. Cambridge: Cambridge University Press, 1974.

Saussure, F. *Course in general linguistics*. New York: Philosophical Library, 1955.

Schank, R. & Abelson, R. *Scripts, plans, goals and understanding*. Hillsdale, N.J.: Lawrence Erlbaum Assoc., 1977.

Snow, C. & Ferguson, C. A. (Eds.) *Talking to children: Language input and acquisition*. New York & London: Academic Press, 1977.

Vygotsky, L. *Thought and language*. Cambridge, MA: M.I.T. Press, 1962.

3

On Transition, Continuity, and Coupling: An Alternative Approach to Communicative Development

Marilyn Shatz
University of Michigan

In recent years considerable attention has been paid to the communicative experiences of the child moving from the prelinguistic to the linguistic period. Whereas the resulting research is by and large a worthy effort that expands our knowledge of early interactive behavior, I submit that much of the work was motivated by inappropriate goals derived from questionable theoretical foundations. To maximize the worth of future efforts in this area, we need to clarify and modify the goals of such research, recognizing how the findings to date bear on those goals. We also need to formulate new research questions, the answers to which will further our attempts to provide both explanatorily and descriptively adequate theories of communicative development. To begin that process, I outline in this chapter what I believe motivated, however tacitly, much of the past research and why such motivation is misguided. Then I present a sketch of an alternative theoretical view of communicative development and defend it on two grounds. First, it avoids some of the pitfalls associated with the theoretical basis behind the earlier research, and second, it takes account of more of the facts we already know about communicative development. Finally, I end with a set of research questions motivated by this new theoretical sketch.

WHY FOCUS ON THE TRANSITION STAGE?

There is little doubt that, in the eyes of the child's family and community, the beginning use of language is an important benchmark in the development of the child. Parents breathe a sigh of relief at the first occurrences of fledgling words and joyously reinforce their use. After all, the ability to use language is traditionally taken in many cultures as evidence of one's humanity and attendant ability to reason. This volume and the conference preceding it are testament to the fact that researchers, too, have assumed that the nonverbal to verbal change is an important one. The question is whether, with regard to its role in an explanatory theory of communicative development, the change warrants its special status, or whether its perceived importance is inflated if not illusory. I argue that the emphasis on the transition to language is to a large extent a consequence of the theoretical controversies surrounding language acquisition research, and that the transition period per se loses some of its significance when a sounder basis on both theoretical and empirical grounds is sought for communicative development.

To clarify why the prelinguistic-linguistic transition has assumed a central position, we need to make excursions into both history and metatheory. As for history, the interest in the period was motivated in part, I believe, by the desire to counteract the strong nativist claims of the 1960s regarding the child's facility for acquiring language. In focusing on universals of language form, the complexity of form, and the lack of structural transparency at the surface level, proponents of the nativist view discounted the possibility of important relations between prelinguistic communicative experiences and later language acquisition. That is, their views implied a discontinuity between early and later stages of development. One effect of this implied discontinuity was to make the onset of language seem quite marvelous and mysterious, requiring a powerful mechanism to account for it. The mechanism suggested by the nativists, of course, was a biological predisposition for language.

There are many reasons why the biological argument was unpalatable to some researchers; among them are the long history of empiricism in psychology and the view that the argument had ''default'' status (that is, it gained force by virtue of evidence against other alternatives rather than evidence for itself). Moreover, the discontinuity aspect of the argument may have been especially disturbing, considering the acceptance continuity has had generally in Western philosophical and scientific thought (see Kagan, 1980). It is not surprising, then, to find that much of the research since the time the biological argument was made has focused on ways of undermining or weakening it. In other papers, I have offered critiques of several lines of work of this sort, such as the attempt to find relations between social development and language development and the study of the role of maternal input on language development (Hoff-Ginsberg & Shatz, 1982; Shatz, 1981; 1982). Here in the same vein, the concern is with another line of research motivated in particular by the discontinuity implication, namely, the search for continuity between prelinguistic and linguistic behaviors.

We needn't search far to find researchers who in the 1970s focused on early behaviors with an eye to later ones. For example, prelinguistic and presyntactic behaviors are described as ''protodeclarative'' and ''protoimperative'' (Bates, Camaioni, & Volterra, 1975), and early interactive patterns between mother and child are characterized as "conversations" (Snow, 1977). On intuitive grounds, at least, the rationale for such research seems reasonable. The more continuity can be demonstrated, the less credibility a theory implying discontinuity will have; the more similarities there are between earlier and later stages of development, the less one requires powerful mechanisms to account for change. On closer examination, however, that rationale and the attendant issues of continuity and discontinuity turn out to be more problematic than might at first appear to be the case. We consider those problems next.

IS CONTINUITY A USEFUL CONSTRUCT?

I begin with a quote from Lewis P. Lipsitt's presidential address in 1981 to division 7 of the American Psychological Association:

> The preservation of sameness is not what development and developmental continuity are about. The essence of continuity is *predictable and explicable* change. That the tadpole and the frog, or the pupa and the butterfly, do not look like one another or behave like one another does *not* mean that the later stages are discontinuous with the earlier. Nor does it mean that the later stages could not, can not, and may not be well predicted and understood in terms of the organism's earlier history. It is the nature of life processes that change will occur, that some later stages of the same organism may bear only superficial resemblances to earlier, and that progressive, orderly, lawful, and understandable rules for these changes will be discovered.

Dr. Lipsitt seems to be saying that continuity has to do with explanatory theory and not superficial similarity. Applied to the topic at hand, his statement suggests that looking to the prelinguistic period for behaviors similar to ones found in the linguistic period is not an activity guaranteed to result in an increased understanding of language acquisition. Even though researchers may identify prelinguistic behaviors that look similar in either their form or function to later ones, they still may be no closer to explaining linguistic behavior. Similarity is neither a necessary nor a sufficient index of continuity.

Dr. Lipsitt's point is a cogent one. In fact, it makes no sense to talk of similarity as the measure of continuity in development. The best example of continuity would then be an organism whose states from time to time were completely similar, or isomorphic; hence that organism would not undergo change. If continuity is identified with lack of change and development with change, then it is a contradiction in terms to speak of continuous development.

Lipsitt avoids this contradiction by establishing continuity not on the basis of similarity of states but on the non-arbitrary basis of change. Since continuity in this sense is obviously demonstrable (pupae develop into butterflies, but tadpoles do not), the issue of continuity becomes vacuous.

Given the previous analysis, the pitfalls of associating similarity and continuity may seem so obvious that one may wonder why it was ever done. The answer to that question, I believe, lies in a deeper consideration of the nature of explanatory developmental theory and the procedural difficulties of building one.

If we consider that development involves change from one state to another, then any theory of development must involve the specification of two parameters: what I shall call the precedence parameter and the mechanism parameter, where precedence refers to the specification of the preceding state and mechanism refers to the means by which the subsequent state is achieved. Prediction of the subsequent state should be possible on the basis of these two pieces of information. The problem then arises of how to specify the parameters. Description of states seems like a tractable problem, but the specification of mechanisms is a notoriously difficult one, often not amenable to direct investigation. Subsequent states, however, are available for examination. A reasonable heuristic strategy has been, not to try to specify the mechanism and predict what will change, but to compare precedent and subsequent stages to specify what it is that has changed, and then, on the assumption that the means of change is related to the nature of the changes to be accounted for, to narrow the set of possible mechanisms of change. Assessing similarity and differences between states becomes useful, then, not because similarity is a direct measure of continuity but because uncovering the degree of similarity between states is one step in discovering what it is that changes, and specifying what it is that changes is one step in discovering what causes change.

Further consideration reveals, however, that assessing similarity is not itself a simple procedure. First, there is the problem of determining the proper description of a particular behavior in a particular state. For example, does the baby who coos in response to his mother's verbal overtures have turn-taking knowledge or is he simply unable to listen and respond at the same time? Second, how does one compare the baby's behavior with the young child who participates in sequential linguistic interactions? To say that they are similar does not necessarily imply that the later one is necessarily dependent on the occurrence of the earlier one. If our purpose in assessing similarity is ultimately to uncover the means of change, we could be misled in that endeavor by assuming on the basis of perceived similarity across states that little changes. If we have judged similarity superficially, or if in fact similar antecedent states are not necessary to later ones, we may postulate mechanisms not fully adequate to account for later states. In short, the similarity assessment strategy is dangerous because we have no clear basis on which to make judgments about crucial similarities and because the assessment of similarity alone is inadequate without some assessment of the necessary relation between earlier and later states.

Moreover, the assumption that the nature of the change and the means of change are related adds still more potential for error to this theory-building strategy, since the nature of the relation between them has been neither clearly specified nor well defended. Rather, one interpretation of the relation, that a small change requires only a weak mechanism and a big change requires a powerful one, seems tacitly to underlie much of the controversy over the roots of linquistic ability. We have at the moment no agreed-upon list of powerful and weak mechanisms. We do not even have a principled set of definitional criteria for deciding how to so classify a mechanism, although theorists of varied persuasions have not felt restrained from arguing as though we do. On one hand, we have had arguments that nothing short of biological predispositions (presumably a powerful mechanism) is sufficient to account for the child's rapid growth in language acquisition, whereas the opposition has argued that the changes involved in becoming a linguistic creature are not so great (and hence presumably do not require a powerful mechanism). Yet, further thought should convince us that there is no necessary connection between the apparent size of a change and the type or strength of the mechanism accounting for it. A concrete example may make the point best.

Consider the growth of bone and muscle that occurs during any one six month period in the middle childhood years. It would seem reasonable to call the amount of such growth relatively small, since during that period it would likely be barely perceptible. Consider now the physical changes apparent after six months during the pubertal period. One would hardly call those changes small. Yet, both can largely be accounted for by genetic mechanisms (although not necessarily the same ones). Are we to conclude from this that one kind of mechanism can be both weak and powerful? In that case, the claim that we need a powerful mechanism or a weak one tells us nothing about the type of mechanism we need. Or, is the magnitude of perceptible change a poor basis on which to define the notion of strength? I would argue for a ''yes'' to the latter question. In the next section an example of an alternative definition of mechanism strength is offered.

Finally, it is somewhat ironic that nativists have argued for large changes and discontinuity in language development, whereas those with more faith in environmental effects have sought continuity. More commonly, it is the discontinuity position that is associated with external influence and changes of large magnitude (Mendelsohn, 1980). This realignment of the more usual relations characterizing the continuity-discontinuity dichotomy is yet another indication of how muddled the continuity construct has become. (See Kagan, 1980, for some of its possible interpretations.) Dichotomous constructs such as continuity and discontinuity serve a useful purpose in organizing our thoughts about areas in which our ignorance outweighs our understanding and we need some framework for research and investigation. However, as Mendelsohn (1980) says, ''Continuity and discontinuity . . . are not constructs of nature, but constructs of the human mind used to interpret nature [p107].'' Like other theoretical constructs they can become obsolete as their inadequacies become more obvious. I would argue that allegiance to the continuity-discontinuity debate is a commitment to a dichotomy that has outlived its worth.

ALTERNATIVE APPROACHES TO COMMUNICATIVE DEVELOPMENT

Given its questionable foundations, it would seem wise to abandon the search for continuity as it has been conducted, and to seek instead other bases on which to explore developmental issues in communication and into which the preverbal and early language periods might fit. For one, we could begin by defining our terms more explicitly.

Defining Mechanism Strength.   As an example of the kind of criteria we could set for determining the strength of mechanisms, consider a distinction found in automata theory, which deals with descriptions of machines in terms of their input-output relations. Such machines are typically described as a set of variables, values on those variables, and operations performed on those valued variables. A distinction is made between a machine which can produce a new output by adding a new value to an old variable and a machine which can create a whole new variable, presumably capable of taking on a range of values. One might define weak mechanisms of change, then, as those procedures which create new values for old variables, and powerful mechanisms of change as procedures that result in new variables capable of taking on a range of values (even if that range expands gradually over time). Of course, the criteria for what count as distinct variables also require more elaboration. For example, a new variable may be one that takes a different set of operations from any of the old variables. This is only one example of the kind of criteria that could be set up to put the investigation of mechanisms of development on a more solid theoretical foundation.

Reassessing the Importance of the Transition Period.   Much like the implicit assumptions about the relation between the magnitude of a change and the nature of the mechanism accounting for that change, the idea that the prelinguistic-linguistic transition is especially significant has been accepted on essentially traditional and intuitive grounds. I do not intend to argue here against according it significance; clearly, the acquisition of linguistic means of expression is an important phenomenon. Rather, I want to put it in more perspective by suggesting that, when viewed from the vantage point of a communicative theory (and not just a theory of language acquisition), it is only one of several significant, or potentially significant, changes.

The idea that other changes besides the transition to language may be significant is not an unusual one. Indeed, the continuity view is based to some extent on such an idea. In particular, the continuist belief is that language behavior is more explainable because one can find early communicative understandings before language that make cracking the language code easier (see, for example, Bruner, 1975, 1978). Note that in this view the significant communicative advances are postulated *in order to* account for linguistic advances, not in order to supplement them.

The point I want to make here is different. I want to argue that the child's communicative understandings are still very *undeveloped* in crucial ways at the time language begins to appear. Nor can the acquisition of language per se fully account for advances in communicative understanding that follow the onset of language use. In terms of the machine analogy, language is not the only variable added to the system accounting for major changes. To defend my view, I begin with a discussion of some criteria for human communication. I then present evidence from various studies suggesting that these criteria do not appear to be fulfilled by children until they are well past the early stages of language acquisition.

It is generally agreed that true communication requires some voluntary action on the part of the sender. In only the most uninteresting sense of the word *communicate* does the radiator communicate to us that the heat is on. Similarly, the baby crying in discomfort does not seem to fulfill this condition completely. At somewhat later points in infancy, the voluntariness of the act seems less questionable (see, for example, Golinkoff, this volume). However, human communication in its highest sense seems to require still more; namely, that the sender understand that his receiver is an independent agent capable of voluntary action, who can understand that the sender intends something and who in his response can recognize that intention without necessarily fulfilling the sender's wants, needs, or goals (beyond the goal of getting the receiver to understand the intention). This condition on human communication is derived from Grice's (1969) analysis of meaning, and as Dennett (1978) notes, it is what distinguishes communication between adult humans from transactions between either men and machines equipped with some form of language or men and animals who have developed expectations about human response behavior on the basis of their experiences with humans. The relevance of all this is that young children have not been shown to meet this condition, even after they begin to speak. In other words, communicative behavior in this sense may not be characteristic of either the prelinguistic, the transitional, or the early linguistic period.

It is, of course, dangerous to argue on the basis of negative evidence that children lack a particular ability, especially in light of the many recent discoveries of early competence (see, for example, Gelman, 1978). Yet several pieces of evidence converge to make my position plausible. The first is a study by

Huttenlocher and Charney (1981), who distinguish between two kinds of verbs, those that describe goal-directed actions (get, put) and those that describe movement (run, jump).[1] They argue that what is salient to the child as actor is his goal-directed plan or the attainment of his goal. What is salient to the child as observer is the perceptual characteristics of movement. Thus, different orders of acquisition of verb use may occur depending on whether the child is describing the child's own or others' actions. The importance of this possibility to the present discussion is that it would suggest the young child does not necessarily view others as having goal-directed plans.

The children in the verb studies did indeed appear to use verbs differentially depending on whether they were talking about their own or others' actions. For example, virtually all uses of *get, take,* and *put* describe an action the child was doing or about to do. Verbs like *come, read,* and *give* were used by some children as descriptions of their own actions and by some as requests, but rarely as both by any one child. On the basis of this sort of evidence, Huttenlocher and Charney conclude that 2-year-olds do not view others in the same way they view themselves, as self-directed agents of planned change. If this is so, then it is difficult to see how such children could be fulfilling the Gricean condition on communication discussed earlier.

The question the Huttenlocher and Charney work raises is really whether the young child has a general concept of person that includes both self and others as capable of intentions, plans, and understandings. Some recent work done by myself and my colleagues at the University of Michigan bears on the same question (Shatz, Wellman, & Silber, in press). Our concern was with the uses of verbs expressing some mental function or mental state such as *think, know,* and *guess.* Such words have been reported to occur fairly early in a child's productions (Limber, 1973). However, these words often can serve conversational functions such as attention-getting ("Know what?") rather than as pure expressions of mental state (Gelman & Shatz, 1977). Hence, the mere occurrence of such words tells us nothing about children's understanding of their own or others' mental life. Thus, Shatz, Wellman, and Silber examined the functions of such verbs in early child speech to determine when children actually begin to use such expressions to encode their thoughts about their own and others' mental states. The data consisted mainly of speech samples collected approximately twice weekly over a 1 1/2 year period from one child beginning when the child was two until the age of four. Of more than 30,000 utterances, 1483 contained at least one mental verb. Additional data come from much shorter transcripts from 30 children who were observed four times during a six month interval beginning when the children were between the ages of 2 and 2; 6.

The first finding of relevance to us here is that the earliest uses of mental verbs

[1]Huttenlocher and Charney's distinctions are considerably more complex than this, involving also the issue of whether the movement involved in the action the verb expresses is specific (e.g. *pull*) or not (e.g. *put*).

are not to express mental state but rather to serve conversational functions. Both data sets suggest this. Second, in the large data set on one child, the first 10 uses of mental state are all references to the child's own mental state. Not until 3 months after he began to produce references to his own mental states did the child produce a clear reference to another's mental state. Also, a consideration of all the data up to age 4 shows that the child persisted in using mental verbs most frequently with first person subjects. Just as the Huttenlocher and Charney data suggest that the young child talks primarily about his own observable goal-directed actions, so our longitudinal data suggest he talks primarily about his own mental actions. However, our smaller data set is not corroborative on these latter points. Seven of the 142 utterances involving a mental verb were mental state expressions. Of these seven, only three involved self-reference. Given the small data set, we cannot be sure these seven utterances are the first uses of mental reference for the six children producing them. In all likelihood, they are not. Still, we cannot conclude with confidence that first mental reference is to the self. Nevertheless, the data do suggest that mental reference is a fairly late acquisition, occurring during the last quarter of the third year of life. Moreover, there is the suggestion in the data that, much like goal-directed action expressions, the first occurrences of mental state expressions are primarily references to the self. Thus, reasonably consistent evidence points to the likelihood that the child does not have a well developed general notion of person until about 3 years of age, long after his early interactive experiences and even after considerable progress has been made on the acquisition of grammar.

We have little comparative data on communicative behaviors before and after the acquisition of the person concept as discussed here. Such a comparison might reveal that the concept is necessary for the occurrence of certain kinds of behaviors. For example, Dennett (1978) argues that lying requires an understanding of the other as a being with beliefs, plans, and goals.[2] Genuine lying, then, should not be found before the fourth year of life.

Other aspects of early interactive behavior similarly argue for the view that basic, major changes in communicative understanding take place after the beginnings of language. The early discourse behavior of children suggests that they sometimes acquire and use devices for maintaining discourse in structurally appropriate ways without an understanding of their communicative import. For example, children have been reported to use *yes* or *no* strategies to respond consistently to questions without regard to the semantic relevance of their an-

---

[2]Again, it is important to distinguish between manipulation of the other on the basis of the manipulator's knowledge of the way the other usually behaves in certain circumstances and true cases of lying which require a clear attempt to affect the other's belief system. Thus, Dennett says, the dog who goes to the door in order to get his master to vacate the chair in which the dog wants to sleep can only be credited with the idea that his master will respond to the dog's door behavior as he usually does (coming to open the door) and not with the belief that the master will believe that the dog wants to go out.

swers. They also have been reported to adopt parental conversational devices such as *hum* or *umm,* but without regard to the pragmatic constraints on such devices (for a review see Shatz, in press). The appropriate uses of such devices depends not only on recognizing them as ''turn-takers'' but on understanding the relation between one conversational partner's intent in making an overture and the other's recognition of that intent in making a response. In other words, we would expect to find a reduction in the production of these ''empty'' conversational devices following the time the child acquires a deeper understanding of the nature of communicative reciprocity between two *persons.*

In sum, the continuists may have been right in arguing that what is basic and unique about human communication may depend on much more than the acquisition of linguistic form. Where they erred, I think, is in assuming that much of the knowledge about communication is acquired before language and that it forms a solid basis for language acquisition itself. When these misconceptions are relinguished, the assumed importance of the transition period dims and the period's role in communicative development can be situated in a broader perspective. The transition period certainly has a place in the study of communicative behavior. The concern here is merely to focus a more objective eye on determining the nature of that role.

The Coupling of Subsystems.   One difficulty with the continuity-discontinuity dichotomy is that it fails to capture the essential nature of communicative development as a multi-faceted phenomenon. As has often been noted, communicative skill is situated at the interface between linguistic, cognitive, and social abilities. As such, its development depends on growth in each of those areas, although growth in any one may be relatively independent of factors in the other. Even within these large domains there are systems of knowledge that affect communicative growth and that may develop at different rates. One thing we have learned from recent research is that communicative and grammatical developments do not proceed in lock step (see, for example, Blank, Gessner, and Esposito, 1979). If we abandon the attempt to explain grammatical development on the basis of early communicative understandings, an alternative model of communicative development that seems consonant with the facts while avoiding the pitfalls discussed earlier begins to emerge. The evidence seems to point to sets of simultaneously developing subsystems (or variables), each with its own set of constraints, precedence conditions, and mechanisms of change. Some of these conditions and mechanisms are undoubtedly shared, but each subsystem is by definition at least partially different on these grounds from other subsystems. The integration of these subsystems, or couplings, is analogous to adding a new variable to the machine mentioned earlier. New levels of performance are attained when couplings occur.

Critical to the theoretical notion of coupling is, of course, the specification of subsystems. That is, to a large extent, an empirical question, determinable by examining both the operations performable on certain kinds of knowledge and the courses of the acquisition of such knowledge. Candidate subsystems include syntactic knowledge, speech act knowledge, understandings of agency, person knowledge, and so on. The point is that these areas of knowledge do not have a unitary acquisition course, all dependent on common constraints and means of change.

As for the conditions necessary for coupling to occur, it is likely that children generally need to build a fairly stable base of knowledge in a subsystem before they consistently couple it with other systems for smooth performance on a broad range of tasks. Support for this notion can be found in the variable performance of children on a variety of cognitive and communicative tasks (see Shatz, 1978; Wilkinson, 1981). Particularly pertinent examples are the inability of young children to utilize fully their syntactic knowledge when they are responding to rather than initiating a conversation (Bloom, Rocissano, & Hood, 1976) or the persistence of nonverbal requests by children with the linguistic means to express them (Read & Cherry, 1978).

This is only the barest outline of an alternative theoretical approach to communicative development. Yet it deserves consideration for several reasons. First, it is not a ''responsive'' approach to communication. By this I mean that it does not attempt to refute an earlier position by arguing the other side of the same theoretical coin. Thus, the coupling approach ignores the continuity-discontinuity issue and seeks as well to define mechanisms of strength in ways independent from those constructs.

Second, it takes account of several aspects of communicative development that we have recently discovered, but which accommodate poorly the continued focus on the transition period. These include major post-linguistic accomplishments such as the maturation of the person concept as well as the tenuous (at best) links found between language development itself and earlier interactive behaviors.

New Research Questions.   Fleshing out the coupling approach will require addressing many remaining questions. Among them are: What is a theoretically sound set of subsystems? What characterizes the development of each? What are the constraints on coupling; that is, what kinds of knowledge systems operate in the presence of others? What are the conditions for coupling? How do coupled systems interact? It is these kinds of questions that I believe would most profitably guide research in early communicative development.

CONCLUSION

It is perhaps worth remembering that even the young child who does not yet have a well-developed concept of person as it has been discussed here is still an active living organism trying to affect and respond to its environment. It should be no surprise, then, that we find the child doing just that with whatever means are currently at his or her disposal. Thus, a preverbal child persists in attempts to get what he or she wants if at first unsuccessful (see Golinkoff, this volume); those attempts can be said to be similar in some sense to later linguistic attempts. Indeed, it would be more surprising if no similarities were observed. Such similarities should not obscure the fact that development does take place over a rather extended time period, often adding new power and maturity to a child's interactive efforts, transforming them into truly communicative actions.

This is not to suggest that young children do not at times appear tremendously clever in their attempts to manipulate the environment. Just as pets often seem well in control of their masters' behavior, so children too are quick to pick up on successful operants. My favorite example of this involved a child about four whom I met in a restaurant as I was eating a luscious bowl of fresh strawberries and cream. "What are you eating," asked the child. "Strawberries," I said. "Do you want one?" "Yes," he said, as he helped himself to one with great relish. Then, in a grand display of clever opportunism, he said, "What are you eating again?" Of course, he got his reward.

We are, as Western adults, biased to think of our children early on as intentional beings. As the previous anecdote shows, they do indeed effectively manipulate the environment to achieve their ends. Yet, we should not let these abilities blind us to important changes that do occur with development, even if those changes are due somewhat to the better integration of prior abilities with newer acquisitions. If we can overcome our preoccupation with only the most primitive attempts at communication and language, we may be rewarded with a broader, more viable theory of communicative development.

ACKNOWLEDGMENTS

A preliminary version of this work was supported in part by the Wisconsin Center for Education Research through a grant from the National Institute of Education (NIE-G-81-0009).

REFERENCES

Bates, E., Camaioni, L., & Volterra, V. The acquisition of performatives prior to speech. *Merrill-Palmer Quarterly,* 1975, *21,* 3.

Blank, M., Gessner, M., & Esposito, A. Language without communication: A case study. *Journal of Child Language,* 1979, *6,* 329–352.

Bloom, L., Rocissano, L., & Hood, L. Adult-child discourse: Developmental interaction between information processing and linguistic knowledge. *Cognitive Psychology,* 1976, *8,* 521–552.

Bruner, J. S. The ontogenesis of speech acts. *Journal of Child Language,* 1975, *2,* 1–20.

Bruner, J. S. From communication to language: A psychological perspective. In I. Markova (Ed.), *The social context of language*. New York: John Wiley, 1978.

Dennett, D. C. *Brainstorms*. Ch. 11, Conditions on personhood. Bradford Books, 1978.

Gelman, R. Cognitive Development. In L. W. Porter & M. R. Rosenzweig (Eds.), *Annual review of psychology, 1978, 28.*

Gelman, R., & Shatz, M. Appropriate speech adjustments: The operation of conversational constraints on talk to 2-year-olds. In M. Lewis, & L. Rosenblum (Eds.), *Interaction, conversation, and the development of language*. New York: Wiley, 1977.

Grice, H. P. Utterer's meaning and intentions. *Philosophical Review*, 1969, *78*, 147–177.

Hoff-Ginsberg, E., & Shatz, M. Linguistic input and the child's acquisition of language. *Psychological Bulletin*, 1982, *92*, 3–26.

Huttenlocher, J., & Charney, R. Children's verb meanings: Evidence about the emergence of action categories. Unpublished manuscript, The University of Chicago, 1981.

Kagan, J. Perspectives on continuity. In O. G. Brim, Jr., & J. Kagan (Eds.), *Constancy and change in human development*. Cambridge, Mass.: Harvard University Press, 1980.

Limber, J. The genesis of complex sentences. In T. E. Moore (Ed.), *Cognitive development and the acquisition of language*. New York: Academic Press, 1973.

Mendelsohn, E. The continuous and the discrete in the history of science. In O. G. Brim, Jr., & J. Kagan (Eds.), *Constancy and change in human development*. Cambridge, Mass.: Harvard University Press, 1980.

Read, B. K., & Cherry, L. J. Preschool children's production of directive forms. *Discourse Processes*, 1978, *1*, 233–245.

Shatz, M. The relationship between cognitive processes and the development of communication skills. In C. B. Keasey (Ed.), *Nebraska symposium on motivation, 1977*. Lincoln, Neb.: University of Nebraska Press, 1978.

Shatz, M. Learning the rules of the game: Four views of the relation between social interaction and syntax acquisition. In W. Deutsch (Ed.), *The child's construction of language*. London: Academic Press, 1981.

Shatz, M. On mechanisms of language acquisition: Can features of the communicative environment account for development? In E. Wanner & L. R. Gleitman, (Eds.), *Language acquisition: The state of the art*. Cambridge, Eng.: Cambridge University Press, 1982.

Shatz, M. Communication. In J. H. Flavell, & E. M. Markman (Eds.), *Cognitive Development*. P. Mussen (Gen. Ed.), *Handbook of Child Psychology*, V. III, 4th ed. New York: John Wiley, in press.

Shatz, M., Wellman, H. M., & Silber, S. The acquisition of mental verbs: A systematic investigation of the first reference to mental states. *Cognition*, in press.

Snow, C. E. The development of conversation between mothers and babies. *Journal of Child Language*, 1977, *4*, 1–22.

Wilkinson, A. C. *Children's partial knowledge of counting*. Unpublished manuscript, University of Wisconsin, Madison, 1981.

4

The Preverbal Negotiation of Failed Messages: Insights into the Transition Period

Roberta Michnick Golinkoff
University of Delaware

Little theoretical or empirical research has been conducted on the transition period between prelinguistic and linguistic communication as compared to the vast amount of research on communication development in the first year of life (see Bullowa, 1979; Lewis & Rosenblum, 1974; Lock, 1978; Schaffer, 1977; Stern, 1977) and language development in the latter half of the second year (see Dale, 1976; Fletcher & Garman, 1979; Nelson, 1978). Therefore, I was surprised and initially unprepared to consider the impressive communicative complexity that characterizes mother-infant communicative interaction during the transition period from approximately 12 to 18 months of age.

Mothers and preverbal infants were observed to engage in lengthy communicative episodes initiated by the infant, apparently about some particular topic. Mothers often appeared eager to disambiguate their infant's signal and presented infants with nonverbal and verbal interpretations of their infants' possible intent. The infants responded to these interpretations in a number of ways, sometimes accepting the mother's interpretation and sometimes rejecting it. The extent to which infants were willing to communicatively persevere in the face of failure to achieve their goals and even to occasionally attempt nonverbal repairs of their original signals was compelling. Having done prior research (Harding & Golinkoff, 1979) with 8-to-12-month-olds on their communicative attempts to use an adult as an agent to achieve their goals, the communicative sophistication of infants just a few months older was all the more striking. While the 8-to-12-month-olds seemed to repeat their initial signal less frequently in the face of failure, not to attempt repairs, and sometimes to revert to less mature behaviors such as whining and crying, infants in the transition period often seemed to single mindedly pursue their goals.

The purpose of this chapter is to introduce and describe an important facet of communicative development which emerges during the transition period from prelinguistic to linguistic communication. I call this phenomenon the "negotiation of failed messages" and I claim that its fortuitous existence permits us to study the refinement and elaboration of the infant's communicative repertoire even before any words have appeared. Such refinement is revealed best in the situation where infants are attempting to convey messages to their caregivers in the face of an initial failure, that is, during the negotiation of failed messages. In addition, individual differences in the course and resolution of such negotiation episodes seem to have implications for the development of language.

The structure of this chapter is as follows: First, two examples of the negotiation of failed messages are discussed to acquaint the reader with the phenomenon and its theoretical underpinnings; second, the components of negotiation episodes are discussed in some detail; and third, the functions of negotiation episodes for the interactants and for the development of communication and language are treated. Thus, this chapter is more theoretical than empirical, describing the basic phenomenon and its potential ramifications. Subsequent papers will include micro-analyses of negotiation episodes.

TWO EXAMPLES OF THE NEGOTIATION OF FAILED MESSAGES

Aside from the first example, which occurred between me and my son, the source of the examples to follow are four lunches between three infants and their mothers, videotaped about once a month during the period from 11 to 18 months. The observer and equipment were concealed behind a screen in each infant's home. Although the focus and force of the infant's initial signals may have been unduly limited during lunch (i.e., to foods and requests/rejections, respectively) there are two virtues to this situation: First, since the infants were confined to highchairs their signals were easier to code than if they moved about freely; second, the infants were forced to signal since they could not attain their goals by themselves.

The First Example.   Jordan is a 14-month-old male infant, being served his lunch.

Example 1.

1.	Jordan:	(Vocalizes repeatedly until his mother turns around.)
2.	Mother:	(Turns around to look at him.)
3.	Jordan:	(Points to one of the objects on the counter.)
4.	Mother:	Do you want this? (Holds up milk container.)
5.	Jordan:	(Shakes his head "no.")

		(Vocalizes, continues to point.)
6.	Mother:	Do you want this? (Holds up jelly jar.)
7.	Jordan:	(Shakes head "no.")
		(Continues to point.)
8, 9, 10, & 11:		(2 more offer-rejection pairs.)
12.	Mother:	This? (Picks up sponge.)
13.	Jordan:	(Leans back in highchair, puts arms down, tension leaves body.)
14.	Mother:	(Hands Jordan sponge.)

Once Jordan has his mother's attention (Turn 2) he produces an initial signal (a point) at one of the objects on the kitchen counter. His mother makes a guess about the focus of his point and presumes that the force of his point is a request when she says in Turn 4, "Do you want this?" while holding up the milk container. Note that the mother does not give him some milk but *asks* if that is what he wants. The mother's behavior is indicative of a *comprehension failure* (independent of the fact that Jordan rejects her interpretation in the next turn) since there is uncertainty in her response to Jordan's signal. By framing her response as a question, Jordan's mother is indirectly indicating that she has failed to immediately disambiguate the message behind Jordan's original signal (the point). These are the first two of the three essential components of a negotiation episode: (1) an initial signal on the part of the infant not produced as a response to something the mother says or does but on a new topic; and (2) a comprehension failure of the message the infant wishes to convey. This comprehension failure may be signaled by either the mother or by the infant, and in this case it is signaled by the mother. The infant's subsequent turn (#5) also signals a comprehension failure since he rejects the mother's tentative interpretation. What follows is a series of four more interpretation/rejection pairs until the mother apparently succeeds in discerning the infant's message.

That the preverbal infant can formulate and retain a specific meaning over several turns is a key theoretical assumption behind this phenomenon and will be discussed at length later. However, having a specific meaning in mind and producing a signal is no guarantee that that meaning will be grasped by the receiver — especially because of the infant's use of nonspecific nonverbal signals. Eventually this episode ends in success; the infant is offered and accepts the sponge, the item he was apparently indicating. This is the third essential component of a negotiation episode—the outcome—and it is always defined from the perspective of the infant. That is, did he or did he not seem to achieve his goal?[1] Other outcomes, aside from success, will also be discussed later.

A Definition of the Phenomenon.   Thus, as the example reveals, the word "negotiation" denotes the essaying back and forth that occurs between the mother

[1]For purposes of referential clarity caregivers will be referred to as "she" and infants as "he."

and the infant until some outcome is reached. The word "negotiate" presupposes that the mother and infant each have their own ideas of what the meaning behind the infant's signal is. A parallel can be drawn with labor negotiations where each negotiant begins with an initial position. The analogy breaks down, however, since during the negotiation of failed messages each negotiant is not equally flexible with regard to modification of his or her initial position. I assume that infants are relatively unyielding with regard to their initial meaning or intent. As far as can be discerned without independent empirical tests, infants seem to strive to accomplish their original goals. Infants do seem to be willing to alter—although not from the first appearance of negotiation episodes—the means they use to convey their message. That is, the *form* of the initial signal will sometimes be repaired through augmenting the original signal or through the substitution of a new signal.

The mother, on the other hand, changes her "position" often. That is, most of the mothers we have observed will flexibly consider many possible meanings in an apparent effort to please the infant. The mother seems to be the negotiant who is more willing to yield and to accommodate to the other negotiant's position.

To summarize, the phrase the "negotiation of failed messages" is meant to label a process which begins in the preverbal period and continues throughout life. It is designed to capture what occurs *after a communication misfire;* it is the process by which a speaker (in this chapter always the preverbal infant) *tries to make his message understood by a listener* (the infant's mother) *after the speaker's initial attempt has failed.*

Negotiation Episodes as One Type of Communicative Exchange. Negotiations of failed messages which take place during the transition period are only a portion of the communicative exchanges that occur between mother and infant. Using the products of much prior research, Fig. 4.1 roughly categorizes the types of communicative exchanges which occur in Western middle-class households when infants are in the transition period. Some exchanges are initiated by the mother and some by the infant. Of those the infant initiates with the intent to communicate, some will initially fail because the mother will fail to comprehend the infant's message. The preverbal negotiation of failed messages occurs only in this portion of the infant's communicative attempts. Of those communicative attempts by the infant that initially fail, some portion will conclude successfully with the infant somehow accomplishing his goal. Thus, negotiation episodes are characterized by: (1) an initial attempt on the part of the infant to send some signal(s) which convey(s) some message; (2) a failure on the part of the mother to understand the child's message; and (3) the subsequent maneuvers the child and mother use to understand or negotiate the child's meaning.

The Utility of Failures for Analyzing Communicative Interactions. Aside from the work of Lock (1979) there are few treatments in the literature which focus

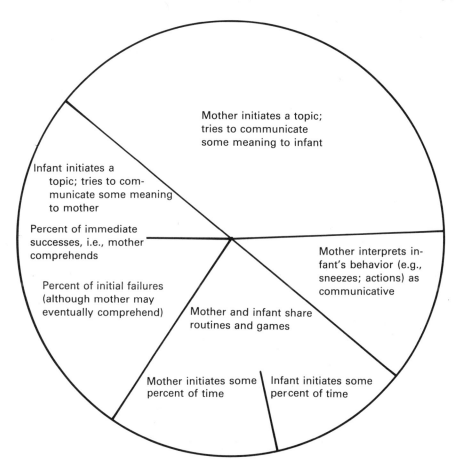

Fig. 4.1   A schematic representation of the approximate relative proportions of communicative interactions which occur between mothers and infants during the transition period from preverbal to verbal communication development.

on the communicative interaction between infants and their mothers during the transition period. Some studies do focus on the transformation of vocalizations into speech (Carter, 1979; Dore, 1974; Halliday, 1975) and some on the use of nonverbal deictic gestures (Bates, 1979). Finally, many have examined language comprehension (for a review see Bloom & Lahey, 1978) and early word use (see Nelson, 1973). Yet few studies examine the emergence of language within an interactional context going beyond the analysis of the individual infant employing his idiosyncratic communicative signals. What appears to be missing in the literature is an account of how the range and complexity of the infant's communicative abilities (both nonverbal and verbal) changes between about 12–18 months, the period before the child uses many words. The infant's attempt to establish his intents through communication with others in the *face of failure* seems particularly well suited to opening the infant's communicative skills for inspection. Under such circumstances the infant is highly motivated to achieve his end, often the attainment of some concrete object. When a payoff is at stake and a failed message occurs, the infant will harness all the tools in his communicative arsenal to accomplish his goals. Bloom, Rocissano, and Hood (1976) report a similar phenomenon in the domain of language production: Children's spontaneous productions, designed to achieve the child's own ends, reflect greater competence (e.g., longer MLU's) than productions used to respond to others' agendas such as question-answering.

The Second Example.   Lest the reader has experienced a comprehension failure due to my inchoate initial signals, let us analyze another example between a 16-month-old and her mother, also at mealtime. This negotiation episode has neither a successful outcome nor a clearly discernible topic for the infant's initial signal.

Example 4.2

1. Nicole: (Turns and points in direction of the refrigerator.)
2. Mother: (Turns in the direction of the point) "Refrigerator."
3. Nicole: (Continues to point.)
4. Nicole: (Turns back to face mother in her high chair.)

The appearance of the initial signal is clear, given that the infant suddenly reorients her body and points in the direction of the refrigerator. The mother seems to think that she understands the baby's focus (unlike in the prior example) since she provides a label for the presumed topic immediately after the infant's signal and with a declarative intonation. However, the infant continues to point, which we interpret to mean that her intention has not been met by the mother's production of a label. For our purposes, it is not possible to know what Nicole had in mind since she turns back in her highchair, apparently to reestablish feeding. This then in our system is a "substitution by the baby" (to be described in greater detail in the following), in which for whatever reason, the infant abandons her attempt to communicate some particular meaning. Thus, in this example, unlike the first example, we have no way of guessing at the infant's intention. Before proceeding with a more detailed theoretical treatment of the components of the negotiation of failed messages the extent to which the preverbal infant is capable of formulating and communicatively pursuing specific communicative intents must be discussed as a separate issue.

What Any Grandmother (In Western Society) Will Tell You: Babies Know What They Want

Let us first return to Example 4.1. On what basis can it be argued that the infant wanted the *sponge,* in particular, the item that he ultimately accepted? There are two reasons to infer that the infant began the episode with the goal of obtaining the sponge. First, if the infant had just wished to gain attention through his communicative efforts or make social contact, he should have stopped signaling when this was achieved. He didn't. Second, if the infant had just wished to be given (or shown) any of the objects present, he should have been satisfied when that goal was met. He wasn't. To the contrary, the infant persisted in signaling, through gaze and gesture, at some particular item from among the array of items present. Such behavior seems to fit nicely under the first and third components of Bruner's (1974) criteria for intentional behavior: Focused persistence on something, the substitution of alternative means when initial means fail, and termination of the behavior when the goal is achieved.

Nonetheless it would be foolhardy to deny that the infant may have had some other intent which is simply inaccessible, either due to its poor formulation by the infant or the insensitive eye of the mother and observer. Perhaps the infant wanted to look out the window behind the food and gave up just at the moment when the mother offered him the sponge. This alternative cannot be conclusively ruled out. However, two arguments can be made for the present method of utilizing the infant's own behaviors for the purpose of attributing specific communicative intents to the infant.[2]

First, during the analysis of negotiation episodes the researcher has access to the infant's acceptance or rejection of the mother's interpretation of the infant's apparent intent. Thus, the infant's *own behavior* is systematically employed to disambiguate the meaning behind the infant's signal. If the infant accepts the mother's interpretation it is assumed that she has succeeded in decoding his message; conversely, if the infant seems to reject the mother's interpretations, that episode would not be assigned a successful outcome.

Using the infant's own behavior to assign communicative intents represents an advance over prior research. Carter (1978), Dore (1974), Halliday (1975), and McShane (1980), among others have proposed that certain functions, such as the "instrumental," "directive," and "regulatory" are encoded by the speech and preverbal communicative signals of the transitional child. Francis (1979) has correctly criticized the approach of assigning intentions to children's preverbal signals as empirically weak. Fine, often questionable, distinctions between func-

---

[2]Taking the child's perspective has had other consequences. For example, we have occasions where a mother interprets some behavior from the baby as though it were a communicative signal and negotiations follow. While these are certainly interesting, we count only episodes which begin with an initial signal from the infant which observers can agree on.

tions are made from the adult's perspective. Most studies also lack external evidence that what the child intends is what the investigator understood.

The second argument for the infant's possession of specific communicative intents is the work on how slightly older infants attempt to repair naturally occurring (Gallagher, 1977; Greenfield, 1980) and experimentally feigned communicative misunderstandings (Wilcox & Webster, 1980). Although these studies are discussed elsewhere later it is worth noting here that young children do attempt to either repeat or recode their signals to get their meanings across. Repetition or recoding of the initial signal suggests that the infant does indeed have a specific intent. When an infant stops signaling after the mother offers a particular interpretation, some evidence is provided for what the nature of that specific intent is.

Thus, two facts support the case for assigning specific intentions to infants' initial communicative signals: (1) the use of the infant's own behavior to make judgments of intent; and (2) the fact that slightly older children do seem capable of rejecting incorrect interpretations of their intents. Clearly, this is not an airtight case. Additional empirical work (e.g., feigning misunderstandings in the transition period; offering a favorite object while the child is presumably signaling for something else) needs to be conducted.

By way of summary of this section, Greenfield (1980) has written an insightful passage which speaks to the value of failed messages for ascertaining the infant's communicative intent:

> Is the negotiated process of interpretation occurring in interaction a meaningful index of [the child's] intention? Or is acceptance of the other participant's interpretation of one's own intention so automatic that it provides no information at all? This question is particularly important in studying early language acquisition where the child's linguistic means to accept or reject an interpretation are limited or nonexistent. But our basic criteria of intentionality reveal instances in which the child rejects the mother's interpretation of the intended content of communication . . . *intentional structure is most visible where the intended consequences do not immediately occur* [p. 268; my underlining].

THE COMPONENTS OF THE NEGOTIATION OF FAILED MESSAGES

As defined earlier, the "negotiation of failed messages" is the *process* by which the preverbal infant endeavors to make his message understood by a receiver (in this case the mother) after the infant's initial attempt has failed. Negotiation episodes have a minimum of three and a maximum of four components: There is (1) an initial signal produced by the infant, followed by; (2) an indication of misunderstanding, optionally followed by; (3) a repair attempt by the infant and, finally; (4) an outcome. Component (3), the infant's repair of failed messages is not a necessary component of negotiation episodes since the infant may not perceive the need to creatively repair his failed messages until having experienced many communicative failures. On another point, the fact that there are four components does not mean that a negotiation episode takes only three or four conversational turns. Some components (specifically (2) and (3)) may occur recursively (see Example 4.1). The rest of this section will describe the four components in detail.

Component 1: The Initial Signal.   The first component in a negotiation episode is the production of an initial communicative signal by the infant which begins the interchange. Since this phenomenon is defined from the *child's* perspective, the form of the initial signal will vary depending on the child. For example, one subject used the following idiosyncratic signal: When she wanted her lunch she leaned forward in her highchair and stared at it fixedly. The intent of this gesture seemed so obvious to the mother and the observer that both laughed and concurred in their interpretation.

Another accommodation to the child's perspective is made by not counting as initial signals communicative behaviors which observers judged were *not* performed in the service of communication.[3] This distinction is made even when an attentive mother interprets such behaviors as initial signals. Differentiating between communicative signals and noncommunicative behaviors is not always easy. Observers of the videotaped interaction, using gesture, prosody, volume, direction of eye gaze, and prior events, judge whether the infant's initial signal was produced with the intent of conveying some meaning. The above behaviors are often cited as evidence of intentional communication in situations where infants use adults as agents to achieve their ends (for a review see Golinkoff, 1981). The form of the intial signals shown on Table 4.1 result from our preliminary analyses. The range of these signals may be constrained by the fact that the infants were always seated in their highchairs. With increased mobility other signals would probably have occurred.

For an infant capable of some speech, the initial signal may be an immature phonological attempt to produce a specific lexical item. While the adult can readily produce specific lexical items and attention-getters in a single turn (e.g., "Hey, got a match?"), the preverbal child may expend considerable effort obtaining the caregiver's attention. The child's work at gaining attention may then have an effect on the length of the negotiation episodes. For our purposes, the first

---

[3]It could be argued that the mother is the best judge of whether the infant has emitted a communicative signal since she shares a common history of communicative exchanges with the infant which she has helped to shape. However, mothers are also notorious (see Snow, 1977) for interpreting every bodily emission as a signal worthy of interpretation and comment.

TABLE 4.1

THE FORM OF INFANTS' INITIAL SIGNALS IN THE PREVERBAL NEGOTIATION OF
FAILED MESSAGES.

Nature of signal and combinations thus far observed

1. Directional sustained eye gaze.
2. Pointing or reaching.
3. Vocalizing (whining, "fake" cry).
4. Giving mother object.
5. Alternating gaze between mother and object; vocalizing; pointing or reaching in various combinations.
6. Primitive lexical attempts with or without nonverbal gestures.

---

turn of a negotiation episode occurs only when the infant attempts to communicate about some content and has already obtained the listener's attention.

Component 2: Comprehension Failure.   The initial signal must be followed by a comprehension failure on the mother's part which can be indicated by either the mother or the infant. Example 4.2 illustrates an episode where the *infant* indicates a comprehension failure. In these cases, the mother seems to think she has correctly interpreted the infant's intent and she takes her turn with assurance. The infant then indicates that the mother has failed to comprehend by continuing to signal. Other behaviors infants use for the same purpose are physically rejecting what the mother offers, shaking the head "no," leaning away from the preferred object, or emitting protest vocalizations. Of course, infants may be doing these things not so much "to indicate" comprehension failure as to express their displeasure at not having achieved these goals. Which of these formulations best describes infants' knowledge is an empirical issue which awaits further investigation.

If the *mother* is the one to indicate a comprehension failure she might say something like "What?" or "I don't know what you want" or she might attempt to formulate the child's nonverbal attempts in the form of a question such as "Do you want the milk?" In practice, it is sometimes difficult to decide when the mother is engaging in such behaviors because she genuinely does not understand, or because she is trying to push the child to express his intentions in a more mature manner. For this reason the term "comprehension failure" should be conceived as labeling a continuum: From complete failure to partial failure (perhaps the topic is understood but not the predication) to indications of failure when the mother is actually fairly certain she knows what the child wants. This latter type of comprehension failure may have its own function, namely to prompt the child to produce a label.

Others in the literature (for a discussion see Cherry, 1979) have noted that mothers or adults interacting with young children will signal comprehension failures and have given these behaviors on the adult's part a variety of labels. Working independently, Corsaro (1977) and Cherry (1979) discussed what they called "clarification requests" and "requests for clarification," respectively. Cherry's analysis approximates the one adopted here. She writes, "The request for clarification is a conversational device which functions to allow *either speaker* to bring a *misunderstanding* in the conversation to the attention of the other. Misunderstandings can be inferred from the presence of clarification questions but *are not limited to them* [pp. 273–274; my underlining]." Thus while Cherry focuses on the adult, she recognizes that either interactant may signal the misunderstanding, as I do. Further, although she focuses only on clarification requests which assume a linguistic form, she is prepared to accept (as in the present analysis), nonverbal indicators of misunderstandings. However, when the clarification request is produced in a linguistic form it can only be in the form of a question.

Corsaro (1977) also defines clarification requests in terms of the interrogative form but he does not admit nonlinguistic signals of misunderstanding in his definition. He writes:

> The clarification request (CR) is defined as an *interrogative* which calls for the clarification, confirmation, or repetition of the preceding utterance of a co-interactant. The CR serves *no substantive topical function* in interaction in that its production does not contribute information in line with the established topic; it is employed rather as a device to keep interaction running smoothly or to repair disruptions in conversation [p. 185; my underlining].

In my rendition of the clarification "request" declarative statements on the mother's part such as "I don't understand what you want.", in addition to interrogatives, function as indications of comprehension failure. Further, since the mothers of our preverbal subjects are often reformulating nonverbal signals or poorly articulated linguistic attempts, their indications of comprehension failure often seem to assist infants in establishing topics they were not able to establish clearly on their own. The mother's signal of comprehension failure then, often "contributes information in line with the established topic" (Corsaro, 1977) in that it serves to clearly *establish* a topic where one was only hinted at by the infant.

Even when mothers interpret their infant's signal incorrectly they are still helping the infant to convey his meaning. Mothers are presenting infants with a dichotomous "yes–no" choice so that all the infants have to signal is acceptance or rejection. This serves to narrow the range of potential referents for infants' signals which in turn serves to assist infants in conveying their meanings.

Cherry (1979) and Corsaro (1977) subdivide their clarification requests into types that are remarkably similar. Both have a category of clarification markers such as "what" or "hmm?" that are presumably designed to request repetition of the prior signal. Both have a category which is designed to get the speaker to confirm or deny the listener's interpretation of the speaker's signal. This confirmation function can be signaled through unaltered full or partial repetition by the listener of the speaker's signal or by a reformulation or expansion produced with a rising intonation. Cherry (1979) has also discussed the "chaining" of clarification questions when the first attempt of the adult to gain insight into the child's meaning fails. "Chaining" certainly occurs in episodes of negotiation which exceed four turns.

The categories I have formulated which seem to capture most of the data for how mothers indicate comprehension failure when negotiating with infants are presented in Table 4.2. These range from nonverbal indicators of comprehension failure to expansions and repetitions of the infant's immature lexical attempts. Thus while two major functions are served by these indicators of comprehension failure (implicit requests for confirmation and implicit requests for repetition), there are differences between these categories in how much the mother seems to know about the infant's intent. When the mother cannot even produce a possible reformulation of the infant's signal (as in categories 1–3) the infant's signal may appear to be maximally ambiguous to the mother. A nonverbal offer (#4) at least indicates that the mother can come up with a potential referent for the infant's signal. A reformulation (#5) may imply further knowledge. Repetitions and expansions (categories 6 and 7) suggest that the mother believes the infant is trying to produce a particular word. Sometimes the mother uses these categories to prompt a more conventional repetition of the item by the infant after she produces a model of the correct form. It remains the task of further research to confirm that these categories do indeed function in the way indicated. A study by Wilcox and Webster (1980) suggests that slightly older children (17–24 months) do indeed distinguish between one type of implicit request for repetition from one type of implicit request for recoding.

Component 3: Repair.   After a comprehension failure is indicated most adult speakers will attempt a *repair* (Jefferson, 1972). While the first two components (initial signal and comprehension failure, respectively) must invariably be present to say that a negotiation episode has occurred, this third component may not always appear due to the communicative immaturity of the infant. Repairs may not be produced for two reasons: (1) infants may not understand that a repair is being requested; or (2) they may recognize that a repair is being requested but may be unable to produce some type of repair upon demand. At least, however, infants will be able to recognize that their intention (whatever it is) is not being honored. For this reason, if nothing else, they may continue to signal. Given this line of argument the first type of repair which we will probably see in our data is *repetition* of the original signal, produced with or without increased urgency. To use Gallagher's (1977) term, *abandonment* of the original intent (failing to produce a repair) will probably appear more frequently early in the transition period.

Two types of repair of the original signal are hypothesized to come later in development in the following order: (1) *augmentations* which involve adding some vocal or nonvocal signal to the original signal; and (2) *substitutions* in

TABLE 4.2
How Mothers (M) Signal Comprehension Failure
of the Infant's (I) Signal

Category	Definition and Example	Function of M's Signal
1. Nonverbal indicators	M uses nonverbal behaviors such as raised eyebrows, quizzical looks, long pauses.	Implicit request for repetition of I's signal
2. Clarification requests	M uses "clarification markers," e.g., "huh" or "what," or full clarification questions, e.g., "What do you want?" M does not name a possible referent.	Implicit request for repetition of I's signal
3. Statements of noncomprehension	M uses declarative intonation and explicitly states she has failed to comprehend, e.g., "I don't know what you want."	Implicit request for repetition of I's signal
4. Nonverbal offer of object	M holds up some object, e.g., the milk container, with or without speech, e.g., "this?".	Implicit request for confirmation
5. Reformulations	M puts I's nonverbal signal into words, e.g., "You want the milk?" in response to I's point. May occur with or without clarification request.	Implicit request for confirmation
6. Repetitions of lexical attempt	M repeats I's lexical attempt with an interrogative intonation, e.g., "milk?"	Implicit request for confirmation plus M models correct form
7. Expansions of lexical attempt	M extends I's lexical attempt to a full sentence, e.g., "Are you saying 'I want the milk'?", using interrogative intonation.	Implicit request for confirmation plus M models correct form

which the infant drops the prior signal and uses another gestural or linguistic signal (not just a phonological variant of the initial signal).

The hypothesized sequence of repair types (first, abandonments and repetitions; second, augmentations and then substitutions) find some support in a slightly older population (17–24 months) in the work of Wilcox and Webster (1980). An experimenter feigned two kinds of misunderstanding during interaction with each subject. In the first type, the adult asked "what?" an implicit request for repetition; in the second, the adult only acknowledged the proposition in a subject's "request" (loosely defined) to obtain some object or activity. Thus, in the latter case, the adult misunderstood the illocutionary force of the infant's utterance by acting as if the infant simply wanted the adult to notice an object. The question "what?" did elicit significantly more repetitions than recodings or abandonments while misunderstanding the force of the utterance elicited more recodings than repetitions or abandonments.

Our data will permit us to examine the first appearance of repairs and to test whether in fact the type of repair employed changes in the hypothesized order with development.

Component 4: Outcome. There are 6 possible outcomes of negotiation episodes: (1) *success* occurs when the mother carries out the infant's apparent goal.
This is signaled by the infant's acceptance of the mother's interpretation; (2) a
compromise results when the mother *grasps* the baby's intent but offers an
alternative which the baby accepts, as in, "No, you can't have more peaches
until you eat your spinach"; (3) *substitution by the mother* occurs if the mother
fails to understand what the baby intended but changes the "topic" in a way that
maintains communication. This often looks to observers as if the mother is trying
to satisfy the force of the infant's intent without understanding the particular
proposition intended; (4) *substitution by the baby* occurs if the baby selects some
alternative. Given the above discussion on repairs, baby substitutions may be one
type of abandonment. Alternatively, such substitutions may mean that the infant
was not much invested in his original intent or got distracted; (5) *failure by the
mother* is signaled by the mother's unwillingness to continue to negotiate; and
(6) *failure by the infant* appears as a regression by the infant—perhaps in response to frustration—to less mature behaviors such as crying, unfocused whining, or tantruming. All but the two types of failure are likely to result in the
appearance of a contented infant. Developmentally, it is expected that failures
(by mother or infant), and substitutions (by mother or infant), will decline as the
mother and infant come to establish their shared meaning system and the infant's
signals become more precise. Compromises may increase for the same reasons.

To summarize, episodes in which meaning is negotiated after an initial failure
have a minimum of three and a maximum of four components. An episode
begins when an infant emits a signal(s) which is not immediately comprehended
by the caregiver. Failure to comprehend may be indicated by the infant or the
mother. Repair attempts on the infant's part may or may not follow before an
outcome is achieved. A frequent outcome is success, in that the infant achieves
his goal, but other outcomes of a more intermediate nature, are possible as, of
course, is failure. Figure 4.2 presents a flow chart of the components of the
negotiation of failed messages. Also included are "missed attempts" at negotiation when for a variety of reasons the mother fails to permit the infant to establish
some meaning. These are discussed in greater detail below.

FAILED UPTAKE OF THE INFANT'S INITIAL SIGNAL:
MISSED ATTEMPTS

A missed attempt occurs when the mother does not pick up on the infant's
apparent attempt to communicate some meaning. This may occur for one of
several reasons, none of which are accessible to observers directly. For example,
the mother may wish to speed up the child's ingestion of food by discouraging
communication. Or, the mother may be preoccupied with her own thoughts or
she may not consider the child's signal to be a signal.

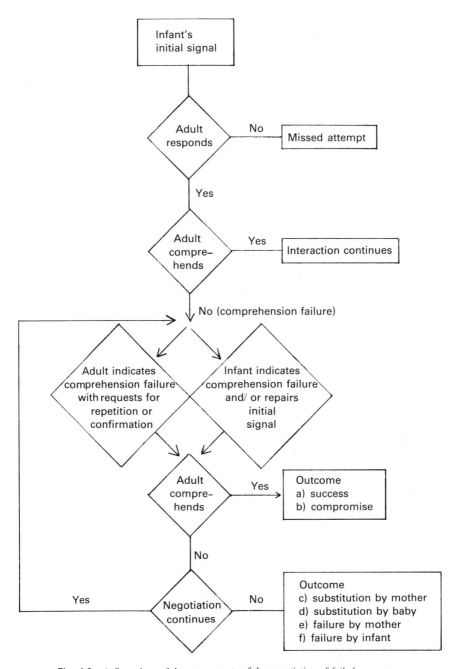

Fig. 4.2   A flow chart of the components of the negotiation of failed messages.

The significance of missed attempts seems to be that a mother who fails to pick up on too many of the infant's attempts to establish meaning may indirectly impede the infant's communicative development. This brings us to the functions that negotiation episodes seem to serve in the discourse that occur between infants and mother.

THE FUNCTIONS OF NEGOTIATION EPISODES

Having outlined the negotiation episode and its components, one must ask how the negotiation of failed messages fits into the general picture of communication and language development. The function of negotiation episodes will be discussed from the perspective of the infant, the perspective of the mother, and in terms of the development of communication and language. All these theoretical points await empirical validation.

1. The Function of Negotiation Episodes from the Infant's Perspective. Readers should imagine themselves in a situation, perhaps in a foreign country, where what they venture to communicate is often met by quizzical expressions, or repetitions, or restatements of what they have just said, all produced with a rising intonation. Very quickly the reader would get the message that his or her communication skills were less than ideal and needed work. To what extent preverbal infants reach this conclusion is another issue. Infants, however, will surely notice they have failed to realize their goals, and perhaps that they are being implicitly requested to clarify their signals. To the extent that a concrete goal is at stake, infants are under highly motivated conditions to get their point across. Indirectly, this may serve to improve infants' communication skills.

Thus, part of what the child may be learning from negotiation episodes is that one can only count on one's communicative attempts meeting with success when they are sufficiently precise. It is probably during negotiation episodes that infants first attempt to clarify and repair their signals. When communication goes smoothly (i.e., when infants emit nonspecific signals and their mothers successfully interpret the signals), infants do not need to augment their communicative repertoires. However, in the face of failure, infants may be pushed to invent new means.

Ochs (1982) has made a related argument. Using a cross-cultural perspective, she asks what a child might be learning about communication in a society where the child's primitive communicative attempts are dwelt upon and expanded (see also Schieffelin & Ochs, this volume). In white middle class society, as opposed to among the Samoans or the Kaluli, mothers' expansions may be teaching the child that clarifying and establishing one's intents is an important goal and one that is culturally valued. This understanding in and of itself may influence the uses to which language is put by the child once it emerges.

2. *The Function of Negotiation Episodes from the Mother's Perspective.* The most obvious function of these episodes seems to be to please the infant and satisfy the infant's needs. All three mothers alluded to trying to figure out what their child wanted and to the techniques they used to interpret their children's signals. Obviously not all middle class mothers have these goals to the same extent. One of the mothers in our sample appeared to ignore many of the infant's initial signals. The mother also seemed to ignore the intent of the infant's signal, substituting topics, for example, foods, she wished the child to eat instead of the food the child was indicating.[4]

The second general function of negotiation episodes is to maintain interaction and communication. Thus, sometimes mothers' requests for confirmation (e.g., "Is it the milk you want?"), which would strictly speaking fall under the rubric of communication failure, seemed to be produced more with the intent of maintaining the child's involvement in communicative interaction. We assumed this to be the case when the mother responded relatively quickly to the infant's signal and when there seemed to observers to be little doubt about the infant's intent. Reformulating their infants' signal in the form of a question, however, cues the child that some response is required. Given that infants can discriminate declarative from interrogative intonation (Kaplan, 1969), and that infants seem to recognize that questions require responses no matter how minimal (see Horgan, 1978), such comprehension failures will increase the likelihood that the interaction continues.

The third function of these episodes seems to be a tutorial one. Once the child produced some primitive lexical attempts it sometimes appeared to us that the mother readily understood the child's garbled phonology and could well have satisfied the child immediately (function #1 discussed earlier). However, mothers sometimes seemed invested in maintaining the communicative interaction in a very particular way: they literally refused to hand over the object of the child's request until they elicited a clearer or more complete communicative signal from the child. One infant, for example, said "tis" for "cheese." His mother held up the cheese out of his reach and said, "Do you want the *cheese?*" and waited. The child seemed to understand that he was being asked to "sing for his supper" and produced a slightly closer approximation to "cheese." Bruner (1975) would refer to such behavior on the mother's part as "upping the ante."

The function of negotiation episodes for the mother seems to shift from function 1—discerning the child's meaning in order to please the child—to function 2—maintaining communicative interaction—to function 3—emphasizing the *form* of the child's utterances with the requirement that the child move in the direction of increased conventionalization of form. That the negotiation of

---

[4]Semi-structured interviews carried out with the three mothers on their beliefs about the capabilities of preverbal infants supports our interpretations about the respective mothers' orientations to child rearing.

failed messages sometimes involved the negotiation of form was suggested by Bloom (this volume). This latter function is also reminiscent of what Dore (this volume) has called "accountability" in that mothers seem to hold their infants accountable to produce more conventionalized linguistic forms.

3. *The Function of Negotiation Episodes for the Development of Commu-*
nication and Language. The special circumstances which surround the negotia-
tion of failed messages may make these episodes especially important for the development of communication and language for several reasons. First, most theoreticians would accept the relatively trivial statement that language and communication development emerge in a social context and in part, to serve the goals of social interaction. However, there is little agreement on which aspect(s) of the social context is (are) the locus of the facilitating effect (see Bruner; Shatz; Snow & Gilbreath, this volume, among others). In my view, the development of communicative competence, including language acquisition, depends on infants having someone (caregiver or sibling) who will permit them to communicate some meaning to attain some material goal. Despite the fact that humans are biologically predisposed to utilize and even invent linguistic symbols (Feldman, Goldin–Meadow, & Gleitman, 1978), such symbols will not emerge when a child is exposed to speech per se (see Braunwald, this volume; Sachs, Bard, & Johnson, 1981). In order for language to develop, infants moving from pre-linguistic to linguistic means of communication must have some individual who will permit them to communicate their intentions. At some primitive level, infants must recognize that meanings which they have can be shared by another and that their communicative efforts can make that sharing come about. The negotiation of failed messages, although only one of the ways in which the child can learn the instrumental uses of communication, presents the child with such an opportunity. Failures per se are essential for infants, else they believe that all they need to do is wish for something, emit a signal, and it will magically appear. Although cross-cultural accounts of communication development have not yet dealt with how infants communicatively pursue goals, there must be times in all cultures when infants signal their wants and fail. Where the cross-cultural dif-ference may occur is in *how* that failure is treated: It may be seized upon until clarification of the infant's signal occurs, as in white middle class culture, or it may be taken as an opportunity to tell the infant that what he requested is what he gets (see Schieffelin & Ochs, this volume). The common denominator across cultures may be that infants' communicative attempts are honored and that in-fants occasionally fail. Such failures may imply to infants that their communica-tive signals: (1) have some power (i.e., can get people to move and act); and (2) are not sufficiently precise to guarantee their success.

Second, infants may show developmental progress in failure situations before they show it in situations where their intentions are correctly interpreted. Given the combination of the infant's high motivation and the mother's initial com-prehension failure, the requirements of the negotiation episode would seem to call for infants' production of what is at the cutting edge of their communicative systems. Many developmental theorists, Piaget and Vygotsky, for example, have stressed the role of failure or conflict as a mechanism which spurs development. Some of the comprehension failures by mothers are genuine and some are apparently feigned by the mother to induce higher levels of performance. Harding (in press, this volume) has explored in detail how this mechanism could operate in communication development.

Specifically with regard to the development of language, mothers' responses to failures in negotiation episodes and infants' information-processing systems may interact in an interesting way. At times when no specific goal is at stake infants may attend to only some of the speech addressed to them. Since infants have limited capacity processors, parental speech may even be ignored when infants are absorbed in consuming tasks such as exploration. In addition, studies of parental speech may artificially inflate the amount and quality of speech mothers produce to their infants (Graves & Glick, 1978). Studies of the negotiation of failed messages where the infant and mother have specific and often conflicting goals may more accurately reflect what the infant takes from the mother's speech than have prior studies.

When mothers reformulate or expand upon infants' signals during failures, highly attentive infants are hearing speech which corresponds to the topics they have in mind. For example, the mother who said "Do you want the *cheese?*" has highlighted the name of the infant's goal for an infant eager to attain that goal. Thus, negotiation episodes may help the infant with the problem of "mapping" speech to nonlinguistic events. When trying to decide if their goal has been met, infants hear the verbal analogues of their thoughts at the same time as they observe their mothers' nonlinguistic behaviors. The study of negotiation episodes may help us better understand the impact of parental speech on children's lexical and syntactic productions (e.g., see Snow & Ferguson, 1977. Furrow, Nelson, & Benedict, 1979). As support for this contention Masur (1982) reports a significant correlation between infants' lexical development and the extent to which mothers produce labels in response to their infants' nonverbal gestures.

FINAL COMMENTS

Bates, Bretherton, Beeghly–Smith, and McNew (1982) have reviewed an extensive body of literature on the social bases of language development. They concluded that there is little evidence, given the variables and age groups that have been studied, that language development can be explained by examining social-interactional variables. Many in this volume have argued that that position may never have been viable. However, a closer look at the transition between pre-linguistic and linguistic communication, the most likely period for an influence of social interaction on language development, may reveal more precisely how the social context facilitates or impedes acquisition.

The origins of individual differences observed in communicative and language development (see Nelson, 1981) may begin at the point when intentional communication for instrumental purposes begins (see Golinkoff, in press), followed by episodes in which failed messages are negotiated. It is at that time that the infant becomes an intentional and relatively skillful partner in the communicative interaction which occurs between mother and infant. However, much prior research on the relationship between communication development and language development has focused on the first year in the infant's life. Attempting to find links between communicative variables in the first year of life and language development in the second or third year has not born fruit (Bates, et al., 1982; Kay, 1979), particularly during the first 6 months of life, when the infant may be genetically shielded from wide environmental variation (Lewis & Ban, 1977; Richman, Howrigan, & New, 1981). Kaye (1979) for example, concluded after an extensive microanalytic longitudinal study that his ability to predict language and cognitive outcomes at 2½ years was not strengthened one whit by using contingent and interactive measures taken before 6 months. The transition period into speech production may well be a more promising time to expect links between social-interactional variables and communicative development. Mothers seem to vary in their acceptance of their children's language attempts (Nelson, 1973) just as we have observed them to vary in their willingness to permit the child to communicate some meaning at the preverbal level.

The study of the preverbal negotiation of failed messages, or the process by which infants make their intentions understood after initial attempts have failed, may assist in charting the range and complexity of infants' communicative abilities as the gradual entry into a linguistic system occurs. Communicative attempts by infants to gain some instrumental end may provide the motivation necessary for infants to refine their communicative skills.

ACKNOWLEDGMENTS

I have received excellent feedback from a number of colleagues who read earlier versions of this chapter. For their efforts I thank Lois Bloom, Laura Gordon, Karen Gouze, Kathy Hirsh-Pasek, Bambi Schieffelin and Marilyn Shatz. In addition, I have been fortunate to have been assisted by some superlative undergraduate students in the coding of my tapes. It has been a pleasure to have worked with Elizabeth Cerny, James Frey, Rita Mazzotta and Patricia Hargett.

REFERENCES

Bates, E. *The emergence of symbols.* New York: Academic Press, 1979.
Bates, E., Bretherton, I., Beeghly-Smith, M., & McNew, S. Social bases of language development:

A reassessment. In H. W. Reese, & L. P. Lipsitt, (Eds.), *Advances in child development and behavior,* Vol. 16. New York: Academic Press, 1982.

Bloom, L., & Lahey, M. *Language development and language disorders.* New York: Wiley, 1978.

Bloom, L., Rocissano, L., & Hood, L. Adult-child discourse: Developmental interaction between information processing and linguistic knowledge. *Cognitive Psychology,* 1976, *8,* 521–552.

Bruner, J. S. From communication to language—a psychological perspective. *Cognition,* 1974, *3,* 255–287.

Bruner, J. S. The ontogenesis of speech acts. *Journal of Child Language,* 1975, *3,* 255–287.

Bullowa, M. *Before speech.* Cambridge, Mass.: Cambridge University Press, 1979.

Carter, A. L. From sensorimotor vocalizations to words: A case study of the evolution of attention-directing communication in the second year. In A. Lock (Ed.), *Action, gesture and symbol.* Cambridge, Mass.: Academic Press, 1978.

Carter, A. L. The disappearance schema: A case study of a second-year communication behavior. In E. Ochs, & B. B. Schieffelin (Eds.), *Developmental pragmatics.* New York: Academic Press, 1979.

Cherry, L. J. The role of adults' requests for clarification in the language development of children. In R. O. Freedle (Ed.), *New directions in discourse processing, Vol. 2.* Norwood, N.J.: Ablex, 1979.

Corsaro, W. A. The clarification request as a feature of adult interactive styles with young children. *Language in Society,* 1977, *6,* 183–207.

Dale, P. S. *Language development: Structure and function.* New York: Holt, Rinehart, & Winston, 1976.

Dore, J. A pragmatic description of early language development. *Journal of Psycholinguistic Research,* 19, 1974, *4,* 343–350.

Feldman, H., Goldin-Meadow, S., & Gleitman, L. Beyond Herodotus: The creation of language by linguistically deprived deaf children. In A. Lock (Ed.), *Action, gesture and symbol: The emergence of language.* London: Academic Press, 1978.

Fletcher, P., & Garman, M. (Eds.), *Language acquisition.* Cambridge, Mass.: Cambridge University Press, 1979.

Francis, H. What does the child mean? A critique of the 'functional' approach to language acquisition. *Journal of Child Language,* 1979, *6,* 201–210.

Furrow, D., Nelson, K., & Benedict, R. Mothers' speech to children: Some simple relationships. *Journal of Child Language,* 1979, *6,* 423–442.

Gallagher, T. Revision behaviors in the speech of normal children developing language. *Journal of Speech and Hearing Research,* 1977, *20,* 303–318.

Golinkoff, R. M. The influence of Piagetian theory on the study of the development of communication. In I. Sigel, D. Brodzinsky, & R. Golinkoff (Eds.), *New directions in Piagetian theory and practice.* Hillsdale, N.J.: Lawrence Erlbaum Associates, 1981.

Golinkoff, R. M. Infant social cognition: Self, people, and objects. In L. Liben (Ed.), *Piaget and the foundations of knowledge.* Hillsdale, N.J.: Lawrence Erlbaum Associates, in press.

Graves, R., & Glick, J. The effects of context on mother-child interaction. *Quarterly Newsletter of the Institute for Human Development,* 1978, *2,* 41–46.

Greenfield, P. M. Toward an operational and logical analysis of intentionality: The use of discourse in early child language. In D. Olson (Ed.), *The social foundations of language and thought.* New York: Norton, 1980.

Halliday, M. *Learning how to mean.* London: Edward Arnold, 1975.

Harding, C. G. Acting with intention: A framework for examining the development of the intention to communicate. In L. Feagans, C. Garvey, & R. M. Golinkoff (Eds.), *The origins and growth of communication.* Norwood, N.J.: Ablex, in press.

Harding, C. G., & Golinkoff, R. M. The origins of intentional vocalizations in prelinguistic infants. *Child Development,* 1979, *50,* 13–40.

Horgan, D. How to answer questions when you've got nothing to say. *Journal of Child Language,* 1978, *5,* 159–165.

Jefferson, G. Side sequences. In D. Sudnow (Ed.), *Studies in social interaction.* New York: Free Press, 1972.

Kaplan, E. L. The role of intonation in the acquisition of language. Unpublished doctoral dissertation, Cornell University, 1969.

Kaye, K. The social context of infant development. Final report to the Spencer Foundation, 1979.

Lewis, M., & Ban, P. Variance and invariance in mother-infant interaction: A cross-cultural study. In S. R. Leiderman, S. Tulkin, & A. Rosenfeld (Eds.), *Culture and infancy: Variations in the human experience.* New York: Academic Press, 1977.

Lewis, M., & Rosenblum, L. (Eds.), *The effect of the infant on its caregiver.* New York: Wiley, 1974.

Lock, A. (Ed.), *Action, gesture and symbol.* Cambridge, Mass.: Academic Press, 1978.

Lock, A. *The guided reinvention of language.* New York: Academic Press, 1979.

Masur, E. F. Mothers' responses to infants' object-related gesture: influences on lexical development. *Journal of Child Language,* 1982, *9,* 23–31.

McShane, J. *Learning to talk.* Cambridge, England: Cambridge University Press, 1980.

Nelson, K. Structure and strategy in learning how to talk. *Monographs of the Society for Research in Child Development,* 1973, *38,* 1–2.

Nelson, K. E. (Ed.), *Children's language: Vol. I.* New York: Gardner Press, 1978.

Nelson, K. Individual differences in language development: Implications for development and language. *Developmental Psychology,* 1981, *17,* 170–187.

Ochs, E. Talking to children in Western Samoa. *Language in Society,* 1982, *11,* 77–104.

Richman, A., Howrigan, C., & New, R. S. Cultural styles of infant-caretaker interaction among the Gusii, Yucatec Mayans, and Bostonians. Paper presented at Society Research in Child Development meetings, Boston, Mass., 1981.

Sachs, J., Bard, B., & Johnson, M. L. Language learning with restricted input: case studies of two hearing children of deaf parents. *Applied Psycholinguistics,* 1981, *2,* 33–54.

Schaffer, H. R. (Ed.), *Studies in mother-infant interaction.* London: Academic Press, 1977.

Snow, C. E., & Ferguson, C. A. (Eds.), *Talking to children: Language input and acquisition.* Cambridge, England: Cambridge University Press, 1977.

Stern, D. *The first relationship: Infant and mother.* Cambridge, Mass.: Harvard University Press, 1977.

Wilcox, M. J., & Webster, E. J. Early discourse behavior: An analysis of children's responses to listener feedback. *Child Development,* 1980, *51,* 1120–1125.

5 DISCUSSION
Of Continuity and Discontinuity, and the Magic of Language Development

Lois Bloom
Teachers College, Columbia University

How do infants learn to include the forms and structures of language in their communication exchanges? Or, more simply, how do children learn to talk? This is the question that motivated the conference. Whether the question will be answered remains to be seen, but certain to be implicated in attempts at an explanation are a complex social context and a complex biological mechanism with, perhaps, a touch of magic.

The prevailing social explanation of the development of language has emphasized the child's acquisition of *communication* competence rather than competence for language *per se*. In the last decade of child language research, there have been four major thrusts in explanations of the development of communicative competence: First, children learn to use language for various functions or purposes, so that one aspect of the development of communication is to learn to get and give information, to get other persons to do things, and to accomplish certain fairly well-defined acts with speech. The functions of speaking and understanding in everyday events provide the context in which language is learned. Second, children learn to recognize and take account of the needs of different listeners in different situations, and learn to monitor how and what they say according to the changing requirements for communication in everyday events. Thus, the actual use of language is socially and contextually conditioned as children learn how to achieve the same purpose by saying more or less the same thing, but in different ways. Third, caregivers' speech to children has been typically characterized as a gradually expanding model from which the child learns the forms of language. At the same time, the language that caregivers use in talking with children is pragmatically motivated by what needs to be accomplished for and with the child in activities of daily living. Fourth, and most relevant to the proceedings of the conference, are studies that have described the origins of communication in the earliest routines and games between infants and mothers (see, in particular, Bullowa, 1979; Lock, 1978; and Schaffer, 1977). The conclusion from this research with infants has been that 'meaning' exists only in the interaction between persons, and shared understandings between infant and mother begin to develop early in the first year of life, long before the conventional forms of language are understood or spoken.

What is often neglected in the emphasis on joint activity in a social context for the origins of communication is, oddly enough, the language. It is clear that social awareness begins virtually at birth to influence the development of joint attention and shared understanding between the infant and caregiver. Development proceeds from relations between infant and other and between infant and object, to the relations among infant, other, and object towards the end of the first year. However, although *communication* begins in this social context, how the *language* is learned in the context of this communication still remains to be determined.

Learning how to communicate is not explanatory for learning language. To say that language develops when shared activity leads to shared understandings, for example, explains something about how children learn to communicate, but explains nothing about how children learn the words and the structure of language. It seems fairly clear that language has not been the object of study in much of the research with infants in the last several years; hopefully, the thrust of the conference may be to shift gears once again and put language back into the study of child language.

The three papers that I am discussing come together to highlight several of the issues that I think need to be considered in determining just how language emerges in the context of communication. Jerome Bruner and Roberta Golinkoff each describe two mutual behaviors that mothers and infants *do,* while Marilyn Shatz calls for a theory of learning to explain how both the language and social interaction are learned in the context of what mothers and infants do. Two of the basic issues that are central to their concerns as well as to much if not all of the infancy literature in the last decade are the relation between nature and nurture, and the question of continuity both within and between different developmental domains. Ultimately, understanding these two issues and the special relation between them in development will lead to an understanding of the transition from nonlinguistic to linguistic behaviors that typically occurs sometime in the second year.

NATURE AND NURTURE

The 1970s was the decade of the discovery of the infant. As a result of a variety of research efforts, considerable respect has grown for the competencies of the human infant in the first few days, weeks, and months of life. Just how competent the human infant is at birth may be a subject of some dispute, but there is a consensus that the infant is far from the bundle of reflexes portrayed in early developmental texts. At the least, newborn infants can discriminate their mothers' voices from other female voices (DeCasper & Fifer, 1980); infants as young as one month of age can discriminate between categories of stimuli, as between the speech sounds /p/ and /b/ (Eimas, Siqueland, Jusczyk & Vigorito (1971). Thus, certain basic capacities that serve communication and language are already in place in the beginning of life.

The 1970s was also the decade of the discovery of the mother, with emphasis on the social interaction between mother and infant for explaining the development of language. Interestingly, the discovery of the mother has taken place independently of the discovery of the infant; the two have come from different research paradigms, with separate conferences and separate publications. Compare, for example, the papers in the present volume and in Lock (1978) and Schaffer (1977) with the papers in Aslin, Alberts, and Petersen (1981), and Yeni–Komshian, Kavanagh, and Ferguson (1980). Nevertheless, whatever the biologically determined endowment of the child may be, the infant develops in a socially determined environment, and the emphasis on the environment, and, in particular, on the mother in the environment, has been considerable in efforts to explain the origins of language.

In this context, it might be worth remembering that the original attraction that Noam Chomsky's nativist idea about language had to begin with was the corrective it offered to the heavy emphasis on the environment that came with the influence of behaviorism on the study of child language (see, for example, Dixon and Horton, 1968). However, a whole generation has now passed since Chomsky's review of Skinner's *Verbal Behavior* in 1959, and once again the balance of influence has become tipped, almost precariously, in the direction of the social context.

There was at least one other influential publication at about the same time that Chomsky's ideas appeared in 1957 and 1959. In 1958, Ann Anastasi published an insightful paper in which she examined the way in which the nature/nurture issue had been dealt with in psychology. The main thrust of Anastasi's analysis was to point out that one reason why the issue resisted resolution for so long was that the wrong questions were being asked. Historically, in psychology and philosophy, the question that was asked in debating the nature/nurture issue was *Which one?* As a result, an either/or tradition had grown up as people sought to establish that *either* nature (the biological endowment of the child) *or* nurture (the social context) determines development. However, nature and nurture are not independent in their effects and certainly do not operate in isolation: Without an environment, there simply would not be any effect from heredity and, conversely, the environment would be empty and possibly would not even exist, wihout heredity. So inasmuch as the question *Which one?* assumes an illogical independence between the forces of nature and nurture, the appropriate question to ask is not *Which one?*, but *How?* (Anastasi, 1958; Lerner, 1976; Richards, 1977).

The question, then, for language acquisition, is *How?* How does the endowment of the child interact with the social context to determine the acquisition of linguistic behaviors? However, most of the studies of the transition from prelinguistic to linguistic communication have implicitly answered the question *Which one?* and they have come up with different answers. For example, according to Jerome Bruner, to John Dore, and to Roberta Golinkoff, it is the social interaction, specifically the exchanges that occur with formats or routines (Bruner, this volume) or with an initial failure in communication attempts (Golinkoff, this volume), that mediates the acquisition of language. And, according to Shatz in another context (1981), it is the "internal properties of the child" that mediate the interaction between the acquisition of syntax and social interaction. Neither answer is wrong, but only together could both of them begin to be correct. That is, in answer to the question *How?*, *both* the endowment of the child *and* the social context act together to mediate the acquisition of language. How that happens remains to be determined, but unless the mutual influence and multiplicative interaction between the two is recognized, the inquiry is doomed.

CONTINUITY AND DISCONTINUITY

In addressing the continuity question, Shatz (this volume) has explored several versions of a continuity hypothesis and pointed out that both of the extreme hypotheses have to be wrong: Language behaviors in the second and third years of life are neither entirely discontinuous nor obviously continuous with infant behaviors. However, it is interesting that, historically, the strong and weak views of continuity were aligned with strong views on the nature/nurture issue. Proponents of behaviorism emphasized the role of the environment, or nurture, in shaping behavior and advanced theories of language development with a strong continuity component. Speech behaviors were considered to be continuous with infant vocalizing or babbling. For example, Thorndike's theory was called the "babble-luck" theory—with a little bit of luck, the infant babbled those sounds that were reinforced by adults in the environment. (See, also, Jenkins & Palermo, 1964; Mowrer, 1954; Staats & Staats, 1963, for other views). Skinner's basic point (1957) was that all behavior, including verbal behavior, was the "result of a continuous shaping process [p. 91]," and could always be traced back to its original, antecedent behaviors, as in babbling. In fact, the relation between babbling and speech seems to have served as the paradigm case in discussions of continuity in developmental texts.

In contrast, nativists have countered the emphasis on continuity from babbling to later speech behavior. For example, Lenneberg (1967) argued that "language development, or its substitute, is relatively independent of the infant's babbling [p. 589]," (see, also, Chomsky, 1959, McNeill, 1970). In 1941, Roman Jakobson (1968) had suggested that features of the sounds that infants babble in their vocalizations in the first year have to be relearned in the second year as phonetic contrasts for learning to say and understand words. Similarly, while infants as young as one month of age are capable of discriminating between categories of speech sounds (such as /p/ and /b/), they need to learn how to discriminate these same sounds when they hear them in words in the second year. Thus, it is not at all clear how the two infant behaviors—being able to hear the difference between /p/ and /b/ in the first few months and babbling the /p/ and /b/ sounds a few months later—are continuous with one another or continuous with the ability to say words like "ball" and "pop" in the second year. It appears, then, that with the relation between continuity and discontinuity, just as with the relation between nature and nurture, the question for language development is not *Which one?*, but *How?* How do the behaviors of infancy relate to language behaviors in the second and third years?

Research that has focussed on social interaction and communication in infancy for the answer to this question appears to be consistent with what Overton and Reese (1981) characterized as a "mechanistic world view"—a view that maintains that change or development is an event that must be explained by something else, rather than the starting point of inquiry as the basic phenomenon to be explained. Communication and social interaction in infancy has been viewed as that "something else" to explain the development of language and, as such, we seem to have come to a conceptual deadend. The first point to consider is that, in large part, the communication behaviors that have been studied in infancy are most probably not the behaviors that are most relevant for communication through language. The studies of communication between mothers and infants have been ethological in style and in the vocabulary of their descriptions.[1] The object of study has been innate, 'biologic' behaviors, and especially that aspect of behavior that produces parallel or alternating patterns when two individuals are together. The participants themselves do not have to consciously interpret such communication to give it meaning, and if they do interpret it, the meaning would not necessarily coincide with an outside observer's view of the shared event. For example, the 'dance' of bees or mating birds or human mother and infant is not intended to be a dance—in the literal sense—by the participants themselves.

---

[1] I am grateful to Geraldine McDonald for pointing out to me the kinesics continuity argument and for allowing me to use her words as well. Much of what follows in the next few paragraphs is attributable to her.

It is difficult to see how this early, rhythmic, affective communication can be continuous in the sense of causing or leading to linguistic communication. For one thing, it is effortless and for another it is largely unconscious, involuntary behavior—even for the adult participant. In contrast, linguistic communication requires intention, effort, and often, especially on the part of the young child, unrhythmical speech behavior. Further, linguistic communication is anything but unconscious or involuntary.

↑ Nevertheless, this early biological, rhythmical communication continues throughout life. Some parts of it (e.g., facial expression), are modified by culture; others, such as the basic rhythm of movement may remain unchanged. Bateson (1971), Birdwhistell (1970), and others have demonstrated that adults in face-to-face communication exhibit a patterning of body posture, gaze, gesture, and turn-taking that is mutually adaptive. Communication in this sense is a framing of the interaction—a 'getting into sync'—that involves a process in which persons act in ways that are responsive to the actions of those with whom they are in communication. The content of any verbal message may be unimportant or at least less important than the affective quality of the relationship, which is conveyed below the threshold of awareness through observation of rhythm sharing, body movement, timing of speech, and silences.

Thus, there are at least these two senses of the meaning of communication. One is the kind of communication that takes place with linguistic messages, which can be characterized most directly as achieving a fit or match between semantic intention and semantic interpretation. Another is the sense in which communication has been most often studied in infancy, which coincides with and is continuous with what has been referred to by such terms as 'interpersonal communication,' 'interactional communication,' 'body motion communication,' 'kinesis,' and which results in a necessary frame or synchrony for communication with language but is probably not otherwise continuous with language.

The second point to consider in regard to mechanistic answers to the question *How?* is that the antecedent events in infancy that appear to be related to later language include considerably more than those behaviors that can be characterized as social and interactional. The early concern with the relevance of infant babbling in continuity theory reminds us that, when you come right down to it, the transition from prelinguistic to linguistic behavior presents a *phonological* problem for the child. In order to say words, the child has to learn something of the sound system just as in the later transition from single-word to multi-word utterances the child has to learn something of the grammar in order to say sentences. Most simply, the infant has to learn the *language*. The more recent emphasis on the continuity of social interaction for explaining language seems to have lost sight of the fact that there are two other components of language in addition to the social component of language use. There are also language *content* or what messages are about—the ideational or information component of language, and language *form* or what messages sound like—the acoustic, articulatory, and structural component of language.

Form, Content, and Use in the Transition to Language

With respect to language form, both the production of sounds in early vocalizing and the perception of speech sound contrasts present evidence of the capacity for phonetic distinctions that figure in later phonemic learning. The traditional linguistic argument for discontinuity was based on the observation that there are different developmental sequences for sound production: (1) in babbling in the first year (from back to front consonants); and (2) in speech in the second and third years (from front to back consonants); see McNeill (1970), in particular. That is, the sequence of consonants that appear in babbling is mirrored in the sequence of sounds that are acquired in words. However, a recapitulation of the same sequence would be, in fact, an even stronger argument for discontinuity. The unsatisfactory implication of such a recapitulation would be that the 1-year-old child would have to back up and start over, rather than capitalize on the progress of developmental change up until that point. The fact that speech evolves out of the matrix of infant vocalization that has itself evolved in the course of the infant's physiological and anatomic maturation would appear to be a stronger argument for continuity than for discontinuity. The articulatory sequence in the first year is determined largely by maturation (see, especially, Lieberman, 1967); the sequence in the second year is determined by the continued maturation of the vocal mechanism *in interaction with* the requirements of the language.

The biologically determined maturation of the vocal mechanism continues in the second year, but linguistic pressures from the environment bring about qualitative changes in vocalization. Much phonological research with 1 and 2-year-old children has indicated that the rules and strategies they use in their phonological development are influenced by words they are learning (e.g., Klein, 1981). While it is still not clear just how such rules and strategies for word learning are related to the earlier perception of phoneme boundaries at 2, 3, and 4 months of age, or to cooing, crying, and babbling in the first year, it is clear that the two aspects of development are not unrelated (see Stark, 1980).

With respect to language content, the facts of sensorimotor intelligence in the first year of development have to do with the movement and location of objects in relation both to the self and to each other (Piaget, 1954). And there is a strong consensus that the referential content of single-words early in the second year, and multi-word utterances later in the second year, has to do largely with objects in general, and movement and location with respect to objects in particular (Bloom, Lifter, & Broughton, 1981).

So it is not only language use that can be traced to antecedent behaviors in infancy; both language content and language form have their antecedents in infancy as well. However, the relatedness of infant behaviors to language behaviors does not guarantee developmental continuity, either within or between the domains of language content, language form, and language use. Within each of these domains infant behaviors are qualitatively different from language behaviors: Babbling is not speech; knowing about objects does not equal talking about objects; and communication without language is not the same as communicating with language. Neither are the behaviors within each of the domains causally related before and after the transition to language: Children do not talk because they are able to perceive and vocalize sound contrasts, or because they know something about objects and events in the environment, or because they are able to participate in communication dialogue with a responsive caregiver. The continuity, then, within each of the separate domains of form, content, and use is only a superficial relatedness; behaviors within one or another domain are not causally related and they are qualitatively different before and after the transition to language.

While there are differences *within* each of the domains of form, content, and use, there is a more important difference *between* the domains before and after the transition to language. The major and definitive difference between them comes from the fact that the development of language as well as language itself depend upon the *intersection* of content, form, and use, whereas in infancy the relevant behaviors constitute *separate* threads of development. The transition from prelinguistic to linguistic behavior comes about when the essentially separate components begin to bump up against one another. Figure 5.1 is meant to schematize the relations between the domains, before and after that transition. The intersection of the three domains involves successive combinations and recombinations of aspects of behaviors, and qualitatively different behaviors emerge as a consequence of their intersection. The result of the intersection among form, content, and use is that the infant begins to become conventionalized—linguistically.

At this point, it may be helpful to remember that there is, in fact, more than one critical transition in the course of language development in the first 3 years. The first transition, and the one that was the focus of the conference, is the transition from prelinguistic to linguistic behaviors. Further down the line, sometime toward the end of the second year, is the transition from single-word utterences to word combinations, and then again, sometime in the third year, is the transition to complex syntax. A critical component in each of these transitions is insight on the part of the child, and it is most often a gradual rather than a sudden insight. The transitions are tedious and usually worked out over some period of time; see the detailed acounts in the early baby biographies, for example Leopold (1939); and, more recently, the account of the transition to first words in Klein (1981) and Lifter (1982); the account of the transition to multi-

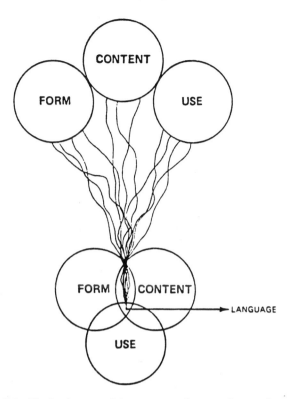

FIG. 5.1   The development of the precursors of content, form, and use, and the contact among these components in infancy, before they are integrated with one another in conventional ways for language (Bloom & Lahey, 1978, p. 70).

word speech in Bloom (1973); and the account of the transition to complex syntax in Bloom, Lahey, Hood, Lifter, and Fiess (1980), and Hood and Bloom (1979). In each case, new behaviors emerge that are related to earlier behaviors and even coexist with the earlier behaviors, but they are NOVEL behaviors in important respects. Each involves an induction on the part of the child. What drives that induction is, in each case, no doubt biologically determined, as, at the same time, the induction proceeds from the child's experience.

In answer, then, to the question *How* do the behaviors of infancy relate to language behaviors in the second and third years of life?, we can at least say, to begin with, that there are both continuities and discontinuities in the changes that occur with development. To understand that development it is necessary to recognize that form, content, and use come together in the process of change, and, indeed, their coming together constitutes that developmental change. Neither of the components alone can explain their intersection.

The Transition to Language

The chapter by Golinkoff offers a potentially productive idea that may begin to answer the question *How?* She proposes that the transition in language development from prelinguistic behaviors (whining, grunting, gestures, facial expressions, etc.) to linguistic behaviors (early words and then multi-word speech) occurs in the context of what she has called the "negotiation of failed messages" between parent and child. That is, certain of the communication exchanges between mothers and their infants are characterized by: (1) some failure on the part of the mother to understand the child's attempt to communicate; and (2) the subsequent maneuvers that the child and the mother use to understand (or "negotiate") the child's intended meaning. In effect, the child has to *learn* to communicate and Golinkoff proposes that this learning takes place in the context in which an attempt fails and it is necessary to persist, try again or somehow revise the original effort to get the message across.

It is a neat idea and a considerable conceptual advance over the prevailing studies that looked at mothers' speech to children for clues to what and how children learn about language. It also represents an effort to explain the acquisition of *language* in the context of *communication*. However, there are at least these three conceptual problems with the notion of the "negotiation of failed messages." The first problem is that it is not at all clear how frequently such negotiations occur. There is no question that they do occur, but they probably occur more frequently for some mother–child pairs than others. Golinkoff seems to suggest a linear, positive relation between the frequency and length of such negotiations and the child's progress in the acquisition of the forms of language—that is, presumably, the more often mothers fail to understand what their children intend to communicate and the longer it takes them to figure it out, the faster and better the child will shape up and use the more acceptable, conventional forms of language. However, this is not intuitively likely to me; I would think that the more often the communication fails, and the harder the mother and child have to work at repairing it, are indications of some difficulty in learning the forms of language and may better characterize the less successful than the more successful language learners.

A second problem with the idea (and with social interactional explanations of acquisition more generally) is that it overlooks the considerable importance of what the child *overhears*. For example, one of the serious problems for deaf children who are taught to speak is that their oral communication is constrained by what they have been specifically taught, in the absence of the opportunity that hearing children have to observe and listen to conversations in many contexts (Fox, 1980). Similarly, in the absence of face to face interaction in non-Western cultures such as Papua, New Guinea (Schieffelin, 1979; this volume) or Samoa (Ochs, in press), much of the language that is learned is no doubt learned through overhearing talk between and among adults and older children.

However, the third problem is, at once, the more important problem as well as the issue that could turn Golinkoff's notion around so that it is more responsive to the question *How?* What happens when the parent fails to understand the child's communication goal is considerably more than a negotiation of meaning. It is not only the meaning or the child's intention that gets negotiated, but, rather, the negotiation involves the way in which the child's original intended meaning gets conveyed. That is, perhaps even more important than a negotiation of meaning, there is also the negotiation of language form and use. Both parties fail in the communication attempt, and both parties need to work out a means for repair: The mother needs to figure out what the child means, and the child needs to figure out how to get the meaning across. The semantic intention probably doesn't change; the meaning or content of the child's message is not manipulated so much as is the form of the message and its use in the communication exchange.

A very straightforward model of communication is captured in the following equation: Most simply, communication occurs when the semantic intention of the speaker coincides with the semantic interpretation of the listener. In many if not most everyday situations that involve adults and older children, the meaning is transparent in the message and communication occurs with relative ease and efficiency. However, when the meaning is not transparent, as it is not for the young prelinguistic child, it becomes necessary to transact, to deal, to bargain— in short, to negotiate the communication exchange, or the means whereby intention and interpretation can coincide.

In contrast to the negotiations that take place in instances of failed communication, Bruner has described another kind of early negotiation of the form, content, and use of language. This time, in the successful communication exchanges between child and parent, there are routines or formats that present a challenge to the child to respond. For example, "What's that?," "You know," "It's a kitty." and then, "What's that?," "Yes, a kitty," "And what's the kitty doing?" There is little question that formats like these occur. The evidence seems to indicate that they are most likely to occur during the period of transition from nonlinguistic to linguistic behaviors toward the end of the first year, although how often they occur is not known.

While it is clear that the formatting Bruner describes figures in an important way in the development of communication, just how it is explanatory for language is less clear. Formatting is behavior that parent and child *do* together, and the behavior that is involved is language behavior. But it has not yet been documented that the formats elicit the child's first words or even any of the child's earliest uses of words. Neither is there evidence for how words presented in formats relate to words that children understand and say in other, less formulated situations. And the bridge to syntax is even more tenuous: Children's first word combinations occur later than the period when formatting has been reported to occur, and the first word combinations are not the same forms as those that the parent provides in formatting. With respect to content, formats typically embrace only naming (of objects and actions), and with respect to use, represent a limited repertoire of communication behaviors.

Nevertheless, formatting provides another context for negotiation whereby adult and child come to agree with one another over just what to say and how to say it. Moreover, both formatting and the behaviors that occur when communication initially fails, as described by Golinkoff, provide opportunities for instances of the kind of accountability between adult and child that Dore (this volume) has described. In all three instances (those described by Bruner, by Dore, and by Golinkoff), it seems that adult and child are—in Dore's terms—holding one another accountable in negotiating the language. While each of these independent investigators has attributed a different underlying motivation or rationale to the parent-infant behaviors they have described, and each has described different forms of such behaviors, it appears that the behaviors they describe share this common function: the negotiation of the form, the content, and the use of language.

In any negotiation, both parties bring a set of resources and competencies to the exchange. In the case of the parent, the resources are considerable, including a full knowledge of the language and a sensitivity to the needs of the child. In the case of the child, the resources consist of the native endowment, talents, and faculties for language that are already in place in the first few months of life. The negotiation in their communication events results in successive adjustments between this basic endowment of the child and the language displays provided by the parent—that is, successive adjustments of the relation between nature and nurture.

Needless to say, negotiations of the form, content, and use of language—and the adjustments that result between nature and nurture—are exceedingly complex. Moreover, negotiation of the language is probably going on all the time, and is not limited to formatting or negotiation in only those situations in which communication initially fails. Attempting to understand the process of this negotiation ought to help us to understand its product—the acquisition of the language in the context of communication. But, we are still a long way from this understanding, and in response to the question "How do children learn to talk?," it often times appears that some part of the answer may be "It's magic."

ACKNOWLEDGMENTS

Preparation of this paper was supported by research grants from The Spencer Foundation and The National Science Foundation. I thank Joanne Capatides for her helpful comments on an earlier draft.

REFERENCES

Anastasi, A. Heredity, environment, and the question How. *Psychological Review,* 1958, *65,* 197–208.

Aslin, R., Alberts, T., & Petersen, M. (Eds.) *Development of perception: Psychobiological perspectives* (2 vols.). New York: Academic Press, 1981.

Bateson, G. *The natural history of an interview.* University of Chicago Microfilm Collection of Manuscripts in Cultural Anthropology, Series 15, Nos. 95–98, 1971.

Birdwhistell, R. *Kinesis and context.* Philadelphia, Pa.: University of Pennsylvania Press, 1970.

Bloom, L. *One word at a time: The use of single word utterances before syntax.* The Hague: Mouton, 1973.

Bloom, L., Lahey, M., Hood, L., Lifter, K., & Fiess, L. Complex sentences: Acquisition of syntactic connectives and the semantic relations they encode. *Journal of Child Language,* 1980, *7,* 225–261.

Bloom, L., Lifter, K., & Broughton, J. What children say and what they know: Exploring the relations between product and process in the development of early words and early concepts. In R. Stark (Ed.) *Language behavior in infancy and early childhood,* Elsevier Science Publishers, 1981.

Bloom, L., & Lahey, M. *Language development and language disorders.* New York: Wiley, 1978.

Bullowa, M. (Ed.) *Before speech.* Cambridge, Mass.: Cambridge University Press, 1979.

Chomsky, N. *Syntactic structures.* The Hague: Mouton, 1957.

Chomsky, N. Review of Verbal Behavior by B. F. Skinner. *Language,* 1959, *35,* 26–58.

DeCasper, A. J., & Fifer, W. P. Of human bonding: Newborns prefer their mothers' voices. *Science,* 1980, *208,* 1174–1176.

Dixon, T., & Horton, D. *Verbal behavior and general behaviour theory.* Englewood Cliffs, N.J.: Prentice Hall, 1968.

Eimas, P. D., Siqueland, E. R., Jusczyk, P., & Vigorito, J. Speech perception in infants. *Science,* 1971, *171,* 303–306.

Fox, D. S. *Teacher–child discourse interactions and the language of pre-school hearing impaired children.* Doctoral dissertation, Teachers College, Columbia University, 1980.

Hood, L., & Bloom, L. What, when, and how about why: A longitudinal study of early expressions of causality. *Monographs of the Society for Research in Child Development,* 1979, *44.*

Jakobson, R. *Child language, aphasia, and phonological universals.* The Hague: Mouton, 1968.

Jenkins, J., & Palermo, D. Mediation processes and the acquisition of linguistic structure. In U. Bellugi, & R. Brown (Eds.), The acquisition of language. *Monographs of the Society for Research in Child Development,* 1964, *29,* 141–168.

Klein, H. Early perceptual strategies for the replication of consonants from polysyllabic lexical models. *Journal of Speech and Hearing Research,* 1981, *24,* 535–551.

Lenneberg, E. *Biological foundations of language.* New York: Wiley, 1967.

Leopold, W. *Speech development of a bilingual child* (4 vols.). Evanston, Ill.: Northwestern University Press, 1939–1949.

Lerner, R. *Concepts and theories of human development.* Reading, Mass.: Addison-Wesley, 1976.

Lieberman, P. *Intonation, perception, and language.* Cambridge, Mass.: M.I.T. Press, 1967.

Lifter, K. *Development of object related behaviors during the transition from prelinguistic to linguistic communication.* Doctoral dissertation, Teachers College, Columbia University, 1982.

Lock, A. (Ed.) *Action, gesture and symbol: The emergence of language.* New York: Academic Press, 1978.

McNeill, D. *The acquisition of language: The study of developmental psycholinguistics.* New York: Harper & Row, 1970.

Mowrer, O. H. The psychologist looks at language. *American Journal of Psychology,* 1954, *9,* 660–694.

Ochs, E. Talking to children in western Samoa. *Language and society, 11,* in press.

Overton, W., & Reese, H. Conceptual prerequisites for an understanding of stability-change and continuity-discontinuity. *International Journal of Behavioural Development,* 1981, *4,* 99–123.

Piaget, J. *The construction of reality in the child.* New York: Basic Books, 1954.

Richards, M. P. M. Interaction and the concept of development: The biological and the social revisited. In M. Lewis and L. Rosenblum (Eds.), *Interaction, conversation, and the development of language.* New York: John Wiley & Sons, 1977, pp. 187–206.

Schaffer, J. R. (Ed.). *Studies in mother-infant interaction.* New York: Academic Press, 1977.

Schieffelin, B. *How Kaluli children learn what to say, what to do, and how to feel: An ethnographic study of the development of communicative competence.* Doctoral dissertation, Teachers College, Columbia University, 1979.

Shatz, M. Learning the rules of the game: Four views of the relation between grammar acquisition and social interaction. In W. Deutsch (Ed.), *The child's construction of language.* London: Academic Press, 1981.

Skinner, B. F. *Verbal behavior.* Englewood Cliffs, N.J.: Prentice Hall, 1957.

Staats, A. W., & Staats, C. K. *Complex human behaviour.* New York: Holt, Rinehart, & Winston, 1963.

Stark, R. E. Stages of speech development in the first year of life. In G. H. Yeni–Komshian, R. Kavanagh, & C. Ferguson (Eds.), *Child phonology: Production and perception.* (Vol. 1). New York: Academic Press, 1980.

Thorndike, E. L. The origin of language. In E. Thorndike, *Selected writings from a connectionist's psychology.* New York: Greenwood, 1949.

Yeni–Komshian, G. H., Kavanagh, R., & Ferguson, C. (Eds.) *Child phonology: Production and perception* (2 vols.). New York: Academic Press, 1980.

6

Setting the Stage for Language Acquisition: Communication Development in the First Year

Carol Gibb Harding
Loyola University of Chicago

This chapter must begin with a caveat. Although the purposes of this volume are to investigate the transition from prelinguistic to linguistic communication and to ascertain the relationship (if any) of developments in the pre-language period to language acquisition, this chapter fulfills neither purpose. Only prelinguistic communication is investigated and its investigation as described here, in no way permits a conclusion about the relationship of prelinguistic communication to language. The rather nebulous description used in the title, "Setting the Stage," reflects this limitation. Communicative developments during the first year do set the stage for language acquisition, but so do other events and probably in even more critical ways, for example, as in conception and birth. The question that I think we would like to answer goes beyond setting the stage. This question is whether or not the development of prelinguistic communication provides the necessary and/or sufficient conditions for linguistic communication. Although in this chapter I will describe achievements of the prelanguage period and make some speculations about how these achievements may culminate in the acquisition of the first words, my caveat remains: Do not expect too much. The infants I have observed were only beginning to use their first word-like vocalizations at the last observation. Although the use of these first words seemed to derive from earlier non-verbal communicative patterns, the findings reported do not eliminate the possibility that: (1) other sources of language learning were present (e.g., innate language structures), as posited by Chomsky (in Piattelli–Palmarini, 1980); or that (2) these first words would have been used even without the earlier communications. In either case, prelinguistic communication might be neither necessary nor sufficient to explain linguistic communication.

Although it is clear that language and communication become related (the term "linguistic communication" presupposes that relationship), the development of the relationship is far from clear. The debate between Chomsky and Piaget (Piattelli–Palmarini, 1980) on the relationship between sensorimotor developments and language acquisition addresses this issue. In response to Piaget's assertion that sensorimotor intelligence provides both the necessary and sufficient base for all later developments including language, Chomsky (in Piattelli–Palmarini, 1980) responded, "I see no basis for Piaget's conclusion. There are, to my knowledge, no substantive proposals involving 'constructions of sensorimotor intelligence' that offer any hope of accounting for the phenomena of language that demand explanation [p. 36]." The outcome of this debate as well as the question of the relationship of prelinguistic communication to linguistic communication await empirical evidence which this chapter will not present.

Given this limitation, what does the chapter offer? First, a discussion about communication will be presented, including definitions and characteristics of what it means to communicate. Second, longitudinal data on 12 infants observed between the ages of 5 months and 10 months will be presented. Third, speculations based on these data will be made about how the interaction of the infant's cognitive abilities and the social environment, particularly the mother's role, in the development of communication may relate to the acquisition of the first words.

A DEFINITION OF COMMUNICATION

There are three characteristics of communication all of which can be (although they not always are) included in its definition.

1. Probably the most simple is the notion that communication can be defined as one organism having an effect on another organism. Using this definition, Konner (1979) described the nursing event itself as communicative. He reasoned that the release of milk from the mother's body triggered by the infant's sucking is a communicative event. Although most researchers require communication to be more than a coordination of physical action and reaction between two bodies, the phenomenon of communicative effect is probably the most easily observed aspect of communication and therefore the one most open to empirical study.

2. The second notion requires the inference of meaning in another's behavior. Although implicit in inference is the first notion of communicative effect, this notion also includes the interpretation by at least one of the organisms involved that "communication" is occurring. This aspect of communication has been defined by speech act theorists (e.g., Austin, 1962) as perlocutionary, that is one partner interprets and reacts to the behavior of the other as communicative even when the other is not necessarily intending to communicate.

3. This second aspect of communication leads directly to the third notion: intentional communication. The concept of intentional communication requires

not only that both the potential for communicative effect exists and the potential for inferring communication in another's behavior but also that one can *intend* to communicate, in other words, that one can use his or her behaviors as a means to signal to another.

Although at times communication has been described by researchers as one or the other of these notions, and although I see the usefulness of each for different types of investigations of communication, I also see these characteristics as outlining (in a simplistic way to be sure) the developmental process of communication. This process may occur in the following way (see Fig. 6.1).

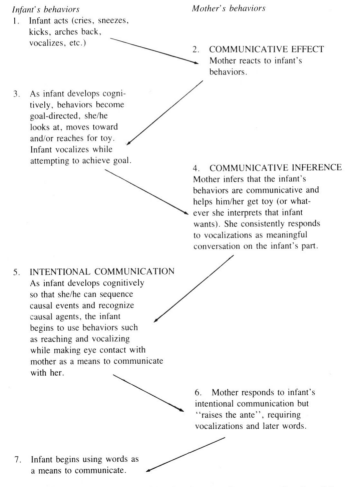

Infant's behaviors

1. Infant acts (cries, sneezes, kicks, arches back, vocalizes, etc.)

Mother's behaviors

2. COMMUNICATIVE EFFECT
Mother reacts to infant's behaviors.

3. As infant develops cognitively, behaviors become goal-directed, she/he looks at, moves toward and/or reaches for toy. Infant vocalizes while attempting to achieve goal.

4. COMMUNICATIVE INFERENCE
Mother infers that the infant's behaviors are communicative and helps him/her get toy (or whatever she interprets that infant wants). She consistently responds to vocalizations as meaningful conversation on the infant's part.

5. INTENTIONAL COMMUNICATION
As infant develops cognitively so that she/he can sequence causal events and recognize causal agents, the infant begins to use behaviors such as reaching and vocalizing while making eye contact with mother as a means to communicate with her.

6. Mother responds to infant's intentional communication but "raises the ante", requiring vocalizations and later words.

7. Infant begins using words as a means to communicate.

FIG. 6.1 A proposed description of the developmental sequence of prelinguistic communication.

The newborn infant's behaviors have a communicative effect on the environment. In addition to the physiological effects described previously (e.g., the release of prolactin in the nursing mother), the infant's behaviors also affect the communicative behaviors of the mother (Brazelton, 1979). As the infant's behaviors become goal-directed the mother also begins to infer communicative intent in the infant's actions. Shotter (1978) described the interactive nature of this process:

> At first, an infant clearly has little power to satisfy his own needs. But to the extent that a mother can interpret her infant's behavior as having an intention to it (no matter how vague and indefinite it may be on his part), she can help him to complete or fulfill it, and in the process "negotiate" a satisfaction of his needs with him. The child's action is thus made to eventuate in a consequence that is at least intelligible to her; and she does it by rendering herself available to him as an "instrument" or "mechanism" acting to produce a result which she feels may be one "intended" in his activity [pp. 68–69].

As the mother interprets the infant's behaviors by inferring intention and reacting to what she thinks that intention is, the infant becomes aware through cognitive processing of the sequencing of the mother's behavior and his own (Harding, 1982a). Therefore, at a sensorimotor level, the infant may begin to make communicative "inferences" of his own. At least the infant begins to expect certain behaviors of the mother to follow certain behaviors of his.

It is hypothesized that this process culminates with the infant's intending to communicate. The development of intentional communication appears to be a gradual process, related to both cognitive ability and social experience, beginning with the awareness of goals in general and leading to the infant acting with communication as a goal (Harding, 1982b). The mother continues to interpret the infant's behaviors as communicative but "raises the ante" (see Bruner, 1978) by beginning to require conventional means of communication (i.e., words).

It may be that during the pre-language period general patterns in mother-infant interactions occur which are related to this developmental sequence of communication. In Fig. 6.1 a sequential diagram of how this process might work is presented. In the next section, an observational study of infants and their mothers is described. Findings from this study will be used to support the proposed sequence.

THE PROCESS OF PRELINGUISTIC COMMUNICATION

Twelve first-born infants and their mothers were observed at approximately 6 week intervals for about 5 months. Initially the infants were 6 months of age ($\bar{X}$ = 5.8). The observation period of 6 to 11 months was selected in order to allow for observation of the developmental period including Piagetian Stage 3 when intentional patterns of behavior begin and the transition from pre-intentional to intentional communication observed by others to occur around 9 to 10 months

(Harding & Golinkoff, 1979; Bates, Camaioni & Volterra, 1975; Bruner, 1976). The mothers were all married, white, middle class, and high school graduates.

An important aspect of this study was that it included three data sources, laboratory and home observations and mother-kept diaries. Each data collection source described below was selected because of its predicted value in adding necessary information in terms of effect, inference, and intention to the investigation of communication development.

1. The laboratory observations were patterned after those used in an earlier study (Harding & Golinkoff, 1979). The lab setting allowed for some behavioral manipulation such as consistency in controlling mothers' input into interactions with the infants. The specific details of this procedure will be described later. The laboratory sessions were videotaped allowing for systematic, intensive coding of the communicative effect of both the infant's and mother's behaviors on the other. This coding also permitted the observation of which behaviors of the infant the mothers inferred to be communicative.

2. The data collected from the observations in the home were expected to add additional information, particularly about the mothers' behavior. It has been observed that context (settings) can affect interactions (Belsky, 1977) and data from the home observations were expected to allow for a more natural investigation of the mother-infant interactions and the infants' communication development. It must be emphasized that there was no planned comparison between the two contexts: home and laboratory settings. Since each source was used for a unique purpose, the data were not viewed as comparable but rather as complementary.

3. The observations and interpretations of the mothers recorded by them in diary format were used as a third source of data. Although some comparisons between mothers' interpretations and the experimenter's observations were planned, in general these data were considered as another complementary source of information. However, the diaries were particularly useful in providing information about the mothers' interpretation of intent in their infants' behaviors.

The procedure for each data source follows:

Laboratory Observations. There were two lab visits; one when the infants were approximately 6-months-old and the other at about 8.3 months of age. During each lab session, which was divided into two parts both of which were videotaped, the mother sat beside the infant who was seated in a tabletop high chair. Part 1 had three 2-minute episodes: Episode 1 was a free-play situation between the mother and the infant with a new toy which the infant could not operate independently (a windup music box). The mother was directed to interact with her child and to operate the toy for him or her. Episode 2 was a "frustration" episode in which the mother was directed to place the toy on a table where it could be seen by the child, but not reached, and to pretend to read. Episode 3 was a reaction episode. For this period, the mother was directed to react to her infant only when she thought the infant wanted her to.

The free play episode was designed to interest the infant in the toy by having the mother demonstrate its use. Also, through her behavior, the mother emphasized to the infant that she was essential for making the toy work. Having the mother read during the frustration episode primarily served to neutralize maternal effects on the infant's use of intentional communication. The infant was required to initiate contact and received no cues or support from the mother. This condition probably made the task more stringent than a natural interactive situation and provided a critical test of the infant's ability to use communicative behaviors intentionally (cf., Harding & Golinkoff, 1979). The reaction episode (Episode 3) permitted the observation of the infant's persistence as well as his behavior when the goal was reached. It also permitted observation of the mother's interpretation of communicative intent in the infant's behavior and her reaction after that inference.

In part 2, Piagetian tasks were administered by the experimenter to assess the infant's object-concept and causal developmental levels (Piaget, 1954; see Harding, 1981).

Home Observations.   Two home visits were made during the observation period, one at about 7 months and the other at about 10 months. The mothers were directed to play or otherwise interact with their infants as they normally would in a one-to-one situation. The observations lasted for about 1 hour although only the middle half hour was recorded in narrative notes by the observer. The observer sat in an obscure corner of the room, wrote and ignored the infant as much as possible.

Mother-kept Diaries.   The mothers were instructed in keeping a diary of their infant's and their own behaviors. Weekly entries were encouraged although the entries were made at the mother's convenience. Although there was no specific format for the diaries the mothers were encouraged to describe what they thought were the important achievements of their infant at the time of the diary entry. The mothers had been told that the study was concerned with the communication development of the infant although they were also encouraged to describe other achievements such as sitting, crawling, and walking.

GENERAL RELATIONSHIPS BETWEEN COMMUNICATION DEVELOPMENT AND MOTHERS' INTERPRETATIONS OF AND REACTIONS TO INFANTS' BEHAVIORS

Although it had been predicted that mothers' behaviors and interpretations would relate to the level of communication development, no specific relationships were predicted. Little prior information was available about the mother's role in communication development at least from this perspective. For example, although micro-analyses of the interactional patterns and contingencies of mother-infant dyads have been made (e.g., Schaffer, 1977), no one has surveyed mothers for their interpretation of their infants' and their own communicative behaviors. Bates, Benigni, Bretherton, Camaioni, and Volterra (1979) interviewed mothers but asked specific questions which allowed for little mother interpretation. Few observational studies in natural or even lab settings have been made examining the changing communicative relationship between the same mothers and infants over time. (Clark-Stewart, 1973, is an exception, although the scope was much broader than communication development.) The findings reported here included data from the mother-kept diaries, home visits, and the reaction episode of the lab observations. Mothers' intuition and their performance over time are both reported.

Results

Each infant's communicative behaviors were coded for each laboratory observation and assigned to the categories described below. "Communicative behaviors" were defined as behaviors identified previously (e.g., Argyle, 1972; Duncan, 1972) as eliciting communicative reaction, that is gaze direction and eye contact, vocalizing, reaching and pointing, whether or not they are used with the intention of communicating.

The categories represent the hierarchical sequence of communicative development:

1. *Procedural behaviors:* This label was used to identify communicative behaviors used as part of global body movements. Piaget (1954) described these undifferentiated movements as "procedures to make an interesting sight last [pp. 267–271]." They are behaviors which may have communicative effect (e.g., vocalizing while banging and kicking on the high chair) but do not appear to be used for communication.

2. *Instrumental behaviors:* These behaviors were directed at the object or mother's hand in an instrumental way, either in an attempt to actually get the object or to "set the mother's hand in motion" (see Piaget, 1954), for example, reaching toward the toy even though it is out of reach. Although easily interpreted as communicative, there was no indication that the infant was trying to communicate. Instead he was trying to achieve the toy through instrumental means.

3. *Intentional gestures:* These behaviors were the coordination of a gesture (in all cases, reaching, since no pointing was observed) with eye contact with the mother and looking back and forth between her and the desired object.

4. *Intentional vocalizations:* These behaviors were vocalizations used in coordination with eye contact with the mother and looking back and forth between her and the object. Since gestures such as reaching had earlier been used as

instrumental means for achieving the toy, an *a priori* hypothesis was that intentional reaching would be observed prior to the intentional use of vocalizations which provide no instrumental connection with achieving the toy.

5. *Coordinated patterns:* This category included reaching, vocalizing, and looking used in coordination as intentional communication. Behaviors assigned to this category were used sequentially by the infant and appeared to represent alternate means the infant had for communicating (see Harding, 1981).

Figure 6.2 depicts the developmental patterns of the 12 subjects across the predicted levels of change in communicative ability. Although one infant's behavior (Infant K) did not change according to this sequence during the observation period, all the other infants who did change progressed according to the predicted sequence. No regressions occurred.

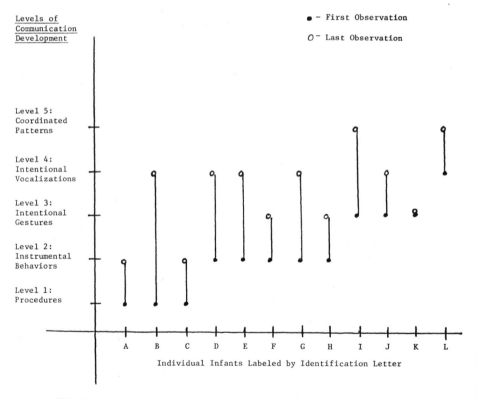

FIG. 6.2   Patterns of Individual Infants' Communication Development Across Time. First Observation: $\bar{X}$ age = 5.8 months. Last Observation: $\bar{X}$ age = 10 months.

Communication Development as Interpreted By the Mothers.   It is interesting that the mothers appeared to respond to and interpret the same types of communicative behaviors that researchers specify as communicative. The behaviors they inferred to be communicative were fairly consistent across mothers for each age of the infant (see Harding, 1982a; Table 6.1).

Most mothers described eye contact, gestures such as reaching and pointing, and sounds such as whines, screams, babbles, and crying as communicative. Eleven of the 12 mothers specifically described eye contact as a critical feature of their infants' communicative behavior. Although prior research has shown that mothers respond to eye contact as communication (e.g., Robson, 1967), it is interesting to know that they are aware of their behavior and knowingly reinforce the infant's eye contact with communication. Four mothers first described eye contact occurring during early social contact interactions but the other seven described it as communicatively important only when the infant used eye contact in coordination with vocalizing and/or attention-directing behaviors such as reaching, in other words, the *a priori* operational definition of intentional communicative behavior.

Seven mothers mentioned the first "da da" or other word at about 7 months and indicated that they did not think it was used as a label at the time. They did describe, however, how they began to teach their infant its meaning; by repeating the sound consistently in context such as when the father was in the room or by taking the baby to "daddy" when the sound "da da" was made. The mothers' descriptions of their response to and interpretations of vocal behaviors such as this give some evidence that may account for vocalizations becoming used more frequently and recognized by the infant as conventional communication. All of the mothers consistently reacted to vocalizations as communicative and encouraged sounds as communications, particularly by identifying them as words and then expanding the conversation based on the infant's use of sound. Differences in what behaviors mothers reacted to follow. However, all mothers reported and were observed reacting to their infants' vocalizations as communicative.

In drawing conclusions from these mother-kept diaries, mothers appeared to accurately (at least in agreement with experimenter observations) assess their infants' communicative behaviors. The infants' uses of communicative behaviors as described by the mothers were coded according to the hierarchical sequence used to code the infants' behaviors observed in the laboratory. Figures 6.3, 6.4, 6.5, and 6.6 depict both the mother-described behaviors and the observed behaviors.

The comparison of these two data sources indicates that mothers' reports concur with the predicted gradual sequence of communication development. Although at 6 months, some mothers tended to underestimate their infants' observed performance (7 of 12 mothers), at each of the other ages mothers' reports in general matched the laboratory observations. Eleven of the 12 mothers

TABLE 6.1

Behaviors Interpreted as Communicative by Mothers;
Listed According to the Infants' Age
at Time of Report in Mothers' Diaries

6 Months	7 Months	8 Months	9 Months	10 Months
crying (7)*	listening (6)	associating consequences with words (usually "no") (8)	waving (12)	associating own actions with words (11)
shrieking (4)	whining (7)	babbling (7)	responding to specific words with correct action (6)	using words (7)
fake cough (3)	"da da" (7)	active participation in games (12)	using sounds with gestures and/or eye contact (7)	using words for communication (4)
procedures (usually described as occurring to continue a game) (6)	imitating noises (7)	expectant waiting (3)	pointing (2)	
eye contact during social contact (4)	reaching (7)	eye contact with vocalizations (5)		
smiling (8)	screaming (4)	using sounds with consistent meaning (5)		
laughing (4)				
making noises (7)				
looking (3)				

*(n) = number of mothers reporting behavior.

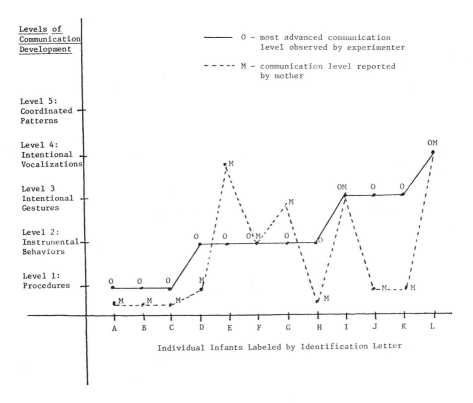

FIG. 6.3   Individual Infants' Communication Development.

reported behaviors that matched those observed at least during one observation time and seven of those mothers' reports matched the observed behaviors at each time. Only one mother's reports (Mother A) never matched with the behaviors observed in the laboratory.

Mothers seemed "tuned in" to their infants' behaviors and, except perhaps at 6 months, were aware of and presumably reacting to the highest level of communicative competence available to the infant. It is particularly interesting in the context of the present discussion that in all instances except two, when infants were observed using intentional vocalizations their mothers also reported this level of development in their diaries. Mothers were in fact more consistent in matching their reports with observed behaviors at the level of intentional vocalizing than any other. (The exception is the level of coordinated patterns which followed and included the use of vocalizations.) This finding supports the hypothesis that infant vocalizations are particularly salient communicative behaviors interpreted and reacted to as communicative.

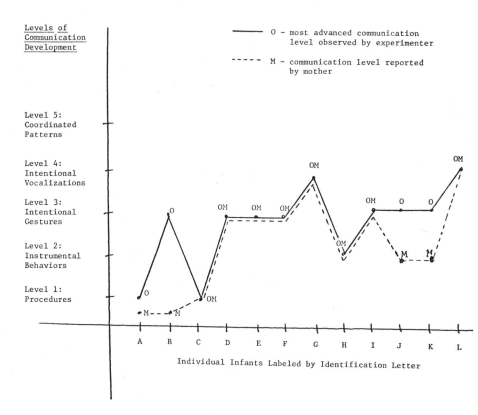

FIG. 6.4   Individual Infants' Communication Development.

General Characteristics of Mother-infant Communicative Interactions.   One characteristic of mothers' behaviors within the mother-infant interactions that was predicted to be important was the mother's inference of intent in the infant's behavior. It had been predicted that the mothers' behavior following an interpretation of communicative intent in the infant's behavior would help the infant achieve goals. In fact the process including mothers' interpretations and reactions to pre-intentional communicative behavior as if they were intentional communication may relate to infants' increasing ability to use communication as a goal (cf. Newson, 1979; Harding, 1982(a),(b)).

Most mothers (10 of 12) according to their diary descriptions inferred intent in their infant's communicative behaviors at least by 10 months of age. At 6 months, four mothers described their babies as communicating intentionally and by 8.3 months, over half of the mothers (n = 8) were inferring intent. (Table 6.2 presents this information.)

The mothers' behaviors also indicated they inferred that their infants intended to communicate with them. The laboratory reaction episode was designed to observe mothers' reactions to behaviors they inferred to be communicative. Even at 6 months, only two mothers did not react to their infants' behavior as communicative. The other 10 mothers began interacting almost immediately and the pattern of their initial reaction indicated that they were inferring communicative intent in their infants' behavior.

A second characteristic that was predicted to be significant in communication development was the consistent reaction of the mother to behaviors which will become communicative. It had been hypothesized that the mothers' consistent communicative reaction to behaviors such as vocalizations, looking and reaching enabled the infant to identify these behaviors as first instrumental in achieving goals and then as means to communicate.

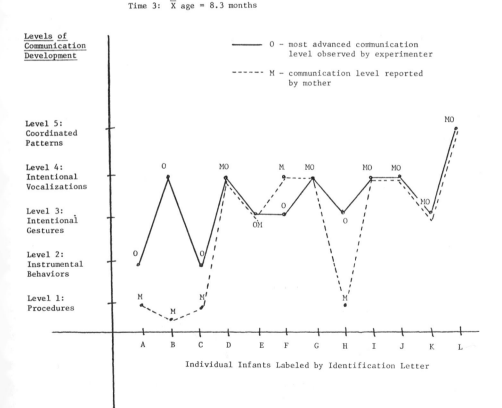

FIG. 6.5   Individual Infants' Communication Development.

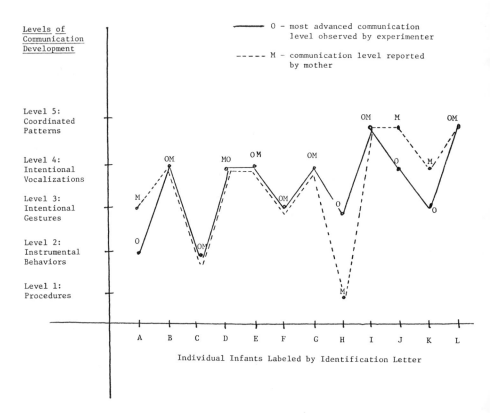

FIG. 6.6   Individual Infants' Communication Development.

It appears that the mothers in the study did react consistently to their infants' behaviors, particularly eye contact and vocalizing. Eye contact appeared to be the primary infant behavior interpreted and reacted to as communicative. At 6 months during the lab reaction episode, 9 of 12 mothers reacted initially to eye contact; six of them only after it occurred simultaneously with vocalizing. Although this combination appears to fit the operational definition for intentionally vocalizing, at 6 months only one infant actually appeared to be using the behaviors for the purpose of communication with the mother. The other infants had been vocalizing for several seconds as they looked around the room and glanced at the mother while still vocalizing. As soon as the eye contact occurred, the mother reacted with comments and/or actions as if in response to intentional communications. This communicative reaction of the mothers to the apparently coincidental co-occurrence of eye contact and vocalizations prior to the infants' intentional coordination of them supports the hypothesis that the mother's inference of intent may precede and contribute to the development of intentional communication.

Eye contact was ignored by only two mothers during the reaction episode. One of these mothers never reacted to her infant during this episode other than to continue to watch her as instructed. The other was the mother of the infant who used intentional vocalizations. She only ignored eye contact until her infant intentionally combined it with vocalizing. It appeared that this mother was waiting for her infant's most advanced usage of communicative behaviors before she reacted. Two mothers responded to eye contact coordinated with reaching (intentional gestures). Only one mother responded without prior eye contact when her infant directed communicative behaviors toward the toy (vocalizing while reaching and looking toward the toy).

All mothers ignored procedures (global body movements, cf., Piaget, 1954) as communicative (six infants performed them) although they had described procedures in the diaries as behaviors they reacted to. One mother ignored her infant as he reached toward her and waited instead until he made eye contact with her. Two mothers ignored their babies for the entire 2 minute episode, except for watching them as instructed to do. One of these infants, as mentioned before, did make eye contact and at one point was even vocalizing while she glanced at her mother but her mother continued to just sit and watch her. The baby ended the episode by whining while looking at the toy and performing procedures, banging

TABLE 6.2
Mothers' Inference of Intent at Each Age of the Infant
and Whether or Not the Infant Was Intentionally Communicating
at the Time

$\bar{X}$ Age	Mother Did Infer Intent			Mother Did Not Infer Intent		
5.8 months	E	I*		A	D	J*
	G	L*		B	F	K*
				C	H	
7 months	D*	I*		A	H	
	E*	L*		B*	J*	
	F*			C	K*	
	G*					
8.3 months	D*	I*		A	H	
	E*	J*		B*		
	F*	K*		C		
	G*	L*				
10 months	A	F*	K*	C		
	B*	G*	L*	H*		
	D*	I*				
	E*	J*				

*Infant observed to be intentionally communicating.

and kicking at the table (an example perhaps of frustration leading to a regression in behavior; Piaget, 1954). The other infant directed all his communicative behaviors at the toy while his mother sat and watched him.

The observation that mothers ignored procedures is interesting in that it indicates that mothers were discriminating in what they were inferring to be communicative. Their general preference for reacting to eye contact and vocalizations may indeed provide some information as to the link between preverbal communication and language acquisition. It could be assumed that more instrumental behaviors such as reaching would be most communicative to mothers since the goal of the infant is more clearly specified. However mothers were observed most often reacting to and encouraging vocalizations as communicative.

A third characteristic that emerged from these observations as an important feature of the mothers' role in communication development concerned the communicative behaviors used by the mothers and the ways they were used during the interactions.

Mothers' communicative behaviors appeared important in at least three ways: (1) the type of behaviors they used in response to their infants' behaviors; (2) the content or focus of their communication behaviors; and (3) the control they exercised over the interactions, for example, how often they initiated turns in the interaction (as coded by an observer) in comparison to the turns they responded to as initiations (intentional or unintentional) of the infant. These characteristics for each mother-infant pair are summarized in Table 6.3 and are described below:

1. Type of mothers' behaviors: In general, the data from the diaries, laboratory observations, and home visits describe maternal responsiveness as verbal comments made in coordination with an action. Some mothers did, however, appear to respond with gestures and actions independent of verbal comments.

During the lab reaction episode at 6 months, of the 10 mothers who responded, six responded with verbal comments coordinated with actions, usually giving the toy to the baby. Two mothers who responded to intentional gestures gave their babies the toy without commenting as did the mother who responded to the infant's communication toward the toy. One mother responded to her infants' eye contact by making faces and laughing.

At 9 months, similar reactions occurred in most of the interactions although when differences occurred they were more pronounced. Nine of the mothers responded to their infants intentional vocalizations or gestures with verbal comments and actions. Although style differences occurred, perhaps reflecting personality variables, the interactional patterns of these nine pairs were remarkably similar. The mother would sit watching her infant, usually leaning toward the baby. The baby would look toward the toy, perhaps vocalizing or even reaching toward it. However, when the mother did not move or interact, the infant would turn toward the mother, make eye contact and vocalize. This usually occurred

TABLE 6.3

Individual Mother-Infant Pairs Scored on Three Characteristics
That May Relate to Communication Development
(Based on Observation Times at 5.8 and 7 Months)

Characteristic		A	B	C	D	E	F	G	H	I	J	K	L
		Mother-Infant Pairs (Labeled by Identification Letter)											
1. Inference of intent (based on mothers' diaries)	Inferred Intent				X	X	X	X		X			X
	Did Not Infer Intent	X	X	X					X		X	X	
2. Type of infant behaviors responded to by mother*	Vocal	X	X		X			X		X			X
	Gestural					X	X		X		X	X	
	Any Motor Behavior			X									
3.1 Mother's focus (based on home visit)	Responsive	X	X	X	X	X		X	X	X	X	X	X
	Directive	X		X	X	X	X	X	X	X			
3.2 Initiations of turns	Primarily Mother Initiated	X	X			X			X	X	X	X	X
	Coinitiated						X	X					
3.3 Type of mother's communicative behaviors	Verbal	X	X	X	X	X		X	X	X	X	X	X
	**Nonverbal						X						

*All mothers responded to vocalizations. However, if they responded to gestures as often as they responded to vocalizations, they were classified as gestural.
**Gestures and actions used without verbal comment for more than 25% of mothers' responses.

109

within the first 30 seconds ($\bar{X}$ time = 25.2 seconds, range ± 6.50 seconds) and the mother would respond with a comment such as "What do you want? Would you like that toy?" The mother then would get the toy and set it on the high chair tray and continue to interact with the infant. Only one mother gave her infant the toy without comment and this occurred as the infant began climbing out of the high chair toward it. Two mothers did not behave in response to their infants' behavior, both of them ignoring eye contact and intentional gestures, although one infant only glanced toward her mother as if maintaining social contact while vocalizing and gesturing toward the toy.

Observations of the mothers' behaviors during the home visits supported the conclusion of the general verbal responsiveness combined with an appropriate action based on the mother's interpretation of the infant's behavior. All mothers were observed responding in this way to at least some of the behavior interpreted as communicative, and eye contact and vocalizations were responded to by all the mothers.

2. Focus of mothers' behaviors: Certain mothers appeared to focus all (or at least most of) their behaviors on what their infants did, closely monitoring infant gaze and other indications of interest. The content of other mothers' behaviors showed more concern with directing the infant's attention. Both types of mother behaviors could be described as instructive (cf., Ryan, 1974) since both included labeling and detailed descriptions, but the content of what was being instructed varied. For what might be called the "responsive" mother the content followed the infant's prior interests at least as indicated by his gaze or on-going activity. For the "directive" mother, content involved activities and objects other than those the infant currently was occupied with. It is not clear what relationship these communication content differences might have to communication development and individual differences in focus may or may not be related to communication development.

3. Initiations: In an earlier study, Harding and Golinkoff (1980) found that mothers who shared initiations of the turns of an interaction with their infants had infants who were more advanced communicatively than mothers who initiated over 50% of the interactions themselves. Sharing initiations may have a positive effect on communication development.

All mothers in this study initiated at least half of the turns; the range for mother initiations was from 51% to 98%. One mother responded to only two of her infant's behaviors as turn initiations. This however seemed to be an exception and most of the mothers (n = 8) responded to at least 25% of the turns rather than initiating them. Five mothers appeared to be "taking turns" with their infants (as discussed in Harding & Golinkoff, 1980) and appeared to be inferring that their infants were intending to initiate communications at least 50% of the time. These interactions appeared conversational whether or not the infant's behavior was intentional.

CONCLUSION

As the infant becomes more organized in interpreting his environment, in other words, as he begins to sequence events and recognize causal agents (Stage 5 behaviors), it appears that he also comes to recognize his mother's role in his achievement of goals and the potential of using her as a means for goal achievement.

Once the infant has mastered the connections between his behaviors, communication with the mother, and the achievement of goals, it appears that he develops alternative plans for communication. As would be expected, the first behaviors used develop from earlier instrumental behaviors such as reaching and only later are more abstract communicative behaviors such as vocalizations used. Mothers played an important role in the development of vocalizations as communicative behaviors. They both responded most often to vocalizations and used verbal responses and comments as they interacted communicatively with their infants. As Ricks (1979) has pointed out, vocalizations are part of a normal infant's behavioral repertoire and as the infant comes to recognize the effect, or in Ricks' words, the meaning his vocalizations have in his world, the infant begins to use his first vocal communications. It would appear that the recognition of the meaning of vocalizations develops first through the recognition of connections, mediated and carried out by the mother, between the infant's behaviors and goal achievement.

The communicative process described is in agreement with Clark's (1978) thesis that symbol systems must derive from sensorimotor actions. There is, however, at least one area of disagreement. Clark assumed that "sounds do not intrinsically have much effect on the world [p. 256]." The data from this research refute this assumption. Sounds in the form of vocalizations appear early in the infant's development to have a major effect on mother's behaviors and become, in fact, a focal point for much of the mother's response and activity concerning the infant. Although the intentional use of vocalizations does not necessarily imply the acquisition of words, the encouragement and repetition observed in mothers as they respond to their infants' vocalizations indicate that early in development mothers begin to selectively "teach" their infants to become word-users. It is not surprising then that when the infant recognizes the usefulness of communication as a goal, he also comes to recognize the usefulness of words as a means of communication.

As I warned at the start of this chapter, these data say nothing about the process of language acquisition. However, it may be that as mothers require certain communicative behaviors before they react, they are not only encouraging those specific behaviors but also "teaching" the infant that a mutual means of communication exists. The development of language as an efficient communicative code may have as its base this early "teaching."

By the end of the first year, the infant has become a communicator, not only through the effect his behaviors have on others but also because he can intentionally use behaviors as means to signal others. In addition, he seems to expect that certain behaviors will be more consistently responded to as communicative, and that usually these behaviors include vocalizations. Although clearly these observations shed no light on how language structures are acquired during the second year, it does seem likely that the process of communication development leading to the use of vocalizations as means of intentional communication is a necessary condition for the acquisition of words.

REFERENCES

Argyle, M. Non-verbal communication in human social interaction. In R. A. Hinde (Ed.), *Nonverbal communication*. London: University of Cambridge Press, 1972.

Austin, J. L. *How to do things with words*. New York: Oxford University Press, 1962.

Bates, E., Benigni, L., Bretherton, I., Camaioni, L., & Volterra, V. *The emergence of symbols: Cognition and communication in infancy*. New York: Academic Press, 1979.

Bates, E., Camaioni, L., & Volterra, V. The acquisition of performatives prior to speech. *Merrill-Palmer Quarterly*, 1975, *21*, 5–226.

Belsky, J. Mother-infant interaction at home and in the laboratory: The effect of context. Paper presented at the biennial meeting of the Society for Research in Child Development, New Orleans, 1977.

Brazelton, B. Evidence of communication in neonatal behavioral assessment. In M. Bullowa (Ed.), *Before speech: The beginning of interpersonal communication*. Cambridge, Mass.: Cambridge University Press, 1979.

Bruner, J. S. From communication to language: A psychological perspective. *Cognition*, 1976, *3*, 155–187.

Bruner J. S. Acquiring the uses of language. Paper presented at the Berlyne Memorial Lecture, March, 1978.

Clark, R. Action, gesture, and symbol. In A. Lock (Ed.), *Action, gesture and symbol: The emergence of language*. New York: Academic Press, 1978.

Clark–Stewart, K. A. Interactions between mothers and their young children: Characteristics and consequences. *Monographs of the Society for Research in Child Development*, 1973, *38*, serial 153.

Duncan, S. D., Jr. Some signals and rules for taking speaking turns in conversation. *Journal of Personality and Social Psychology*, 1972, *23*, 283–292.

Harding, C. G. A longitudinal study of the development of the intention to communicate. Unpublished dissertation, 1981.

Harding, C. G. Acting with intention: A framework for examining the development of intention. In L. Feagans, R. M. Golinkoff, & C. Garvey, (Eds.), The origins and growth of communication. New York: Ablex, 1982.(a)

Harding, C. G. The development of the intention to communicate. *Human Development*, 1982(b), *25*, 140–151.

Harding, C. G., & Golinkoff, R. M. The origins of intentional vocalizations in prelinguistic infants. *Child Development*, 1979, *50*, 33–40.

Harding, C. G., & Golinkoff, R. M. Preverbal communication: The role of cognitive development and maternal style. Paper presented at the Second International Conference on Infant Studies, New Haven, Connecticut, April 24, 1980.

Konner, M. Communication. Paper presented at SRCD Summer Institute on Communication, 1979.

Newson, J. The growth of shared understandings between infant and caregiver. In M. Bullowa (Ed.), *Before speech: The beginning of interpersonal communication.* London: Cambridge University Press, 1979.

Piaget, J. *The construction of reality of the child.* New York: Ballentine, 1954.

Piattelli-Palmarini, M. (Ed.) Language and learning: The debate between Jean Piaget and Noam Chomsky. Cambridge, Mass.: Harvard University Press, 1980.

Ricks, D. Making sense of experience to make sensible sounds. In M. Bullowa (Ed.), *Before speech: The beginning of interpersonal communication.* London: Cambridge University Press, 1979.

Robson, K. S. The role of eye-to-eye contact in maternal-infant attachment. *Journal of Child Psychology and Psychiatry,* 1967, *8,* 13–25.

Ryan, J. Early language development. In M. P. M. Richards (Ed.), *The integration of the child into a social world.* London: Cambridge University Press, 1974.

Schaffer, H. R. (Ed.), *Studies in mother-infant interaction.* London: Academic Press, 1977.

Shotter, J. The cultural context of communication studies: Theoretical and methodological issues. In A. Lock (Ed.), *Action, gesture, and symbol: The emergence of language.* New York: Academic Press, 1978.

7

A Cultural Perspective on the Transition from Prelinguistic to Linguistic Communication

Bambi B. Schieffelin
Graduate School of Education
University of Pennsylvania

Elinor Ochs
Department of Linguistics
University of Southern California

ETHNOGRAPHIC ORIENTATION

To most middle class Western readers, the descriptions of verbal and non-verbal behaviors of middle class caregivers with their children seem very familiar, desirable, and even natural. These descriptions capture in rich detail what does go on in many middle class households, to a greater or lesser extent. The characteristics of caregiver speech (Baby Talk register) and comportment that have been specified are highly valued by members of white middle class society, including researchers, readers, and subjects of study. They are associated with good mothering and can be spontaneously produced with little effort or reflections. As demonstrated by Shatz and Gelman (1973), Sachs and Devin (1976), and Andersen and Johnson (1973), children as young as 4-years-of-age can speak and act in these ways when addressing small children.

From our research experience in other societies as well as our acquaintance with some of the cross-cultural studies of language socialization (Blount, 1972; Bowerman, 1981; Fischer, 1970; Hamilton, 1981; Harkness, 1975; Harkness & Super, 1977; Heath, in press; Miller, 1982; Philips, in press; Schieffelin & Eisenberg, in press; Scollon and Scollon, 1981; Stross, 1972; Ward, 1971; Wills, 1977), the general patterns of caregiving that have been described in the psychological literature on white middle class are neither characteristic of all societies nor of all social groups (e.g., all social classes within one society). We would like the reader therefore, to reconsider the descriptions of caregiving in the psychological literature as *ethnographic descriptions*.

By ethnographic, we mean *descriptions that take into account the perspective of members of a social group, including beliefs and values that underlie and organize their activities and utterances*. Ethnographers rely heavily on observations and on formal and informal elicitation of members' reflections and interpretations as a basis for analysis (Geertz, 1973). Typically the ethnographer is not a member of the group under study. Further, in presenting an ethnographic account the researcher faces the problem of communicating world views or sets of values that may be unfamiliar and strange to the reader. Ideally such statements provide a set of organizing principles that give coherence and an analytic focus to the behaviors described.

Psychologists who have carried out research on verbal and non-verbal behavior of caregivers and their children draw on both of the methods articulated above. However, unlike most ethnographers, typically the psychological researcher *is* a member of the social group under observation. (In some cases, the researcher's own children are the subjects of study.) Further, unlike the ethnographer, the psychologist addresses a readership familiar with the social scenes portrayed.

That researcher, reader, and subjects of study tend to have in common a white middle class literate background has had several consequences. For example, by and large, the psychologist has not been faced with the problem of cultural translation, as has the anthropologist—there has been a tacit assumption that readers can provide the larger cultural framework for making sense out of the behaviors documented. A consequence of this in turn is that the cultural nature of the behaviors and principles presented is not explicit. From our perspective, *language and culture as bodies of knowledge, structures of understanding, conceptions of the world, collective representations, are both extrinsic to and far more extensive than any individual could know or learn. Culture encompases variations in knowledge between individuals, but such variation, while crucial to what an individual may know and to the social dynamic between individuals, does not have its locus within the individual.* Our position is that culture is not something that can be considered separately from the accounts of caregiver-child interaction; it is what organizes and gives meaning to that interaction. This is an important point, as it affects the definition and interpretation of the behaviors of caregivers and children. How caregivers and children speak and act towards one another is linked to cultural patterns that extend and have consequences beyond the specific interactions observed. For example, how caregivers speak to their children may be linked to other institutional adaptations to young children. These adaptations in turn may be linked to how members of a given society view children more generally (their 'nature', their social status and expected comportment) and to how members think children develop.

We are suggesting here that sharing of assumptions between researcher, reader, and subjects of study is a mixed blessing. In fact, this sharing presents a *paradox of familiarity*. We are able to apply without effort the cultural framework for interpreting the behavior of caregivers and young children in our own social group; indeed as members of a white middle class society, we are socialized to do this very work, that is interpreting behaviors, attributing motives and so on. The paradox is that in spite of this ease of effort, we can not easily isolate and make explicit these cultural principles. As Goffman's work on American society has illustrated, articulation of norms, beliefs, and values is often possible only when faced with violations, that is with gaffes, breaches, misfirings, and the like (Goffman, 1963, 1967; Much & Shweder, 1979).

Another way to see the cultural principles at work in our own society is to examine the ways in which *other* societies are organized in terms of social interaction and in terms of the society at large. In carrying out such research, the ethnographer offers a point of contrast and comparison with our own everyday activities. Such comparative material can lead us to reinterpret behaviors as cultural that we have assumed to be natural. From the anthropological perspective, every society will have its own cultural constructs of what is natural and what is not. For example, every society has its own theory of procreation. Certain Australian Aboriginal societies believe that a number of different factors contribute to conception. Von Sturmer (1980) writes that among the Kugu–Nganychara (West Cape York Peninsula, Australia) the spirit of the child may first enter the man through an animal that he has killed and consumed. The spirit passes from the man to the woman through sexual intercourse, but several sexual acts are necessary to build the child. (See also Montagu, 1937; Hamilton, 1981.) Even within a single society, there may be different beliefs concerning when life begins and ends, as the recent debates in the United States and Europe concerning abortion and mercy killing indicate. The issue of what is nature and what is nurture (cultural) extends to patterns of caregiving and child development. Every society will have (implicitly or explicitly) given notions concerning the capacities and temperament of children at different points in their development (see for example, Ninio, 1979; Snow, de Blauw, & van Roosmalen, 1979; Dentan, 1978). The expectations and responses of caregivers will be directly related to these notions.

TWO DEVELOPMENTAL STORIES

At this point, using an ethnographic perspective, we will recast selected behaviors of white middle class caregivers and young children as pieces of one 'developmental story.' The white middle class 'developmental story' that we are constructing is based on various descriptions available, footnote on individual variation and focuses on those patterns of interaction (both verbal and non-verbal) that have been emphasized in the literature. This story will be compared with another developmental story; the Kaluli (Papua New Guinea), a society that is strikingly different.[1]

One of the major goals in presenting and comparing these developmental stories is to demonstrate that communicative interactions between caregivers and young children are culturally constructed. In our comparisons, we will focus on three facets of communicative interaction: (1) the social organization of the verbal environment of very young children; (2) the extent to which children are expected to adapt to situations or that situations are adapted to the child; and (3) the negotiation of meaning by caregiver and child. We first present a general sketch for each social group and then discuss in more detail the consequences of the differences and similarities in communicative patterns in these two groups.

These developmental stories are not timeless, but rather are linked in complex ways to particular historical contexts. Both the ways in which caregivers behave towards young children and the popular and scientific accounts of these ways may differ at different moments in time. The stories that we present represent ideas currently held in the two social groups.

The two stories show that there is more than one way of becoming social and using language in early childhood. All normal children will become members of their own social group. But the process of becoming social including becoming a language user is culturally constructed. In relation to this process of construction, every society has its own developmental stories that are rooted in social organization, beliefs, and values. These stories may be explicitly codified and/or tacitly assumed by members.

Anglo-American White Middle Class Developmental Story[2]

Middle class in Britain and the United States covers a broad range of white collar and professional workers and their families including lower middle, middle middle, and upper middle class strata. The literature on communicative development has been largely based on middle middle and upper middle class households. These households tend to consist of a single nuclear family with one, two,

---

[1]A third developmental story based on research in Western Samoa has been written by E. Ochs. See E. Ochs & B. B. Schieffelin 'Language acquisition and socialization: Three developmental stories and their implications' in R. Shweder and R. LeVine (eds.) *Culture and its acquisition,* University of Chicago Press, in press.

[2]The data for this story consists of the numerous accounts of caregiver-child communication and interaction that have appeared in both popular and scientific journals. Our generalizations regarding language use are based on detailed reports in the developmental psycholinguistic literature which are cited throughout this paper. In addition we are drawing on our own experiences and intuitions as mothers and members of this social group. We invite those with differing perceptions to comment on our interpretations.

or three children. The primary caregiver almost without exception is a child's natural or adopted mother. Researchers have focused on communicative situations in which one child interacts with his or her mother. The generalizations proposed by these researchers concerning mother–child communication could be an artifact of this methodological focus. However, it could be argued that the attention to two-party encounters between a mother and her child reflects the most frequent type of communicative interaction to which most young middle class children are exposed. Participation in two-party as opposed to multi-party interactions is a product of many considerations, including the physical setting of households, where interior and exterior walls bound and limit access to social interaction.

Soon after an infant is born, many mothers will hold their infants in such a way that they are face-to-face and will gaze at them. Mothers have been observed to address their infants, vocalize to them, ask questions, and greet them. In other words, from birth on, the infant is treated as a *social being* and as an *addressee* in social interaction. The infant's vocalizations, physical movements, and states are often interpreted as meaningful and will be responded to verbally by the mother or other caregiver. In this way, proto-conversations are established and sustained, along a *dyadic, turn-taking* model. Throughout this period and the subsequent language-acquiring years, caregivers treat very young children as communicative partners. One very important procedure in facilitating these social exchanges is the mother's (or other caregiver's) *taking the perspective of the child*. This perspective is evidenced in her own speech through the many simplifying and affective features of baby talk register that have been described and through the various strategies employed to identify what the young child may be expressing.

Such perspective-taking is part of a much wider set of accommodations by adults to young children. These accommodations are manifested in several domains. For example, there are widespread material accommodations to infancy and childhood in the form of cultural artifacts designed for this stage of life, that is baby clothes, baby food, miniaturization of furniture, and toys. Special behavioral accommodations are coordinated with the infant's perceived needs and capacities, for example, putting the baby in a quiet place to facilitate and insure proper sleep; 'baby-proofing' a house as a child becomes increasingly mobile, yet not aware of or able to control the consequences of his own behavior. In general, *situations and the language used in them are adapted or modified to the child* rather than the reverse. Further, the child is a *focus of attention,* in that the child's actions and verbalizations are often the *starting point* of social interaction with more mature persons.

While developmental achievements such as crawling, walking, and first words are awaited by caregivers, the accommodations noted above have the effect of keeping the child dependent on and separate from the adult community for a considerable period of time. The child is protected from certain experiences which are considered harmful (e.g. playing with knives, climbing stairs), but such protection delays his knowledge and developing competence in such contexts.

The accommodations of white middle class caregivers to young children can be examined for other values and tendencies. Particularly among the American middle class, these accommodations reflect a *discomfort with the competence differential* between adult and child. The competence gap is reduced by two strategies. One is for the adult to simplify her or his speech to match more closely what the adult considers to be the verbal competence of the young child. Let us call this strategy the *self-lowering* strategy, following Irvine's (1974) analysis of intercaste demeanor. A second strategy is for the caregiver to richly interpret (Brown, 1973) what the young child is expressing. Here the adult acts as if the child were more competent than his behavior more strictly would indicate. Let us call this strategy the *child-raising* strategy. Other behaviors conform to this strategy, such as when an adult cooperates in a task with a child but treats that task as an accomplishment of the child.

For example, in eliciting a story from a child, a caregiver will often cooperate with the child in the telling of the story. This cooperation typically takes the form of posing questions to the child, such as "Where did you go?", "What did you see?," and so on, to which the adult knows the answer. The child is seen as telling the story even though she or he is simply supplying the information the adult has preselected and organized (Ochs, Schieffelin, & Platt, 1979; Schieffelin & Eisenberg, in press; Greenfield & Smith, 1976). Bruner's (1978) descriptions of scaffolding, in which a caregiver constructs a tower or other play object, allowing the young child to place the last block, are also good examples of this tendency. Here the tower may be seen by the caregiver and others as the child's own work. Similarly, in later life, caregivers playing games with their children may let them win, acting as if the child can match or more than match the competence of the adult.

A final aspect of this white middle class developmental story concerns the willingness of many caregivers to interpret unintelligible or partially intelligible utterances of young children (cf. Ochs, 1982). One of the recurrent ways in which interpretation is carried out is for the caregiver to offer a paraphrase ((or 'expansion' (Brown & Bellugi, 1964; Cazden, 1965)), using a question intonation. This behavior of caregivers has continuity with their earlier attributions of intentionality directed towards ambiguous utterances (from the point of view of the infant). For both the prelinguistic and language-using child, the caregiver provides an explicitly verbal interpretation. This interpretation or paraphrase is potentially available to the young child to affirm, disconfirm, or modify.

Through exposure to and participation in these clarification exchanges, the young child is being socialized into several cultural patterns. The first of these is a way of recognizing and defining what constitutes unintelligibility, that an utterance or vocalization may in fact not be immediately understood. Second, the child is presented with the procedures for dealing with ambiguity. Through the successive offerings of possible interpretations, the child learns that more than one understanding of a given utterance or vocalization may be possible. The child is also learning who can make these interpretations, and the extent to which they may be open to modification. Finally the child is learning how to settle upon a possible interpretation and how to show disagreement or agreement. *This entire process socializes the child into culturally specific modes of organizing knowledge, thought, and language.*[3]

A Kaluli Developmental Story[4]

The Kaluli people (population approximately 1200) are an example of a small scale, nonliterate egalitarian society (E. L. Schieffelin, 1976). Kaluli, most of whom are monolingual, speak the Kaluli language, a non-Austronesian verb final ergative language. They live in the tropical rain forest on the Great Papuan Plateau in the Southern Highlands of Papua New Guinea. Kaluli maintain large gardens and hunt and fish in order to obtain protein. Villages are composed of 60–90 individuals who traditionally lived in one large longhouse that had no internal walls. Currently, while the longhouse is maintained, many families are living in smaller dwellings so that two or more extended families may live together. It is not unusual then for at least a dozen individuals of different ages to be living together in one house which consists essentially of one semi-partitioned room.

Men and women utilize extensive networks of obligation and reciprocity in the organization of work and sociable interaction. Everyday life is overtly focused around verbal interaction. Kaluli think of and use talk as a means of control, manipulation, expression, assertion, and appeal. It gets you what you want, need, or feel owed. Talk is a primary indicator of social competence and a

---

[3]We would like to thank Courtney Cazden for bringing the following quotation to our attention, "It seems to us that a mother in expanding speech may be teaching more than grammar; she may be teaching something like a world-view (Brown & Bellugi, 1964, p. 143)."

[4]The data on which this analysis is based were collected in the course of 2 years of ethnographic and linguistic fieldwork (1975–1977) among the Kaluli in the Southern Highland Province. This research was sponsored by the National Science Foundation and the Wenner-Gren Society for Anthropological Research, New York. During this time, E. L. Schieffelin, a cultural anthropologist, and S. Feld, an ethnomusicologist, were also conducting ethnographic research. This study on the development of communicative competence among the Kaluli focused on four children who were approximately 24-months-old at the start of the study. However, an additional 12 children were included in the study (siblings and cousins in residence) and their ages ranged from birth to 10 years. The spontaneous conversations of these children and their families were audiotape recorded for 1 year at monthly intervals with each monthly sample lasting 3–4 hours. Detailed contextual notes accompanied the audiotaping and these annotated transcripts along with interviews and observations form the data base. A total of 83 hours of audio tape were collected and transcribed in the village. Analyses of Kaluli child language acquisition data are reported in Schieffelin, B. B. (1981, in press).

primary way to be social. Learning how to talk and become independent is a major goal of socialization.

For the purpose of comparison and for understanding something of the cultural basis for the ways in which Kaluli act and speak to their children, it is important to first describe selected aspects of a Kaluli developmental story which I have constructed from various kinds of ethnographic data. Kaluli describe their babies as helpless, 'soft,' (*taiyo*) and 'having no understanding' (*asugo andoma*). They take care of them they say, because they 'feel sorry for them.' Mothers, who are the primary caregivers, are attentive to their infants and physically responsive to them. Whenever an infant cries it is offered the breast. However, while nursing her infant, a mother may also be involved in other activities, such as food preparation, or she may be engaged in conversation with individuals in the household. Mothers never leave their infants alone and only rarely with other caregivers. When not holding their infants, mothers carry them in netted bags which are suspended from their heads. When the mother is gardening, gathering wood, or just sitting with others, the baby will sleep in the netted bag next to the mother's body.

Kaluli mothers, given their belief that infants 'have no understanding' never treat their infants as partners (speaker/addressee) in dyadic communicative interactions. While they greet their infants by name and use expressive vocalizations they rarely address other utterances to them. Furthermore, mothers and infants do not gaze into each other's eyes, an interactional pattern that is consistent with adult patterns of not gazing when vocalizing in interaction with one another. Rather than facing their babies and speaking to them, Kaluli mothers tend to face their babies outwards so that they can be seen by, and see others that are part of the social group. Older children greet and address the infant and in response to this, the mother while moving the baby, speaks in a high pitched nasalized voice "for" the baby. Triadic exchanges such as the one that follows is typical of these situations.

When a mother takes the speaking role of an infant she uses language that is well-formed and appropriate for an older child. Only the nasalization and high pitch mark it as "the infant's." When speaking as the infant to older children, mothers speak assertively, that is, they never whine or beg on behalf of the infant. Thus, in taking this role the mother does for the infant what the infant cannot do for itself, appear to act in a controlled and competent manner, using language. These kinds of interactions continue until a baby is between 4–6 months of age.

Several points are important here. First, these triadic exchanges are carried out primarily for the benefit of the older child and help create a relationship between the two children. Second, the mother's utterances in these exchanges are not based on, nor do they originate with anything that the infant has initiated—either vocally or gesturally. Recall the Kaluli claim that infants have no understanding. How could someone with "no understanding" initiate appropriate interactional sequences?

EXAMPLE 1
Mother is Holding Her Infant Son Bage (3 Months).
Abi (35 Months) Is Holding a Stick on His Shoulder in a Manner
Similar to That in Which One Would Carry a Heavy Patrol Box
(The Box Would Be Hung On a Pole Placed Across the Shoulders
of Two Men).[a]

Mother	Abi
(Abi to baby)	[1]Bage! / do you see my box here? / do you see it? / do you see it? /
(high nasal voice talking as if she is the baby, moving the baby who is facing Abi):	
[2]My brother, *I'll* take half, my brother.	
(holding stick out)	[3]mother, give him half / give him half / mother, my brother—here, here take half / X /
(in a high nasal voice as baby):	
[4]My brother, what half do I take? What about it, my brother, put it on the shoulder!	
[5](to Abi in her usual voice): "Put it on the shoulder."	
(Abi rests stick on baby's shoulder)	
[6]There, carefully put it on. (stick accidentally pokes baby) Feel sorry, stop.	

[a]For all examples transcription conventions follow Bloom & Lahey (1978).

However, there is an even more important and enduring cultural construct that helps make sense out of the mother's behaviors in this situation and in many others as well. Kaluli say that "one cannot know what another thinks or feels." Now, while Kaluli obviously interpret and assess one another's available behaviors and internal states, these interpretations are not culturally acceptable as topics of talk. Individuals often talk about their own feelings (I'm afraid, I'm happy, etc.). However, there is a cultural dispreference for talking about or making claims about what another might think, what another might feel, or what another is about to do, especially if there is no external evidence. As we shall see, these culturally constructed behaviors have several important consequences for the ways in which Kaluli caregivers verbally interact with their children, and are related to other pervasive patterns of language use which shall be discussed below.

As infants become older (6–12 months) they are usually held in the arms or carried on the shoulders of the mother or an older sibling. They are present in all on-going household activities, as well as subsistence activities that take place outside the village in the bush. During this time period babies are addressed by adults to a limited extent. They are greeted by a variety of names (proper names, kinterms, affective and relationship terms) and receive a limited set of both negative and positive imperatives. In addition when they do something they are not to do, such as reach for something that is not theirs to take, they will often receive such rhetorical questions such as "Who are you?!" (meaning "not someone to do that") or "It is yours?!" (meaning "it is not yours") to control their actions by shaming them (*sasidiab*). What is important to stress here is that the language addressed to the preverbal child consists largely of "one-liners" which call for no verbal response. Either an action or termination of an action is appropriate. Other than these utterances, very little talk is directed to the young child by the adult caregiver.

This pattern of adults not treating infants as communicative partners continues even when babies begin babbling. Kaluli recognize babbling (*dabedan*) but say that this vocal activity is not communicative and has no relationship to speech that will eventually emerge. Adults and older children occasionally repeat vocalizations back to the young child (ages 12–16 months) reshaping them into the names of persons in the household or into kinterms, but they do not say that the baby is saying the name nor do they wait for or expect the child to repeat those vocalizations in an altered form. In addition, vocalizations are not generally treated as communicative and given verbal expression. Nor are they interpreted by adults, except in one situation, an example of which follows.

When a toddler shrieks in protest of the assaults of an older child, mothers will say "I'm unwilling" (using a quotative particle) referring to the toddler's shriek. These were the only circumstances in which mothers treated vocalizations as communicative and provided verbal expression for them. In no other circumstances in the four families in the study did adults provide a verbally expressed interpretation of a vocalization of a preverbal child. Thus, throughout the preverbal period very little language is directed to the child, except for imperatives, rhetorical questions, and greetings. A child who by Kaluli terms has not yet begun to speak is not expected to respond either verbally or vocally. What all of this means is that in the first 18 months or so very little sustained dyadic verbal exchange takes place between adult and infant. The infant is only minimally treated as an addressee, and is not treated as a communicative partner in dyadic exchanges. One immediate conclusion is: The conversational model that has been described for many white middle class caregivers and their preverbal children has no application in this case. Furthermore, if one defines language input as language directed to the child then it is reasonable to say that for Kaluli children who have not yet begun to speak, there is very little. However, this does not mean that Kaluli children grow up in an impoverished verbal environment and do not learn how to speak. Quite the opposite is true. The verbal environment of the infant is rich and varied, and from the very beginning the infant is surrounded by adults and older children who spend a great deal of time talking to one another. Furthermore, as the infant develops and begins to crawl, engage in play activities, and other independent actions, these actions are frequently referred to, described, and commented upon by members of the household speaking to one another especially by older children. Thus, the ongoing activities of the preverbal child are an important topic of talk between members of the household, and this talk about the here-and-now of the infant is available to the infant, though only a limited amount of talk is addressed to the infant. For example, in referring to the infant's actions, siblings and adults use the infant's name or kinterm. They will say, "Look at Seligiwo! He's walking." Thus the child may learn from these contexts to attend the verbal environment in which he or she lives.

Every society has its own ideology about language, including when it begins and how children acquire it. The Kaluli are no exception. Kaluli claim that language begins at the time when the child uses two critical words, 'mother' (nɔ) and 'breast' (bo). The child may be using other single words, but until these two words are used, the beginning of language is not recognized. Once a child has used these words, a whole set of inter-related behaviors are set into motion. Kaluli claim once a child has begun to use language he or she then must be "shown how to speak" (Schieffelin, 1979). Kaluli show their children language in the form of a teaching strategy which involves providing a model for what the child is to say followed by the word ɛlɛma, an imperative meaning "say like that." Mothers use this method of direct instruction to teach the social uses of assertive language (teasing, shaming, requesting, challenging reporting). However, object labeling is never part of an ɛlɛma sequence, nor does the mother ever use ɛlɛma to instruct the child to beg or appeal for food or objects. Begging, the Kaluli say, is natural for children. They know how to do it. In contrast, a child must be taught to be assertive through the use of particular linguistic expressions and verbal sequences.

A typical sequence using ɛlɛma is triadic, involving the mother, child (between 20–36 months), and other participant(s). An example follows. *In this situation, as in many others, the mother does not modify her language to fit the linguistic ability of the young child. Instead her language is shaped so as to be appropriate (in terms of form and content)* for the child's intended addressee. Consistent with the ways she interacts with her infant, what a mother instructs her young child to say usually does not have its origins in any verbal or nonverbal behaviors of the child, but in what the mother thinks should be said. The mother pushes the child into ongoing interactions that the child may or may not be interested in, and will at times spend a good deal of energy in trying to get the child verbally involved. This is part of the Kaluli pattern of fitting (or pushing) the child into the situation rather than changing the situation to meet the interests or abilities of the child. Thus, mothers take a directive role with their young children, teaching them what to say so that they may become participants in the social group.

In addition to instructing their children by telling them what to say in often extensive interactional sequences, Kaluli mothers pay attention to the form of

EXAMPLE 2

Mother, daughter Binalia (5 years), cousin Mama (3½ years), and son Wanu (27 months) are at home, dividing up some cooked vegetables. Binalia has been begging for some but her mother thinks that she has had her share.

[1]Mother → Wanu → > Binalia:[a]
Whose is it? say like that.

[2]whose is it?! /

[3]Is it yours?! say like that.

[4]is it yours?! /

[5]Who are you?! say like that.

[6]who are you?! /

[7]Mama → Wanu → > Binalia:
Did you pick (it)?! say like that.

[8]did you pick (it)?! /

[9]Mother → Wanu → > Binalia:
My G'ma picked (it)! say like that.

[10]my G'ma picked (it)! /

[11]Mama → Wanu → > Binalia:
This *my G'ma* picked! say like that.

[12]this *my G'ma* picked! /

---

[a]   →   =   speaker → addressee
      → >   =   addressee → > intended addressee

---

their children's utterances. Kaluli will correct the phonological, morphological, or lexical form of an utterance or its pragmatic or semantic meaning. Since the goals of language acquisition include a child becoming competent, independent, and mature sounding in his language, Kaluli use no Baby-Talk lexicon, for they said (when I asked about it) that to do so would result in a child sounding babyish which was clearly undesirable and counter-productive. The entire process of a child's development, of which language acquisition plays a very important role, is thought of as a hardening process and culminates in the child's use of "hard words" (Feld & Schieffelin, 1982).

The cultural dispreference for saying what another might be thinking or feeling has important consequences for the organization of dyadic exchanges between caregiver and child. For one, it affects the ways in which meaning is negotiated during an exchange. For the Kaluli the responsibility for clear expression is with the speaker, and child speakers are not exempt from this. Rather than offering possible interpretations or guessing what a child is saying or meaning, caregivers make extensive use of clarification requests such as "huh?" and "what?" in an attempt to elicit clearer expression from the child. Children are held to what they say and mothers will remind them that they in fact have asked for food or an object if when given it they don't act appropriately. Since responsibility of expression does lie with the speaker, children are also instructed with εlεma to request clarification (using similar forms) from others when they do not understand what someone is saying to them.

Another important consequence of not saying what another thinks is the absence of adult expansions of child utterances. Kaluli caregivers will put words into the mouths of their children but these words originate from the caregiver. However, caregivers do not elaborate or expand utterances initiated by the child. Nor do they jointly build propositions across utterances and speakers except in the context of sequences with εlεma in which they are constructing the talk for the child.

All of these patterns of early language use, such as the lack of expansions or verbally attributing an internal state to an individual are consistent with important cultural conventions of adult language usage. The Kaluli very carefully avoid gossip and often indicate the source of information they report. They make extensive use of direct quoted speech in a language that does not allow indirect quotation. They utilize a range of evidential markers in their speech to indicate the source of speakers' information, for example, whether something was said, seen, heard, or gathered from other kinds of evidence. These patterns are also found in early child speech and as such, affect the organization and acquisition of conversational exchanges in this small scale egalitarian society.

A DISCUSSION OF THE DEVELOPMENTAL STORIES

We propose that infants and caregivers do not interact with one another according to one particular 'biologically designed choreography' (Stern, 1977). There are many choreographies within and across societies. Cultural systems as well as biological ones contribute to their design, frequency, and significance. The biological predispositions constraining and shaping social behavior of infants and caregivers must be broader than thus far conceived in that the use of eye gaze, vocalization, and body alignment are orchestrated differently in the social groups we have observed. As noted earlier, for example, Kaluli mothers do not engage in sustained gazing at, or elicit and maintain direct eye contact with their infants as such behavior is dispreferred, associated with witchcraft.

Another argument in support of a broader notion of biological predisposition to be social concerns the variation observed in the participant structure of social interactions. The literature on white middle class child development has been oriented, quite legitimately, towards the two-party relationship between infant and caregiver, typically infant and mother. The legitimacy of this focus rests on the fact that this relationship is primary for infants within this social group. Further, most communicative interactions are dyadic in the adult community. While the mother is an important figure in the Kaluli developmental story, the interactions in which infants are participants are typically triadic or multi-party.

As noted, Kaluli mothers will organize triadic interactions in which infants and young children will be oriented away from their mothers towards a third party.

This is not to say that Kaluli caregivers and children do not engage in dyadic exchanges. Rather, the point is that *such exchanges are not accorded the same significance as in white middle class society*. In white middle class households that have been studied the process of becoming social takes place predominantly through dyadic interactions, and social competence itself is measured in terms of the young child's capacity to participate in such interactions. In Kaluli and Samoan households, the process of becoming social takes place through participation in dyadic, triadic, and multi-party social interactions, with the latter two more common than the dyad.

From an early age, Kaluli children must learn how to participate in interactions involving a number of individuals. To do this minimally requires attending to more than one individual's words and actions, and knowing the norms for when and how to enter interactions, taking into account the social identities of at least three participants. Further, the sequencing of turns in triadic and multi-party interactions has a far wider range of possibilities vis-a-vis dyadic exchanges and thus requires considerable knowledge and skill. While dyadic exchanges can only be ABABA . . . , triadic or multi-party exchanges can be sequenced in a variety of ways, subject to social constraints such as speech act content and status of speaker. For Kaluli children, triadic and multi-party interactions constitute their earliest social experiences and reflect the ways in which members of these societies routinely communicate with one another.

CONCLUSIONS

This chapter contains a number of points but only one message—that the process of acquiring language and the process of acquiring socio-cultural knowledge are intimately linked. In pursuing this generalization, we have formulated the following proposals:

The specific features of caregiver speech behavior that have been described as simplified register are neither universal nor necessary for language to be acquired. White middle class children, Kaluli children, and Samoan children all become speakers of their languages within the normal range of development and yet their caregivers use language quite differently in their presence.

The use of simplified registers by caregivers in certain societies may be part of a more general orientation in which situations are adapted to young children's perceived needs. In other societies, the orientation may be the reverse, that is, children at a very early age are expected to adapt to requirements of situations. In such societies, caregivers direct children to notice and respond to other's actions. They tend not to simplify their speech and frequently model appropriate utterances for the child to repeat to a third party in a situation.

The cross-cultural research raises many questions. The extent to which we are developing culturally specific theories of development needs to be considered. To add to what we know we must examine the prelinguistic and linguistic behaviors of the child of the ways in which they are continually and selectively affected by the values and beliefs held by those members of society who interact with the child.

It is tempting to speculate about what differences these differences make. Cross-cultural research invites that. However, at this point in our research it seems premature to focus on answers. Instead we prefer to use these data to generate questions—questions that will suggest new ways to think about language acquisition and socialization. And when we identify a new phenomenon or find old favorites missing—such as the absence of expansions and lack of extensive modified speech to the child in diverse societies—we must identify the socio-cultural factors that organize and make sense of communicative behaviors. Because these behaviors are grounded in culturally specific norms we can expect that the reasons for the "same" phenomenon will be different.

While biological factors play a role in language acquisition, socio-cultural factors have a hand in this process as well. It is not a trivial fact that small children develop in the context of organized societies. Cultural conditions for communication organize even the earliest interactions between infants and others. Through participation as audience, addressee, and/or 'speaker," the infant develops a range of skills, intuitions, and knowledge enabling him or her to communicate in culturally preferred ways. The development of these competencies is an integral part of becoming a competent speaker.

REFERENCES

Andersen, E. S., & Johnson, C. E. Modifications in the speech of an eight-year-old to younger children. *Stanford occasional papers in linguistics,* 1973, *3,* 149–160.

Bloom, L. & Lahey, M. *Language development and language disorders.* New York: John Wiley and Sons, 1978.

Blount, B. Aspects of socialization among the Luo of Kenya. *Language in society,* 1972, 235–248.

Bowerman, M. Language development. In H. C. Triandis & A. Heron (Eds.), *Handbook of cross-cultural psychology,* volume 4. *Developmental psychology.* Boston, Massachusetts: Allyn and Bacon, 1981.

Brown, R. *A first language: The early stages.* Cambridge, Mass.: Harvard University Press, 1973.

Brown, R., & Bellugi, U. Three processes in the child's acquisition of syntax. *Harvard Educational Review,* 1964, *34,* 133–151.

Bruner, J. S. The role of dialogue in language acquisition. In A. Sinclair, R. J. Jarvella, & W. J. M. Levelt (Eds.), *The child's conception of language.* New York: Springer-Verlag, 1978.

Cazden, C. Environmental assistance to the child's acquisition of grammar. Unpublished Ph.D. dissertation, Harvard University, 1965.

Dentan, R. K. Notes on childhood in a nonviolent context: The Semai case. In A. Montagu (Ed.), *Learning non-aggression: The experience of nonliterate societies.* Oxford: Oxford University Press, 1978.

Feld, S. & Schieffelin, B. B. Hard talk: A functional basis for Kaluli discourse. In D. Tannen (ed.) *Analyzing discourse: Talk and text.* Washington, D.C.: Georgetown University Press, 1982.

Fischer, J. Linguistic socialization: Japan and the United States. In R. Hill & R. Konig (Eds.), *Families in east and west.* The Hague: Mouton, 1970.

Geertz, C. *The interpretation of cultures.* New York: Basic Books, 1973.

Goffman, E. *Behavior in public places.* New York: Free Press, 1963.

Goffman, E. *Interaction ritual: Essays on face to face behavior.* Garden City, New York: Anchor Books, 1967.

Greenfield, P. M, & Smith, J. H. *The structure of communication in early language development.* New York: Academic Press, 1976.

Hamilton, A. Nature and nurture: Aboriginal childrearing in north-central Arnhem land. Institute of Aboriginal Studies, Canberra: Australia, 1981.

Harkness, S. Cultural variation in mother's language. In W. von Raffler-Engel (Ed.) *Child language, 1975, Word 27,* 495–8.

Harkness, S., & Super, C. Why African children are so hard to test. In L. L. Adler (Ed.), *Issues in cross cultural research. Annals of the New York Academy of Sciences, 1977, 285,* 326–331.

Heath, S. B. *Ways with words: Language, life and work.* London: Cambridge University Press, in press.

Irvine, J. Strategies of status manipulation in the Wolof greeting. In R. Bauman, & J. Sherzer (Eds.), *Explorations in the ethnography of speaking.* New York: Cambridge University Press, 1974.

Miller, P. *Amy, Wendy and Beth: Learning language in South Baltimore.* Austin, Tex.: University of Texas Press, 1982.

Montagu, A. 1937. *Coming into being among the Australian Aborigines; a study of the procreative beliefs of the native tribes of Australia.* London: G. Routledge and Sons Ltd.

Much, N., & Shweder R. Speaking of rules: The analysis of culture in breach. In W. Damon (Ed.), *New directions for child development: Moral development,* No. 2. San Francisco, Ca.: Jossey-Bass, 1979.

Ninio, A. The naive theory of the infant and other maternal attitudes in two subgroups in Israel. *Child Development 1979, 50,* 976–980.

Ochs, E. Talking to children in Western Samoa. *Language in society.* 1982, *11,* 77–104.

Ochs, E., Schieffelin, B. B., & Platt, M. Propositions across utterances and speakers. In E. Ochs & B. B. Schieffelin (Eds.), *Developmental pragmatics.* New York: Academic Press, 1979.

Philips, S. in press. *The invisible culture.* New York: Longman, Inc.

Sachs, J., & Devin, J. Young children's use of age-appropriate speech styles. *Journal of child language 1976, 3,* 81–98.

Schieffelin, B. B. Getting it together: An ethnographic approach to the study of the development of communicative competence. In E. Ochs & B. B. Schieffelin (Eds.), *Developmental pragmatics.* New York: Academic Press, 1979.

Schieffelin, B. B. A developmental study of pragmatic appropriateness in word order and case marking in Kaluli. In W. Deutsch (Ed.) *The child's construction of language.* London: Academic Press, 1981.

Schieffelin, B. B. *How Kaluli children learn what to say, what to do and how to feel.* New York: Cambridge University Press, in press.

Schieffelin, B. B., & Eisenberg, A. Cultural variation in children's conversations. In R. L. Schiefelbusch, & J. Pickar (Eds.), *Communicative competence: Acquisition and intervention.* Baltimore, Md.: University Park Press, in press.

Schieffelin, E. L. *The sorrow of the lonely and the burning of the dancers.* New York: St. Martins Press, 1976.

Scollon, R., & Scollon, S. The literate two-year old: The fictionalization of self. Abstracting themes: A Chipewyan two-year-old. In R. O. Freedle (Ed.), *Narrative, literacy and face in interethnic communication, Vol. VII in Advances in discourse processes.* Norwood, N.J.: Ablex, 1981.

Shatz, M., & Gelman, R. The development of communication skills: Modifications in the speech of young children as a function of listener. *Monographs of the society for research in child development.* 1973, No. 152, 38, No. 5.

Snow, C., de Blauw, A., & van Roosmalen, G. Talking and and playing with babies: The role of ideologies of childrearing. In M. Bullowa (Ed.), *Before speech: The beginnings of interpersonal communication.* Cambridge: Cambridge University Press, 1979.

Stern, D. *The first relationship: Infant and mother.* Cambridge: Harvard University Press, 1977.

Stross, B. Verbal processes in Tzeltal speech socialization. *Anthropological linguistics* 1972, *14*, 1.

von Sturmer, D. E. Rights in nurturing, unpublished M.A. thesis, Australian National University, Canberra, 1980.

Ward, M. *Them children: A study in language learning.* New York: Holt, Rinehart and Winston, 1971.

Wills, D. *Culture's cradle: Social structural and interactional aspects of Senegalese socialization.* unpublished Ph.D. dissertation, University of Texas, Austin, 1977.

DISCUSSION

8

Empirical Versus Logical Issues in the Transition from Prelinguistic to Linguistic Communication

Susan Sugarman
Princeton University

It is undeniable that children develop intellectually and socially before they talk and that those around them respond to what they do and have ideas about why they do it. What we make of these phenomena is another matter. This discussion will center on two problems with the way in which these observations have been conceptualized. One is the tendency of set up false oppositions, that is, oppositions between alternatives that are either inconceivable or that are orthogonal to one another. The other is the tendency to treat as empirical problems issues that are logical or interpretive. Related to this is a tendency to count as fact interpretations based on circumstantial evidence. One response to these problems might be to formulate more "testable" hypotheses than has been done and gather more data. I will argue otherwise. We need to sort out and reclaim the larger issues and exploit more fully the circumstantial evidence we have.

Thus, the discussion will critically examine the larger questions that have been asked of the relation between preverbal experience and language development. The two preceding papers will serve as a vehicle for the discussion, but the points made are in no way restricted to them.

Four issues will provide the context for the discussion. The first two are very broad and set the stage for the next two, more specific, concerns, which I will consider in some detail. The first issue is the question of whether there is continuity or discontinuity between prelinguistic and linguistic communication. I will argue that this is a false opposition and that to the extent it does bear on valid concerns, it is a theoretical issue masquerading as an empirical one. The second issue is that of whether we are innately constrained to develop language or whether language acquisition is conditioned by prelinguistic developments and/ or environmental practices. I will argue that these alternatives are orthogonal.

The third issue has to do specifically with the causal role of preverbal communication in language development. This, again, is a theoretical issue that has been treated as a matter of empirical fact. The fourth issue concerns the causal implications for language development of environmental practices and cross-cultural differences in them. This, too, is an interpretive issue that has passed as a factual one.

FROM PRELINGUISTIC TO LINGUISTIC
COMMUNICATION: CONTINUITY OR
DISCONTINUITY?

As this volume testifies, it is now agreed that infants communicate before they talk and that this is an ability that evolves over the first year of life (see also selections in Bullowa (1979) and Lock (1978), as well as Bates (1976, 1979), Bruner (1975), Dore (1974), Ryan (1974), and Sugarman (1978, in press)). The question that has arisen is whether preverbal communication has anything to do with language.

The question is unviable as stated. We must take as a first assumption the existence of both continuity and discontinuity in the transition from preverbal communication to language. That we normally grant this assumption is evident in the way we usually describe the relevant developments: Children move from communicating by nonverbal means to communicating by predominantly verbal means. They are communicating in both cases (continuity) but are using different means to do so (discontinuity).

A more workable phrasing of the question would be: What is the locus of the continuities and discontinuities between preverbal communication and language, and with reference to what unit of analysis? For example, if we are considering language as a means of communication we come up with one answer. If we are considering it as a complex rule system for symbolic representation we come up with another. In the first instance language has more in common with preverbal communication, and in the second instance, less.

Differently put, rather than phrasing the question in terms of just any relation between preverbal communication and language, we must specify the dimension(s) along which the comparison is to be made; presumably language will represent the end state on this dimension. We might ask: To what extent do children's preverbal interactions involve communication in the sense that linguistic communication is communication? That is, what do their most clearly communicative acts look like, and how do those acts compare with communication by language (which is presumably better still)? To address this question we need a concept of what fully adapted communication is so that we can decide which of a given child's behaviors approximate it most closely. Some idealization of this sort is implicit in Harding's (this volume) emphasis on behaviors, or combinations of behaviors, that make the infant's signaling look intentional. This emphasis on the intention to convey, as opposed to the intention to do (to achieve some other goal), has figured prominently in other accounts, and there is converging evidence that children distinguish these intentions by the end of the first year—before they communicate by talking (Bates, 1976; Sugarman, 1978).

With this evidence we can assert that preverbal communication has at least one component of linguistic communication that it did not necessarily have to have (intentional signaling), and one can proceed to examine in what way linguistic communication still exceeds preverbal communication on that same dimension.

In summary, we must begin by assuming the existence of both continuity and discontinuity in comparing preverbal communication and language. Then we must select a dimension of comparison, and then we can organize our observations on that dimension (or dimensions, as the case may be). The critical step is the selection of the dimension, and it is a theoretical step. The relation of preverbal communication (or any other events of the first year of life) to language is an empirical issue only within this context.

LANGUAGE: INNATELY PROGRAMMED OR DEVELOPMENTALLY CONDITIONED?

Discussions of language development often reduce to the alternative either that we are innately disposed to acquire language *or* that language builds on the acquisitions or experiences of the prelinguistic period. This is a false opposition, because both possibilities could exist.

Chomsky's (1968) statement that "We must postulate an innate structure that is rich enough to account for (the) disparity between experience and (linguistic) knowledge [p. 69]" does not mean that the events of the prelanguage period are irrelevant to the onset of language. That we are somehow constrained to develop the language that we do does not say *how* we do it. Chomsky (1968), acknowledged this. The general point about the inadequacy of nativist claims for a theory of developmental mechanism was forcefully made by Lehrman (1970), who argued that nature selects for outcomes in a species and not, after a certain point, for the developmental pathways to that outcome. These considerations clearly leave open the possibility that prelinguistic developments condition the acquisition of language. To the extent that they do, however, this does not refute the claim that language is innately constrained to develop in one direction and not another.

There is the further issue of how much of language is accounted for by prelinguistic developments, as opposed to innate constraints. This question has no clear answer at present. It is extremely unlikely, on the one hand, that prelinguistic developments could ever account for the details of linguistic structure (Slobin, 1981). On the other hand, language and sensorimotor intelligence should show global parallels simply because they are each developing systems of knowledge (Sinclair, 1971). Some preverbal experiences and acquisitions may nonetheless be critical to *some aspects* of language development. For example, it may be that unless children have learned something about communication prior to speaking they would have little motivation to look for a language to learn (though even here autistic children, whose understanding of communication is aberrant, do develop a kind of language). Such claims are virtually untestable but they do seem more inherently meaningful than claims that link prelinguistic developments to syntax.

In brief, we may be innately disposed to develop linguistic structure but may be helped along the way by developments, including preverbal communication, that are nonlinguistic, or at least not specifically linguistic. Rather than making blanket claims about whether language is innate or conditioned by other developments, we need to think about which aspects of language are likely to be the direct outgrowth of other developments and which are more likely to be emergent.

THE RELATION OF PREVERBAL COMMUNICATION TO LANGUAGE: ANTECEDENT, PRECURSOR, OR PREREQUISITE?

We have concluded that there is probably a nontrivial relation between preverbal communication and language. In this section we consider further what that relation might be.

The problem is this. Preverbal communication comes before language, but so does eating with a spoon. Are there more compelling reasons for believing that preverbal communication plays a role in language acquisition than that eating with a spoon plays a role?

To facilitate this discussion I will distinguish three types of relations between earlier and later behavior. My use of terms converges with some, but not all, uses in the literature. *Antecedent* will denote a behavior that reliably precedes another behavior in development. *Precursor* will denote a behavior that precedes another behavior and shares some feature(s) with it: For instance, the behaviors are structurally similar or share the same function. *Prerequisite* will denote a behavior that precedes another behavior and is causally necessary to its emergence. Precursors and prerequisites must be antecedents, by this analysis, but an antecedent need not be either a precursor or a prerequisite. A precursor may be a prerequisite but it need not be, and a prerequisite may be a precursor but need not be. To clarify these points: Both preverbal communication and eating with a spoon are antecedents to language, since they both precede it. Preverbal communication, but not eating with a spoon, is a precursor as well, since it shares a function with language. But either preverbal communication or eating with a spoon (or both) could be a prerequisite to language, or neither could be.

The only one of these three relations that is empirically demonstrable is the antecedent relation: Either A reliably precedes B or it does not. The issue of whether A and B share similar features, and therefore exist in a precursory relationship, is a matter of judgment. Note, for example the controversy over whether meaningful parallels exist between sensorimotor action patterns and linguistic structure (Piatelli–Palmarini, 1980). Prerequisite relations are virtually untestable. We will deal below with prerequisite relations, because these are what is at issue when one speaks of prelinguistic acquisitions as "setting the stage" for language, as Harding has done.

To say that skill A is prerequisite to skill B means not only that B follows A in development, but that it builds in some way from A. Harding's data (this volume) show temporal succession: She documents the infant's increasing ability to act with intention and shows that this happens before language begins. We might even make the case that the kind of intentional signaling she describes (eye contact plus vocalization, or eye contact plus gesture) shares at least some functional properties with the intentional signaling that is entailed in using a linguistic code and thus constitutes a precursor to language. There is no evidence here, however, of a prerequisite relation, that is, evidence that in order to talk children must engage in a phase of intentional signaling prior to speech. This possibility is certainly plausible, but it has not been demonstrated.

The same problem exists with other data. I will review three of my own studies which examined the relation between preverbal and verbal communication across different settings and then show that even this cross-context evidence does not conclusively demonstrate that children *must* engage in preverbal communication before they can talk, though this experience may be very helpful (the data are reported in full in Sugarman (in press)). The studies focused on the children's development prior to speech of a coordination of goal-oriented behavior involving external objects (referred to below as object-oriented behavior) and social signaling (person-oriented behavior), for example, combining bids for some desired object with direct solicitation of adult aid (through eye contact, vocalization, pointing, and so on). Several authors have cited this coordination as evidence of an intention to communicate (see Sugarman, in press). There is evidence from a number of studies that children achieve this coordination in their nonlinguistic behavior between 10 and 12 months of age, that is, just before they begin to speak their first words (Bates, 1976, 1979; Harding & Golinkoff, 1979; Sugarman, 1978). Prior to that time they engage either in goal-oriented behavior, for example, trying to grasp a desired toy that is near the mother but out of reach, or in socially focused behavior, for example, exchanging vocalizations with the mother and looking at her. They do not do both at once, even though by 9 months individual object-focused and person-focused exchanges may be quite complex (Sugarman, 1978).

Children progress through this sequence under a variety of conditions. In the three studies I have reported these conditions include normal children in a normal home environment, (otherwise normal) children in an institution, and an autistic child at home. The institutionalized children passed through the sequence of preverbal developments, including person-object coordination, at the same rate as the normal home-reared children. However, they began to speak considerably later than the normal children, that is, several months after achieving person-object coordination nonverbally. The autistic child progressed through the preverbal sequence at a much slower rate than the normal home-reared or institutionalized children; he began to engage in coordinated person-object interactions at around his third birthday. Limited data suggest that he began to speak shortly afterwards, and hence at the same point in the developmental sequence as the normal home-reared child and (relatively) earlier than the institutionalized child.

This pattern of results suggests that the development of preverbal intentional (coordinated person-object) communication may be necessary, but not sufficient, to the emergence of language. The development of the autistic child, in particular, suggests the presence of a strong relationship of this type, since the child's preverbal and verbal communication were both delayed and then appeared in rapid succession. This could mean that language simply cannot emerge unless the child has some sense of what communication is, some need to engage in it, and some practice at doing so.

Unfortunately, there are a variety of other potential explanations for the mutual delay and close sequencing of preverbal intentional communication and first words. The autistic child's (non-communication) cognition was not formally tested. The possibility therefore exists that the delay in communication and language was simply part of a broader cognitive deficit, as others have suggested occurs in autism (Fay & Schuler, 1980; Snyder, 1975). However, this child's object-focused routines were fairly complex at the beginning of the observation period (18 months). Social contact was extremely rare and was simple and fleeting when it did occur. It was this that developed substantially over the year-and-a-half of observation, and it was only after this development that the child began to integrate social and object pursuits in one exchange. Perhaps the child's cognition of the physical world (or at least those aspects of it that are not socially mediated) was fairly well developed, and his deficit had more to do with extending an available cognitive capacity to a domain, which, for independent reasons, was difficult for him to assimilate. Again, however, we can draw no firm conclusions since no formal observations were made of cognitive development, and the case record is insufficiently detailed to permit an adequate retrospective analysis.

Even if the autistic child's language delay was mediated by a specific communicative (as opposed to general cognitive) deficit, this would not necessarily imply that fully developed person-object coordination (intentional communication manifested nonverbally) is necessary to language emergence in normal

development. Autism is a syndrome that pervasively affects sociability and communication. It may be that the only way an afflicted child becomes oriented
toward language is through the development of an interest and competence in
communication as such. In a related vein, Urwin (1978) emphasizes the importance to the development of language in blind children of both a build-up of rich
caretaker-child exchanges (as occurred in play sessions with the autistic child;
see the full report) and the development of an explicit, studied coordination of
social and object schemes. She bases her position on the particular cognitive and
social problems presented by blindness. The implication is that different routes
may be taken into language, depending on the problems, or absence of problems,
involved.

Thus, the development of fully coordinated (intentional) preverbal communication may not be necessary to the emergence of language. The two may be
linked, but in a weaker way. They may be the normal manifestations of two links
in a higher-order chain that consists of general cognitive and general social
development. If these broader developments are proceeding normally (and if
there is adequate social and linguistic input from the environment), then children
will exhibit intentional communication by around 1 year, and language shortly
thereafter. But the emergence of language may not *depend* on the previous
development of any particular behavioral manifestation of intentional communication.

Importantly, the absence of a necessary link between preverbally manifested
intentional communication and language onset has no direct implications for the
possible facilitating effects of the former on the development of the latter. Even
if fully coordinated preverbal communication were to turn out to be an optional,
rather than a requisite, stepping stone to language in normal development, facilitation of it might prompt attention to language in cases of disorder. This is the
implication of Urwin's (1978) work, as well as of the study of the autistic child.
There is additional evidence that the facilitation of an earlier ''non-necessary''
behavior may accelerate the appearance of a later, related behavior. Bower
(1974) reports instances in which very young infants were trained to exercise
behaviors that do not normally appear spontaneously; as an apparent result,
plausibly related skills that do normally develop spontaneously appeared earlier
than usual. For instance, some toddlers walked early if they had been trained to
exercise the neonatal walking reflex in the first month or so of life. Given the
rarity of this experience in normal development, the exercise of neonatal walking
can hardly be said to be necessary to later walking (i.e., it may be a precursor but
not a prerequisite). The exercise of certain early behaviors may therefore facilitate the appearance of later skills, but this does not mean that the same link
operates in normal development.

In summary, we can document preverbal developments in interpersonal exchanges that make children's intention to communicate increasingly clear. These
developments seem to occur in both normal and (at least one type of) atypical

development and occur whether children are growing up at home or in an institution. It seems that in all these contexts children engage in exchanges that may properly be called communicative before they begin to speak. Therefore, a behavior pattern that looks like a precursor of verbal communication appears before language. We do not have conclusive evidence that this development is a necessary condition for language, however invariantly it may precede it. It is certainly a more likely stepping stone, if an optional one, than are other acquisitions of the first year such as crawling, walking, or eating with a spoon.

The major purpose of this analysis of developmental interrelationships was to stress once again the limits of empirical inquiry, and, correspondingly, the need for very careful *a priori* consideration of which skills are necessarily entailed in later ones and which skills *may* figure in later ones. If we want to look for precursors or prerequisites to later behaviors, we must decide which aspect of the later behavior we are interested in accounting for and which aspect of the earlier experience is likely to do the accounting. That is, we must try to specify the level of abstraction at which developmental causation is likely to exist. For instance, there is a good chance that if a child is going to learn to *communicate* through language, then the child must learn what *communication* is and probably does this before talking—otherwise, why talk? What causal links there are between preverbal and verbal communication are more likely to exist at this general level (of the communicative function itself) than at the level of specific behavior patterns that instantiate this general knowledge. The exercise of specific patterns may be used, however, to facilitate communication by language, but that is a separate issue. In any event, the data alone will never be sufficient to specify the level at which causal continuity exists between earlier and later communication. All the more reason to think through the alternatives and to bring the data to bear on them in as compelling a way as possible.

THE IMPACT OF ENVIRONMENTAL PRACTICES ON LANGUAGE: FACT OR CULTURAL FICTION?

Thus far we have been considering the child's own previous development as possible prelinguistic preparation for language. Prelinguistic experience also includes the environment's treatment of the child. How does this input contribute to language acquisition?

The problems that arise in attempting to make sense of the relevant observations parallel those that arise in attempting to interpret the relation between (the child's) preverbal and verbal communication. We begin with observations like the following. Caregivers (in the Western middle class) respond reliably to their children's preverbal behaviors and interpret them as communicative, that is, as having a meaning and as involving an intention to express that meaning to someone else (see descriptions by both Harding, this volume; and Schieffelin, this volume). It turns out, however, that not all cultures treat their preverbal children as communicative partners. Schieffelin reports, for example, that Kaluli caregivers do not interpret their infants' behavior (including babbling) as meaningful, that they hardly ever address their speech to them, and that to the extent they do do so, they do not leave room for the children to respond. In short, Kaluli caregivers are far less directive of communicative interaction during the preverbal period than are Western middle class caregivers. This pattern reverses during the early language period. Kaluli caregivers seem to give their children more direct instruction in talking than do Western middle class caregivers (see Schieffelin & Eisenberg, in press). To supplement these observations, both Harding and Schieffelin have provided data on the way in which caregivers rationalize their behavior. Harding's Western caregivers see themselves as teaching meaning, and the infant as (intentionally) expressing it. Schieffelin's Kaluli caregivers see themselves as nurturing infants who are helpless and "have no understanding," but they then see themselves as explicitly teaching the children how to talk once certain critical signs of language appear.

One might conclude from these observations, as Harding (this volume) does, that (Western) caregivers "are 'teaching' the infant that a mutual means of communication exists" and that "the development of language as an efficient communicative code may have as its base this early teaching." Or, one might conclude, as Schieffelin implies, that different cultural practices and beliefs differentially affect what children learn about language.

As with the observation that gestural communication precedes language, the observation that given cultures adopt certain postures with respect to language learning does not imply that these postures cause, or are necessary to, the child's development of language. Further, whether right or wrong, such a claim does not specify what aspect of the child's communicative/language development is affected by these cultural practices. This difficulty parallels the problem with the claim that preverbal communication contributes to language acquisition: What aspect of the earlier experience is contributory, and what aspect of later behavior does it affect?

Consider the claim that different environments do different things while children are learning to talk or while they are developing in other ways before they talk. How different is different? Whether or not the "choreography" (Schieffelin's term, after Stern (1977)) of caregiver–infant interactions varies across cultures depends on one's level of analysis. For instance, on the one hand, Kaluli mothers rarely address utterances to their infants, and the utterances they do address are not prompted by the infant's signals; Western middle class caregivers differ on both counts. On the other hand, Kaluli mothers are physically responsive to their infants, for example, they offer them the breast when they cry. Further, Kaluli adults engage in rich and varied verbal exchanges with each other, and as the infant develops these exchanges focus increasingly on the infant's activity.

One reasonable interpretation of these findings is that *verbal* interpretation and *verbal* responsiveness to the preverbal infant are not decisive for the subsequent development of communication by language, in any culture. Perhaps what is operative is more general responsiveness, along with the general availability of linguistic input.

There is some evidence to support this more basic relationship. In a study of individual differences among American mother–infant dyads, Bell and Ainsworth (1972) found that mothers' consistent and contingent response to crying was associated with the infants' development of a differentiated repertoire of noncrying communicative behaviors (they did not look at language per se). Consider also patterns of language development in institutionalized children. Caregiver responsiveness to infants' signals, as well as overall linguistic input, are greatly reduced in institutions, because of the rotating staff, the high infant–caregiver ratio, and the consistently enforced schedule of feeding, napping, and other activities (Tizard & Tizard, 1971, 1974). Consistent with the proposed link between language development and general environmental responsiveness, language is often delayed in these settings (though children seem to catch up by 3 years of age (Tizard, Cooperman, Joseph, & Tizard, 1972)); broad structural changes in preverbal communication and other prelinguistic behavior seem unaffected (Sugarman, in press). Though the evidence is not definitive (many factors vary along with general responsiveness and overall availability of linguistic input (see Sugarman, 1978)), it is quite plausible that those cultural practices that affect language development are far more global than we often make them out to be.

If there is a problem with the way we construe the environmental factors that affect language acquisition, there are even more severe problems with discussions of the impact of those factors on what children learn. There seems to be almost a tendency to buy into a culture's interpretation of that impact; to assume, along with the Western mothers, that they are teaching their children to communicate, and to assume with the Kaluli mothers that they are not teaching their preverbal infants to communicate and *are* teaching their nascently verbal toddlers how to talk. The consequences of different cultural practices for learning to communicate (by whatever means) must be established on independent grounds—either that, or we should not be making claims about causal influences (see Geertz, 1973). One way to at least approach these claims, if we want to entertain them, would be to compare the course of language (or other communicative) development in the two cultures. In what ways do Kaluli and English acquisition differ? Are there major structural differences in the pattern of acquisition, or just differences in some of the minor forms and in when they get learned? It could turn out, for example, that the Kaluli mothers' efforts to directly "teach" language to their children have about as much impact on overall linguistic structure as American mothers' efforts to teach their children polite forms, which is to say not very much impact at all.

As Schieffelin points out, however, those cultural practices that are oriented around children's development of language and communication do socialize the child into a particular culture, that is, into a particular way of organizing knowledge and experience. Again, what it is these practices socialize is an open question. As we found in our consideration of the socializing agent, it may be that what is socialized is more global than is often suggested. Perhaps these practices engender a general attitude toward social interaction and toward the way in which language may be used in that interaction. But they do not, in and of themselves, explain what language is or how it is learned.

These "language socialization" practices might serve another kind of function altogether. They may fulfill some purpose for the adults who are raising children, and not just for the children themselves. Why, for example, do Western middle class mothers see every preverbal twist and turn as meaningful, while Kaluli mothers do not? What are the needs of the already-enculturated members of the group that are served by culturally received ideas about how language gets learned?

Finally, whatever differences there may be in the cultural practices related to language development, and however these differences affect what is learned, we must still explain the fact that children in all cultures learn language and that the languages they learn are in many fundamental ways the same. The variations that exist in "language socialization" cannot explain what is universal across languages and language learning—just as the universals of human cognition, development, and biological make-up cannot explain how languages differ.

To summarize, adult caregivers engage in behaviors and have beliefs that are related to children's development of communication and language. These behaviors and beliefs vary across cultures and across different settings within the same culture. They doubtlessly have some impact on the way children are socialized into a culture and on how they communicate, by language or other means. It is not presently clear precisely what the locus of these differences is, and it is not clear what aspects of language development those differences affect. Despite these differences—whatever they eventually turn out to be—human languages are in many significant ways the same and pass through similar phases of acquisition. A theory of how children learn to talk is going to have to account for both the similarities and the differences.

CONCLUSION

It might seem by now that we cannot ask any interesting questions about the relation between preverbal communication and language, or at the very least, that we have little hope in answering them. So many of the claims are unprovable (or unfalsifiable), or the field is sufficiently far from having the necessary data that the claims might as well be unprovable.

Questions about the role of prelinguistic experience in language acquisition are inherently important, however, for both theory and intervention. This is particularly true of preverbal communication, which more than other preverbal developments, seems *prima facie* related to at least one central aspect of language.

The message is simply that we need to be more discerning about the questions our data do and do not address so that we can know where to turn to address the questions we really want to ask. One of the major problems with recent thinking in the area is that the problem space is inadequately dimensionalized, and hence many of the questions as currently formulated miss their mark. All the questions this discussion has considered—continuity vs. discontinuity in development, the role of innate factors vs. acquired experience in language development, causal relations between earlier and later developments, causal relations between environmental practices and the way children communicate—make sense only with respect to a particular dimension of comparison. That dimension needs to be made explicit. Though it is already implicit in much that has been done, more theoretical work may be necessary to keep it from unwittingly shifting.

Once we have sorted out the questions that are inherent in our larger theoretical concerns and that seem answerable in principle, we will still probably find that we cannot definitively answer those questions. We will have to put up with more circumstantial evidence in exploring developmental relationships than perhaps our ideals of "science" say we should. But this is not bad. We need, rather, to know how to exploit the wealth of circumstantial evidence that is currently or potentially available to us, as does a good judge, who once in a while reaches a true verdict.

ACKNOWLEDGMENTS

I thank Ellice Forman, Sam Glucksberg, Ellen Junn, Joan Stiles-Davis, Addison Stone, and James V. Wertsch for comments on this paper.

REFERENCES

Bates, E. *Language and context: The acquisition of pragmatics*. New York: Academic Press, 1976.

Bates, E. *The emergence of symbols: Cognition and communication in infancy*. New York: Academic Press, 1979.

Bell, S., & Ainsworth, M. D. S. Infant crying and maternal responsiveness. *Child Development*, 1972, *43*, 1171–1190.

Bower, T. G. R. *Development in infancy*. San Francisco, Ca.: W. F. Freeman, 1974.

Bruner, J. S. From communication to langue: A psychological perspective. *Cognition*, 1975, *2*, 255–287.

Bullowa, M. (Ed.), *Before speech: The beginning of interpersonal communication*. New York: Cambridge University Press, 1979.

Chomsky, N. *Language and mind*. New York: Harcourt, Brace, and World, 1968.

Dore, J. A pragmatic description of early language development. *Journal of Psycholinguistic Research*, 1974, *4*, 343–350.

Fay, W. H., & Schuler, A. L. *Emerging language in autistic children*. Baltimore, Md.: University Park Press, 1980.

Geertz, C. *The interpretation of cultures*. New York: Basic Books, 1973.

Lehrman, D. S. Semantic and conceptual issues in the nature-nurture problem. In L. R. Aronson, E. Tobach, D. S. Lehrman, & J. S. Rosenblatt (Eds.), *Development and evolution of behavior: Essays in memory of T. C. Schneirla*. San Francisco, Ca.: W. H. Freeman, 1970.

Lock, A. (Ed.), *Action, gesture, and symbol: The emergence of language*. London: Academic Press, 1978.

Piattelli–Palmarini, M. (Ed.), *Language and learning: The debate between Jean Piaget and Noam Chomsky*. Cambridge, Mass.: Harvard University Press, 1980.

Ryan, J. Early language development. In M. P. M. Richards (Ed.), *The integration of a child into a social world*. Cambridge, England: Cambridge University Press, 1974.

Schieffelin, B., & Eisenberg, A. Cultural variation in dialogue. In R. L. Schiefelbusch, & J. Pickar (Eds.), *Communicative competence: Acquisition and intervention*. Baltimore, Md.: University Park Press, in press.

Sinclair, H. Sensorimotor action patterns as a condition for the acquisition of syntax. In R. Huxley, & E. Ingram (Eds.), *Language acquisition: Models and methods*. New York: Academic Press, 1971.

Slobin, D. I. Universal and particular in the acquisition of language. In L. R. Gleitman, & E. Wanner (Eds.), *Language acquisition: The state of the art*. New York: Cambridge University Press, 1981.

Snyder, L. S. Pragmatics in language-deficient children: Prelinguistic and early verbal performatives and presuppositions. Unpublished doctoral dissertation. University of Colorado, Boulder, 1975.

Stern, D. *The first relationship: Infant and mother*. Cambridge, Harvard University Press, 1977.

Sugarman, S. Some organizational aspects of preverbal communication. In I. Markova (Ed.), *The social context of language*. New York: Wiley & Sons, 1978.

Sugarman, S. The development of preverbal communication: Its contribution and limits in promoting the development of language. In R. L. Schiefelbusch, & J. Pickar (Eds.), *Communicative competence: Acquisition and intervention*. Baltimore, Md.: University Park Press, in press.

Tizard, B., Cooperman, O., Joseph, A., & Tizard, J. Environmental effects on language development: A study of young children in long-stay residential nurseries. *Child Development*, 1972, *43*, 337–358.

Tizard, J., & Tizard, B. The social development of two-year-old children in residential nurseries. In H. R. Schaffer (Ed.), *The origins of human social relations*. New York: Academic Press, 1971.

Tizard, J., & Tizard, B. The institution as an environment for development. In M. P. M. Richards (Ed.), *The integration of a child into a social world*. Cambridge, England: Cambridge University Press, 1974.

Urwin, C. The development of communication between blind infants and their parents: Some ways into language. Unpublished D. Phil. thesis, Cambridge University, 1978.

9

The Redundancy Between Adult Speech and Nonverbal Interaction: A Contribution to Acquisition?

David J. Messer
Child and Family Research Branch, NICHHD, NIH

The past 2 decades have provided us with a wealth of information about the verbal input that children receive and about the verbal output that they produce. These studies have led to a better understanding of the characteristics of these dimensions but only have provided a limited insight into the nature of the transition from nonverbal communication to speech. By its very nature data concerned exclusively with speech is unlikely to reveal the way in which children normally begin to produce and comprehend single words. The utilization of some form of nonverbal information would appear necessary to enable infants to make the connection between words and objects or events. Of the various relationships between speech and nonverbal information which can be examined, the relationship that exists between referential words and nonverbal information is perhaps one of the more interesting. This is primarily because the child's early vocabulary is largely composed of these words, and that the speech of adults to children contains a high proportion of referential words (Benedict, 1979; Nelson, 1973; Phillips, 1973). There is also a particular fascination with this relationship because it involves the issue of understanding the meaning of words, a topic long debated by philosophers.

Current perspectives about the development of speech give emphasis to the *productive* aspects of both nonverbal and verbal communication. At present, a widely held view is that the child's behavior develops into communicative acts because of the responsiveness of the adult (see Lock, 1978). The ideas of Vygotsky (1962, 1966) and Ryan (1974) are central to this perspective. It is stressed that the child produces actions and that adults will respond to such actions as if they were a request for a response. Such reactions are supposed to transform the child's behavior so that eventually there develops an intention to communicate and a desire to influence adult's behavior.

Although these ideas have made an important contribution, there are some difficulties in applying them to the process whereby children begin to use words. A prediction from this perspective would be that the infants' early vocalizations are transformed by the adults' responses into words. It is true that adults' responses are likely to play some role in the acquisition process, but previous discussions of Skinner's ideas concerning the adult shaping the childs' vocalizations into words have usually rejected this as an important mechanism. These difficulties appear to have led to the postulation of the use of pointing and labeling by the mother, and the subsequent imitation of speech by the infant as being part of the bridge between nonverbal and verbal communication (Carter, 1978; Clark, 1978). Associated with this has been the belief that when infants first produce a word they have little or no understanding of it (Clark, 1978; Lock, 1980). The understanding is supposed to develop later during social word games. I would like to argue that this bridge between nonverbal and verbal communication is also built by children utilizing a variety of forms of nonverbal information which enables them to comprehend the relationship between words and their referents. Studies are reviewed to show that infants are supplied with information which could help them understand the relationship between words and objects, and an examination is made of studies that investigate whether children make use of such information. It is suggested that the nonverbal information available to children is not restricted simply to the activities of one member of the pair or to gestural indication like pointing, but it is argued that the adult and child are involved in a communication system in which the very structure of social interaction provides information which can assist the understanding of speech.

NONVERBAL INFORMATION ABOUT THE REFERENT OF SPEECH TO YOUNG CHILDREN

Before considering various studies of nonverbal behavior, the definition of this term should briefly be considered, especially the status of some of the properties of speech. Harper, Wiens, and Matarazzo (1978) have pointed out that there is a range of definitions that have been applied to nonverbal behavior. They themselves considered paralinguistic phenomena (including the stress and timing of speech) as one form of nonverbal behavior. In this chapter their scheme is adopted.

In reviewing the nonverbal behavior which could assist the comprehension of adult's speech, a specific concern is with the way the adult's utterances and the child's attention come to be centered on one referent out of a number of possibilities. The classic answer to this question has often been that the adult points to an object and labels it. My aim is to show that we have progressed far beyond this simple model. Studies which have investigated this topic have shown that establishing joint attention is a much more complex process. Various studies will be reviewed, with some recent studies that I conducted being presented in greater detail. There are five topics that are considered: (1) the indication of a referent by an adult; (2) the importance of behavior rituals; (3) social interaction and the identification of a referent; (4) the identification of referential words; and (5) the evidence that children utilize nonverbal information.

The Indication of a Referent by an Adult

Two areas of indication are considered: pointing and head turning.

Pointing.   By the second year of life infants are able to follow adults' points. The infants' ability depends on the spatial configuration of referent, infant, and indicator. Lempers (1976) found that most 9- and 10-month-old infants could follow points to proximal objects but not to distal ones, although both abilities were present in 12- and 14-month-olds. Murphy and Messer (1977) have reported that the orientation between infant, pointing arm, and referent influenced the infants' performance. A 9-month-group was only able to follow points directed to objects in front of them. In this position the mother's pointing arm was usually aligned with the child's body. As a result attention to the pointing hand could easily be transferred to the target object. In contrast, a 14-month-group could follow points across as well as in front of their body. The former requires a more sophisticated response from the infant as he or she has to locate the target object by utilizing the angle between the mother's arm and body. Simply gazing at the pointing arm and transferring the gaze to the nearest object would result in incorrect identification of the target object.

Murphy and Messer (1977) used a semi-natural situation. Consequently, it was possible to study pointing in relation to other maternal activities. This revealed that pointing was augmented by additional attention obtaining devices, such as finger waving and finger clicking. Another finding was that mothers invariably looked at the object when they started to point at it and looked back at the infant just over 1 second afterwards. The findings of Scaife and Bruner (1975) and of Lempers (1976) suggest that this head turning at the target object could provide the infant with an additional clue to the identity of the referent. More importantly, such a pattern of gaze may help infants interpret the pointing gesture as an indication of interest to which they are expected to respond.

Murphy (1978) has examined pointing in relation to maternal speech during book reading. She reports that with infants from 9 months to 20 months maternal points were accompanied by maternal naming significantly more often than would be expected by chance, the same was true for infant points from 14 to 24 months. The highest level of naming occurred at 14 months, an age at which infants would be expected to be especially receptive to this form of input. Interestingly, the frequency of naming with maternal points declined from 14 months, whereas from this age questions increased in frequency. Murphy suggests that this is a change of maternal conversation style from providing the label to asking for the label.

Headturning.   A more subtle form of indication is turning one's head towards an object. A number of tests have been conducted on the infant's ability to utilize this behavior (Lempers, 1976; Lempers, Flavell, & Flavell, 1977; Masangkay, McCluskey, McIntyre, Sims-Knight, Vaughn, & Flavell, 1974; Scaife & Bruner, 1975; and Strayer, Bigelow & Ames, 1973). These findings suggest that before the age of 12 months, infants are able to follow another's head and eye movements (Lempers, 1976; Scaife & Bruner, 1975), but it is not at all certain how frequently and in what circumstances infants make use of the ability. The reason for uncertainty is that the studies used an experimental paradigm to test the child's abilities. Typically, the infant and experimenter were seated face to face and established eye contact before the experimenter looked away. Furthermore, the head turns were often of 90°, an extreme postural change. Thus, there is uncertainty about whether the results can be generalized to normal social interaction. If the behavior occurs in normal settings, then infants undoubtedly possess an important ability which will help them understand the adults' interest.

These studies of pointing and headturning suggest that young infants do have the ability to follow the adult interest in a referent. They are also able to indicate objects themselves. Consequently, adult speech can be integrated with objects that the adult indicates or objects that the child indicates. Both processes provide information which should help the child understand the adult's speech about objects.

Behavior Rituals

The work of Bruner and his associates has considered a variety of themes related to language acquisition and it would be impossible to do justice to all the ideas in this chapter. Instead, two aspects of this corpus of writings are focused upon. First, (Ninio & Bruner, 1978) there is the opinion that "participation in a ritualized dialogue, rather than imitation is the major mechanism through which labeling is achieved [p. 1]." Ninio and Bruner have described social interaction during book reading for one child between 8- and 18-months-old. They found that most maternal utterances occurred in a specific order: a demand for attention, "look"; a question about the referent, "what's that"; and a label, "its an X." Moreover, in the majority of occasions the child responded in a way that allowed the mother to interpret his action as a reply to her utterance. Thus, a ritualized sequence of behavior was built up between mother and child. If dialogues such as these are to help language acquisition then it would appear that the child's understanding of labeling utterances and questioning utterances are of fundamental importance to the process; the child has to recognize when a label is asked for and when a label is supplied. Ninio and Bruner (1978) appear to suggest that such understanding is possible because the child has become familiar with the "reciprocal dialogue rules that govern exchanges . . . into which labeling is inserted [p. 14]."

The second and related issue is that ritualized formats are important because they allow the adult and child to achieve a shared sense of topics to which they attend (Bruner, 1975a, 1975b). Clark (1978) has made a similar argument that interaction allows the child-world and mother-world to meet, so that mother and child have a shared view of what is important and relevant. We can see the result of this in the adults' use of language that is appropriate to the child's level of functioning. As Brown (1958) has pointed out, adults do not hand an apple to a young child and say "eat some fruit;" they say "eat this apple." Similarly, Murphy (1978) and Ninio (1980) have reported that mothers tend to refer to whole objects rather than its parts, attributes, or actions. Consequently, although philosophers have problems with deciding what attribute is being referred to, mothers and children may be able to side-step such difficulties. This is particularly important, because if mothers and infants share a common idea of the specificity of referencing expressions, then the mother's speech is likely to be appropriate to the child's conceptual schemata of the world, thereby facilitating the match of speech and concepts. Such processes can be seen as part of the socialization of the child into his or her culture. Patterns of social interaction may define the most relevant concepts for the child, speech is meshed with these patterns.

Social Interaction and the Identification of a Referent

Infants are able to follow specific forms of indication such as pointing to locate a referent, they also may be able to utilize information from less obvious movements such as head turning. In addition, in certain circumstances adults appear to use ritualized sequences of dialogue which could help infants understand and respond to conversation about objects. I would like to suggest that normal adult–child interaction also contains a number of sources of information about the identity of the referent which are part of the basic flow of social behavior. In this section attention will be paid to such behavior which could assist the young child's comprehension of speech about objects.

During adult-child interaction adults often integrate their behavior with that of the infant. A study of behavior that highlights this phenomenon has been reported by Collis and Schaffer (1975) who carried out a careful analysis of the timing of looking behavior. Children between 5- and 10-months-old were seated on their mothers' lap. Collis and Schaffer report that mothers usually followed the direction of the infants' gaze. In a later study of the same situation, Collis (1977) reports that between one fifth and one third of all mutual looks at the same object were accompanied by labeling. Thus, it would appear that the child does not always have to locate the referent of maternal speech, rather, the mother frequently synchronizes her speech with objects in which her child is interested.

Interaction between mother and child often involves an object that one of the pair is manipulating. A study that I conducted attempted to examine various forms of nonverbal behavior (either mother's or the child's) that would help the infant understand referential speech when toys were being manipulated. In particular, the interest was in looking at features of nonverbal behavior which provided a continuous source of information about the identity of the referent of maternal speech. Such behavior was investigated because it might provide children with assistance in understanding a large proportion of the speech that they hear.

During the observations the children were seated on their mother's lap in front of a table on which they could play with seven small toys. There was a preliminary warm up session and then a 5 minute play session between the mother and child was recorded on videotape. The sessions took place in a child welfare clinic, and the mothers were asked to play with their children as they might do at home. Three age groups were studied: 11 months, 14 months, and 24 months, with 14 mother–infant pairs in each age group. Over three thousand maternal utterances were transcribed. Each utterance was coded so as to preserve information about the identity of the toy that was being referred to (if any) and the most specific form of reference used about a toy. The different forms of reference were coded as the use of a noun or name, a pronoun or an "indirect reference." The latter code was used when a toy was not referred to by a name or pronoun but the utterance did concern a particular object, for example, "see the wheels." If the mother or child held the toy being referred to then its identity and the behavior being performed on it were recorded. The precise details of the methods used in these studies have been presented elsewhere (Messer, 1978; 1980; 1981).

Manipulation of objects by the infant often provides the adult with an important source of information about the focus of the child's interest. Moreover, manipulation of objects by an adult easily captures the child's interest. Thus, manipulation appears to be an important dimension of nonverbal behavior which allows the mother and the child to attend to the same object. The first analysis was undertaken to investigate whether information provided by the manipulation of objects could help the child locate the referent of maternal speech. It appeared unlikely that maternal speech would be related exclusively to either the child's activities or to the mother's activities. For this reason maternal speech was examined in relation to the behavior of both members of the dyad. The data were entered into 7 × 7 contingency tables according to which of the seven toys was being referred to, and which of the seven toys was being manipulated at the time of the utterance. These tables were constructed separately for each age group, each reference type, and occasions when the mother or the child were manipulating the toy (a total of 18 tables). A very close relationship existed between the object the mother referred to and the object being held at the time of the utterance. There was a remarkable consistency in the findings across the 18 tables. Between 73% and 93% of the references occurred when the toy referred to was being held at the time (see Table 9.1). Moreover, the frequency of this behavior exceeded the figure that would be expected from a chance agreement between the identity of the toy referred to and of the toy being manipulated ($p < 0.001$, from kappa coefficients, Fleiss, 1973).

In addition, there appears to have been a temporal relationship between speech and manipulation. Maternal utterances were classified according to whether a reference was made by the mother to an object that: (1) was being simultaneously manipulated; (2) had just been picked up or put down; or (3) was held at another time. Most references were to toys held at the same time. There were fewer references to toys that had been held on preceding or subsequent occasions, and the least number of references to toys held at other times ($p < 0.001$ for each age group and each form of reference, Page's L Test, Bradley, 1968). This suggests that as time from contact with the toy increased, the probability that it would be referred to decreased. The basic integration of speech and contact with a toy appeared to occur throughout the observation session and was not limited to the activities of either mother or child. In other words, the relationship between speech and contact appeared to be part of the basic structure of social interaction.

The relationship between speech and manipulation was also examined to

TABLE 9.1
Agreement between Toy Referred to
and the Identity of the Toy Being Held at the Time

	Agreement When Infant Manipulated a Toy			Agreement When Mother Manipulated a Toy			Total[a] Agreement
	Names	Pronouns	Indirect Reference	Names	Pronouns	Indirect Reference	
11 Months							
% Agreement	85	83	82	90	96	96	72
Total Utterances	170	152	114	147	110	106	1074
14 Months							
% Agreement	79	79	78	88	92	91	71
Total Utterances	221	136	79	177	125	88	1095
24 Months							
% Agreement	73	81	84	86	91	93	76
Total Utterances	279	217	144	148	124	97	1253

[a]The % of total agreement is lower than the average agreement for mother and infant because a number of utterances occurred when no toy was being held, or when both individuals held a toy.

determine whether maternal reference was associated with certain behaviors. In general, references were more likely to be associated with activities of the child which involved their sustained interest or associated with maternal behaviors which would capture the child's interest. The child's act of picking up a toy was strongly associated with labeling. There was also one maternal behavior that was especially closely associated with labeling; this consisted of picking a toy up, bringing it to a position close to the child's midline and holding it stationary. One might almost say this was a behavior which was ritualized in such a way that it conveyed the message that the mother was engaging in a labeling activity.

It could be objected that the behavior observed in this situation does not give an accurate impression of the speech that children usually hear. In particular, there is the possibility that mothers normally use a much lower proportion of references to current activities. In this sample of speech about three quarters of all utterances were to objects being held at the time (72% at 11 months, 71% at 14 months, and 76% at 24 months). This is comparable to figures provided about mother–infant interaction at home. Howe (1975) reported that on 50% of the occasions when mothers named objects, they themselves were holding the relevant object within 2½ seconds of the start of an utterance. Snow found between 64% and 80% of maternal utterances were to objects being held at the time (Snow, 1977), and Cross (1977), observed that with slightly older children (19–32 months), 63% of maternal utterances were to objects and events in the immediate context. These findings suggest there is similarity between observations reported here and the mothers' behavior in their home.

A second analysis was undertaken to examine whether not only *simultaneous* relationships could help comprehension of adult speech but whether *sequential* relationships could also play a part in this process. Speech should be easier to understand if it was organized so that any utterance was likely to refer to the same referent as the previous utterance. The presence of strings of utterances which all referred to the same object should make it less difficult for children to identify the referent in the sequence. For this reason the importance of *verbal episodes* in maternal speech was determined. These are defined as a string of successive utterances which all refer to the same toy, irrespective of the form of reference used. For example, ''That's a dolly. She's pretty. That's a horse. What does he say?'' would constitute two verbal episodes. The referent of the first verbal episode being a doll and of the second verbal episode being a horse.

Transition tables were constructed to provide data about the sequencing in maternal speech. Pairs of successsive utterances were entered into the tables according to the identity of the toy referred to in the first utterance and the identity of the toy referred to in the second utterance. This produced a 7 × 7 table where the cells on the diagonal contained the frequency of transitions in which the same toy was referred to in two successive utterances. Over half of the pairs of utterances contained a reference to the same toy (between 59% and 64% depending on the age group). Furthermore, for every mother–infant pair this result was unlikely to occur by chance ($p < 0.001$, kappa coefficient, Fleiss, 1973).

A problem facing the preverbal child is identifying these verbal episodes. Were there any forms of nonverbal behavior which marked out this organization? Three types of behavior were found to occur at the beginning of verbal episodes: manipulating a new object, a pause, and naming. The majority of verbal episodes began after a new toy had been manipulated (70% at 11 months, 71.0% at 14 months, and 45.9% at 24 months), suggesting that changes in the verbal and nonverbal referent tended to coincide. This should have the effect of making it easier for the child to identify when a new verbal episode would begin.

There are findings which suggest that slightly older children are able to process and respond to pause intervals in conversation (Garvey & Berninger, 1981). An issue of interest is whether the start of verbal episodes were highlighted by longer pauses. Six subjects were randomly chosen from each age group for this analysis. The recordings of these subjects were replayed at half the normal speed using a Lexicon Varispeech cassette recorder. This corrected the pitch of the speech and thereby made the slower speech more intelligible. The intervals between maternal utterances were timed by a stopwatch to the nearest 1/10 sec. This analysis revealed that the interval between utterances which referred to a different toy was half as long as the interval between utterances which referred to the same toy (mean interval in seconds between utterances; 11 months, same toys 3.3, different toys 7.2; 14 months, same toys 3.1, different toys 9.4; 24 months, same toys 2.0, different toys 5.4; this difference was consistent in all subjects selected for analysis; $p < 0.032$ in each age group, two-tailed sign test). The organization of pauses in this way could aid the detection of the start of verbal episodes.

It is also worth noting that names were especially likely to be included in the first utterance of a verbal episode, even though this cannot be considered a nonverbal behavior (percentage of verbal episodes beginning with a name, 52.3% at 11 months, 56.9% at 14 months, and 53.6% at 24 months). As a result, both nonverbal behavior and naming would make it easier to detect the start of verbal episodes. The integration of these behaviors could reduce the child's difficulty in understanding utterances, because the redundancy present in the use of verbal reference would be easier to detect. For example, the child would not have to identify the referent of each utterance separately, and would be able to develop procedures to establish when an object previously referred to is still being talked about.

The Identification of Referential Words in Adult Speech

Most of the studies of adults' speech to children have been concerned with demonstrating that the syntactic input children hear is not as complex as once was thought. Examination of these studies also indicates that these modifications could help children process speech more easily and help them to identify referential words from the stream of speech that they hear.

In general, adult to child speech contains shorter utterances than adult to adult speech, whether the length is measured in morphemes (Drach, 1969), or number of words (Longhurst & Stepanich, 1975; Phillips, 1973). The use of short utterances means that the chance of a child selecting the relevant words is improved, and if complete utterances are stored there will be fewer demands on memory. A lower type-token ratio has been found in speech directed at infants (Broen, 1972; Drach, 1969; Fraser & Roberts, 1975; Phillips, 1973; Remick, 1976). The use of a limited vocabulary means that a smaller number of words are used more often; in consequence, infants have more opportunities to hear the same word. Furthermore, adult to child speech contains a high proportion of function words and concrete nouns (Broen, 1972; Phillips, 1973), so both these aspects of speech to infants might help the identification of verbal labels.

Beside the modifications of the style of speech, there are also modifications of the lexicon. A review of the modifications which are common to six different languages has been made by Ferguson (1964). The modified lexicon mainly contains words which refer to objects and events which are of potential interest to infants. Ferguson suggests the modified lexicon may help the initial acquisition of words by making the sounds more suitable for the infant's productive capacity. It is also possible that because the form of the word is similar to the infant's vocalization he or she is more likely to attend and reproduce these words.

There is another feature of the baby talk lexicon which may help referential (and other relevant) words to be identified. Ferguson describes the use of diminutive affixes as being common characteristics of baby talk (Spanish: ito and ita; Comanche: ci; Gilyak: k and q; Marathi: k; ula and ulba; Arabic: o; English, y). Inflexional affixes are uncommon, so the diminutive is an invariant feature of the lexical items. Relevant words could be identified from the affix and it is possible to imagine circumstances in which children after acquiring a few of these terms will look for and attend to similar phonological forms. For example, in English, -y is often used as an affix with nouns which refer to objects or persons with which the infant interacts. Interestingly, verbs are modified less frequently, and in cases when a word can be used as a noun or a verb (drink, walk), modifications usually occur when the word is used in its nominative form. Thus, there is a possibility that in English speech affixes may help infants identify names.

Another feature of English baby talk is that there often exists a variety of labels for the same referent. A dog might be called by a personal name, 'doggy,'' 'woof woof,' 'bow-wow' or any similar onomatopoeia. Casual observations suggest that adults will use a variety of these forms with their prelinguistic children. An interesting question concerns whether they restrict their usage after the child has started to produce one particular form of a label.

A surprisingly large proportion of adult to child utterances are single words. Broen (1972) found 15% of material utterances were single words, with "here," there,'' and ''see'' being the most common ones. Verbs accounted for 32% of this sample, nouns 21%, and adjectives 13%. This type of input, while being of potential help to identify names, at first sight appears to be of limited assistance because according to Broen's results, single names only constitute 3% of all utterances. However, one should bear in mind that in some circumstances, the use of single words may have a significance out of all proportion to their frequency.

Even with these characteristics present in adult speech to children it still may be difficult to identify referential words from the stream of adult speech. The use of emphasis may provide an additional aid to this process. In many communication systems signals of low amplitude are often treated as background noise and special attention is paid to high amplitude signals. It would also appear that stressed words are more likely to be recalled (Frith, 1969; Hermelin & O'Conner, 1970). In addition, Brown (1965) has argued that the words emphasized in adult speech to children tend to be included in the child's telegraphic utterances. Consequently, words of higher acoustic amplitude may be more attention worthy, more likely to be recalled, and more likely to be included in the child's later utterances. For these reasons I conducted a study to examine whether acoustic amplitude was used in a way which could help children identify the name of an object. Fifteen mothers and their 14-month-old children were observed for 8 minutes playing with five toys in a situation similar to that already described. The acoustic amplitude of the mother's speech was displayed visually on the video recordings. An array of lights were arranged so that the stronger the acoustic signal the greater number of lights were illuminated. As a result, it was possible to establish identity of the loudest word in each utterance.

Transcriptions were made of the 739 maternal utterances which contained the name of one of the toys. Those utterances which were accompanied by an extraneous noise were discarded from the sample. Utterances in which several words were equally the loudest were also discarded; often this was because the mothers spoke softly so that none of the lights were illuminated or so loudly that the maximum level was obtained for several words. The remaining sample of speech consisted of 487 utterances which contained 1850 words. Names were highly likely to be emphasized. In 47% of the utterances a toy name was the loudest word. Moreover, of the different classes of words (e.g., names of toys, qualifiers, interrogatives, verbs, etc.), names were the class most likely to be emphasized.

Ervin–Tripp (1973) has suggested that the last word in an utterance is more likely to be recalled and imitated. Consequently, it is of interest that names were highly likely to be the last word of an utterance (75% of the utterances contained a name in the last position). It is also of interest that names were especially likely to be the loudest word of an utterance after a new object had been picked up by the mother or infant; the use of emphasis would appear to coincide with the introduction of a new topic. Both these features of the patterning of behavior may provide additional assistance to help children identify the names of objects from the stream of adult speech.

Thus, adult-child interaction appears to be organized so that the adults' speech corresponds with the object to which the pair is attending. In addition, adults' speech may assist children in identifying the semantically important words in an utterance. As a result the children's difficulty in relating labels to current activities should be minimized, and their comprehension and production of speech facilitated.

The Utilization of Nonlinguistic Information

Do young children use nonlinguistic behavior to help them understand referential speech? The fact that children have been involved in social interaction since birth suggests that they will both attend to and make use of nonlinguistic information similar to that which has been described here. There are also a number of experiments which have examined the influence of nonverbal behavior on the comprehension of speech. These suggest that young children rely more on nonverbal than verbal information when attempting to interpret utterances, and that with increasing age this reliance declines. A series of ingenious experiments by Macnamara (1977) presented instructions in both English and French which were accompanied by different forms of nonverbal gestures. The children were monolingual. As a result, the use of two languages allowed Macnamara to examine the effectiveness of nonverbal information while controlling for the influence of linguistic knowledge. He found that nonverbal behavior rather than speech guided the identification of a referent by 12-month-olds. When words and gestures were in conflict the children were more likely to rely on gesture. Even at 17 months nonverbal behavior was more likely to guide behavior than was speech. Sinha and Carabine (1981) examined comprehension strategies and have suggested that young children (less than 3 years) primarily rely on contextual rather than linguistic information when intepreting utterances. Older children of 3–9 years also have been reported to have difficulty following instructions when the verbal and nonverbal information are in conflict; as for example, when the toy a child holds is the object rather than the subject of instructions (Bem, 1970; Huttenlocher, Eisenberg, & Strauss, 1968). Thus, for young children nonverbal information appears to be very influential in mediating the child's interpretation of verbal instructions.

What evidence do we have that the match between speech and current nonverbal activities of the dyad influences the rate of language acquisition? Experimental training sessions have been able to change the child's responsiveness to labels when names are matched to their referents. Nelson and Bonvillian (1973) have reported details about the acquisition of new words after mothers produced labels in the presence of their referents during mother–child interaction. Oviatt (1980) has reported a change in the infant's responsiveness to labels during short training sessions in which a referent held by the infant was labeled by the experimenter and mother. At 12–14 months, after training half the infants when tested responded appropriately to the labels, by 15–17 months most infants when tested were able to respond.

Indirect evidence for the importance of the relationship between adult speech and the child's current activities comes from studies by Cross (Cross, 1977, 1978) and by Wells (Wells, 1979; in press; Wells & Robinson, in press). The studies of Cross and of Wells were primarily concerned with mothers' speech to children who had already started to use words, and in consequence can only be extrapolated to the initial acquisition process. The adult's contingent reply to child utterances was found to occur at a higher frequency with more linguistically advanced children (Cross, 1978) and to be correlated with later linguistic progress (Wells, in press; Wells & Robinson, in press). Cross (1978) has concluded that the important principle underlying these findings is that speech is related to the child's *own behavior*. Wells and Robinson (in press) draw a similar conclusion, that acquisition will be assisted by adult's speech being contingently related to the child's preceding utterance, their *activity,* or *focus of attention*. Thus, it may be that the existence of a relationship between speech and current activities will assist the progress of language acquisition; what needs to be established is whether this is true of all speech and all activities or whether it is certain forms of speech and certain actions that are more critical to the process.

The evidence about the importance of the relationship between maternal speech and the current manipulation of objects is of a more tentative nature. Cross (1977) found a negative correlation between the child's linguistic skill and the amount of references to objects that were being held, about to be held, or had just been held. This suggests that mothers of older, more linguistically sophisticated children (19 months to 32 months) talked about objects not involved in current activities. In the study by Wells (Wells, in press; Wells & Robinson, in press), data extraction was from audio not video recordings so that accurate interpretation of the nonverbal context would be difficult. Even so, Wells (1979) has reported provocative differences in a comparison between more and less linguistically advanced children, the advanced group received more references about shared activities. He also has reported a positive correlation between the number of references to shared activities and later progress in language acqusition.

DISCUSSION

Observations of adult–child behavior suggest that social interaction provides the infant with a variety of forms of nonverbal information which can be used to understand the relationship between words and their referents. Adults are able to draw a young child's attention to an object they wish to talk about, also adults can identify the object in which a child is interested and integrate their speech with this interest. Writing about behavior in this way suggests that there is an unidirectional influence; the adult is either leading or being lead by the child. The actual relationship appears to be a more subtle and reciprocal one, with both partners negotiating about the identity of the topic of interest. Mothers integrate their speech with the behavior of the dyad; they carefully time their utterances so that they are related to an object either they themselves or the child is manipulating. As a result, the activity of manipulation provides a very useful clue about the identity of the verbal referent, even though this activity is not a conventional gesture. Adult utterances to young children tend also to be organized into verbal episodes. The beginning of verbal episodes are marked out by nonverbal behavior; by the mother or child manipulating new objects, or by pauses in the mother's speech. This should make it less difficult to identify the referent of any one utterance in a sequence and should make it easier to identify when a new referent is introduced. Again, with this data, a simple lead or follow model of interaction breaks down. The use of verbal episodes by the mother cannot be said to direct the child's attention to an object, nor can the nonverbal marking of verbal episodes be said to depend exclusively on the mother's behavior. What we see is that the structure of dyadic interaction provides information in a form which could help the child understand referential speech. Another feature which could assist the comprehension of adult speech to young children is the emphasis of referential words. This may resemble the adult leading the child's attention to an object, but even here the use of emphasis is integrated with other features of interaction. Emphasis is more likely to be used after a new object has been manipulated by the mother or the child.

It is possible that identifying a referent from nonverbal behavior and the comprehension of speech are two different processes; it is also possible that the relationship between speech and nonverbal behavior has little bearing on the development of the ability to produce words. However, almost all theories of word acquisition postulate that children acquire the ability to comprehend and produce words by relating sounds they hear to objects and events that they identify in their environment. This is not to say that the acquisition of words is simply the result of forming an association between labels and referents. The child is also having to learn about semantic relations and pragmatic uses of different expressions. In other words, the child is likely to be integrating these contingencies with existing knowledge of communication and with knowledge about the status of objects and events. A difference between theories is in the importance that is attributed to formation of these relationships.

Perspectives which suggest that the acquisition occurs by the development of the infants' ability to produce communication tend to discount the possibility that social interaction has a number of features which can help the infant comprehend speech. Instead it is proposed that adults transform the actions of children into intentional communication. Associated with this has been the idea that the infant's imitation of words when the mother points to an object is part of the bridge between nonverbal and verbal communication. Lock (1980) and Clark (1978) have suggested that imitation first takes place without infants understanding a word's significance and that this capacity develops from later use in conversation and social word games. Certainly, the ideas from the Vygotsky tradition maintain that children will produce communication before understanding its significance. If this argument is correct, subtle forms of information are unlikely to be of assistance to the acquisition of words, because children can utilize more obvious information such as that provided by the adult's reaction to the use of words or by becoming involved in the "original word game." However, there are reasons to doubt that the acquisition of words is this simple (see, Bloom, 1974). A number of studies indicate that comprehension precedes production at the one word stage and during later development (Bates, Bretherton, Shyder, Shore, & Volterra, 1980; Benedict, 1979; Cocking & McHale, 1981; Goldin-Meadow, Seligman, & Gelman, 1976; Huttenlocher, 1974; Ingram, 1974; Nelson, 1973; Oviatt, 1980). Thus, imitation may occur when children already have some understanding of the word's significance; such understanding may arise because of the exposure to contingent relations between words and objects or events that occur during social interaction.

Experimental studies provide findings which suggest that nonverbal behavior may be relevant to the acquision process. Comparisons indicate that young children often use nonverbal rather than verbal information to help them interpret verbal messages, sometimes to the extent of placing greater reliance on nonverbal behavior (Macnamara, 1977). Experimental investigations also provide evidence that the match between words and referents is sufficient to enable infants to comprehend and later produce words (Nelson & Bonvillian, 1973; Oviatt, 1980).

Thus, the bridge between nonverbal and verbal communication may be built by the infants' comprehension of speech from nonverbal information prior to and during the stage at which they begin to produce words. However, potentially sterile arguments concerning whether comprehension precedes production should be avoided. Studies by Nelson (1973) and by Dore (1975) raise the possibility that different children may acquire language in different ways. The important question is not the order of emergence (in a comprehension-production controversy) but the circumstances in which the different processes occur and with which children.

A different issue concerning word use is whether children break the linguistic code because of participation in behavior rituals, or whether interaction at a more general level has a role to play in the process. There is more redundancy in behavioral rituals than in the rest of interaction. This suggests that it will be easier to break the linguistic code in these situations rather than in less structured social interaction. However, because the difference between these two contexts appears to be one of degree, we should not exclude the possibility that normal interaction may make a contribution to acquisition. Moreover, studies of other cultures are beginning to suggest that behavioral rituals are not a universal feature of adult–child interaction (Schieffelin, this volume).

Although there are findings and reasons which suggest that nonverbal behavior assists the acquisition process, we should remember that there remains a gap in the argument. We have limited empirical evidence about the actual importance of different dimensions of nonverbal behavior. Infants who lack exposure to the intense social interaction that is common in Western societies can develop language, even though their culture or the institution in which they are placed may provide only a minimal amount of linguistic and nonverbal information (Dennis, 1973; Kagan & Klein, 1973). At first sight this implies that the system that allows the acquisition of language to take place is so robust that the process can take place in very limited circumstances; differences in input are unlikely to have any long term consequences. The inference may not be correct; we should remember that children's verbal scores on developmental tests during the third year are highly correlated with later scores on intelligence tests (McCall, Eichorn & Hogarty, 1977). Perhaps infants can acquire language with limited information, but it may also be the case that a suitable input will accelerate the acquisition process and provide a basis for continuing advances in cognitive development. Because of these issues there is a pressing need for longitudinal studies. Admittedly, there are problems with longitudinal studies other than logistic ones. The identification of dependent and independent variables is difficult, especially as it is possible that some relationships are facilitative rather than necessary. In addition, a threshold effect could exist with most children having enough exposure to the relevant events to allow language acquisition to take place. Therefore, crosscultural studies which will allow us to look at different patterns of childrearing and studies with deaf or blind children are especially important.

Some of these issues are being addressed in a collaborative study in which Dr. Lorraine McCune–Nicolich, Eileen Holzhauer, and I are participating. Longitudinal observations of social interaction during infancy will be examined in relation to the childrens' later linguistic progress. The variables we are focusing on are: the overall match between maternal speech and nonverbal activities; the tendency of the mothers to comment on their own or their child's activity; and the mothers responsiveness to child communication. Hopefully, this and similar studies will begin to identify the forms of nonverbal behavior which are related to the word acquisition process.

During the last 20 years the scope of research on child language has greatly expanded. Incomplete understanding of the nature of adult's speech to children provoked a blossoming of studies of this topic. In a similar manner, I hope that our incomplete understanding of the relevance of nonverbal behavior to the acquisition process may encourage further research. The use of gesture and imitation have been the most widely quoted process through which children start to acquire words. We are beginning to see that these are just some of the behaviors that could play a part in the acquisition process. It is becoming apparent that parent-child social interaction is organized in ways that provide a variety of different opportunities for children to make the transition from nonverbal communication to language. Despite the difficulties of attempting to integrate techniques from the different traditions in linguistics and the study of nonverbal interaction it is to be hoped that there will be further research on this promising topic.

ACKNOWLEDGMENTS

The research conducted by the author was supported by a S.S.R.C. Grant to Professor H. Rudolph Schaffer, University of Strathclyde, Scotland. This chapter was written while the author was a Visiting Fellow at the Child and Family Research Branch, NICHD, NIH. I would like to thank Glyn Collis and Rudolph Schaffer for their help, advice, and encouragement. I would also like to thank Martha Zaslow and Roberta M. Golinkoff for their helpful comments about this paper.

REFERENCES

Bates, E., Bretherton, I., Snyder, L., Shore, C., & Volterra, V. Vocal and gestural symbols at 13 months. *Merrill-Palmer Quarterly*, 1980, *26*, 407–423.

Bem, S. L. The role of comprehension in children's problem solving. *Developmental Psychology*, 1970, *2*, 351–358.

Benedict, H. Early lexical development: Comprehension and production. *Journal of Child Language*, 1979, *6*, 183–200.

Bloom, L. Talking, understanding, and thinking. In L. L. Lloyd (Ed.), *Language perspectives: Acquisition, retardation, and intervention*. Baltimore, Md: University Park Press, 1974.

Bradley, J. V. *Distribution-free statistical tests*. Englewood Cliffs, N.J.: Prentice-Hall, 1968.

Broen, P. A. The verbal environment of the language learning child. *Monograph of the American Speech and Hearing Association*, 1972, *17*, 1–103.

Brown, R. How shall a thing be called? *Psychological Review*, 1958, *65*, 14–21.

Brown, R. *Social Psychology*. London: Free Press, 1965.

Bruner, J. S. From communication to language—a psychological perspective. *Cognition*, 1975a, *3*, 255–287.

Bruner, J. S. The ontogenesis of speech acts. *Journal of Child Language*, 1975b, *2*, 1–19.

Carter, A. L. From sensorimotor vocalizations to words. In A. Lock (Ed.), *Action, gesture and symbol: The emergence of language*. London: Academic Press, 1978.

Clark, R. A. The transition from action to gesture. In A. Lock (Ed.), *Action, gesture and symbol: The emergence of language*. London: Academic Press, 1978.

Cocking, R. R., & McHale, S. A comparative study of the use of pictures and objects in assessing children's receptive and productive language. *Journal of Child Language*, 1981, *8*, 1–13.

Collis, G. M. Visual co-orientation and maternal speech. In H. R. Schaffer (Ed.), *Studies in mother-infant interaction*. London: Academic Press, 1977.

Collis, G., & Schaffer, H. R. Synchronization of visual attention in mother–infant pairs. *Journal of Child Psychology and Psychiatry*, 1975, *16*, 315–320.

Cross, T. G. Mothers' speech adjustments: The contributions of selected child listener variables. In C. Snow, & C. A. Ferguson (Eds.), *Talking to children*. Cambridge, Mass.: C.U.P., 1977.

Cross, T. G. Mothers' speech and its association with rate of linguistic development in young children. In N. Waterson, & C. Snow (Eds.). *The development of communication*. Chichester State: Wiley, 1978.

Dennis, W. *Children of the Creche*. New York: Appleton-Century-Crofts, 1973.

Dore, J. Holophrases, speech acts, and language universals. In I. Markova (Ed.), *The social context of language*. New York: Wiley, 1975.

Drach, K. The structure of linguistic input to children. *Language behavior research lab. Working paper No. 14*. Berkeley, Ca.: University of California, 1969.

Ervin-Tripp, S. M. Some strategies for the first 2 years. In T. E. Moore (Ed.), *Cognitive development and the acquisition of language*. New York: Academic Press, 1973.

Ferguson, C. A. Baby talk in six languages. *American Anthropologist*, 1964, *66*, 103–113.

Fleiss, J. L. *Statistical methods for rates and proportions*. New York: Wiley, 1973.

Fraser, C., & Roberts, N. Mothers' speech to children at four different ages. *Journal of Psycholinguistic Research*, 1975, *4*, 9–16.

Frith, U. Emphasis and meaning in normal and autistic children. *Language and Speech*, 1969, *12*, 29–38.

Garvey, C., & Berninger, G. Timing and turn taking in children's conversations. *Discourse Processes*, 1981, *4*, 25–57.

Goldin-Meadow, S., Seligman, M., & Gelman, R. Language in the 2-year-old: Receptive and productive stages. *Cognition*, 1976, *4*, 189–202.

Harper, R. G., Wiens, A. N., & Matarazzo, J. D. *Nonverbal communication: The state of the art*. New York: Wiley, 1978.

Hermelin, B., & O'Connor, N. *Psychological experiments with autistic children*. Oxford: Pergamon Press, 1970.

Howe, C. *The nature and origins of social class differences in the propositions expressed by young children*. Unpublished doctoral dissertation, University of Cambridge, Cambridge, England, 1975.

Huttenlocher, J. The origins of language comprehension. In R. Solso (Ed.), *Theories in cognitive psychology*. Hillsdale, N.J.: Lawrence Erlbaum Associates, 1974.

Huttenlocher, J., Eisenberg, K., & Strauss, S. Comprehension: Relation between perceived actor and logical subject. *Journal of Verbal Learning and Verbal Behavior*, 1968, *7*, 527–530.

Ingram, D. The relationship between comprehension and production. In L. Schiefelbusch, & L. L. Lloyd (Eds.), *Language perspectives: Acquisition, retardation, and intervention*, Baltimore, Md.: University Park Press, 1974.

Kagan, J., & Klein, R. E. Cross cultural perspectives on early development. *American Psychologist*, 1973, *28*, 947–61.

Lempers, J. D. *Production of pointing, comprehension of pointing and understanding of looking behavior in young children*. Unpublished doctoral dissertation, University of Minnesota, 1976.

Lempers, J. D., Flavell, E. R., & Flavell, J. H. The development in very young children of tacit knowledge concerning visual perception. *Genetic Psychology Monographs*, 1977, *95*, 3–53.

Lock, A. *Action, gesture, and symbol: The emergence of language*. New York: Academic Press, 1978.

Lock, A. *The guided reinvention of language*. London: Academic Press, 1980.

Longhurst, T. M., & Stephanich, L. Mothers' speech addressed to one-, two-, and three-year-old children. *Child Study Journal*, 1975, *5*, 3–11.

Macnamara, J. From sign to language. In J. Macnamara (Ed.), *Language learning and thought*. New York: Academic Press, 1977.

Masangkay, Z. S., McCluskey, K., McIntyre, C., Sims-Knight, J., Vaughn, B., & Flavell, J. The early development of inferences about the visual percepts of others. *Child Development*, 1974, *45*, 357–366.

McCall, R. B., Eichorn, D. M., & Hogarty, P. S. Transitions in early mental development. *Monographs of the Society for Research in Child Development,* 1977, *42*(3).

Messer, D. J. The integration of mothers' referential speech with joint play. *Child Development,* 1978, *49,* 781–787.

Messer, D. J. The episodic structure of maternal speech to young children. *Journal of Child Language,* 1980, *7,* 29–40.

Messer, D. J. The emphasis of names by mothers. *Journal of Psycholinguistic Research,* 1981, *10,* 69–77.

Murphy, C. M. Pointing in the context of a shared activity. *Child Development,* 1978, *49,* 371–380.

Murphy, C. M., & Messer, D. J. Mothers, infants and pointing: A study of gesture. In H. R. Schaffer (Ed.), *Studies in mother–infant interaction.* London: Academic Press, 1977.

Nelson, K. Structure and strategy in learning to talk. *Monographs of the Society for Research in Child Development,* 1973, *38,* Nos. 1–2, Serial No. 149, 1–135.

Nelson, K. E., & Bonvillian, J. Concepts and words in the 18-month-old: Acquiring concept names under controlled conditions. *Cognition,* 1973, *2,* 435–450.

Ninio, A. Ostensive definition in vocabulary teaching. *Journal of Child Language,* 1980, *7,* 565–573.

Ninio, A., & Bruner, J. The achievement and antecedents of labeling. *Journal of Child Language,* 1978, *5,* 1–15.

Oviatt, S. L. The emerging ability to comprehend language: An experimental approach. *Child Development,* 1980, *51,* 97–106.

Phillips, J. R. Syntax and vocabulary of mothers speech to young children: Age and sex comparisons. *Child Development,* 1973, 44, 182–185.

Remick, H. Maternal speech to children during language acquisition. In W. von Raffler–Engle (Ed.), *Baby talk and infant speech.* Amsterdam: Swets and Zeithinger, 1976.

Ryan, J. Early language development: Towards a communicational analysis. In M. P. M. Richards (Ed.), *The integration of a child into a social world.* Cambridge: Cambridge University Press, 1974.

Scaife, M., & Bruner, J. S. The capacity for joint visual attention in the infant. *Nature,* 1975, *253,* 265–266.

Sinha, C., & Carabine, R. Interactions between lexis and discourse in conservation and comprehension tasks. *Journal of Child Language,* 1981, *8,* 109–129.

Snow, C. E. The development of conversation between mothers and babies. *Journal of Child Language,* 1977, *4,* 1–22.

Strayer, J., Bigelow, A., & Ames, E. W. *I, you, and point of view.* Manuscript, Simon Fraser University, 1973.

Vygotsky, L. S. *Thought and language.* Cambridge, Mass.: MIT Press, 1962.

Vygotsky, L. S. Development of the higher mental functions. In *Psychological Research in the U.S.S.R.* Moscow: Progress Publishers, 1966.

Wells, C. G. The role of adult speech in language development. Paper presented at a conference on ''Social Psychology and Language,'' Bristol, England, 1979.

Wells, C. G. Adjustments in adult–child conversation: Some effects of interaction. In H. Gites, W. P. Robinson, & P. M. Smith (Eds.), *Language: social psychological perspectives.* Oxford: Pergamon, in press.

Wells, C. G., & Robinson, W. P. The role of adult speech in language development. In C. Fraser, & K. Scherer (Eds.), *The social psychology of language.* Cambridge: Cambridge University Press, in press.

10 Feeling, Form, and Intention in the Baby's Transition To Language

John Dore
Baruch College and the Graduate School, The City University of New York

In our concern to explain how children learn language, we have invariably assumed one or another source of development as primary. Either the infant's mind or his environment has dominated inquiry, thus sustaining the infamous nature-nurture controversy. Investigators have presumed either that the child somehow invents (creates, etc.) language and then merely adapts to conventional expressions of it; or that the child discovers (induces, etc.) it from the speech of others and must then somehow make it his own. Though both processes may well be involved, the locus of their interaction and manner of relationship are, at best, unclear. Of course, major variations appear in each theoretical camp: Mind theorists argue about whether language is essentially a genetically given faculty versus a cognitively constructed system (see the Chomsky–Piaget debate in Piattelli-Palmerini, 1980); social theorists conceive the environment in radically different ways, ranging from a reinforcement system (Skinner, 1957) to a cultural map to be progressively internalized (Vygotsky, 1962). And, despite claims by everyone that both organism and milieu must be attended to, a dichotomy of choice of primary source still inheres in theories of development.

George Miller (personal communication) compared the failure of behaviorist explanations to the mystery in nativist ones, concluding that we are caught between "the impossible and the miraculous." Perhaps in response to this theoretical stalemate, and to many years of the dominance of structural models, psycholinguists have begun to turn to functional theories for frameworks to describe language. We have tried to apply to development notions from the philosophy of language (e.g., Austin, 1962; Searle, 1969; Wittgenstein, 1953), from the "ethno" sciences (Gumperz & Hymes, 1972), from British functionalism (Malinowski, 1923) and from literary/psychological/social theorists as diverse as Burke (1950), Mead (1934), and Goffman (1974). Concerning earliest words, for example, Bates (1976), Bruner (1975), Cross (1977), Dore (1975), Halliday (1975), Ochs and Schieffelin (1979), and Snow (1977) have all stressed the social aspects of language acquisition. This chapter emerges out of this tradition, complementing many other chapters in this volume. However, four areas will be stressed which have thus far not been well-developed by interactional approaches: The personal relationship between mother and infant, the affective nature of prelinguistic communication, the centrality of dialogue, and the functional analyses of affective expression.

I propose, as a necessary component of language emergence, the dialogue *between* caregiver and infant, as distinct from locating language *in* the mind or *out* there in speech and social routine. First words will be seen to emerge in the infant as consequences of dialogical functions of affective expressions across members of an intimate dyad. This treatment is, therefore, not a contribution to a theory of mind, language, or society. Rather, it focuses on the transformation of babbling to words by means of the caregiver's inducement of, first, the anxiety leading to the intention to communicate and, second, the conventional forms of expressions. It argues that, apart from any cognitive invention and social discovery, the origin of words occurs in the immediate context of affective conflict, arising as solutions to maintain and negotiate relationship through dialogue. In short, I plan to describe the affective inputs to intentionality and reference.

Briefly and roughly put, the argument proceeds as follows. Prior to his first words the baby (B) experiences a period that is transitional between words and babbling, usually occurring near the end of the first year. He or she comes to this point with at least these abilities: (1) to act on objects deliberately, to achieve physical goals by means of sensorimotor coordinations; (2) to express affect directly, vocally and/or gesturally, either as an accompaniment to his or her actions (often as though talking to objects), or while gazing at the face of the primary adult caregiver (A), but not alternating gaze with object manipulation; and (3) to attend to A's activity and to respond directly to some of A's vocalizations and gestures directed to him or her (B). These prelinguistic accomplishments are well-documented by numerous investigators (e.g., Bruner, 1978; Stern, 1977; Sugarman-Bell, 1978; and Trevarthen & Hubley, 1979).

I offer here a two stage hypothesis about how mother and infant interact during this period, and suggest that such interaction is a necessary condition for language onset. First, when B expresses affect in a marked way, A *matches* it (for original conception, see Stern, 1982) by either "*analoguing*" to the same affect-state, *complementing* it with a different state, or *imitating* the external form of his behavior. These communicative matches intervene in B's affect-state in the sense that they "analog" it with a differing intensity and often in a different behavioral channel, or they contrast B's affect with an opposing state, or reproduce an observable form of his own affect (recall that initially he expresses spontaneously, so only after A's match can he observe a form for his own affect). On the basis of such behavioral descriptions, I hypothesize that A's interventions in B's affect expressions *transform* them into intents to express those affect-states.

A simple example, from early on in this period, will illustrate this hypothesis. When babies in our culture express delight in any way at some unusual sight, mothers typically clap to express joy along with them. *How can* such a match transform an unmediated expression of delight into an intention to express it? First, B initiates the interaction by his expression; A's clapping provides an analog in an observable form of his own affect. Since B has been observing A all along, and may not have identified with it, he can now observe his own feeling in her behavior. When he claps in response to her clap, he is not merely imitating some form out there in another person. At that moment he discovers a gesture for what he is feeling. Since her form matches his feeling, his clapping expresses his own state, not hers; even though his affect had to "loop through" her to become observable. This may be the original moment of "cognizing" a connection between internal state and external sign for it. The behavioral form can then be reproduced when feeling the same affect, thereby allowing both B and A together to "*re*-cognize" and share the same affect state. Perhaps without her analog of his state in another form, he could not become aware of his own state—there would be nothing to observe. This awareness may be the origin of intention—the moment when the motivation for an expression finds an observable form that can be focussed upon and then reproduced.

But this does not explain *why* a B *would* change from expressing to intending. For this we must postulate that the B is motivated to maintain some intimate state of communion with A. He needs to adapt to her ways of doing and expressing in order to achieve, maintain, repair, and later renegotiate their relationship. So, by clapping, for example, he can invoke in her and himself a pleasurable affect state to share, and therefore to ensure solidarity. This is a familiar enough assumption in psychodynamic theories, but it does not go far enough. It is the negative case, with its conflict of affect, that better accounts for the emergence of intention.

Conflict arises when A's communicative match *contravenes* B's affect-state. For example, when the baby we describe tries to mouth an object, his mother prohibits it; this occasions B's affect expression of a "protest" with an abrupt, high-pitched, vowel-like utterance accompanied by arm-flapping in apparent anger; A then reprimands B with an obviously angry, intense "Don't you yell at your mother!"; to which B responds with a still higher pitched, indeed violent, "protest." B here again initiates interaction with the positive affect action of mouthing. A blocks that affect, in a sense knowing his pleasure but contravening it. B of course can not "cognize" her behavior as a form for his affect. However, his protest is provoked by her prohibition, thereby providing a potential link between his affect and her *complement;* that is, his protest is an unmediated expression of negative affect which analogs her negative act of prohibition. Moreover, the hypothesis that *A induces intentions in B* is seen more clearly in the subsequent round of this interaction. After matching intense prohibitions and protests, A shifts her tone to a lower pitch with a repeated "I said 'no' " while pulling the piece away from him again; at this he protests most violently, looking at her. It seems as though at this moment he has become aware, through her contravention, of his own negative affect, and can begin to *intend to express* it for the first time. Thus, what began as a complement of her prohibition of his pleasure, concludes as a double, crossmodal "analoguing" of the same affect: her pulling the piece away matched by his reaching and pulling it back, her intense reprimand matched by his intense protest. Out of such conflicts his marked motivated expressions become transformed into intentions to express.

But, again, *why*? If B's affect is breached by prohibition, rather than attuned to, the conflict threatens communion. Anxiety arises. Being able to express his state intentionally allows B to invite a match of positive affect and to deny negative matches. It allows him *to test the state of their relationship*. The intent to express becomes the first cognitive tool for communicating about their relative states in their dialogue with one another. Because the same affect can be differentiated into two forms and communicated cross-modally, partnership in dialogue emerges. But *the analog of affect is the foundation of dialogue*.

The second part of this two stage hypothesis is that *A induces in B conventional forms* for expressing shared affect-states. Given that B can already intend to express his state, the question arises: How does A intervene in B's expressions to change their form? But we are not concerned with the mere echoing of forms, so much as the shared meaningfulness of expressions for the dyad. Now, some degree of meaningfulness must already inhere in B's intentions to express a shared state, some minimal awareness that a form somehow matches an internal state. Although this requires some cognitive processing, the content of what B is aware of is not yet a cognitive category; it is an affective match. The problem is then not, as in cognitive approaches, to identify the overlap in semantic features of the B's first words and his caregiver's. Rather, it is to identify the procedures they use to effect "meaningful" exchanges (i.e., effective, consequential, motivating, interactions) and to specify the processes by which word meanings emerge from expressions intended and interpreted as shared affect states.

One possibility here, adumbrated by Vygotsky's (1978) dictum that intrapsychic events first occur on an interpsychic level, would be that *their* conversational procedures become *his* psycholinguistic processes: That her ways of staging scenes, indicating objects, searching for words to fit them, contrasting meanings, and so on, in their affectively meaningful and shared interactions become his ways of, say, sorting information into distinctive semantic sets. In this way A would at least highly constrain possible interpretations of their shared affect. The central problem would then become the means whereby affectively meaningful communicative actions *between* A and B are transformed into personal meanings-for-words *in* B. This shifts emphasis away from asking what biological and cognitive categories B brings to the task of language learning toward asking how categories emerge from interpersonally shared affect states and the behavioral forms in which they are expressed. Thus, we assume that word meanings are consequences in B of what AB feel and do. The dialogue they engage in is the interface between his functional intents and her formal requirements for interpretation. Though A cannot give B his needs, motives and intents, she does supply him with the forms necessary to express them.

When B intends to express affect to A, A matches B's expression with a conventional form. This intervenes in B's expressive form, transforming it toward conventional recognizability. A either *analogs* B's expression with a more specific form, or *complements* it with a contrasting one, or *imitates* his form closely without marked affect. *Formal analogs,* even when they are not affective attunements as well, nevertheless serve to replace B's idiosyncratic forms for expressing himself. That is, assuming that they already share affect and that B initially expresses it idiosyncratically, A's imposition of conventional form merely supplies a close substitute for what B is already expressing. A's utterance gives form to B's intent. And this may well be the moment that B first realizes that his form expresses some content, and the moment when he originally cognizes some connection between his own content and his mother's form for expressing it.

When the mother of the 12-month-old girl in our second example below asks "Wanna play with the castle?", the B turns to gaze at her. A then points to the pile of "castle" blocks and says "This!", emphatically stressing both her vocalization and her pointing gesture. B replies with an unintelligible utterance, low in pitch, volume, intensity, and duration, resembling an aspirated stop followed by a back vowel (roughly /hkyɔ/). A responds with a high-pitched, rising "No?" in a pleasant tone of surprise. At this B repeats "No!" with an intense, abrupt tone and emphatic head nod. However, contrary to the expected semantically negative "answer", B proceeds to knock over some of the blocks.

Describing this complex communicative match, it is clear that B intentionally expresses her response to A, behaviorally manifested by her body orientation to A and the blocks, her gazing toward A and her vocalizing to her. A interprets B's unintelligible utterance as negative, but she is either unsure, surprised, or both; so A produces what might have been the B's "answer." But this is no mere imitation. A marks her semantically negative content with positive affect; simultaneously giving B's utterance conventional form and soliciting clarification. Further, for B's part, when she repeats "No!" it is not with A's surprise tone, but with an emphatic one, perhaps analoguing A's emphasis on "This!" earlier. Here we see a conversion from B's initial intent to "answer" vocally but unintelligibly to her accomodation to A's form of answering. Again, like clapping for gleeful affect, here A *trans*-forms B's expression to conventional status!

However, in this case there is no direct affect attunement. Rather, a more complex interplay of affect and form takes place. B apparently takes the form of A's negative content, but omits the pleasant tone of surprise on that form, and assimilates the emphatic marking of A's prior "This!" to her own "No!" Moreover, this reply constitutes a move in a conflict of the agendas they are negotiating for B's behavior: B has been playing with a phone while A is recommending block play. (In fact, A's behavior may be an elaborate distraction from B's playing with the real phone, not unlike in principle from our first mother's prohibitions.) Thus, we have a degree of tension, if not anxiety, in their agenda clash, motivating B's apparent rejection. Finally, however, B's "no" has not quite acquired word status since she does go to the blocks, and during this same time period she does not contrast "yes and no" in a semantically consistent way.

We can ask the same two questions of this word-*like* emergence that we asked of the origin of the intention to express: How can a B do it and why would he? The first has been the concern of most approaches to acquisition; most recently cognitive theories have dominated the market. And, indeed, some degree of cognitive processing must occur if a B is to, say, contrast positive and negative semantic features in the form of "yeses" and "nos." Moreover, the infant must be able to adapt and produce linguistically contrastive sounds. Both cognitive and phonological contrastivity are necessary inputs to language. Here I suggest that the interpersonal matching of affect is also necessary, and the three together may be sufficient to "cause" language.

The salience of motivation in this account leads to the conclusion that the dialogical basis of language occurs when dyadic partners match, analog, complement, imitate, and mismatch each other's affect, but express themselves in different forms. Adaptation to each other's affect and form constitutes the dyad's very identity (from which B derives his identify; see Mead, 1934). In Piagetian terms, A accomodates to B's affect and assimilates it to her forms; B accomodates to A's forms and assimilates them to his affect and cognition. Tension always exists from the disequilibrium of their matches, at all levels. Mismatches of both kind and intensity abound in every dyad. After intentionality emerges the only solution to mutual comprehension in dialogue is a shared system of linguistic symbols.

Again, to be in communion, to be understood, to be effective in conveying intent and content, B must adapt to A's forms. Not only uncertainty and ambiguity, but also anxiety is reduced by being able to express states, needs, desires for objects, and so on by unequivocal symbols; that is, words that disambiguate among items desired at the right moment. Words reconstitute the dyad's intersubjectivity. Trevarthen and Hubley (1979) describe a "secondary intersubjectivity" evident at 9 months of age in the form of interactional synchronies between dyadic partners across several behavioral modalities. Words transform this into a symbolic intersubjectivity that allows for convenient reproducibility of form and interchangeability of speaker. This contributes directly to the emergence of both ego identity and social competence (see Erikson, 1968).

INDEXICALITY, INTENTIONALITY, AND ACCOUNTABILITY

In order to clarify earlier hypotheses, fuller analyses of our two examples will be necessary. But, first, a few related notions must be mentioned which will help with the data analyses. These include the status of the baby's vocalizations at this period, changes in his intentionality, and the social nature of the mother's motivation and behavior at this time. This section will be an attempt to show how the baby's "indexical forms" and intentional expressions change under the influence of the adult's pervasively "accountable" behavior.

Investigators agree, almost unanimously, that between babbling and the first genuinely referential words the child progresses through an intermediate phase of word-like productions. Piaget (1952) called these "symbols" (tied to sensorimotor schemata) as distinct from linguistic "signs" and Halliday (1975) described this period as "proto-language." In Dore (1975) I called them "primitive speech acts,"; Dore, Franklin, Miller, and Ramer (1976) described them as "phonetically consistent forms,"; and here I refer to them as "indexical expressions."

Unlike babbling, "indexicals" have a well delimited shape, bounded by pause and often directed at objects. They include expressions of affect (early in this phase especially forms like squeals of joy and cries of frustration) as well as syllable-like sequences, often combining phoneme-like sounds with marked affect. They occur repeatedly, though in variable phonetic form, in a child's repertoire of sounds, and can be loosely correlated with recurring internal and environmental conditions. In fact, indexicals do not appear to be detachable from the child's affect state at first; that is, not appearing to be mediated by intention to express to another initially. Nor are they displaced, in the sense that words are, in time and place from their moment of articulation. Although they function systematically from the point of view of the adult's interpretation, they are not organized into contrastive sets in semantic domains the way first words are. Dore et al. (1976) grouped these forms into four categories: *affect expressions,* such as /ei::/ for pleasure; *instrumentals,* such as //ʌʔ/ while reaching for something; *indicating expressions* to take note of or point out some aspect of the environment, often accompanied by pointing; and *groupings* that appear to reflect an interaction between subjective state and attention to objective properties, such as when two different groups of sounds are used with the same group of objects but differ in the affect they express.

Thus far in our analyses of the data from this project there seem to be two types and two phases of development of indexical expressions. The first, *affect indexicals,* seem to emerge from early crying and delight sounds, at the beginning of the transitional phase being exemplified primarily by grunts of protest or squeals of glee. They are occasionally directed to someone via gaze, and are dominated by gestures, facial expressions, and tones typical of aroused affect states; an example is the B's protest described earlier. In such behavior the affect is more salient than the form is conventional, and it tends to be replaced by forms like "stop" and "no" later in development. The second type, *formal indexicals,* exhibit less affect-indicating behaviors, and increasingly approximate the surface forms of adult speech. They are better-defined syllabically, phonemically more stable, and more varied prosodically than the affective type. For example, the B in the same prohibition episode above produced /i::⌢/ in a tone which, although it manifested some mild pleasure, was marked by much lower pitch, less intensity, slower and less abrupt features than the protest. This type ranges from such conventional seeming "vowels" through B's imitations of A's words to apparent word-forms.

A majority of investigators currently consider such forms to be "widely over-generalized word uses" (Bowerman, 1978), as though they *refer* in a linguistic sense. Here I suggest that, although they do indicate empirical complexes, they lack the semantically discrete, contrastive, displaced, referential features of gen-uine words. In Dore (1978a), for example, a boy as late as 15 months used the term "bee" to index such diverse occurrences as falling leaves, crawling ants, spots on a wall, bleeps on a T.V. screen, and his father slapping a table. It is difficult to see the commonality in such extensions, and the indexical did not contrast with others in a set for movement terms. Assuming that such an indexi-cal expression does intend something prior to becoming a word proper, the question here is: What occurs between infant and interlocutor that transforms the indexical to a word?

A direct answer requires an adequate characterization of adult behavior, but first I want to specify two phases within the indexical period in terms of inten-tionality. The difference between the affective and formal *type* of indexical corresponds roughly to the *time* of their emergence; in general, indexicals marked heavily with affect eventually give way to more formally marked indexi-cals, though an affective stratum of word use continues. Recall that we are discussing a period between two other kinds of intentionality: the intent to achieve a physical goal and the intention to convey a word meaning. In the first the infant is aware of a practical end and can institute various means to achieve it, largely by sensorimotor actions on objects, best described in terms of Piaget's (1952) middle stages of sensorimotor intelligence. The baby, typically crawling, moves to, grasps, manipulates, and otherwise explores the properties of objects, including his own body and the face of his caregiver. A prototypical example is the mouthing of objects which, however elementary, satisfies most investigators' criteria for inferring an *intent-to-act.* This type has been widely described as a cognitive acquisition. It is used here as input to the transitional phase in that such actions are what mothers typically react to, comment on, match and otherwise intervene in.

At the other end of development we have the much discussed *intention-to-convey* lexical content. This is what is acquired by the end of the transitional period. The intention-to-convey presupposes the development of recognizable words whose intensional meaning features partly overlap the adult's. Their forms are phonemically stable and largely conventional; their use is displaced in time and space, detached from the immediate context and well established in memory; the choice of one over another routinely exhibits a semantic contrast among a limited set of items (like "yes-no" or "ball-baby" from a set of responses or toys); and toward the end of the single-word utterance period, the term chosen will function as a predicate (e.g., B will point to a cookie and say "eat." See Bloom 1973; Dore 1978a; Greenfield & Smith, 1976; deLaguna, 1927/1963 for details). Moreover, in addition to semantic information, word conveyances also function to communicate expectations. With them B induces in A the recognition that: (1) B is referring to some particular conceptual domain; (2) he intends to communicate some illocutionary function like requesting or answering; (3) B expects A to recognize both his intent and content; and (4) he expects A to do something about it, like complying or at least acknowledging him (see Dore 1978b).

Between the intent-to-act on objects and the intention-to-convey word meaning, there occurs a transitional phase of intentionality, coinciding with what we have formally described as the period of indexical expressions. Intentional expressions of this sort are more than physical actions, but less than intended word meanings. This is the period that requires closer empirical scrutiny and clearer theoretical formulation than has been available in previous explanations of language acquisition. From our preliminary analyses it appears that, for many children at least, this period itself can be subdivided into two phases: an "intending-*in*-expressing" and "intending-*to* express" (to distinguish these from the intent-to-act and the intention-to-convey, where forms of the word-root "intend" are meant to mimic development). The empirical difference between the two subtypes of intentional expression should be apparent from the earlier discussion of how mothers induce intentionality from motivation in their children. Recall that our 9-month-old addresses /i::/ to the doll he is about to mouth and /æ↗/ in protest, swinging at his mother's arm. Although these differ in form type (formal and affective, respectively), they both exemplify "intending-*in*-expressing."

Such vocalizations are closer to the intent-to-act insofar as they accompany actions and are not addressed directly to people. They express some state, but are not *intended* to express a specific state. They are not mediated, premeditated, or planned, but rather immediate, spontaneous, and reflexive. Philosophers like Langer (1972) call them "presentational" intentions: automatic ways of reacting to a particular event, as opposed to a choice of possible responses from among a set of known, appropriate, alternative ones. Empirically, intendings-*in*-expressing incorporate two behavioral modalities: vocal plus gesture or gaze-at-object, but not both. Vocalizations are either accompaniments to actions, or, when addressed in the direction of another, are not intoned, with onset and pause, to solicit responses, even though they may receive routine responses from an attentive adult.

In contrast, "intending-*to*-express" is closer to the intention to convey words. It does not merely add more of the same to an action, but rather supplement it with an amplifying concern, usually involving something to be done or said about the object. They are directly addressed to someone, with sharp focus of personal gaze to indicate the other's status as addressee. They are premeditated expressions, evidenced by the time delay between onset of personal gaze and onset of vocalization. Thus they seem to be cognitively mediated. They are "representational" intentions to the extent that some kind of deliberation takes place, some rudimentary cognitive content is executed. The empirical evidence for such a characterization consists in the integration of three modalities, synchronized across persons, movements, and objects. That is, the infant can alternate rapidly between acting on an object and vocalizing to someone about it, the behaviors therefore ensembled within a single theme. A typical example is the "no" by the 12-month-old girl previously described. While it does echo the A's preceding phonemes, its prosody expresses a quite different internal state from A's. Yet it is not quite a word insofar as it does not actually contrast with "yes," but rather fulfills the general function of responding to solicitations. (Recall that B went on to act as if she said "yes" and that the two words were not semantically productive for her at this time.) The phenomena described here as two kinds of intentional expressions before words have been reported widely in the diary literature on language development, but have not been isolated for study, nor related to affect development and interaction in the dyad. Whether they occur in the chronological order we found in our babies is a matter for further, quantitative research. We turn now to A's contribution in order to explain how her behavior interacts with B's development of indexical forms and intentional expressions as described earlier.

In principle, the dialogue between A and B can be construed as the influence of A's culture on B's mind, of A's socialized forms on B's motivated actions; but also as the influence of B's needs on A's responses. What are the properties of A's socialized responses and how do they interface with B's motives and intents? We must assume that A is herself highly motivated to socialize her baby successfully, not only to consciously provide her B with words (the hallmark of normalcy and intelligence in our society); but, more pervasively, as a thoroughly socialized agent she can not help but act in culturally appropriate and pragmatically effective ways. All her behavior is meaningful and *accountable in form*. Not only are all words and almost all actions of A's conventional in form; they constitute the totality of what is acceptable behavior for the child.

Garfinkel (1967) describes "everyday activities as members' methods for making these same activities visibly-rational-and-reportable-for-all-practical-purposes [p. vii]." These methods are *accountable* in that they are "situated practices of looking and telling . . . which consist of an endless, ongoing, contingent accomplishment [p. 1]." To talk "accountably" then, is to display mutually recognizable rules of usage for a situation at hand. The two primary properties of accountable talk, according to Garfinkel, are *indexicality,* the displaying of a part of a circumstance, making it sharable; and *reflexivity,* that indexical expressions constitute the very accomplishment of the circumstance. See Dore and McDermott (1982) for an example of how talk both creates and is determined by its contexts.

Five other properties of accountability, which Garfinkel adapted from Schutz (1962) are the following: (1) accountable practices function against a background of assumed *relevancies;* that is, taken-for-granted, known-in-common, sensible expectancies of acting in terms of "what everyone knows," which operate tacitly until they are breached; (2) The *"et-cetera-ness"* of such relevancies consists in there existing "more than one can say at the moment," but which nevertheless functions as an expectancy that is an unspecified part of our agreement in behaving accountably; our agreement, whatever it turns out to be specifically, is therefore inherently incomplete and subject to upcoming contingencies, and thus always subject to further revision; (3) conversation is a *situated* accomplishment of a mutual context of interaction consisting of mutually sensible displays of concerted efforts toward consensus; (4) such situated displays must be temporally *sequenced* vis-a-vis each other, and aligned so as to be recognizably sensible (i.e., accountable); and (5) because of these features of relevant expectancies, et-cetera-ness, situatedness, and sequentiality, conversation must be interpreted procedurally in terms of a *prospective-retrospective* analysis; that is, members must await future developments in order to "locate" past displays, which themselves "project" prospects for future clarification.

Garfinkel (1967) argued that a "common understanding consists of an inner-temporal course of interpretive work [p. 25]"; that shared agreement derives from "social methods for accomplishing the member's recognition that something was said-according-to-a-rule and not the demonstrable matching of substantive matters [p. 30]"; and that common understanding consists in "the enforceable character of actions in compliance with the expectancies of everyday life as a morality [p. 53]." He continues, "The features of the real society are produced by persons' motivated compliance with these background expectancies [p. 53]." When such expectancies are breached, the member "should have no alternative but to try to normalize the resultant incongruities." Such breaches lead to bewilderment, a "specifically senseless environment" and ultimately to "internal conflict, psychosocial isolation, acute and nameless anxiety along with various symptoms of acute depersonalization [p. 55]."

Regarding language acquisition, first words can be construed as the acquisition of accountable objects, as well as the more traditional intentional objects. In this view the word acquired is not merely the symbolic consequence of intentional development. It is, specifically, the consequence of *interpreted* intentions; and, still more specifically, B's intending expressions are interpreted *accountably* by A. The crux of development is, thus, how B's intentions become account-

able. Insofar as words exhibit the aforementioned features, words are accountable objects par excellence.

We have already discussed how express*ings* are indexical, but early AB
utterances are reflexive as well in that they constitute part of their accomplishment *in* talking. That is, the talk not only indexes their mutual attention to
context, but it *performs* it in that such talk *is* the doing of "what we are now
doing is playing, eating, etc."; and it displays how "we are together" or not on
this. In analoguing B's affect, A gives form to *their* feeling. This form integrates
B's state with an accountable form for expressing it. And A's form also *is* their
most immediate context; the external, accountable, mutually recognizable form
of their shared affect.

Since word uses must always function against a background of relevancies, A
must know both more than she can say and more than B could know. Her word
uses relative to B's intendings-in (to)-express will foreground only a small part of
a word's meaning, and only that part relevant to the circumstances at hand.
Future uses of the "same word" will be applied to different circumstances (i.e.,
objects, events) and thus will contingently exhibit different meanings. Her work
at expanding B's form uses *in any way* must constitute a revision of meaning for
his form. To that extent the mother must pervasively *breach* any expectancies of
relevant meaning that B has begun to acquire for a form.

The "et-cetera" clause for any word's meaning, and of course any minimal
meanings B may have for a form, entails that its application will be subject to
contingencies not-knowable-in-advance. While a schema, although open to
change, is entirely contained cognitively at any given moment, a word, being an
accountable object as well, can never be entirely stabilized in that way. So, when
A revises B's word use, she is in effect not only breaching what he may have
thought they agreed to as that word's meaning, but she also conveys to him
something like "that's what it meant all along, from the start." This may of
course be quite disorienting for the child. It certainly must compete with any
tendency to cognitively fix discrete meanings. And, of course, such change-
from-without is quite distinct from creation-from-within. Such competition and
conflict may motivate B's need to learn more language.

Since A in a sense operates "inside of" B's affect, her interventions into his
indexical expressions can introject into them three dimensions of meaning. Her
words have a distinctness and specificity and effectiveness relative to the circumstances A and B have jointly focussed upon; they have a discreteness and con-
trastiveness relative to other words in a semantic system; and, most deeply, her
words inherently reflect the *moral* status of something like "that's the only *right*
way to say this here." If B is motivated to adapt to A's forms and their uses,
these dimensions of meaning automatically accrue to his accomodation to her
forms. He has many hundreds of opportunities to realize their meanings, especially since she routinely interprets his forms as meaningful before he can
intend them as such.

However, at the same time we have seen how A pervasively breaches and unconsciously revises any degree of meaningfulness B may have constructed for his affective experience expressed by her forms. B's acquisition of meanings progresses from his first attempts to act with and "index with" word-like forms, to A's breaches of such attempts, to his bind of being "overthrown again," to his learning more about the word's accountable meaning so as to stabilize his linguistic cognition as a *defense* against the pervasive incursion of her breaches. In other words, the disequilibrium between her communicative matches and his affective state and cognitive awareness becomes a motivational (even moral) crisis for him if his personal identity with her as partners in communion (now communication) is threatened by too many mismatches or failures on her part to "uptake" his affect or intent to express.

The emergence of word meaning must also depend upon the situatedness of word uses. It is perhaps this that prompted Wittgenstein (1953) to view the meaning of a word as its collection of uses. In developmental studies, the emphasis on cognitive processes and products has obscured the importance of use preceding meaning. When meanings are treated as calculable and computable inten*s*ional features of words, the influence of accountable uses is devalued. In that case, too, the extensions of words to newer circumstances, the dyad's methods for establishing meanings and the very motivation for their emergence are neglected as well. Ultimately, with the neglect of such rich inputs, it is tempting to postulate innate linguistic knowledge, but here we are recommending that we should first explore fully how prelinguistic intentional expressions become accountable in form. By "use-preceding-meaning" here I mean B's indexical expressions before they are transformed into accountable word forms. Indexicals become increasingly specified for meaningfulness because of their situated uses, A's revisions and B's cognitive readjustments. Innateness in the above case would not be epistemological (as Chomsky, 1965 argued), but would involve B's natural expression of affect and A's innate tendency to attune to it *cross-modally* (see Stern, 1982).

This accountable viewpoint of the social situatedness of early word usage sheds new light on the well-known "here-and-now-ness" of early language. Situatedness includes more than the "action bases" for concepts that words refer to (cf. Piaget). More crucially, earliest acquisition seems to be *inter*actionally situated. Not only does B's form increasingly approximate A's, but, since some forms continue to function as indexical expressions, they are idiosyncratic rather than accountably conventional. These are "projections" or prospects that B tries out; the indexical uses of "bee" mentioned earlier. In such cases A often adapts to B's usage temporarily; but she eventually orients *automatically* to its more accountabl uses. Thus, such *un*accountable functions disappear.

Also, sequentiality allows for the method of interpretation Garfinkel calls prospective—retrospective analysis. For word learning, we suggest this works in the following way. For some affect-state or intent-to-express B produces some indexical form associated with it. This serves to project a potential connection between the two, which is both imitated from the A and recognized by her as a communicative attempt on B's part. In a sense the projected sound has "prospects" for meaning which the B cannot know beforehand. It is the A's investiture of the sound with situated meaningfulness that retrospectively supplies the B's prospect with meaning. Similarly, across many usages B retrospectively recognizes what he meant by previously projected prospects of word meanings.

In this way the AB dyad co-constructs his lexicon. They create word meanings together such that: (1) B gets to know more about what A knows, thereby increasing his "communing" power with her; (2) A knows what B knows, thereby allowing her to socialize him properly, to know what to work on next; and (3) to create a domain between them in which B can creatively "play" with meanings and change them around, while for accountable purposes they both have tools with which to negotiate concerted activity, including more word learning. In Garfinkel's terms, all of this *is* the origin of a *reciprocity of perspective* whereby the world known in common can be objectively expressed.

ILLUSTRATIVE ANALYSES OF INTERACTIONS DURING THE TRANSITIONAL PERIOD

The analyses here attempt to demonstrate the sequencing and alignment, as well as the ambiguity, of A's forms with B's functions. Several levels of interaction are referred to, ranging from the agenda being negotiated to the multiple functions of the behavioral bits. The examples are excerpts from transcripts of interactions from a corpus of 10 mother–infant pairs who were videotaped for one hour in a playroom at New York Hospital in a study conducted by Dr. Daniel Stern. The scenes involved changes in personnel and props (e.g., mother–baby alone, stranger with mother, mother absent, new toy attraction, etc.) and were repeated at intervals of 4,6,9,12,18,24, and 36 months. The study was originally concerned with such issues as infant individuation, changes in interactional patterns, and infant's responses to mothers' prosodies. Thus far it is clear that, before speech production, babies orient systematically to their mothers' vocal tones. The babies' exact responses to changes in mothers' voice qualities (along dimensions of pitch, intensity, etc.) are now being studied, but for our purpose here it is sufficient to refer to tones impressionistically. Finally, the two examples here were chosen because they illustrated differences in sex, age, level of development, the "mood" of the scene, and two styles of AB interaction in general.

The examples analyzed here are organized around the notion of a communicative match (derived from Stern's notion of affective attunement, 1982). A match occurs whenever some *marked motivated behavior,* as an affect expression by B is directly responded to by A. Thus, on the one hand the notion of an AB affect match is a theoretical postulate, on the other such matches are identifiable in a fairly rigorous empirical way. These occur in sequences of at least two moves in a round: the B's initiation, A's response, with optional moves related to these first two which do not initiate another round. Here three types of match are scored: analogs are matches of affect wherein a partner responds to another's affect expression in the same dimension (i.e., positive or negative); complements are contrastive matches, manifested in the opposite dimension of the initiation; and imitations are non-affect matches of external form, with no apparent marked affect.

The data here are also described at the levels of agenda and of *specific communicative function*. "Agenda" is defined as a verbal and/or gestural focus on a topic or activity; play routines, "word-work," and prohibition agendas. These are executed in rounds by specific functions, such as playfully intoned indexical and acknowledgement, invitation-answer, or prohibitable-prohibitive rounds. Each example here exhibits a different kind of agenda conflict which locally motivates the communicative functions and more generally motivates the infant's acquisition of language. In Example 10.1, a prohibition-and-protest sequence, a mother and her 9-month-old boy negotiate a conflict between playing with a puzzle board (her explicitly recommended agenda) and mouthing a piece of the puzzle (his repeatedly "behaved agenda"). But apart from the superordinate puzzle-play agenda, A alternates between two subagendas of prohibiting him from mouthing and interpreting his vocalizations as words. These are referred to as play, prohibition, and "word-work," respectively.

A sets B up for her puzzle-play agenda by arranging him physically next to the board, telling him where to put the leaf. B's /i::/ initiates a round of behavior insofar as it is a marked motivated behavior. This indexical expression combines a vowel-like form with mild positive affect; for descriptive purposes it is more of a formal indexical than an affective one. It may be echoing A's "leaf," but there is no evidence that it (nor any of B's forms at this time) approach word status. Perhaps because of the dual form-affect properties of /i::/, A replies in a correspondingly double way: Her word "eat" expands his form into an accountable one (which incorporates his mouthing action also); and her intonation is "playful" relative to what preceded and followed it, thus, analoguing his pleasure. His raising the piece toward his mouth is scored as a "preventable" functionally, not yet a prohibitable, while her utterance functions as a preventive. Round 2 begins with his mouthing, prohibitable action. First she expands to another /i/-word, "leaf," but her "no" shifts to a tense, elongated, slow rising-falling tone which, together with her pulling the piece away, constitutes a prohibitive. Round 2 continues because B immediately protests her prohibitive with an "angry" vocalization and arm flaps. She responds by reprimanding him and pulling the piece away again.

Regarding communicative matches in round 2, A's "leaf" imitates B's /i/ from round 1 (though this time she labels the object involved rather than the

EXAMPLE 10.1

A Prohibition Episode Negotiated between a Mother
and Her Nine-Month-Old Boy

Match # Type	Adult Behaviors	Baby Behaviors	Communicative Functions
1	Put the leaf in there.	(holding a piece of a puzzle in hands)	directive
	That's a part of a puzzle.		comment
		/ i::: ʔ / (raising piece to mouth; hesitates, then looks around to A)	"pleasure" indexical preventable
IMI	No. It's not to eat. (play-ful tone; shaking head)		preventive
ANA		(puts piece in his mouth)	prohibitable
2 IMI	That's a *leaf*.		prohibitive
COM	No / :: ʔ / (pulling piece away with her finger)		
ANA		/ ŋ:ʔʌ̃/ (flapping arms angrily)	protest-1
ANA	Don't you yell at your mother (moving piece away from B)		reprimand

182

#	Speaker	Utterance / action	Vocalization / action	Interpretation
3	COM		/ m::m ⊃ / (reaching for piece)	elicitive
	COM	I said *NO!* (high, intense, abrupt, angry tone; but she gives the piece back to him)		denial
4	COM		(puts piece in his mouth)	compliance
				prohibitable
				prohibitive
	COM	(pulls piece out of mouth)		protest-2
	ANA	I said no. (low, lax; pulling piece away)	/æ ↗/ (high-pitched; arm flapping)	warning
	COM			
5	COM		/æ ↗/ (highest pitch; examining piece)	protest-3
	COM	Does that taste good? (rocking head up and down)	(puts piece in mouth) / m::m /	"pleasure" indexical
				accusation
		It's only cardboard.	(takes it out; examines it)	compliance
			(puts it back in mouth)	comment
6	COM	Huh? Does that taste good? Let's put it back! (taking it out of his mouth)		prohibitable
				accusation
				directive
				prohibitive
	ANA		(flaps arm weakly) /ʌʔ/	protest-4

183

action "eat"). But her tone shift on "no" and accompanying act complement his mouthing because of the contrast between his presumed pleasure and her clear displeasure. Then we see *B* analoguing her displeasure in his angry protest. Still more negative affect is displayed by her reprimand. Thus, the conflict between their preferred agendas mounts, as displayed both by communicative match and function type. Regarding the accountability work, A interprets the vocalization in his protest as a "yell," and moving the piece away from him confirms that she is attempting to hold him accountable *not* to mouth. Further, while A's initial complement induces him to protest the first time, her moving the piece away occasions his next act of trying to retrieve it.

Round 3 is initiated by his elongated nasal and reaching. This is scored as an *elicitive* function, as distinct from a *solicit,* because it is an "intending-in-expressing" or "presentational act" and not an intent to express *to* A that he wants the piece; that is, not a representational and illocutionary act of soliciting it, as might be manifested by personal gaze that *references* A as well as the object. A treats the elicitive *as if* B might be soliciting the piece from her. (Such *as-if* interpretations intervene in B's state, and his subsequent observation of them provides the beginning of the transformation of them from presentational to representational intentions, e.g., from elicitive to solicitive; initial solicitives in our data are often manifested behaviorally in the following sequence—onset of personal gaze, onset of vocalization, offset of vocalization, offset or alternation of gaze with object manipulation.) Additionally, while A's angry vocalization here complements B's affect by blocking his desire, her giving him back the puzzle piece at the same time complies with his desire. This ambiguous double signal of denying vocally what she complies with gesturally must bind B, perhaps inducing further anxiety and leading to the violent protests to come. Her giving and taking of the piece may even induce the change from elicitive to protest.

After A complements his pleasure in mouthing at round 4, it is then B who analogs A's negative affect with his second, more emphatic protest. A's tone then shifts downward, as though to contrast with his anger. But she retains the same words—"I said no," and pulls the piece away again! This occasions his most aggressive protest which, relative to her lowering of tone, complements her state with a much more negative one. This is their climax. He triumphs temporarily. Then, in round 5, she complements his pleasure indexical with an ironically intoned accusation, continuing the commentary as he examines the piece. In round 6, he performs the prohibitable mouthing again; she again complements it with an accusation. But this time she takes the piece away permanently, to which he weakly protests, and ultimately loses the skirmish. A's agenda of not-mouthing holds sway over his mouthing.

Example 10.2 involves a 12-month-old girl engaged in her "behaved agenda" of telephone play-and-talk in contrast to her mother's mildly recommended "castle-block" play for her. Moreover, the example is critical for showing how

A's forms complete B's speech functions. We offer a brief analysis of this example primarily as a contrast with the "prohibition" scene. This mother can not be characterized as "prohibitive" in any sense, since she rarely blocks her baby from doing what she wants. However, she is "interventional" in our sense in that she does try to distract her B's attention away from prohibitable actions (or, conversely, attract B to hers). An example from the same session as our excerpt was when the B knocked the phone handle off its cradle; A, having failed with mild (playfully intoned) pleas like "Okay, let's hang it up now," waits until B goes to another toy before rearranging the phone herself. Even when B is handling the electric outlet, A merely tries to distract her. A almost always matches B's play efforts with a playful or encouraging tone.

B initiates this example with a characteristic, continuous, babble-like "cackle" while reaching for the phone. But, after a pause, B's final syllable terminates with a rise. Because personal gaze follows her terminal rise, almost immediately and *before* A's response, B's utterance is scored as a solicitive. A's acknowledgement of it analogs her daughter's positive state. Then A "imitates" B by carving out of her cackle three syllables, labeling the object of attention, "telephone." This is an orientation to external form, rather than internal state. B then imitates the prosody of A's "telephone," almost perfectly, but she continues to use her own idiosyncratic segmental phone types and terminates again with a rise. Because of the absence of personal gaze this time, the utterance is scored as an elicitive. A analogs it with an acknowledgement. B then turns to face A and initiates round 3 by producing a solicitive with a rising terminal contour. Again A analogs it with an acknowledgement. B walks away, vocalizing, this time without a rise, communicatively functioning as an accompaniment.

The episode shifts to a mild agenda conflict when in round 3 A invites B to play "castle" with the blocks on the floor between them. After getting B's attention, A nods, emphatically points to the blocks and prosodically stresses her invitation with a second part, "this!" B's first attempt at an ostensible "answer" is phonetically uninterpretable for content. It is a complement on the match level because of the stark contrast behaviorally between A's excited offer and B's apparently negative attitude. Then A in turn complements B's response with a more excited, surprised "no?" This functions as a clarification question, and apparently influences B's more conventionally formed answer. Here again, A's form intervenes in B's prior "quasi-function," transforming its response status into an accountable form. More interestingly, B's "no" not only adapts to A's segmental phonemes but also utilizes the emphatic stress and head nod from A's earlier "this." While in round 2, B adapted to the prosody of "telephone," here she *re-envoices* A's prosody, phonemes, and gestures to give full conventional form to what earlier was a "quasi-answer" at best. In other words, in both cases B is becoming accountable to the appropriate forms for expressing her intents.

EXAMPLE 10.2
A Play-with-Competitive-Agenda Episode between Mother and 12-Month-Old Girl

Match # Types	Adult Behaviors	Baby Behaviors	Communicative Functions
1	Boy, there's so much to do.	/ dɪkədæ. . . / pause / dæ ↗ / (while reaching toward telephone; then turns to A)	comment
ANA	Yea! (high-pitch, elongated slow rising, playful tone)		solicitive acknowledgement
IMI	Telephone. / ↗ / (slow rising and falling contour)	(turns to phone)	label
2 IiMI		dætəkæ ↗ / (same prosody as A's "telephone," with rising terminal contour)	elicitive
ANA	Aha.	(turns to A)	acknowledgement
3 ANA	Yea. / /	/ dɪkæ ↑ / (emphatic stress)	solicitive acknowledgement

	Utterance	Nonverbal / phonetic	Function
		(walking toward corner) / dəkɪdæ /	accompaniment
	Wanna play with the castle?		invitation
		(turns to A)	
4 COM	This! (emphatic stress and emphatic pointing)	/ hkyɔ / (very low pitch, intensity)	"answer"
COM	NO? (high-pitch, "surprise")		clarification
IMI		NO! (high, abrupt tone; emphatic head nod)	answer
COM	Okay.		acknowledgement
5		(walks to A; hesitates; then knocks some blocks over) / dəkæ ↗ / ("joyful," emphatic stress; glances at A)	solicitive
ANA	Yea. (breathy, laughed) Knocked it over, didn't ya? Let's see. Whata ya gonna do with the rest of the castle?		acknowledgement
		(turns to phone)	"questionings"
	Nothing! ("ironic" tone)		"ignore"
			self-answer

Yet, despite its form, B's "no" is apparently not semantically contrastive, since she proceeds to violate the putative truth value of "her" answer by playing with the blocks. At this point the answer is only negligibly hers, and more of a ventriloquating of A's answer for her. A gives conventional form to B's functional capacity to answer, but she cannot give her semantic contrastivity itself. The main point here is that As show Bs how to answer before they can comprehend the forms they use. Also, apart from the semantic mismatch, B's going to the blocks here signals solidarity with A, just as A's tones do with her.

However, B's hesitation before knocking the block down suggests (as did our "prohibition" baby's hesitation) that she is becoming aware of the clash in agenda between her and A, and perhaps beginning to reflect upon her choice of game. Here this A accepts her B's choice to forego the "castle" game. Although A mildly prefers block-play for B in her subsequent questioning, she ultimately accepts B's reorientation to the phone (unlike the mother in Example 10.1). A's final remark of "nothing" (like the above mother's "it's just cardboard") seems to be addressed to someone other than the child—some adult audience or herself or perhaps such ironies are played to the camera. At any rate, utterances of this sort remind us of the multiple "voices" we all perform from the dialogical point of view. Just as B's "no" is more "their" word than hers, "nothing" is less their word (or even A's word) than it is the word of some wider social grouping.

CONCLUSION

The approach to language proposed here is obviously attempting to integrate and extend the social-interactional (Mead, Vygotsky, Bruner, etc.) and the affective (Langer, Erikson, Stern, etc.) traditions. I assume that, while affect is the primary dimension of early communication, it is the cross-personal dialogue of affect that is most crucial for language emergence. Cognition is secondary in two senses: (1) it operates to construct meaning systems already begun by connections between affective states and socialized forms of expressions; and (2) intentionality itself emerges out of the more fundamental motivation toward persons and the objective world. The difference between this approach and current cognitive, linguistic, and social ones is best reflected in the nature of dialogue. This "dia-" logic of the dyad is different in kind, chronologically prior, and theoretically more fundamental than the "mono-" logics assumed by most philosophies of science. Instead of, for example, the logic that A is only A and not B, Adult and Baby here are one, irreducible unit. Thus, the problem of language emergence is reversed: It is not how A communicates to a separate B, so much as how AB become differentiated into distinct language-using ego entities.

A final note regarding the definition of "word." In the psycholinguistic (and dominant) definition, contrastive, semantic, intensional features of words are "known" (computed, chosen, etc.) somehow by the child. To explain their origin one must appeal to innate linguistic knowledge or some specific cognitive function. But, defined pragmatically, the word is the symbolic consequence of intended and interpreted affect form complexes, used first as indexical expressions of personal (social, objective, etc.) contexts to express one's self and to commune with others, only secondarily accruing to a system of displaced meanings.

I do not claim to have fully explained word emergence here. However, I hope that I have at least pointed to a possible type of explanation that neither appeals to innate linguistic knowledge nor to the primacy of cognition, but rather to an interpersonal dialogue of affect expression as the (possibly innate) basis of symbolic consciousness.

ACKNOWLEDGMENTS

The data for this paper came from a project conducted by Dr. Daniel Stern of the New York Hospital. Without these data and his insights into the attunement of affect between mothers and babies, this paper could not exist. I thank him and Helen Marwick of Edinburgh University for their description of the prohibition segment reported herein. I am deeply indebted to Lois Bloom for her close reading and helpful recommendations for revision of a prior draft. I also thank our editor, co-contributor and conference organizer, Roberta Golinkoff, for her patience, the challenging ideas of her paper which so closely relates to mine, and her helpful comments on mine. Finally, I thank Catherine Snow and Bambi Schieffelin for their constant encouragement, and Ray McDermott for his constant criticism, and their feedback during the long writing of this paper. None of the above of course agrees with my account completely. That is the beauty of our dialogue.

REFERENCES

Austin, J. *How to do things with words.* New York: Oxford University Press, 1962.

Bates, E. *Language and context: The acquisition of pragmatics.* New York: Academic Press, 1976.

Bloom, L. *One word at a time: The use of single word utterances before syntax.* The Hague: Mouton, 1973.

Bowerman, M. Systematizing semantic knowledge: Changes over time in the child's organization of word meaning. *Child Development,* 1978, *49,* 977–987.

Bruner, J. The ontogenesis of speech acts. *Journal of Child Language,* 1975, *2,* 1–20.

Bruner, J. From communication to language: A psychological perspective. In I. Markova (Ed.), *The social context of language.* London: Wiley, 1978.

Burke, K. *A rhetoric of motives.* Englewood Cliffs, N.J.: Prentice-Hall, 1950.

Chomsky, N. *Aspects of the theory of syntax.* Cambridge, Mass.: M. I. T. Press, 1965.

Cross, T. Mothers' speech adjustment: The Contribution of selected child listener variables. In C. Snow & C. Ferguson (Eds.), *Talking to children: Language input and acquisition.* Cambridge, Mass.: Cambridge University Press, 1977.

Dore, J. Holophrases, speech acts, and language universals. *Journal of Child Language,* 1975, *2,* 21–39.

Dore, J. Concepts, communicative acts, and the language acquisition device. Invited address to the Boston Child Language Conference, September, 1978a.

Dore, J. Conditions for the acquisition of speech acts. In I. Markova (Ed.), *The social context of language*. London: Wiley, 1978b.

Dore, J., Franklin, M., Miller, R., & Ramer, A. Transitional phenomena in early language acquisition. *Journal of Child Language*, 1976, *3*, 13–28.

Dore, J., & McDermott, R. Linguistic indeterminacy and social context in utterance interpretation. *Language*, 1982, *58*, 374–398.

Erikson, E. *Identity: Youth and crisis*. New York: Norton, 1968.

Garfinkel, H. *Studies in ethnomethodology*. Englewood Cliffs, N.J.: Prentice-Hall, 1967.

Goffman, E. *Frame analysis*. New York: Harper, 1974.

Greenfield, P., & Smith, J. *The structure of communication in early language development*. New York: Academic Press, 1976.

Gumperz, J., & Hymes, D. *Directions is sociolinguistics: The ethnography of communication. New York: Holt, Rinehart & Winston, 1972.*

Halliday, M. Learning how to mean. London: Edward Arnold, 1975.

deLaguna, G. *Speech: Its function and development*. Bloomington, Ind: Indiana University Press, 1963. (Originally published 1927.)

Langer, S. *Mind: An essay on human feeling*. Baltimore, Md.: The Johns Hopkins University Press, 1972.

Malinowski, B. The problem of meaning in primitive languages. In C. Ogden, & I. Richards, *The meaning of meaning*. New York: Harcourt, Brace, & World, 1923.

Mead, G. *Mind, self, and society*. Chicago, Ill.: Chicago University Press, 1934.

Miller, G. Personal communication, 1979.

Ochs, E., & Schieffelin, B. *Developmental pragmatics*. New York: Academic Press, 1979.

Piattelli–Palmarini, M. (Ed.), *Language and learning:* The *debate between Jean Piaget and Noam Chomsky*. Cambridge, Mass.: Harvard University Press, 1980.

Piaget, J. *The origins of intelligence in children*. New York: International Universities Press, 1952.

Shutz, A. *Collected papers II: Studies in social theory*. The Hague: Nijhoff, 1962.

Searle, J. *Speech acts*. Cambridge, Mass.: Cambridge University Press, 1969.

Skinner, B. *Verbal behavior*. New York: Appleton-Century-Crofts, 1957.

Snow, C. The development of conversation between mothers and babies. *Journal of Child Language*, 1977, *4*, 1–22.

Stern, D. *The first relationship*. Cambridge, Mass.: Harvard University Press, 1977.

Stern, D. "Attunement of internal states by way of 'inter-modal fluency'". Paper delivered at International Conference of Infancy Studies. Austin, Texas, March 1982.

Sugarman–Bell, S. Some organizational aspects of pre-verbal communication. In I. Markova (Ed.), *The social context of language*. London: Wiley, 1978.

Trevarthen, C., & Hubley, P. Secondary intersubjectivity: Confidence, confiding, and acts of meaning in the first year. In A. Lock (Ed.), *Action, gesture and symbol*. London: Academic Press, 1979.

Vygotsky, L. *Thought and language*. Cambridge, Mass.: M.I.T. Press, 1962.

Vygotsky, L. *Mind in society*. (Edited and translated by M. Cole, V. John-Steiner, S. Scribner, & E. Souberman). Cambridge, Mass.: Harvard University Press, 1978.

Wittgenstein, L. *Philosophical investigations*. New York: Macmillan, 1953.

11

DISCUSSION
Text, Context, and Interaction
in Language Acquisition

Catherine Garvey
The Johns Hopkins University

Both authors of the papers under discussion agree that the production and the comprehension of first words take place in situations that are rich in interpersonal communication. While David Messer emphasizes the 'nonverbal' aspects of the communication that might assist the child in comprehending the link between reference and referent object, John Dore stresses the interpsychic experiences that might lead the preverbal child to words. They recommend that the scope of investigations of the transition period be widened to include features of the extralinguistic input, or to include the affective events in which the communications are embedded. I concur, in general, with these recommendations. However autonomous the linguistic system may become, its roots are tangled in the network of the textual, contextual, and interpersonal properties of early communication. To anticipate Dore's argument, the same might be said about the ontogeny of the self. The task is to specify these properties as precisely as possible.

In a review of Bullowa's (1979) *Before Speech,* Alison Gopnik (1981) suggests that "The line of development from prelinguistic to paralinguistic communication seems much clearer than the line from prelinguistic communication to language [p. 499]." Although she does not go on to specify exactly what she means by paralinguistic communication, she does allude to intonation and gesture and their role in expressing "emotional states," in accomplishing social ends, and in establishing rapport. Thus, paralinguistics is used by Gopnik to mean more than the term designates in Crystal and Davy's (1969) system, in which it refers to vocal effects caused by different configurations of the glottal and supraglottal organs, for example, whisper, falsetto, creaky voice. While we might leave some vocal modifications such as whisper, falsetto, or giggle outside the linguistic *system,* there are other effects created by the contrastive (i.e. phonemic) and the noncontrastive accompaniments of pitch, loudness, duration of segmentals, and pause that have important roles in the linguistic code (language) and in the use of the linguistic code (verbal communication) . . . and these are not solely expressive or phatic in function.

David Messer, in dealing with aspects of communication that he calls nonverbal or nonlinguistic, indicates how the prosodic feature of amplitude is collocated with response timing, gesture, gaze, and repetition of verbal reference to make the child's task of comprehending linguistic references easier or more transparent. John Dore's examples of mothers' prohibitions suggest that these might well have some distinctive 'tones of voice' that an infant could come to recognize as signaling negative affect.

It is important to consider what we mean by the term language as acquired or achieved by a child and to consider also what other systems may be involved. Shatz (this volume) deals with language acquisition specifically targeting syntax. She finds little evidence of direct mapping from gestural systems to syntactic development. Dore is primarily concerned with the acquisition of the word, what Vygotsky might call word meaning, the conjunct of word and thought, or concept. Messer is primarily concerned with the comprehension of referring terms that select object concepts, and thus, it seems to me that he joins the comprehension of the *acts* of referring and naming to the linguistic *means* for referring. When we use the term linguistic we can thus select syntax, semantics, pragmatics, phonology, or combinations of these. We cannot neglect, however, in any realistic account of language learning the contrastive prosodic systems which contribute to phonological and syntactic structure. We should not, I believe, neglect the other, expressive-interpretative systems, which also utilize frequency, amplitude and duration, and which are vital to oral-aural communication. Further, we should not neglect the use of prosodic, especially rhythmic, features to group and organize phrases and utterances, a function vital both to syntax on the sentence level and to coherence and cohesion in discourse. These features are used in conjunction with words, segmental forms; they are conventionalized and appear to be rule governed, though they have proved to be difficult to describe. They appear to be less difficult to begin to learn to use and discriminate, though mature control of these systems is probably achieved rather late in the course of language acquisition; as is the case for mature control of certain syntactic structures. As an example of one product of these systems one might listen to the 'motherese' of a 2½-year-old girl attending to her Baby (doll). "Oh? oh Baby. Are you wet? You are? Awh." When compared with a real mother, the child might be faulted on failure to observe a number of cooccurrence rules of the motherese register, but she does capture some of the essential markers of that register, using raised pitch, wider pitch excursions, and greater vocalic length than in her normal speech. She also leaves pauses for Baby's (imaginary) responses.

There are a number of analytically distinct subsystems involving pitch, loudness, duration, and pause, and some also employ nonlexical and lexical segments as well. Where to make the cut between what is linguistic and what is nonlinguistic is not a simple matter. Wherever we slice it, though, verbal, linguistic communication cannot and does not proceed without the simultaneous operation of these prosodic and paralinguistic systems and features.

In regard to language, one of its primary characteristics is that emphasized by Lenneberg (1973) who sees the basic nature of language, at every level of its organization, as relational. This nature is embodied in the formula (w_1, w_2) phi; to be read as a command to relate elements from an open set of words, object words, perhaps, in a manner indicated by phi, which is a potentially open set of relations. In real life, however, the formula is incomplete and must be expanded by instructions for the context of the formula (e.g. put) and the mood or force of the relationship. (E.g. imperative, question, statement): $[(w_1, w_2)$ phi $w_3]$ gamma.

The capability for symbolic representation and the conceptualization of relational meanings are achieved very closely in time. When we credit the child with syntax, the use of two words in construction, the conservative criteria for syntax would include, though not always explicitly, the production of the two or more words under a single intonation contour and in close temporal sequence, that is, without a noticeable pause, for example, Mòmmy sôck versus Mòmmy (pause) sòck. Thus, intonation and temporal integration of constructions are already implicated in the first phases of language learning.

What I am proposing is that what the child has to learn in order to be credited with language is vastly more complex than our discourse suggests. Granted, we do not have a 'syntax' of discourse, but we do have certain hints as to the nature of the combinatory and sequencing rules of communication. The hints point to what is essentially relational, that is, structures of the type discussed by Lenneberg (1973). An example of the role of the prosodic systems in defining these structures seems to me as clear as the use of word order to signal a given type of construction—a given type of relationship. I refer now to Halliday's (1979) observations of the means his son Nigel employed to signal the within-speaker discourse meaning of 'next in a sequence of same acts.' The child at 15 months used as signal to start a game of naming pictures in a book, [á::dà] roughly corresponding to 'What's that?' but with the force of a request for the adult to name the picture. After the mother responded, ''That's a ball,'' the child pointed to the next page and said [á::dâ] glossed as 'And what's that?' Halliday interprets this as ''already a form of interaction that has texture to it. The relation to this utterance to what preceded it is foregrounded by the use of a special intonation pattern.''

Nigel also used tone to signal the meaning that a word represented a second attempt at a failed communication. At 18 months, he was listing things he had seen on a walk [tìk lòu bà dòubā]. When his father who had been responding to each item, didn't understand and tried to interpret, incorrectly, Nigel repeated what he had said as [dōubà]. This was an emphatic repetition, clearly not a first mention, thus the command was relate [dōubà] to [dòubā] as repetition of a failed message.

Such text-forming devices are surely examples of the use of the contrastive prosodic features to indicate relational meanings. Relationships are also formed between speakers as well as in one person's text. In the first vocal interactions of toddlers, vocal copy games are observed, following closely on motor copy games. Exchange of vocal segments, of very similar frequency, amplitude and duration with the whole exchange produced at an invariable rhythm are means of indicating that 'I understand what we are doing and show this by doing the same thing.' Exact rhythmic repetition is also a mark of the play orientation, so the message would read: 'I relate what I do to what you do in a playful fashion.'

Now, it is well established that infants have a special sensitivity to prosody, to pitch, amplitude, and timing, first for the detection of mood, perhaps, but also for the detection of linguistic contrasts. Relatively early they use the prosodic parameters of speech in babbling, some time before these parameters have entered into a system of phonemic contrasts. These capabilities are available for eventual use in language, but before that they are used in sharing in the interactions in which language is learned. I see early interaction as providing the opportunity for learning some of the dynamics intrinsic to the linguistic system. For a provocative account of how mothers' speech to pre-verbal and to neo-verbal infants changes, accommodatively, with developmental changes in the communicative goals of the dyads' interactions, see Stern, Spieker, Barnett, and MacKain, (in press).

What could the infant learn at this time? I suggest such discoveries as 'the direction of pitch can signal a different message,' 'cognitive prominance is associated with auditory prominance,' 'this act or this word, is related to the prior act or word in some way, and is so marked.' Such learnings are part of what we conservatively call language and must surely be prerequisites (and not merely antecedents or precursors) to the comprehension and production of linguistic expressions. And it is these dynamic properties of language that might well lead to 'breaking the code.' Some specific features will come to be phonemically organized by that code, some will remain as diacritics to encoded messages, and some will also be employed in defining the texture of discourse.

As an example of the last function let us take Messer's finding that mothers temporally segregate talk about one referent from talk about a different referent. This is done by the use of short pauses between successive utterances within an episode and longer pauses between episodic units. Such an arrangement might be interpreted by the child as something like 'no long pause, probably the messages are coherent,' or, 'long pause, probably these messages do not cohere, or 'long pause, here comes something new.'

That this pattering of coherent discourse is well learned as it *applies to linguistic production* is suggested by our (Garvey & Rae, in preparation) findings that 2 ½-year-olds in interaction with peers do essentially the same thing. Though some between-speaker pauses are a little bit longer than the mothers of the 2-year-olds permit in their episode internal speech to the child, the relative pattering of between-speaker pauses in coherent and noncoherent speech is the same in child-child interaction. The expectation of a response *in good time* is so well developed by 2 ½-year-olds that failure of the peer partner to respond to a directed utterance can trigger a replay of the failed message (with appropriate intonational markings of its status as a replay). The replay usually occurs within an interval that just exceeds the normal speaker-switching pause (i.e., 1.1 + seconds, as if the switching pause + wait a fraction of a second for replay + repeat message were nicely calibrated to the system of verbal exchange).

I am suggesting that while the temporal integration and segregation of reference may contribute, along with kinesic and other cues, at an earlier stage to the child's ability to focus on the name of the referent object, this subsystem of timing will also come to be used as part of the turn-taking mechanisms of interactive speech, though it must, of course be reintegrated with other systems. More than one thing is being learned during the interactions Messer describes.

Messer has very usefully pointed to the complexity of the episodes of face-to-face interaction in child-caregiver pairs and has shown convincingly how several systems operate simultaneously to assist the child in comprehending what another says, specifically, to what another refers. He analyzes amplitude, repetition, rough concordance between naming and touching or holding the referent object, and temporal organization delimiting and integrating reference to one object. Examination of tone or pitch contour would probably provide still another distinctive cue for first mention of a referent in the naming-game format or the explore-these-objects format. The child might well deduce that object reference is always action oriented, gaze linked, simultaneous with action and proximal. If he does form this hypothesis, he will of course have to discard it as inadequate sometime early in the third year of life.

While I am in agreement with Messer that the early communicative situation i highly redundant, I am not so certain that any of the cues to reference or all of them taken together would assure comprehension of reference terms. They would not unless the child were aware in advance of the relevance of the message thus redundantly signaled. Here, again, I believe that we come close to the role of social interaction and social knowledge in language learning. I suggest that in order to utilize the redundancy of messages the child must be able to place the message in an intelligible context, that is, he must know that 'we are doing a naming game' or 'naming is what we are doing.' Or 'we are exploring a set of objects, one after the other.' From experience he will know that in this game he will have a chance to hold the object, and further that each object topic will be accompanied by a predication or comment. In recognizing the format (and thus we see the importance of behavioral routines), the child can come to utilize the multiple and delicate cues mothers provide to focus on a specific word, the label, or the name of the referent object.

The importance of this prior social knowledge of what we are doing becomes perhaps a bit clearer when we realize that although the same referent may be linguistically indicated several times in a sequence, or episode, mothers do not and cannot make it easy for the child to grasp the *linguistic means for referring*. To quote from one of the samples in Messer's (1980) article, "Oh, there's a super car. You like cars don't you? What are you going to do with it? Are you going to make it go?" (Mother brings the car to child, both hold, child retains car.) Mother rementions the object, indeed, but she does so in a different linguistic form, that is, car/cars/it/it, and the position of the term changes across messages as does its syntactic function. Of course, in the pronominal form, amplitude and pitch prominence are reduced.

It would seem that the changing forms of reference within episodes makes the task of learning the names of objects a difficult one. Perhaps, however, something other than object names is being learned. Perhaps discourse relations are being learned as well, for example, the conjoining of nominals as topic with successively shifting predication. The child already knows that referring requires a common focussing of attention. On that basis he can go on to build word-concept-object correspondences, as they are built up over episodes in the familiar formats he and his caregiver have constructed. Given some familiarity with a context and recognition of textual patterns that may cooccur in that context, what are the dynamics of the interpersonal exchanges that motivate the changes toward conventional linguistic expression? This question is the central concern of Dore's paper.

In searching out the underlying forces that work together to impel the development of language out of the communicative base of mother–child interaction and communion, Dore proposes an interpretative framework that might be characterized as a dialectic. On the one hand is the infant, actively engaged in constructing his physical and social world. Unlike Piaget's more independent, constructing infant, however, Dore's infant will construct his world from the affect-rich experiences with the mother. On the other hand is the adult, who enters into the infant's affective experiences, but who is imbued with the 'relatively natural conception of the world' which informs her reactions to the infant. The affective forces within the infant evolve with maturity and with experience in the dyadic setting from mere intent to act through intending to express to eventual intention to convey (something). The force within the adult is a compulsion to accountability in respect to both linguistic and nonlinguistic behavior on the part of the infant. Her communications with the infant mirror the forms that accountability must take. Schutz (1962) realized the intimate relation of language and social knowledge:

> The native language can be taken as a set of references which, in accordance with the relatively natural conception of the world as approved by the linguistic community, have predetermined what features of the world are worthy of being expressed, and therewith what qualities of these features and what relations among them deserve attention, and what typifications, conceptualizations, abstractions, generalizations, and idealizations are relevant for achieving typical results by typical means [p. 349].

From this perspective, learning a language is tantamount to acquiring a social identity.

The adult (A) has no choice, then, but to move the baby (B) toward membership in the community of which she is a part. She insists on his accountability. The baby (B), if he is to retain his essential communication with her, must move toward this accountability. Dore sees the beginnings of language in the first words, which are a joint product of the B's inchoate, or, at least, primitive intentions and A's principled interpretations and interventions in B's behavior. In this framework, "Word meanings are a consequence in B of what AB feel and do." As such, B's initially achieved word meanings are continuously subject to change as AB's activity shifts and as the context changes. The locus of the process of language development is thus, the relationship of AB and the process itself resides in the dialogue that A and B create between them.

The transactions that Dore sees as most critical are communicative "struggles." It is "anxiety" on the part of B that leads to the intention to communicate. Dore discovers the "origin of words . . . in the immediate context of affective conflict [p. 2]." Further, as B begins to grasp the meanings of his experiences, A must necessarily continue to revise what B has just learned in the direction of full accountability. Thus A breaches B's attempts at acquiring meaning and he must learn more about the word "so as to stabilize his linguistic cognition as a *defense* against the pervasive incursion of her breaches [p. 22]."

As the single or the primary motivational process, this reactive characterization fails to account fully for the frequently documented discrepancy between level of comprehension and production; for infant-initiated communicative acts, specifically, the early appearance of what often appears to be gratuitous rejection and negation of adult nurturant acts (Pea, 1980; Wenar, 1982); and for the infant-paced communicative achievements of the transition period.

The centrality of the affective dimension in language acquisition is not in question. The ubiquity of affective polarity, or positive and negative evaluation in both language and cognition, (Deese, 1973) is evidence of its importance. My view of the infant, however, is more positive than that of Dore's and would include more than one motivating force. As Dan Stern (1977) has shown, the infant's fascination with a world which is not that of his mother and himself, begins to intrude in the pure play of mother and infant at about 6 months. The child's interest in objects is followed and supported by mothers though some mothers may be disconcerted at losing the status of principal focus of infant attention. New kinds of games then become possible, along with the entrance of objective reference. Mother and infant now attend jointly to 'a thing out there' rather than solely to each other. This fascination is fed by and grows with increasing mobility and experiences of doing, handling, and having an effect on things. Two other forces or 'motives' in addition to those proposed by Dore impel the child. One is the biological determination to do what it can do, what it was designed to do: crawl, walk, run, explore, make sounds. That the child is determined, in more ways than one, is quite clear. One need only try to hold a squirming infant who "wants down" or feed one who is engrossed in banging a spoon. The exercise of component acts in the development of new levels of skill is, it appears, inherently pleasurable. Or differently stated, voluntary exercise of preliminary stages of an innate capacity seems to be its own reward—even though the state that it leads to may prove to be even more rewarding. We see this process operating in early babbling, in vocal play, and in the verbal practice play of the young child (Labov & Labov, 1978). We could call this motive the operation of the sense of efficacy, the delight in control of emerging capabilities. That, of course, is by no means an original suggestion. The motive operates on immediate satisfaction.

As to the second motive, it is a related one. As the determined toddler or crawling infant speeds off, he often looks back. As the child knocks a bottle off the high chair, he usually looks at the adult. I maintain that the infant is motivated by the recognition that he has an effect on the adult. Having an effect on others, and even more, having a predictable effect, is perhaps the major motive behind much social learning in young children. Thus, I see the infant motivated not primarily by anxiety or frustration, but rather, using the processes of contingency awareness of long standing and benefiting by the extremely prompt responses of adults to most of his directed actions, motivated by the desire to create an effect on the other. Production of phonetically stable forms has powerful and immediate effects, as do other gestures that the adult can interpret as (potentially) social behavior. The headshake that precedes and comes to accompany vocal, then verbal rejection is an example of what may begin as an involuntary gesture of aversion that becomes a voluntary communicative act by virtue of its effect.

The minimum requirement for the operation of such a 'motivational' system is the ability to perceive and discriminate the positive or negative valence of others' reactions; it should be able to operate over a number of different activities and over a number of different developmental stages; and it should be robust enough to operate in interactions with familiar adults other than the primary caregiver. If this view sounds somewhat like a theory of reinforcement for operant behavior, that is not a coincidence. One need not espouse a stimulus-response view of the nature of language acquisition, however, to advocate such a view of motivation. The view of the child as operant is not in conflict with the view of the child as operator and as active initiator of communicative events.

Young children seem to be spontaneously drawn to acquiring conventional uses of objects. The developmental history of object play reveals a steady progression toward conventional usage of objects and replicas. The advantage of the child's attempt to reproduce adult behaviors in play is that many of these attempts are intelligible (or, accountable) to the adult; the adult can acknowledge them as if they were meaningful and go on to expand or elaborate them. Most importantly, it is those, perhaps, barely intelligible acts that receive acknowledgment that will be shared and thus will be subject to further *joint* reference, repetition, perhaps elaboration.

Once acknowledged as intelligible, a playful act can then be used instrumentally to obtain adult attention and further interaction; this is just what we see young children doing. Once a child has held a toy telephone receiver up to his ear, looked at an adult, and has had his act immediately validated by smiles, and rounds of "Hi" or "Hello," he can and does use that telephoning gesture to obtain adult participation, if he finds himself ignored or excluded from an adult conversation. In such successful use of a socially meaningful behavior, which occurs in a playful mode, the infant comes to experience his own effectiveness and control. He may also have acquired another use for the powerful greeting form, "Hi."

It is consonant with the framework that Dore has adopted in his chapter to recognize that the forces toward accountability that inform the mothers' interpretations and interventions in the infants' behavior also operate on the investigator whose in-depth interpretive work is ultimately indexical. (An actual participant in a communicative episode has an additional motive for making sense of the proceedings beyond the motives that shape the investigator's understanding. The participant as potential next speaker must follow the proceedings *in order to* insert his turn at speaking or acting at the appropriate moment in the temporal sequence with literally split-second timing, and his turn must display his understanding of what is transpiring.) Although the observer/investigator necessarily shares in the relatively natural conception of communicative activity, this is not necessarily a reason for questioning the 'objectivity' of such interpretive work; rather, it might be advantageous to take note of the important insights into the construction of social behavior that this approach offers and of the view it provides of the dynamic interactions of interpersonal behavior with the text and context of talk.

The process of temporal sequencing and alignment and the process of recursive, prospective-retrospective analysis are of particular interest here in that they contribute to our perception of the textual features of what we accept as episodes of interpersonal communication. For example, the tentative identification of a gesture (vocal, verbal, or kinesic) as functioning as a "preventable" or as a "prohibitable" constrains us toward interpretation of a subsequent gesture or utterance as functioning as a "preventative" or as a "prohibitative," respectively. Next moves (and not only the next contiguous move—see, for instance, round 6 of Example 10.1) are inspected in light of the expectations set up by the first tentative categorization of a move. If the expected next move is not to be found, we would then look for evidence that the participants had marked its noticeable absence. It is also possible that the observer (or participant) might first encounter what he takes to be a "prohibitive" and would then scan the prior moves for what might function as the antecedent "prohibitable." In fact, a decision to identify a strip of communicative behavior as an episode depends in part on the ability to detect an accountable linkage between alternating moves of the participants throughout some portion of the strip and failure to detect such linkage at some other point in the strip, which failure would lead us to identification of that point as an episode boundary.

It is clear from Dore's examples (as well as from his discussion of them) and from some of the work that Messer reports that investigations of partners' reciprocal influence during the transition to linguistic communication and studies of the changes in the infants' communicative expressions cannot afford to neglect the situated flow of interactive exchange. Both the adult and the baby behaviors reference, by both linguistic and nonlinguistic signals, not only what is done at that moment, but what has been done and what the participants expect will occur. Often by linguistic markers, even by explicit reference, for example, emphatic stress on 'leaf' in round 2 and the mother's reference to her verbal action in round 2 in both round 3 and round 4 (Dore's Example 10.1), the moves and exchanges display their role in and their dependence on recognizable, and probably repeatable, units of interaction that extend beyond the utterance or the sentence.

REFERENCES

Bullowa, M. (Ed.), *Before speech: The beginning of interpersonal communication.* Cambridge, Mass.: Cambridge University Press, 1979.

Crystal, D., & Davy, D. *Investigating English style.* Bloomington, Ind.: Indiana University Press, 1969.

Deese, J. Cognitive structure and affect in language. In P. Pliner, L. Krames, & T. Alloway (Eds.), *Communication and affect: Language and thought.* New York: Academic Press, 1973.

Garvey, C., & Rae, G. The temporal organization of mother-child and child-child conversation. Manuscript In preparation.

Gopnik, A. Review of M. Bullowa (Ed.) *Before speech. Journal of Child Language,* 1981, *8,* 495–499.

Halliday, M. Development of texture in child language. In T. Meyers (Ed.), *The development of conversation and discourse.* Edinburgh: Edinburgh University Press, 1979.

Lenneberg, E. What is meant by knowing a language? In P. Pliner, L. Krames, & T. Alloway, (Eds.), *Communication and affect*. New York: Academic Press, 1973.

Labov, W., & Labov, T. The phonetics of *cat* and *mama*. *Language*, 1978, *54*, 816–852.

Messer, D. The episodic structure of maternal speech to young children. *Journal of Child Language*, 1980, *7*, 29–40.

Pea, R. The development of negation in early child language. In D. Olson, (Ed.), *The social foundations of language and thought*. New York: W. W. Norton & Co., 1980.

Schutz, A. Collected papers I: The problems of social reality, The Hague: Nijhoff, 1962.

Stern, D. *The first relationship*. Cambridge, Mass.: Harvard University Press, 1977.

Stern, D., Spieker, S., Barnett, R., & MacKain, K. The prosody of maternal speech: Infant age and context related changes. *Journal of Child Language,* (in press).

Wenar, C. On negativism. *Human Development*, 1982, *25*, 1–23.

12 Implications of the Transition Period for Early Intervention

Phyllis Levenstein
Adelphi University

Although syntax was the most prominent aspect of language studied in the mid-60s, it was the contribution of such scholars as Brown, Bruner, Cassirer, Sapir, and Vygotsky to the *semantics* of language which helped to form the theoretical base for the Verbal Interaction Project's Mother–Child Home Program. Impelled by the school problems of low income children, which tend to perpetuate the cycle of poverty, we began the development and research of the Mother–Child Home Program with a pilot program in 1965 (Levenstein & Sunley, 1968). We believed that an intervention program to tackle the problem should start very early and take place in the home, at the very roots of cognitive socialization. We at the Verbal Interaction Project (VIP) were convinced that the cognitive socialization leading eventually to adequate school performance begins with the exchange of language in the family. Indeed, its probable basis is in the oldest long term human dialogue in the world—the exchange of non-vocal and vocal signals, of labels, and of language symbols between a mother and her young child, within the context of their perhaps equally ancient dyadic participation in interactive play.

For Sapir (1921/1962) language played a critical role in cognitive development. Because language, as he pointed out, is an easily utilized, vocal actualization of the human ability to abstract and symbolize reality, he believed that human language is a perfect symbol system, superseding its communication function. His guess was that humans had developed it through their vocal summarization of abstractions derived from numerous concrete perceptual—conceptual encounters with the real world. So unique among animals is this human accomplishment that a philosopher, Cassirer (1944) following Sapir's lead, suggested that man be redefined as an "animal symbolicum" rather than as an "animal rationale."

In the first two decades after publication of Cassirer's essay, empirical support began to accumulate for Sapir's and Cassirer's beliefs about the primary function of language as a symbol system. Vygotsky (1962) presented evidence for the efficiency of language as a conceptual summarizer of the common traits which people abstract from unlike experiences. Parallel to Vygotsky's work, Brown (1958) had noted that language, which forms an inventory of its culture, is taught to the culture's children in the "original world game" whose players are parent and child. Bruner commented, in a book reporting work done with his co-authors (Bruner, Oliver, & Greenfield, 1966), that "What Roger Brown calls the original world game ends up by being the human thinking game." Bruner's (1966) book supported his (1964) hypothesis that the "cognitive coin" consisting of labels for specific human experiences—coins exchanged in the verbal interaction of mother–child discourse—add up to the golden coins of human concepts (Bruner, 1964).

Other investigators in the same decade were discovering that the number of such verbal interaction "coins" in the home, like other coins of the realm, was related to the socioeconomic status of the family. Bernstein (1965) was the first investigator to point this out, based on his sociological research in Britain. Hess and Shipman (1965) found that black middle class and low income families in America differed along a similar socioeconomic class dimension. Their memorable conclusion was that "the meaning of deprivation is the deprivation of meaning."

Their work in the United States, along with that of many others such as Deutsch (1965), and along with reviews like those of Bloom (1964) and Freeberg and Payne (1967), provided a consistent explanation for the frequently observed relationship between children's school competencies and socioeconomic status. As Freeberg and Payne concluded: "The sheer amount of verbal activity and . . . books and other devices that supply a wide range of opportunity for language usage are the consistent predictors of verbal and problem solving abilities [p. 85]."

These predictors were found more often in middle class than in low income homes. They seemed to be part of middle class parents' casual, unplanned interactions with their preschoolers. They came, therefore, to be called the "hidden curriculum" of the middle class home.

The strong relationship of children's preschool and school competencies to family verbal interaction, and the latter's relationship to family socioeconomic status, have continued to be explored and demonstrated by many investigators since those earlier findings. Notable recent examples using a variety of measures and subjects are to be found in Bradley and Caldwell, 1976; Clarke-Stewart, 1973; Clarke-Stewart, Vander Stoep, and Killian, 1979; Elardo, Bradley and Caldwell, 1977; Laosa, 1980; Nelson, 1973; Ninio, 1980; Ramey, Farran, and

Campbell, 1979; Schacter, 1979; Tulkin and Kagan, 1972; and Van Doorninck, Caldwell, Wright, and Frankenberg, 1981.

In response to the social problem posed by the resulting SES inequities in the children's vulnerability to school disadvantage, many investigators of the 1960s began to devise and evaluate verbally-oriented preschool intervention programs for low income children. Their research projects were usually conducted independently but tended to share a common empirical background, similar to the one just described, often with the addition of Hunt's influential 1961 review, and with the goal of aiding low income preschool children through an enriched cognitive curriculum. For center-based programs, these investigators were, principally, Kuno Beller, Carl Bereiter, Bettye Caldwell, Martin and Cynthia Deutsch, Susan Gray, Rick Heber, Merle Karnes, Francis Palmer, and David Weikart. Their programs were uniformly excellent, each in its own way, although their methods and even philosophies differed, sometimes drastically. The programs almost always produced promising short-term results in terms of children's cognitive outcomes. However, early follow-up studies for most of them were either equivocal or showed fading effects.

Three early intervention investigators of the mid-60s believed that prevention of school disadvantage should occur in the home, where the "deprivation of meaning" appeared to have its sources. They were Ira Gordon, Phyllis Levenstein, and Earl Schaefer. Without awareness of the others' work, each of these investigators devised a home-based program which was, in effect, a version of the "hidden curriculum" of the middle class family, since each incorporated goals related to the verbal stimulation found in so many studies to be antecedent to children's school competencies. These programs were first described in publications by Gordon (1969), Levenstein (1970), and Schaefer (1969). Except for Levenstein's program, the early follow-up results showed fade outs of short-term program effects.

However, a recent meta-analysis (Lazar & Darlington, 1982) which combined later follow-up data on most of the programs developed and researched in the 1960s, whether center-based or home-based, reversed the disappointing early follow-up trends, by demonstrating significant "sleeper" effects.

Of all the programs of the 1960's, Levenstein's is one of the few to have continued its existence, and to do so in exactly the same format in which it had been researched. It also continues to use the same program name: The Mother–Child Home Program.

It seemed to us, in developing the program out of the theoretical and empirical framework cited earlier, that one of the most critical phases of the mother–child dialogue and thus the time for intervention, is the latter part of that very period of transition from prelinguistic to linguistic communication which is the subject of this book. Both Cassirer (1944) and Vygotsky (1962) commented that the appearance of language begins the period when the infant can be said to join the human race. The baby leaves infancy, passes from the emotion laden, experienced-bound non-verbal communication which may well be essentially infra-human, into his rightful heritage: the uniquely human capacity for spontaneous symbolization through language (Sapir, 1921/1962).

These ideas of the 1960s, which were so fundamental to the Mother–Child Home Program, are the psycholinguistic clichés of the 1980s. But it is evident that at least two of the still-fresh contributions of the late 70s and the early 80s are also singularly relevant to the Mother–Child Home Program. These are: (1) the recognition of developmental psycholinguistics as a separate category for empirical research; and (2) the application of "pragmatics" to the study of children's language development. It has now become apparent that the very young child's presuppositions within the dyadic dialogue can hardly be voiced or understood without reference to the common situational context of both mother and child. The Program enriches that context to enlarge the child's repertoire of interesting referents through books and toys that stimulate verbal interaction. The Program also influences, and is influenced by, a developmental variable that is the subject of another recent psycholinguistic observation. This is that the child's presuppositions are colored by the course of his or her cognitive development. For example, Ochs points out (1979), that there is now documentation of the child's increasing sensitivity to the perspective of the viewer, away from reliance on the immediate situational context, and toward greater reliance on non-situational knowledge.

The infant's emergence into linguistic communication and thought, occurring from about 18 months to about 30 months of age, is paralleled in that transition period by a rapid, almost explosive, unfolding of a whole repertoire of sensorimotor, social, and affective developmental skills which turn him from a baby to a "toddler." The saccharinity of this label, the only English one available for this stage, is matched only by its inaccuracy. Two-year-olds don't so much toddle as race from one new wonder to another. But no matter how much they explore, they usually return to home base, and to the most stable person there— the mother. Attachment to mother (or whoever is the primary stable nurturer) appears to be at its height at this stage.

All of these developmental concepts and events, including other perhaps dimly perceived ideas which would be explicated in the 80s, converged to suggest the Program's *locus* (home), the *agent* (mother), the *curriculum* (teaching labels for multiple instances to build into symbolized concepts), the curriculum *materials* (self-motivating toys and books), and the *home visitor* ("Toy Demonstrator").

The necessity for the dyadic dialogue to occur in a pragmatic *context* comprehensible and motivating to both mother and toddler was also fundamental to the Program. However, the concept was grasped only intuitively when it was incorporated into the Program's creation in 1965. It remained for developmental psycholinguists many years later to expand on the influence of context and to demonstrate it empirically. This is shown with special clarity in a recent report whose erudition is in sharp contrast to the somewhat naive approach of the VIP in 1967 and yet whose title echoes some of the Mother–Child Home Program's most basic assumptions: *Language and context* (Bates, 1976).

In brief, the Mother–Child Home Program (MCHP) encourages mothers' verbalized play with their own children and gives them the equipment (toys and books) to do it. The situational context for the Program was constructed around play and playthings because of the success of a toy in eliciting verbal interaction between mothers and their 4-year olds in Hess and Shipman's study of maternal teaching styles (1965). That this use of toys was not simply another cliche of the 60s was demonstrated by the central, and charming, role of hand puppets in a more recent investigation (Bates, 1976) of young Italian children's knowledge of the polite forms of their language. However, the Program added to the toys another even more important ingredient: picture books, developmentally sequenced to match the children's increasing age in the program. Thus, the program became explicitly a pre-literacy method to prepare the child for later school-related books and for enjoying their own selections of books.

The MCHP has been described in detail elsewhere (e.g., Levenstein, 1977). It consists of 92 semi-weekly, half-hour Home Sessions spread over 2 school years, conducted by home visitors called "Toy Demonstrators." The first MCHP year is called "Program I;" the second year is "Program II." The Toy Demonstrators are trained to model for the mother, rather than to directly teach, verbal interaction with the child. It is parent education, with the purpose of guiding the mother to enhance the child's acquisition of concepts and social-emotional development. The interaction centers around commercially available toys and books which are permanently assigned to the child. The Toy Demonstrator, after involving the mother early in the Home Session, gradually fades into the background; the mother is free to adopt the modeled behavior, or not, as she wishes.

The 46 Home Sessions during each year roughly follow, for both Program I (first year) and Program II (second year), the local school calendar for a total of about 7 months from October to May. Altogether the program requires about 23 hours of the dyad's time with a Toy Demonstrator each year, aside from the time mothers might spend outside of the sessions playing and reading with their children each day (suggested but not stressed to the mothers). The cost of giving low income mothers the materials, and access to the techniques, of the hidden cognitive curriculum of many middle income families, is currently estimated at about $700 a year for each child. The cost can be kept relatively low because it includes the free labor manpower of the mothers acting as their children's main teachers, and the free working space contributed by the participating families.

In 1967, the first full research year, social workers with masters' degrees were the Toy Demonstrators. After that, the Toy Demonstrators have been paid former mother-participants, with high school education, and unpaid women volumteers, usually college educated. They are trained together in an initial 8 session Training Workshop, and in weekly group supervisory conferences through the program year. Twelve books and 11 toys, selected on 26 explicit criteria by VIP staff, are given to the mother for the child each year, in a planned weekly sequence of increasingly complex curriculum materials. The Toy Demonstrators model verbal interaction techniques, and interpersonal behavior functional to learning, focused on the toys and books (Verbal Interaction Stimulus Materials, or "VISM"). The structured cognitive curriculum is spelled out in a set of Guide Sheets, one of which is prepared for each VISM. The curriculum consists of a list of concepts and behaviors which remains the same on every Guide Sheet but are illustrated and elaborated differently by each new toy or book.

The chief lesson conveyed to the Toy Demonstrator in supervision is that the program is aimed primarily at the mother rather than at the child; that the main and enduring responsibility for the child must be the mother's, not the Toy Demonstrator's; and therefore, that the ability to eliminate her active participation from Home Sessions is the Toy Demonstrator's best sign of success.

Newer home based programs have borrowed from the MCHP, but some features still seem to be unique to the MCHP: (1) an explicit, written program procedure that does not depend on special staff skills or charisma; (2) an explicit, written, 2-year curriculum provided in small, comprehensible bits; (3) home visitors of minimal experience and education, trained to *model* interaction techniques and not to teach didactically or to counsel; (4) permanent assignment of a carefully chosen set of commercially available curriculum materials (books and toys); (5) choice of the transition period to address the mother–child pair as a dyadic social system; and (6) explicit precautions to protect the family from Program intrusiveness.

It is perhaps these features that account for the Program's popularity with children and mothers, and with sponsors of program relications throughout the country. The popularity with families is evidenced by very high rates of mothers' acceptance of offers to participate in it (close to 100%) and of home session appointments kept by mothers (about 85%) as well as by relatively low attrition (about 25% over 2 years); and with Sponsors, by 81 MCHP adoptions (replications) in 16 states, and Bermuda, over 10 years. The method is described in full detail in training manuals used in replications of what is now called the Model Program and in such publications as Levenstein, 1975 and 1977.

Twelve years of evaluative experimental research with about 700 subjects entering in annual cohorts at the VIP significantly supported our theory-based guesses about what would constitute an effective program, after solution of research methodology problems indicated in Madden, Levenstein, and Levenstein (1976). In 1978 the MCHP was nationally validated by the Joint Dissemination Review Panel (U.S. Office of Education and National Institute of Education) for having demonstrated its effectiveness in preventing educational disadvantage in low income children. Third graders who had had the program showed normal reading and arithmetic scores, and had relatively few school problems or grade failures. Mothers in the Program demonstrated markedly increased verbal interactive behavior which lasted at least into the child's kindergarten years (the last point measured).

Having accomplished its mission to develop a program validated as effective, the VIP is now chiefly engaged in helping agencies throughout the country implement the Program and continuing research of the links between parenting in preschool years and child's school age competencies. Our aim is to investigate whether there are demonstrable correlations between specific maternal behaviors in the child's early years and the child's later ability to cope with school and other tasks. In other words, we are tracing the parent–child network which we postulated would be built by the Mother–Child Home Program.

It seemed reasonable to assume that in a supportive parent–child network, the parents' behavior would be antecedent to the child's even allowing for dynamic parent–child interactive patterns. This was the hypothesis on which was based one of the Program's short-term major aims: To foster the interactive, and particularly the verbally interactive, elements of the mother's behavior toward her child. A necessary research corollary to that aim was to find or develop a reliable, valid measure of its directly observed accomplishment. Since no such measures could be found already developed in the Program's early years, we constructed instruments to measure and quantify some of the less elusive elements of maternal interactive behavior. One of these is "Parent and Child Together" (PACT), and the other is "Maternal Interactive Behavior" (MIB).

PACT's development began in 1970. It has been used with every annual cohort since then as both a measuring instrument and a teaching device for Toy Demonstrators. The Toy Demonstrators rated Program mothers from Home Session observations on 20 items along four parenting dimensions: Nurturance, Encouragement of Autonomy, Verbal Interaction, and Control. The Program mothers showed a significant pre-post difference in their PACT scores. However, no conclusions could be drawn from this, since the non-Program, Comparison mothers could not be observed at home to be measured in the same way, in order to conduct the more important between-group comparisons.

It took us until 1973 to devise the MIB, a maternal-behavior measurement method and instrument by which Program and non-Program mothers could be compared with each other. We videotaped at our office Program and non-Program mothers in 10 minutes of play with their almost 4-year-old children, after the Program dyads had completed the MCHP. The video taping took place at the time of the child's post-Program cognitive evaluation at the VIP, a regular event for all cohorts. The videotape was then rated on the MIB along 10 dimensions of maternal interactive behavior.

The 10 MIB items were "program referenced"—that is, the maternal interactive behaviors were selected from maternal behaviors explicitly promoted by the Program's curriculum. The selection was made by the Program's author (the author also of this chapter) on the basis of two major considerations: the intrinsic importance of the behavior, and the liklihood of a particular behavior's emerging clearly during 10 minutes of videotaped mother–child interaction. No upper limit was set on the number of items to be so selected. Theoretically, the selection could have contained 58 positive maternal behaviors. In actuality, only nine such behaviors could be identified as filling both criteria, and these comprised the nine "Postive Behavior" items of the MIB. A tenth item of "Negative Behavior" was added, after some pilot testing of what kinds of negative behaviors mothers were likely to demonstrate in a 10 minute videotape. As a more general VIP staff effort, the 10 items were then incorporated into an instrument for rating mothers on them, the "Maternal Interactive Behavior," or MIB.

An equally important task, along with the selection of MIB items and developing them into an instrument, was to ascertain that the ratings had high interrater reliability so that they would not be influenced by differences among raters. This was assured by two teams of MIB Raters producing Pearson coefficients of .96 and .97, respectively, when their total scores of the videotaped frequencies of MIB items for 39 mothers were correlated with each other.

The 10 MIB items are listed, along with examples of each, in Fig. 12.1. The MIB Rater was instructed to view the videotape *four* times, tallying the raw frequencies of the mother's behavior in the items listed for each viewing, and then adding the tallies for Items 1 through 9 to reach a "Positive Behavior Total Score," and for Item 10 to reach for a "Negative Behavior Score."

The setting for the MIB videotaping was semi-naturalistic: A rather bare playroom furnished mainly with a child's table and two chairs for mother and child; toys on the table; and a videotape camera on one corner, with the recorder operated and monitored in a room next to the playroom via a cable (to reduce reactive effects). Two toys were pre-arranged on the table in a standard way: (1) a stylized wooden freight train composed of two cars and a locomotive detached from each other, each of different colors, with hook-eye links; and (2) a Form Board puzzle surrounded by its 8 colored forms of 4 differing shapes (circle, square, oblong, triangle) which are made to fit on backgrounds of the same or contrasting colors.

The mother was invited to participate when the evaluation appointment was made and was reminded by the Driver who brought her and the child to the evaluation that the child would be videotaped playing with some toys. *If the mother objected, the MIB procedure was terminated at this point.* (Each year from 7% to 12% of the mothers did object and were not videotaped.) Otherwise, when the mother and child arrived at the playroom, the Driver explained: "This is the playroom and toys we talked about in the car. Here's a chair for (child) and one for you. (Child) may play with the toys after I leave you, and, of course, you may help in any way you like. That video camera (pointing) will take the pictures. I'll turn it on just before I leave you and (child). I'll turn it off when I come back. I'll be back in 10 minutes."

FIGURE 12.1
Maternal Interactive Behavior (MIB) Items and Examples

MIB Item	Examples
1. GIVES SPECIFIC LABEL INFORMATION. For specific nouns or proper noun names, whether object, person, abstraction, etc., *except* for "color," "shape," "number," "one."	"This is a PUZZLE."
2. GIVES SPECIFIC COLOR INFORMATION.	"The big BLUE circle."
3. VERBALIZES ACTIONS, such as turning, fitting, matching, linking, building, etc. Describes any ongoing manipulation. Omit forms of "to be" but include "must," "know," "see," "have," "need," "try," "do," "hear."	"You can't FIT the big blue circle into that puzzle."
4. GIVES SPECIFIC NUMBER AND SHAPE INFORMATION. Includes "another," "first," "last," "more," "less," "other," but NOT "how many?".	"This big blue CIRCLE is different from MANY others."
5. QUESTIONS, OR SOLICITS INFORMATION OTHER THAN "YES" OR "NO." Stimulates child to verbalize information.	"What shape is this puzzle piece?"
6. VOCALIZES PRAISE. Communicates vocal pleasure with child or child's behavior by vocalization, NOT tone of voice.	"Um-hmm!" "There we go!"
7. STIMULTES DIVERGENT OR FANTASY USE OF TOY. Encourages child to use toy differently from obvious purpose, or as part of make believe. May be verbal or non-verbal.	"Let's ROLL this big blue circle." "Doesn't this puzzle LOOK LIKE A FACE?"
8. SMILES OR MAKES OTHER POSITIVE GESTURE. Demonstrates communication of warmth for 3 seconds.	SMILES in any direction or HUGS child.
9. REPLIES TO CHILD'S VOCALIZATION. Within 3 seconds of child's vocal utterance, expands on, affirms or otherwise *verbally* follows child's vocalization.	"Good." "Yes." "It *is* like your own ball."
10. DOES NOT REPLY TO CHILD'S VOCALIZATION. Does not answer within 3 seconds.	

TABLE 12.1
Means and Standard Deviations[a] of MIB Items at Posttest (1978) as a Function of Treatment Status

					MIB Item and Total Scores							
Treatment Status	Item 1 Gives Labels	Item 2 Gives Colors	Item 3 Describes Actions	Item 4 Gives Numbers, Shapes	Item 5 Asks Information	Item 6 Praises[a]	Item 7 Aids Divergence	Item 8 Smiles	Item 9 Replies to Child	Item[b] 10 No Reply	Total[c] Positive Score	Total[d] MIB Score
MCHP N = 25	37.24 (19.68)	17.88 (12.72)	95.00 (27.07)	18.48 (16.96)	20.68 (12.92)	9.76 (6.15)	15.76 (17.76)	8.48 (5.80)	54.92 (20.65)	11.60 (7.33)	278.20 (87.85)	266.6 (91.85)
Control N = 23	17.96 (7.58)	20.00 (19.52)	67.83 (27.95)	6.26 (7.25)	11.65 (12.57)	6.04 (5.71)	4.78 (6.40)	5.09 (6.32)	34.87 (15.81)	18.00 (11.25)	174.48 (175.25)	156.48 (82.14)
Significance Level	<.001	NS	<.01	<.01	<.05	<.05	<.01	NS	<.001	<.05	<.001	<.001

[a]The number in parentheses is the standard deviation.
[b]Item 10 is the negative item.
[c]Total Positive Score = Σ Items 1 to 9.
[d]Total MIB Score = Σ Items 1 to 9—Item 10 ("negative item").

The Driver answered the mother's possible questions about procedures by saying pleasantly, "That's up to you."

The Driver then turned on the camera and left, shutting the door behind her. After 10 minutes she returned and shut off the camera. Provision was made for the mother to view the videotape at a later date, if she so wished.

The MIB was a simple, even simplistic, instrument whose scores were the frequencies of the 10 program-related maternal behaviors (Fig. 12.1), easily observable on the videotapes, and their summative scores. The scoring was by raters who were blind to the treatment status of the mother–child pairs.

The mean MIB scores of three different annual cohorts of Program mothers were markedly superior to those of the non-Program mothers immediately after completion of the 2-year program for each cohort. Table 12.1 shows the 1978 posttest MIB scores for 91% of the 1976 cohort, with levels of significance (determined by analysis of variance) entered for the between-group differences on every item as well as total score. The MIB superiority of the Program mothers is reflected in the Total Positive Score (Item 10, "No reply" excluded) and in every Item Score except Item 2, "Gives colors," and Item 8, "Smiles or makes other positive gesture." The differences were significant on all other Items, even on the non-verbal Item 6, "Vocalizes praise."

To illustrate the post-Program contrast between Program and non-Program mothers on the MIB, two transcripts of the same videotape segment are presented here, one for a Program mother and one for a non-Program mother, both from the same subject cohort. Each transcript contains all words and sounds vocalized by the mother during Minutes Three and Four of the 10 minute videotape. The child's speech is represented by the usual ". . ." convention.

PROGRAM MOTHER

Now, what are these colors? . . . Show me some colors that are not on the train. Do you have any colors that are not on the train? . . .

What other color? . . . Look careful, that's on the train. See there . . . Show me one color, two colors that are not on the train . . . Two colors, that's right, where's the other? . . . Right. What color is that? . . . Right, okay.

What you want to do now? Let's take them fast . . . I'm gonna scramble them up, and see can you get them right. Okay. Let me mix them up. Okay. . . . Now get the right ones . . . Hurry up, let's see how fast you can go . . . I'm gonna race you. Ah Ah. Hurry up. Right . . . Ooh he works fast . . . MMMM . . . You are a winner. I'm gonna do you yourself.

Okay let's play with the train for a while. Robert, what else can you do with the train? What else can you do? What does the people carry on the train? . . . No, not that . . . What other purpose, does this type of train . . . you can't ride in it, but what can you do? Can't you carry things on it? Do you have anything to put in this

TABLE 12.2

Means and Standard Deviations[a] of MIB Items at Follow-Up (1980) as a Function of Treatment Status

MIB Item and Total Scores

Treatment Status	Item 1 Gives Labels	Item 2 Gives Colors	Item 3 Describes Actions	Item 4 Gives Numbers, Shapes	Item 5 Asks Information	Item 6 Praises[a]	Item 7 Aids Divergence	Item 8 Smiles	Item 9 Replies to Child	Item[b] 10 No Reply	Total[c] Positive Score	Total[d] MIB Score
MCHP N = 19	36.90 (26.10)	13.53 (17.21)	88.47 (37.46)	12.74 (11.54)	21.63 (17.68)	7.00 (6.50)	9.37 (11.42)	2.74 (2.73)	48.74 (23.22)	12.32 (9.17)	241.11 (109.82)	228.79 (114.09)
Control N = 18	14.78 (12.19)	4.72 (4.35)	58.83 (26.77)	5.22 (4.65)	9.50 (10.07)	3.28 (5.51)	3.83 (5.18)	2.56 (3.22)	32.11 (18.66)	17.89 (9.76)	134.81 (60.50)	116.94 (62.82)
Significance Level	.01	.05	.05	.05	.05	NS	NS	NS	.05	.05	.01	.01

[a]The number in parentheses is the standard deviation.
[b]Item 10 is the negative item.
[c]Total Positive Score = Items 1 to 9.
[d]Total MIB Score = Σ Items 1 to 9—Item 10 ("negative item").

214

type of train? . . . You know this type of train it carries wood, it carries direct, it carries, umm, refrigeration boxes for fruit and things like that. Did you know that? . . .

And this type of train they don't have people ride on it. It's passengers are going to particular places. They use it to haul different things . . . Okay. Let her go.

NON-PROGRAM MOTHER

You want another one? . . . There are no more, just those three . . . Mhmm.

Come here, Ellen . . . Come here . . . Tell me what color is this? What color is this? And this color? What color? . . . This color? This? What is this one? What is this? This is red. Ha.

That's people? Where they going to? Where they go to? . . . Kentucky Fried Chicken. Mhh? . . . They like it? Kentucky Fried Chicken is delicious right?

But if it don't fit you can leave it over there. It is okay. Okay. Mhmm. Mhmm.

The dramatic difference in the amount of each mother's vocal expression for this videotape segment is evident at a glance. The Program mother's superority in volume alone is matched by the amount of information she gives, by her encouragement of the child's imagination, and by the number and variety of responses she tries to elicit from the child.

However, the reader will perhaps note that both mothers demonstrate syntactic errors to approximately the same degree. Correction of mothers' pronunciation and grammar is not part of the MCHP method. Our belief is that synatax has no appreciable relevance to the role of the mother's verbal interaction in the very young child's cognitive growth. No evidence has emerged to challenge this assumption, either in our own research or in that of others.

The MIB procedure was once more utilized with 88% of the 1976 cohort in a follow-up evaluation, when the children were in mid-kindergarten. The follow-up results are to be seen in Table 12.2, "Mean and Total Positive Scores for Maternal Interactive Behavior (MIB) at Kindergarten Follow-up." The Program mothers' marked superiority remained for the Total Positive Score and seven out of the 10 items. This time Program mothers were superior on Item 2, "Gives colors" but lost their statistical superiority on Item 6 ("Vocalizes praise") and Item 7 ("Aids divergence"). They still showed no statistical superiority on Item 8, "Smiles or makes other positive gesture."

A further important follow-up finding was that the correlation between the post-program MIB scores and the follow-up MIB scores yielded a markedly significant coefficient, .68, $p < .001$. This supported the conclusion from the information in Table 12.1 and Table 12.2. Not only did the Program have an immediate positive effect on maternal interactive behavior, but this effect was maintained for almost 2 years.

These MIB findings were essentially part of our evaluative research of short-term and long range effectiveness of the Mother–Child Home Program. Our next research step, which we have already begun, will bring us into the realm of basic research. We are attempting to trace the strands of a possible supportive parent–child network, postulated when the Program was first conceived, by exploring the relationships between specific maternal interactive behaviors in preschool and kindergarten years, and children's specific competencies at school age. The children's variables to be related to maternal behavior are reading and arithmetic achievement; Stanford-Binet IQ; and 20 social-emotional behaviors grouped under Social Responsibility, Task Orientation, and Self-Confidence. Those for mothers are the 10 MIB items (Fig. 12.1).

Through simple correlations and through step-wise multiple regressions, we will put one of the most basic assumptions underlying the Mother–Child Home Program to the test. This is that the mothers' positive interactions, and especially verbal interactions, with the child in the transition period will promote the development of his or her coping skills in school years. Empirical support for this hypothesis will support also our use of the transition period for early intervention.

However, we have become aware that we may encounter in this task at least one pair of formidable methodological obstacles. On the one hand, the crudity of our measures, in both content and scoring (especially the MIB), omits completely the kinds of contextual considerations which have enriched the field of developmental psycholinguistics, and are to be found in studies of pragmatics by such authors as Bates (1976). On the other hand, the lack of reliability between correlations of parent and toddler behavior across different samples has been recently pointed out all too clearly by Clarke–Stewart and her colleagues (1979). How we will steer between Scylla and Charibdys is one of the challenges in our current quest for the predictive links between early parental verbal behavior and later child competencies.

Nevertheless, the research has already produced significant empirical evidence for the effectiveness of a theory-based early intervention program conducted during the little child's transition from prelinguistic to linguistic modes of communication and thought. It appears to validate the theories of the giants on whose shoulders we stand and of the developmental psycholinguists whose ideas were elaborated long after the Program arranged its first Home Session with a mother–child dyad.

ACKNOWLEDGMENTS

The current follow-up research reported in this chapter is funded by National Institute of Education through NIE Grant No. G 80-0042. Previous research and the Mother-Child Home Program, also cited, were principally supported by the Marion R. Ascoli Fund;

Carnegie Corporation of New York; Children's Bureau, U.S. Department of H.E.W.; Education Commision of the States; Foundation for Child Development; General Mills Foundation; W. T. Grant Foundation; Irving B. Harris and Harris Foundations; Joe and Emily Lowe Foundation; National Institute of Mental Health, U.S. Dept. of H.E.W.; North Shore Unitarian Society Veatch Program; Rockefeller Brothers Fund; and the U.S. Department of Education.

REFERENCES

Bates, E. *Language and context*. New York: Academic Press, 1976.

Bernstein, B. A Socio-linguistic approach to social learning. In J. Gould (Ed.), *Penguin survey of the social sciences*. Baltimore, Md.: Penguin, 1965.

Bloom, B. B. *Stability and change in human characteristics*. New York: Wiley, 1964.

Bradley, R. H., & Caldwell, B. M. The relation of infants' home environments to mental test performance at fifty-four months: A follow-up study. *Child Development*. 1976, *47*, 1172–1174.

Brown, R. *Words and things*. Glencoe, Illinois: The Free Press, 1958.

Bruner, J. S. The course of cognitive growth. *American Psychologist*. 1964, *19*, 1–15.

Bruner, J. S., Oliver, R., & Greenfield, P. *Studies in cognitive growth*. New York: Wiley, 1966.

Cassirer, E. *An essay on man*. New Haven, Ct.: Yale University Press, 1944.

Clarke–Stewart, K. A. Interactions between mothers and their young children: Characteristics and consequences. *Monographs of the Society for Research in Child Development, 1973, 38* (6–7, Serial No. 153).

Clarke–Stewart, K. A., VanderStoep, L., & Killian, G. Analysis and replication of mother–child relations at 2-years of age. *Child Development*, 1979, *50*, 777–793.

Deutsch, M. The role of social class in language development and cognition. *American Journal of Orthopsychiatry*, 1965, 35, 78–88.

Elardo, R., Bradley, R., & Caldwell, B. M. A longitudinal study of the relation of infants' home environments to language development at age three. *Child Development*, 1977, *48*, 595–603.

Freeberg, N. E., & Payne, D. T. Parental influence on cognitive development in early children: A review. *Child Development*, 1967, *38*, 66–87.

Gordon, I. J. Stimulation via parent education. *Children*, 1969, *16*, 57–59.

Hess, R., & Shipman, V. C. Early experience and the socialization of cognitive modes in children. *Child Development*, 1965, *36*, 869–886.

Hunt, J. McV. *Intelligence and experience*. New York: Ronald Press, 1961.

Laosa, L. Maternal teaching strategies in Chicano and Anglo-American families: The influence of culture and education on maternal behavior. *Child Development*, 1980, *51*, 759–765.

Lazar, I., & Darlington, R. Lasting effects of early education. *Monographs of the Society for Research in Child Development*, 1982, *47*, (Serial No. 195).

Levenstein, P. Cognitive growth in preschoolers through verbal interaction with their mothers. *American Journal of Orthopsychiatry*, 1970, *40*, 426–432.

Levenstein, P. A message from home, In M. J. Begab, & S. S. Richardson, (Eds.), *The mentally retarded and society: A social science perspective*. Baltimore, Md.: University Park Press, 1975.

Levenstein, P. The Mother–Child Home Program. In M. C. Day, & R. K. Parker (Eds.), *The Preschool in action*. Second edition. Boston, Mass.: Allyn and Bacon, 1977.

Levenstein, P., & Sunley, R. Stimulation of verbal interaction between disadvantaged mothers and children. *American Journal of Orthopsychiatry*, 1968, *38*, 116–121.

Madden. J., Levenstein, P., & Levenstein, S. Longitudinal IQ outcomes of the Mother–Child Home Program. *Child Development*, 1976, *47*, 1015–1025.

Nelson, K. Structure and strategy in learning to talk. *Monographs of the Society for Research in Child Development*, 1973, *38*, (1–2, Serial No. 149).

Ninio, A. Picture-book reading in mother-infant dyads belonging to subgroups in Israel. *Child Development*, 1980, *51*, 587–590.

Ochs, E. Introduction: what child language can contribute to pragmatics. In E. Ochs, & B. B. Schieffelin (Eds.), *Developmental pragmatics*. New York: Academic Press, 1979.

Ramey, C. T., Farran, D. C., & Campbell, F. Predicting IQ from mother–infant interactions. *Child Development*, 1979, *50*, 804–815.

Sapir, E. *Culture, language, and personality*. Berkeley, Ca.: University of California Press, 1962. (Originally published in 1921.)

Schacter, F. F. *Everyday mother talk to toddlers*. New York: Academic Press, 1979.

Schaefer, E. S. A home tutoring program. *Children*, 1969, *16*, 59–61.

Tulkin, S. R., & Kagan, J. Mother–child interaction in the first year of life. *Child Development*, 1972, *43*, 31–41.

Van Doorninck, W. J., Caldwell, B. M., Wright, C., & Frankenburg, W. K. The relationship between twelve-month home stimulation and school achievement. *Child Development*, 1981, *52*, 1080–1083.

Vygotsky, L. S. *Thought and language*. Boston, Mass.: MIT Press, 1962.

13

Early Stages of Discourse Comprehension and Production: Implications for Assessment and Intervention

Robin S. Chapman
University of Wisconsin-Madison

Jon F. Miller
Waisman Center on Mental Retardation and Human Development

This volume has reviewed the communicative achievements of children passing through the first half of the second year of life. The range of research topics and their microanalytic detail give new clarity to our theories and descriptions of development in the transition period. The work reported here brings us closer to identifying causal antecedents of the acquisition of language and communication skills.

Such understanding is especially important for work with language disordered children from various populations. Clearly, a variety of factors contribute to the acquisition process. Language and communication skills can be fragile or resilient in response to a variety of physiological and psychological deficits. Speech and language deficits are associated with conditions arising from congenital and genetic abnormalities, disease processes, trauma, and environmental deficits. At the same time, even the most profoundly damaged individuals acquire some degree of environmental responsiveness that can be communicative.

The question addressed in this chapter is how the facts and processes uncovered by detailed research on normal development can contribute to our ability to identify and treat children who fail to acquire language skills at a rate expected for their age and cognitive status. We discuss the applications of developmental data to early identification efforts and show how new data can enhance our ability to find young children at risk for communicative disorders. We also show how mother–child interaction patterns contributing to language acquisition in normal children can provide strategies for intervention in certain types of language disorders.

FINDING THE CHILDREN

Who can be identified as at risk for language disorders early in the transitional period? The multiple factors affecting language acquisition and use mean that multiple things can go wrong (Miller, 1982). Cognitive development, perceptual integrity, information processing, and environmental support, all make their contributions to language development, and impairment of one or more is associated with deficits in language acquisition or use. The etiological categories of mental retardation, learning disabilities, hearing impairment, and deprivation of cognitive and linguistic stimulation, as in cultural familial retardation, all stem from impairment of one of these factors and are associated with deficits in language and communication. Primary etiology then becomes useful as an indicator of "at risk" status for communication development.

Etiology alone will not predict the specific language outcome, given the multiple factors that affect performance in each of the previous categories. Severity of the primary etiology, time of onset, and the age at which the problem was identified can result in diverse patterns of language acquisition. But etiology as a primary indicator of at-risk status can serve as one screening device in the first year of life. Cognitive and perceptual deficits of moderate to severe degree and associated conditions identifiable at birth such as genetic syndromes, inherited metabolic disease, trauma, low birth weight, and prematurity are the earliest indicators. Identification of mild to moderate processing deficits must await further development.

The identification of environmental deficits must focus on the family, rather than the child. Low socioeconomic status has been associated with slower language development, but the cause of this correlation has not been clear. Recently, Ramey, Sparling, and Wasik (1981) reported an at-risk scale for family characteristics within the low SES population of their study that predicted developmental deficits. The factors in their scale included maternal age and maternal educational status. Others have reported children of teenage mothers to be particularly at risk for language delay. Prenatal nutrition and chemical ingestion have also been recently linked to birth defects and developmental disorders; for example fetal alcohol syndrome and children of mothers on methadone.

While screening for known conditions associated with language disorder can allow us to identify a number of children who are at risk for communication development in the first year of life, there remain whole populations of children who will be missed by such screening procedures even though they will ultimately exhibit a variety of language disorders. The identification of these children must be accomplished by directly assessing the developmental status of the child's communication skills. To carry out such an assessment requires a map of communicative development in the first two years of life; the developmental accounts offered in this volume become important.

To illustrate just how important the use of recent information on communicative development could be, consider the following example of current practice. An 8-month-old child is having his routine pediatric examination. The usual physiological data are taken, the mother is queried as to sleeping and elimination habits, and the immunization schedule is reviewed. At this point, developmental questions are centered around motor activities such as crawling, pulling to standing position, and (in Cambridge) walking. An inspection of the developmental scale most used by pediatricians, the Denver Developmental Screening Test, confirms this focus. Language items begin to appear on the Denver at 10 to 12 months with first words in production. Comprehension items do not appear until 20 months. Further, the scale cannot confirm developmental delay in communication skills until the child is at least 2 years of age and more generally 2½ to 3 years old. Critical years of language learning have been lost.

Recent work, however, identifies a number of factors that can signal developmental problems in communication within the first year of life. In order to confirm developmental delay, sufficient data must be gathered over time to determine progress in both comprehension and production. With the research methods and data available, it is possible to confirm developmental delay for language at 12 months of age. If these procedures are made cost effective by incorporation into routine medical evaluations, they will greatly improve our ability to find children early in life who need additional help in language learning.

The procedures must include developmental milestones for both language comprehension and language production; and for the interactional achievements associated in pragmatic development. These milestones can then be used as a measure with which we can compare the performance of children we assess. Table 13.1 and Table 13.2 are examples of the entries which such scales might contain. Table 13.1 summarizes the performance of a group of normal children on discourse comprehension and production tasks. Table 13.2 summarizes communication-related skills which should be acquired by the ages indicated.

Developmental charts for communicative skills such as Tables 13.1 and Table 13.2 must be based on a multidimensional view of the process, sampling items at each age level reflecting developmental status along each dimension. Ideally such scales should quantify the variability both among individuals, in the acquisition of a milestone; and within individuals, in the relation among milestones along different dimensions. At present, knowledge of variability is one of the most serious gaps in our documentation of development during the transitional period. We are beginning to identify the critical milestones, but the variability to be expected in attaining them and the normal variability in the acquisition of one skill as compared to another remain to be quantified.

How can developmental charts such as these currently be used? First, checklists like Table 13.1 are useful in identifying children who require further monitoring. For example, children who are not comprehending their own name or "mama"; who are not eventually responsive most of the time, their mothers

TABLE 13.1

The Development of Discourse Comprehension and Production
Skills in 48 Children Aged 10–21 Months (4 at Each Month)

Skill	10–12 Mos.	13–15 Mos.	16–18 Mos.	19–21 Mos.
DISCOURSE COMPREHENSION: LEXICAL[a]				
Understands only one word in utterance:				
Looks at present person	100%	100%	92%	92%
Looks at present object	42%	100%	100%	100%
Carries out action verb	8%	33%	75%	83%
Looks for absent person or object	0%	8%	42%	67%
Understands more than one word in utterance:				
Demonstrates action on object	0%	8%	42%	67%
Shows possessor's possession	0%	8%	42%	83%
Demonstrates toy agent action	0%	0%	8%	58%
Demonstrates toy agent action on object	0%	0%	0%	8%
COMPREHENSION IN CONTEXT: LEXICAL GESTURAL AND SITUATIONAL CUES[b,c]				
Looks at objects that mother requests (episode outcome)	84%	83%	89%	82%
Acts on objects in the way requested (episode outcome)	15%	27%	26%	37%
DISCOURSE PRODUCTION[d]				
Frequency of vocalization in 20 minutes of free play:				
Child	47	103	111	134
Mother	367	337	287	318
Turntaking: per cent of child's vocalizations overlapping mother's	6%	5%	4%	2%
Topic continuation:				
After mother initiates topic	2%	9%	12%	22%
After silence > 2 sec.	5%	11%	12%	11%
Topic initiation:				
After mother continues topic	1%	2%	3%	3%
After silence > 2 sec.	3%	9%	12%	13%
Mother continues child's topic initiation	57%	71%	63%	72%

[a]Miller, Chapman, Branston, and Reichle (1980).
[b]Chapman, Klee, and Miller (1980).
[c]Chapman (1981a).
[d]Chapman, Miller, MacKenzie, and Bedrosian (1981).

ask attention to objects with gesture; or who do not take turns in games such as "Hi" or "peekaboo" or the cultural equivalent by 12 months—these are examples of children whose progress should be monitored for at least the next 6 months. A set of comprehension tasks allowing monitoring of that dimension is given in Miller, Chapman, Branston, and Reichle (1980). These tasks have been used successfully in the Waisman Center clinics for the past 5 years; they are an

TABLE 13.2
Developmental and Criterion Referenced Scale for Identification of
Communication Deficits in the First Two Years of Life (Adapted from
Miller, 1982)

PHYSIOLOGICAL/BEHAVIORAL INDICES OF PROBLEM STATUS AT BIRTH	IMPLICATION OR POTENTIAL PROBLEM AREA
• Feeding problems	At risk for communication development
• Weak cry	At risk for communication development
• Congenital Anomalies	At risk—developmental delay
• Syndrome	At risk—developmental delay
• Orofacial anomalies	Medical decisions surgery—timing
• Laryngeal anomalies	Implications for speech motor control
• Motor deficits—Cerebral Palsy	Implications for speech motor control
• At risk—low birth weight	Long term follow-up

BEHAVIORS WHICH SHOULD BE PRE-SENT AT SIX MONTHS	
Comprehension	
• Consistent orienting to sound	Hearing sensitivity
Production	
• Productive vocalization continues or increases	Hearing, or general developmental milestones
• Syllable repetition (ba ba ba)	Speech mechanism or general developmental delay
• Duration of cooing, singing and babbling 2–3 sec.	Speech mechanism
• Variable intonation, both during crying and cooing	Speech mechanism
• Voiced/voiceless contrast: /p/ vs. /b/	Speech mechanism
• Discrete tongue movements: /d/ /n/ /d/	Speech mechanism or general delay

BEHAVIORS WHICH SHOULD BE PRE-SENT AT 12 MONTHS	
Production	
• Produces MA-MA or DA-DA, pet name referentially. Low frequency and intelligibility. Imitates speech sounds.	Developmental delay, cognitive deficits, minimal hearing loss
Comprehension	
• Understands his own name, or a name for present familiar person	Hearing or developmental delay
• Responsive to mother's gestured requests to attend to objects	Hearing, vision, or developmental delay
Use of language for communication	
• Turntaking vocalizations in communication games such as peek-a-boo, pat-a-cake	

(*continued*)

TABLE 13.2 (*Continued*)

BEHAVIORS WHICH SHOULD BE PRE-SENT AT 18 MONTHS	IMPLICATION OR POTENTIAL PROBLEM AREA
Comprehension	
• Understands single words, names for familiar people and objects within visual field	Developmental delay, hearing loss
Production	
• Few intelligible words	
• Words frequently note familiar people and objects	
• Frequency of vocalization increasing	
Use of Language for Communication	
• Requests	
• Comments	
• Rejects with motor and vocal or vocal behavior	Absence of intention to communicate
• Hi and Bye with gesture or vocal behavior	

BEHAVIOR WHICH SHOULD BE PRE-SENT AT 24 MONTHS	
Comprehension	
• Understands at least two words in an utterance, such as, "Throw Ball" indicating action-object relation	Developmental delay
• Understands action verbs and reference to absent objects	Specific communication delay
Production	
• Vocabulary increase to 20 words minimum	Developmental delay
• Two word utterances	Developmental delay
Use of Language for Communication	
• Request names, locations "What's that," "Where's that"	Developmental delay
• Uses words for multiple functions	
• Initiates topics in conversation following a pause	

example of an instance in which experimental methodology proved sensitive to clinically relevant variables.

Analyses of language production during the transitional period usually employ sampling techniques; recording mother and child at play with a set of toys, diaries, or parental report. Language sample analyses require extensive context and a long time to carry out, but they yield important information (see Miller, 1981). We are currently working on computerized methods to reduce analysis time for free speech samples (Miller & Chapman, 1982). The information we currently have is useful in determining "at risk" status; but confirmation, given present knowledge, must await the child's further development.

A second use to which checklists can be put, once expected variability is clearly established, is to identify children who are candidates for intervention programs. Table 13.2 is a provisional example of such a checklist; it lists milestones according to the ages at which children should have already acquired the skills, given current knowledge of variability. Such checklists flag children with significant delays in communicative skill.

When children are known to be developmentally delayed, direct assessment of communication skills allows the identification of children who have further, specific language deficits in production alone or both production and comprehension. To carry out such a comparative assessment of cognitive and communicative status, however, requires a nonverbal means for cognitive assessment. One such set of items for sensorimotor evaluation has been adapted from the Piagetian literature (Uzgiris & Hunt, 1975; Miller, Chapman, Branston, & Reichle, 1980). Such comparative evaluation is important because additional, specific language problems may be relatively common in mentally retarded children (Miller, Chapman, & MacKenzie, 1981).

Identifying children as candidates for language intervention, then, can come about in three ways. First, children with primary etiologies associated with language disorder or delay should be considered for intervention. Second, children who fail to reach communication milestones at the expected time should be monitored. Third, children who show significant delays in milestones should be considered for intervention. In all three cases, confirmation that a language problem exists must be accomplished through direct assessment of language and communication at relevant ages. Deciding which of these children to include in intervention programs can then be based on the program resources available. Over-inclusion is ideal, offering children who are marginal performers early intervention services as a preventative measure to preclude future and potentially more devastating deficits.

DESIGNING INTERVENTION PROGRAMS

Once children have been identified for an intervention program, we must decide who is to be the agent and who the object of change in our intervention efforts. Clearly, where at-risk factors are those associated with the mother, intervention efforts must focus on her as the object of change rather than the child. As the mother's behavior changes, she becomes the change agent and intervention focuses on the child.

In other populations the decision to make the mother or teacher or therapist the chief agent of change must be made in more ambiguous circumstances. Given the child's developmental level, the amount of time for which intervention is possible, and the need for natural intervention contexts, the mother emerges as the logical choice. She can spend more time in facilitative interaction with her child, both in play and in the context of the child's daily routines and communicative needs. It is the child's caregiver—mother or other—who is likely to know best the child's behavioral repertoire; and it is the caregiver's repertoire that the child is likely to know best, allowing the development of mother and child strategies for communication.

Mechanisms of Acquisition in Normal Children

Mothers adjust their speech in the transitional period on the basis of what is happening in the situation (Chapman, 1981b), but which of these changes are useful to the child? What aspects of interaction are critical to the early stages of language learning? Much has been made of the well-formedness and syntactic simplicity of the mother's utterances, and these aspects may indeed be important when the child is able to understand more of the utterance—most of its words, as opposed to one or two. Similarly the repetitive forms and content in mothers' successive utterances within an episode have been pointed to as a set of textbook illustrations of constituent substitution possibilities (e.g., Broen, 1972; Messer, 1980). But such relationships between utterances are well beyond the means of the transitional child who is working to grasp the relation between one aspect of the situation and one word of the utterance. In the transitional period the most critical aspect of the mother's input is lexical: the extent to which she provides words for what the child is attending to or trying to do.

Lexical Development.   There is evidence to support the view that amount and timing of the mother's lexical input affects lexical development. Masur (1982), in a longitudinal study of four children, demonstrated that the mothers were linguistically responsive to their children's early gestural communication, offering labels in response to their children's pointing gestures two to three times as often as in response to reaching or extending object gestures. Further, those children whose mothers were most likely to provide labels in response to the child's points later acquired larger production vocabularies.

Developmental differences between lower and middle socioeconomic class infants do not ordinarily arise until the second year of life. This is especially clear in measures of language comprehension and production, and is predicted by measures of mother–child linguistic interaction (Bee, Barnard, Eyres, Gray, Hammond, Spietz, Snyder, & Clark, 1982). Similarly, Clarke-Stewart (1973) has shown that variation in lower class children's linguistic skills can be accounted for by variation in the sheer amount of communicative interaction available to the child. Investigators have demonstrated differences as a function of social class in the amount of talking that children hear. The effectiveness of a daycare program in reversing at 30 months some of the language delay identifiable at 18 months has been shown by O'Connell and Farran, (1980) and Ramey, MacPhee, and Yeates (in press).

Swenson (1981) and Fowler and Swenson (1979) have experimentally demonstrated long lasting effects on both vocabulary and, later, syntax, of intervention between 8- and 16-months for normal, middle class children. Mothers were encouraged to talk to their children in one-word and short sentences, labelling target objects and actions typical of early vocabulary; to call attention to objects, labelling them; to play action games with labelling; and to label the objects and actions to which the infants spontaneously attended.

Beginning the same intervention 4 months earlier in another group of infants produced some word comprehension for every infant by 5 months of age; spontaneous word use in all children by 8 months; productive vocabularies averaging 70 words by 17 months; two-word utterances in half the children by 12 months; and in five of the six by 17 months (Swenson, 1981). In both intervention groups, the rapid increase in comprehension vocabulary preceded a similar acceleration in production vocabulary by about 5 months. Advances in comprehension and production were still present 1 to 2 years later compared to normative expectations. This work is particularly important for its demonstration of the effects in comprehension of very early modification of mother input (well before the infant age when mothers ordinarily shift to simplified speech).

How children come to segment out the phonetic segments that correspond, as labels, to the objects and action of their attention is an unresolved issue. The high proportion of one-word utterances, and their success in the experimental intervention programs, offer one avenue of resolution. There are a sufficient number of instances where the child doesn't have to identify the appropriate segment in the input; the input is the word itself. Alternatively, stressed syllables or utterance-final segments may have privileged status as potential lexical items, or utterances in which the word in question is the only additional content to a recognized or frequently occurring carrier phrase. These questions need to be explored in studies where the child's comprehension of lexical items, rather than his use of them, is the dependent measure.

Expansions and the Development of Syntax. What about the importance of mother's expansions of children's utterances? In all of the studies of 18-to 36-month-old children, expansions have been shown to be very frequent in stage 1 speech, decreasing thereafter, and to be the best predictor of later syntactic acceleration. We propose that expansions are effective particularly in the case where the added elements are already in the comprehension of vocabulary in other, shorter contexts, but not yet easily integrated into the child's multiword speech. Thus, expansions should be particularly useful to the child in the early multiword period where the intent to produce multiword utterances so clearly exceeds the ability to express lexical relationships. Branston (1979) has experimentally demonstrated the efficacy of an intervention program for mentally retarded children in which expansions of a targeted semantic relation during spontaneous play led to a significant increase in the multiword utterances coding that relation.

With respect to the development of comprehension skills, in contrast, expansions serve to segment the novel phonological content from the already produced and understood segment. To the extent that the added content maps meaning to which the child is attending, some expansions may serve lexical development. In the transitional period of interest, however, this mechanism is a less likely one for lexical acceleration, simply because comprehension is limited to one element in the sentence for most of the period. It may, however, be a mechanism for accelerating the time when the child comes to understand two lexical items in a sentence relative to context.

Operating Principles for Intervention Programs

The development of intervention programs for various populations of language disordered children has been a continuing activity over the past 12 years as a part of our clinical work at the Waisman Center on Mental Retardation and Human Development. Given the diversity of these children in terms of language, cognitive and perceptual abilities, and environmental support, several operating principles have been developed to assist in the design of specific intervention programs for individual children. Three are discussed here.

The first principle is that the focus of treatment should be *communication:* What is to be taught should, in itself, be functional for the child in his or her present circumstances and the environment he or she is moving toward. Most particularly, the child will need the means to communicate his or her own needs and comments, to interact. This means that the treatment environment must be responsive to the child's communicative attempts and provide him or her with the means for making them. Further, the treatment environment must provide the basic stuff about which to communicate: experience appropriately geared to the child's cognitive level that leads to the development of expectations; social interaction that leads to play and communicative interchange; variation that leads to surprised expectations and reasons to communicate; linguistic input to mark the experiences, plans, goals, and outcomes that the child is likely to communicate about.

The development of program content is guided by the second principle, *developmental theory.* Our basic premise is that intervention is the process of teaching a first language. Such an enterprise should in principle be directed by our best guess as to the acquisition processes operating in the natural environment. This second principle recognizes the perceptual processes, cognitive characteristics, and learning style that the child brings to the language learning task. Intervention programs motivated by developmental theory provide for continuity from initial teaching to functional use, capitalizing on the child's inherent motivation to communicate. This approach is particularly appropriate for the 10 to 18 month period of development.

The third principle guiding program development is that of *individual differences:* There is a need to recognize the diversity of language disordered children and to describe their functioning in detail before planning therapy. Two populations are relevant in discussing the application of developmental fact and theory for the transitional theory. The first group are those children identified because their communicative development has not kept pace with the rest of their development. These children are essentially normal in all other respects, at least as far as can be determined at this early stage of development. For this group, language is significantly delayed relative to cognitive development; the language skills to be acquired are assumed to be well within the child's cognitive capacity. Our expectation is that the proper environmental organization for language intervention should lead to relatively rapid acquisition rates unless unidentified processing factors are at work.

The second group for whom developmental data are relevent is the mentally retarded, where a significant gap exists between chronological and mental age. These children pose a particular challenge for careful description because of the heterogenous nature of the classification. Mental retardation is the result of a wide variety of etiological conditions, including metabolic, genetic, traumatic, and environmental problems. Each of these conditions represents potential differences in perceptual, information processing, and cognitive characteristics. These differences potentially have consequences for language learning over and above the generally slower rate to be expected. Careful comparison of the children's cognitive, comprehension, and talking skills is especially important to identify which children resemble the language-delayed population previously discussed in having specific language deficits; and which children have commensurate language and cognitive skills that require a general program of language and cognitive enrichment. In the latter case, the expectation for acquisition rate is guided by the rate of cognitive advancement. Consider the following examples of sequences that we might pursue for intervention programs with these two populations.

Two Examples

The first example is that of an initial program for a moderately retarded 3-year-old functioning between 12 and 15 months. The general strategy is to establish comprehension of an initial vocabulary, moving to produce those same elements in pragmatically appropriate contexts, shifting from highly structured situations to naturalistic environmental control (see, e.g., Miller & Yoder, 1974). First, select a frequently occurring event or experience from the child's daily routine in school or home that is of interest to the child. In that context make the meaning to be verbalized clear nonverbally—or better yet, follow the child's lead by providing input about those aspects of the event to which he is attending. Vocabulary modeled in these contexts should be selected for its usefulness to the child, and his ability to approximate an interpretable version of the word. The first intervention goal should be to establish comprehension of the word for a referent. Once that is established, intervention goals branch in three directions: a new word to learn to understand in another context; a new referent for the word just learned; and use of the word in the original teaching context. A broad vocabulary allowing comprehension and expression of here-and-now events in the child's environment should be taught prior to any expansion of goals to multiword utterances. The major objective is to provide as many learning opportunities as possible. This population acquires new information at a slower rate, meaning that more exposures to language in context will be needed for acquisition to occur.

The instructional strategy for both the mentally retarded child just discussed and the retarded child with specific language disability, to be discussed here, must incorporate those naturalistic teaching devices that maintain the natural flow of interaction in the normal patterns of mother–child interaction described in this chapter and throughout this book. They are even more critical for the specifically language delayed child. Input must be simplified to the point that the child can recognize words; relations between language and event must be predictable; the mother must recognize and be responsive to the child's communicative attempts; the mother must make her meaning evident from the situation. Such maternal strategies for communication may be sufficient in and of themselves to promote learning for those children who have advanced cognition relative to language skills, if the complexity of input is matched to the child's linguistic rather than cognitive level. Thus, the focus of a program for a specifically language delayed child within the retarded population would be reciprocal communicative interaction.

In all intervention programs the child's spontaneously initiated behavior would be treated as communicative. In this respect our intervention programs assume, with Western mothers, that children understand what they hear and intend to communicate. That assumption, if only limitedly warranted, provides the basis for the mother to respond appropriately to the child. However, the intervention programs share with the Kaluli mothers of Schiefflin's chapter (this volume), the practice of giving the child the language he can use and of modeling for him how to speak. In this way the child's problem in learning what to say is simplified—just as American mothers simplify it in book reading and play episodes where speaking roles can be exchanged. In this way the child learns to respond appropriately to the mother. Both American and Kaluli mothers' assumptions are important for successful communicative interaction.

CONCLUSION

Given the material covered in this chapter and the research discussed in this volume there are several concluding comments that seem warranted. First, research must be put in practice. Recent research has given us an improved understanding of the sequences and the complex relational dependencies involved in communication development. With improved theory and data comes the responsibility of putting this new knowledge to work. The communicative needs of children who have failed to develop normally, for whatever reason, make this charge clear and urgent. Second, the solution to the complex problems embodied in those children with developmental disabilities lies in careful scientific study. The careful research on normal processes of acquisition exemplified in this volume must be extended to the disordered population.

This chapter has discussed two major thrusts in the application of developmental data to disordered development: early identification and intervention. In the case of early identification, prevention of long lasting deficits is the primary goal. Prevention, by the very nature of the limited developmental data, will require the monitoring of development for six months to a year for a large number of children for whom communication development is the only question. This monitoring process must become a part of the health care delivery system if application of what we know is to be seriously put to use. The second year of life is the critical period for identifying these children.

The reported work on the effects of early intervention clearly support its effectiveness in improving productive language skills. As we consider the effect of early intervention beyond language stimulation programs, we must seek to understand the interaction between environmental variables and various physiological deficits. Current intervention programs provide directed stimulation through more talking, listening, and responding, guided by patterns of normal mother–child interaction. These programs assume, then, the same intellectual and information processing capabilities that are available to normal children of similar cognitive levels.

When this assumption cannot be made, what are the guiding principles for early intervention? In order to answer this question researchers must document childrens' performance characteristics in great detail. Such descriptions must include medical as well as behavioral data. In populations like the mentally retarded, the only solution to intervention research will likely be with individual children using single subject designs. The diversity of this population and others will require a long-term systematic effort to begin to understand the ways that the environment can be altered to either facilitate communication in specific contexts or to teach the child language skills to communicate in any situation. We need to know when to alter the environment so that the child can function, and when to alter the child.

Research on children with disorders will in turn make contributions to normal theory through documenting the limits of learning and performance under extreme conditions. Research on the language performance of disordered children offers a challenge to those who undertake it; and the reward of making fundamental progress in the identification and treatment of language disorders.

REFERENCES

Bee, H. L., Barnard, K. E., Eyres, S. J., Gray, C. A., Hammond, M. A., Spietz, A. L., Snyder, C., & Clark, B. Prediction of IQ and language skill from perinatal status, child performance, family characteristics, and mother-infant interaction. *Child Development*, 1982, *53*, 1134–1156.

Branston, M. E. *The effect of increased expansions on the acquisition of semantic structures in young developmentally delayed children: A training study*. Unpublished doctoral dissertation, University of Wisconsin-Madison, 1979.

Broen, P. A. The verbal environment of the language-learning child. *American Speech and Hearing Association Monograph*. 1972, *17*.

Chapman, R. S., Cognitive development and language comprehension in 10- to 21-month-olds. In R. Stark (Ed.), *Language behavior in infancy and early childhood*. New York: Elsevier, 1981(a).

Chapman, R. S. Mother-child interaction in the second year of life: Its role in language development. In R. Schiefelbusch, & D. Bricker (Eds.), *Early language: Acquisition and intervention*. Baltimore, MD: University Park Press, 1981(b).

Chapman, R. S., Klee, T. M., & Miller, J. F. *Pragmatic comprehension skills: How mothers get some action*. Paper presented to the American Speech and Hearing Association, Detroit, Nov. 1980.

Chapman, R. S., Miller, J. F., MacKenzie, H., & Bedrosian, J. *The development of discourse skills in the second year of life*. Paper presented at the Second International Congress for the Study of Child Language, University of British Columbia, Vancouver, Canada, August 13, 1981.

Clarke-Stewart, K. A. Interactions between mothers and their young children: Characteristics and consequences. *Monographs of the Society for Research in Child Development*, 1973, *38*, (6–7, Serial No. 153).

Fowler, W., & Swenson, A. The influence of early language stimulation on development: Four studies. *Genetic Psychology Monographs*, 1979, *100*, 73–109.

Masur, E. F. Mothers' responses to infants' object-related gestures; influences on lexical development. *Journal of Child Language*, 1982, *9*, 23–30.

Messer, D. J. The episodic structure of maternal speech to young children. *Journal of Child Language*, 1980, *7*, 29–40.

Miller, J. F. *Assessing children's language production: Experimental procedures*. Baltimore, MD: University Park Press, 1981.

Miller, J. On identifying children with language disorders and describing their language behavior. In J. Miller, D. Yoder, & R. Schiefelbusch (Eds.), *Contemporary issues in language intervention*. ASHA Reports No. 21: American Speech-Language-Hearing Association, November, 1982.

Miller, J. F., & Chapman, R. S. *SALT: Systematic analysis of language transcripts*. A computer program developed on the Harris/5 Computer, the Research Computing Facility, Waisman Center on Mental Retardation and Human Development, University of Wisconsin-Madison, December 1982.

Miller, J. F., Chapman, R. S., Branston, M., & Reichle, J. Comprehension development in sensorimotor stages V and VI. *Journal of Speech and Hearing Research*, 1980, *9*, 243–260.

Miller, J. F., Chapman, R. S., & MacKenzie, H. *Individual differences in the language acquisition of mentally retarded children*. Paper presented at the Second International Congress for the Study of Child Language, University of British Columbia, Vancouver, B.C., Canada, August, 1981.

O'Connell, J., & Farran, D. C. *The effects of daycare intervention on the use of intentional communicative behaviors in socioeconomically depressed infants*. Paper presented at the Sixth Biennial Southeastern Conference on Human Development, Alexandria, VA, April 1980.

Ramey, C. T., MacPhee, D. M., & Yeates, K. O. Preventing developmental retardation: a general systems model. In L. Bond, & J. Joffe (Eds.), *Facilitating infant and early childhood development*. Hanover, NH: University Press of New England, in press.

Ramey, C. T., Sparling, J. J., & Wasik, B. H. Creating social environments to facilitate language development. In R. L. Schiefelbusch, & D. D. Bricker (Eds.), *Early language: Acquisition and intervention*. Baltimore, MD: University Park Press, 1981.

Swenson, A. *Long term effects of infant language stimulation*. Paper presented at the Society for Research in Child Development, Boston, MA, April 5, 1981.

Uzgiris, I., & Hunt, J. McV. *Assessment in infancy*. Champaign, IL: University of Illinois Press, 1975.

14

Why Social Interaction Makes a Difference: Insights from Abused Toddlers

Susan R. Braunwald
Los Angeles, California

There is widespread empirical consensus that infant–caregiver interaction during the first year of life is the source of prelinguistic accomplishments in the child that seem to set the stage for language acquisition (see Harding, this volume). Theoretically, there is agreement that the infant and his mother[1] play complementary but developmentally unequal roles in the transactional process of interaction that leads to these prelinguistic accomplishments. Although the infant is an active interactional partner, his mother is the psychological and cultural arbitrator whose interpretations of his emergent behavior define the intentions and meanings being transacted between them (Braunwald, 1976; Bruner, 1975; Dore, this volume; Kaye, 1979; Lock, 1978, 1980; Newson, 1979; Richards, 1974a, b; Schaffer, 1977; Shotter, 1974). Thus, the infant must depend upon his mother to provide him with caregiving and to create for him a psychological environment of cognitive, social, and emotional experiences that is sufficiently predictable to permit him to develop internalized expectations of his world and intentional communicative skills.

Given this scenario of the infant's development of prelinguistic communication, it appears that the minimal environmental input necessary to trigger the onset of language acquisition involves far more than the quality of the linguistic

---

*Throughout this chapter the gender of the pronoun refers to the gender of the person. However, in the introduction the masculine pronoun has been used to refer to the infant in order to avoid possible grammatical ambiguity in one of the sentences.

[1]In reality an infant experiences interaction with multiple caregivers. The term ''mother'' is used because so much of the research on prelinguistic communication and the linguistic input to the child is based upon observations of mother–infant dyads. For grammatical clarity, the masculine pronoun is used to refer to the infant.

input per se. Whatever linguistic input the child does receive is embedded in a cumulative and evolving matrix of cognitive, social, and affective experiences, many of which are mediated by his mother's expectations and perceptions of his developmental competence. Insofar as the infant is concerned, this experiential matrix has to be sufficiently rich and consistent to facilitate his development of the prelinguistic accomplishments that temporally co-occur with the onset of the transition to symbolic communication.

Despite theoretical speculation and a number of careful correlational studies, it is not known to what degree prelinguistic communication relates to the child's ability to acquire language in the sense of a creative and rule generated linguistic system. Are the infant's prelinguistic achievements developmental prerequisites, precursors or merely facilitative accomplishments that optimize his genetic potential to acquire a symbolic means of communication (see Shatz, this volume; see Sugarman, this volume)? Moreover, the implication that social interaction is the developmental mechanism for prelinguistic communication does not mean by extension that it is the explanation for how and why the child then goes on to acquire language. The fundamental question still remains: To what extent is the human infant born with a genetic capacity to acquire the structure of language that is buffered against a wide range of experiential variability (Bates, 1979)?

Obviously, it would be inadmissible to deprive children of a normal infancy in order to probe for the lower limit of the experiential and linguistic input necessary to language acquisition. It is not possible to ask a mother to default on her role as the empathic interpreter of her infant's behavior in order to discover *whether* and *how* less sensitive and culturally appropriate patterns of mothering relate to the child's prelinguistic accomplishments and thereby to language acquisition. Non-accidental trauma (NAT) or child abuse is a naturally occurring "experiment by nature" (Bronfenbrenner, 1979) in which to begin to delineate how social interaction, prelinguistic communication, and language acquisition relate to one another.

The insights in this chapter come from a therapeutic language intervention which I conducted with two severely abused toddlers, Alan and Brian. My observations of Alan and Brian are used to identify by default prelinguistic accomplishments that may facilitate the child's ability to make the transition from prelinguistic communication to language. In order to highlight how the transition period differs for Alan and Brian and to clarify how social interaction relates to these differences, I compare my observations to descriptions from more optimally functioning mother–child dyads. Throughout this chapter I keep in mind two questions: Are the form, content, and use of language separable aspects of communicative competence that are differentially sensitive to experiential variation? What are some of the variables in the quality of social interaction that may have consequences for the timing and ease of the child's transition from prelinguistic to linguistic communication and for the degree of elaboration of his initial symbolic capacity?

DATA

The data on Alan and Brian come from their general file, the daycare staff's notes, and my clinical notes. Although I recognized the research potential of these cases, I decided against a formal study and media documentation for both ethical and practical reasons. Nonetheless, I was aware of the theoretical implications of my clinical impressions.

My clinical notes are an anecdotal record of the course of the language intervention. They describe whatever struck me as developmentally pertinent during any given session. They contain examples of the child's language and communication, objective descriptions of his social and cognitive development, clinical impressions of his emotional state, and my own thoughts and hypotheses about the progress of the intervention. Because both children's expressive language was brief and infrequent, I was able to keep notes on much of what they said.

The comparative examples come from my own longitudinal diary data and from published research on prelinguistic communication and the one-word stage of language development. The scope and method of the diary studies on Laura Braunwald and on Cheryl Brislin are described in detail elsewhere (Braunwald & Brislin, 1979).

Ultimately, my insights in this chapter are the outcome of my own personal experience as a theoretically informed participant–observer. The juxtaposition of my theoretically motivated observations and my clinical experiences proved to be a valuable perspective for understanding how qualitative differences in the experiential input to language acquisition relate to the *process* of making the transition from prelinguistic to linguistic communication. My own meta-awareness of how interacting with these abused toddlers differed from my experiences with normal children is the source of my theoretical speculation in this chapter. As I reflected upon my daily experience of trying and often failing to communicate with these ambivalent and lackluster toddlers, I began to appreciate the many ways in which positive experiences during infancy optimize the child's potential to make the transition from prelinguistic communication to language.

INTERVENTION

Theoretical Philosophy

The language intervention was a practical application of my knowledge as a developmental psychologist to a situation in which I assumed that the children's delayed verbal communication was related to pathology in the infant–caregiver relationship. In planning the intervention, I assumed that the disruption in the infant–caregiver relationship interfered with the children's development in multiple ways, some or all of which could have consequences for their ability to acquire and to use language. The goals of the intervention were: (1) to enrich the children's general experiences as a basis for developing the content and functions of language; (2) to provide them with linguistic input in which the mapping of form onto meanings and intentions was consistent, differentiated and clear; (3) to extend the range of interpersonal contexts in which they communicated; and (4) to model for them how to use language in an effective and appropriate manner in their interpersonal transactions (i.e. "Tell Tommy 'mine!'" as an alternative to snatching the ball back from him).

Description of the Sessions

Physical Setting.   The language intervention was carried out in the mainstream of a large and modern daycare center in which one of three units was set aside for the abuse program. The daycare center was not modified to create a therapeutic setting, and the basic design of the building permitted almost no visual or auditory privacy. My solution to this lack of privacy was to take the child out alone with me for a walk around the neighborhood.

Working with the children in the public and unstructured settings of the daycare center and the neighborhood was advantageous as an ecological approach to language intervention (Mahoney & Weller, 1980). The public setting was useful for expanding the experiential knowledge necessary to meaning, for teaching vocabulary and pragmatic skills in relevant contexts, and for gradually helping the children to communicate with people other than myself. However, these public and unstructured settings were not an ideal therapeutic milieu, and it was stressful to interact in them when the children were working out emotional issues.

Duration of the Intervention.   I saw Alan and Brian daily for individualized sessions that lasted for as little as 5 minutes to as long as 2 hours with an average length of 1 hour. The length of the session depended upon the child's willingness to interact with me and whether he and I became engaged in working through an emotional issue which had to be resolved before I left. Whenever the child became emotionally overwhelmed, I remained for as long as it took to calm him down and to leave him with some reassurance that he was safe (i.e., Example 9). Because I was in the unit for longer than the length of the child's session, the caregivers and I established clearly marked ritualized routines for beginning and ending the individualized session. The children did learn to recognize and participate in these routines and to accept the difference between their special time alone with me and my general presence in the unit.

Content.   In lieu of a sequenced program of language intervention, I tried to approximate a normal process of mother–child interaction in which the contexts and content of verbal communication are embedded in a framework of predictable and gratifying shared experiences. I tried to create this experiential framework by "mothering" the children in the sense of responding contingently to their immediate needs as I perceived them. As in normal mothering, these needs ran the gamut from physical care to structuring developmentally appropriate experiences. I changed the children's diapers, cuddled them when they were sick or sad, taught them all kinds of skills from eating with a spoon to riding a tricycle, gradually extended the scope of their cognitive and linguistic experiences and tolerated the fluctuations in their mood. Thus, I tried to create a situation in which the children's motivation to communicate and the content and contexts of their language could evolve gradually as a consequence of establishing a predictable and satisfying relationship with an adult caregiver.

Insofar as the content of the linguistic input per se is concerned, I saturated the children with language in a form that was relevant to the immediate situational context. I described their actions, labeled the objects in the environment, and called their attention to perceptually salient events. I helped them to establish communicative rituals for repetitive interactions and events. I demonstrated how language could be used in interpersonal transactions and modeled symbolic play. Since the children had to communicate with multiple caregivers, I tried to keep the form of their language and play as conventional and comprehensible to a general listener as possible.

Therapeutic Relationship.   Although the goal of my intervention was to provide the children with the experiential and linguistic stimulation to facilitate language acquisition, their emotional disturbance was so profound that they could not benefit from this enrichment outside of the context of a "therapeutic" relationship to me. Their willingness to establish social contact, the quality of that contact, the topics of their communication and the content of the language which they learned became intertwined with the therapeutic issues which they themselves introduced into their relationship to me. In essence, the children's psychological need to work through their ambivalence toward an adult whom they perceived as a caregiver took precedence over any other task which I tried to introduce into the language intervention. Thus, the children used their relationship to me as if it were a therapeutic opportunity to work on emotional problems relating to separation and individuation, attachment, and the establishment of trust.

Once I realized that the children's "therapeutic" relationship to me was the critical ingredient in the language intervention, I consulted regularly with a psychiatrist whom I knew. Although he never observed the children, he helped me to understand the dynamics of the ambivalent attachment that they were working out in relationship to me. He gave me specific suggestions about how to respond to the children's emotional outbursts and helped me to cope with my own feelings about being the target of their displaced anger and fear.

THE CHILDREN

Language in the Therapeutic Daycare Unit

In general, the frequency and quality of the abused children's language and communication were subjectively different from that of the same-aged lower SES children in the other units of the daycare center. These abused infants and toddlers were unwilling and/or unable to initiate and to sustain age-appropriate forms of communication. For example, the infants, some of whom babbled, rarely engaged in spontaneous and playful prelinguistic communication such as "protoconversations" (Bateson, 1979; Schaffer, 1977) or games of give-and-take (Bates, 1979; Bruner, 1975; Gray, 1978). The toddlers in their second and third year of life were reluctant to carry on a conversation, to engage in reciprocal rounds of language play (Garvey, 1977), or to accompany their own activity with private speech (Zivin, 1979).

The therapeutic unit was at once too silent because there was so little spontaneous speech and too noisy because there was so much whining, crying, and tantruming. These abused children were either unwilling and/or unable to use consistent and differentiated verbal and nonverbal communication to express themselves. Many of their attention-getting and communicative devices were annoying amorphous behaviors such as stubborn silence, fussing, whining, crying, and tantruming. This undifferentiated communicative style often led to misunderstandings in which the process of negotiating meaning degenerated to the level of angry interpersonal confrontations. Day-to-day variations in the children's motivation to use differentiated interpersonal communication were a reliable barometer of their emotional state.

Even when it was possible to engage these abused children in positive interpersonal communication, their style of participation was subdued and lackluster. Their faces failed to "light-up" with that spontaneous smile and those bright eyes which make communicating with normal infants and toddlers so delightful and gratifying. In general, their characteristic pattern of interaction was comparable to the "abusive" and "rejecting" style which George and Main (1979, 1980; Main, in press) found in abused toddlers in daycare centers. The ten abused toddlers in their sample, who were compared to matched controls from families under stress, were reluctant to interact with their caregivers. When they did so, there was often a hostile quality to their interaction including episodes of unprovoked harassment such as biting and hitting (i.e., Example 9).

Selection of the Children

Alan and Brian were not in the therapeutic unit simultaneously. Each of them was selected for individualized intervention because he was the most significantly language-delayed and emotionally disturbed child in the unit at the time.

Table 14.1 is a comparative summary of these two cases including the child's presenting symptoms, the focus of the intervention, and the outcome of his development to the present time. As can be seen from the table, the children's lack of spontaneous age-appropriate language and communication was alarming even within the context of the therapeutic unit.

TABLE 14.1
Comparative Summary of the Cases

Dimension	Alan	Brian
Presenting Symptoms	Language delay; excessive drooling; awkward gait; fine motor problems; minimal attention span; extreme left hand dominance.	Language delay; absence of interpersonal contact; self-stimulating behavior; abnormal unmodulated affect; lack of attachment; wariness.
Diagnosis	Expressive aphasia complicated by traumatic life-history.	Emotional disturbance.
Possible Etiology	Organic deficit—CAT scan shows damage to left hemisphere of brain.	Environmental deprivation—minimal experiential input during infancy.
Initial Level of Communication	Intentionality expressed by "eh" + point and eye-contact; sociability.	Almost no prelinguistic communication; avoidant.
Intervention		
Length	One year.	Five months.
Developmental Focus	Make form accessible—various strategies including "home sign" and 8-week bi-weekly sessions with speech pathologist; clarify diagnosis.	Provide minimal experiential input to language—regressed to infancy and retraced sequence of prelinguistic communication.
Relationship	Worked through ambivalent attachment to become positively attached.	Worked through fear of social contact to become ambivalently attached.
Response to Author at Follow-up	Positive memory—hugs; indicated memory of walks by getting jacket.	Anger—avoidance; took me to door and said: "Bye. Go."
Outcome		
Strengths	Motivation to communicate; pragmatic skills	Symbolic communication.
Weaknesses	Symbolic communication.	Integration of structure and function of language; emotional disturbance.
Future	Likelihood of continued severe expressive language delay and increasing developmental deficits as a consequence.	Likelihood of progress in appropriate developmental environment; intervention was early and improvement continues in new secure foster home.

Emotionally, the language intervention was intended as a token-compensation for the fact that neither Alan or Brian had a mother who could come to the daycare center. The mothers of the other children stayed with them at the daycare center for several hours each week. The language intervention was the only chance for Alan and Brian to have the undivided attention of a caregiver at the daycare center, and I became their mother-surrogate.

Alan

Case History.   Alan was placed in the therapeutic daycare by court order at the time that he was returned from foster care to his mother's custody. At that time, he was 20-months-old. I saw Alan regularly once a week beginning at 20 months but did not begin the intensive language intervention until he was 26-months-old. I worked with Alan for 1 year until he left the program for placement in an aphasia classroom. The etiology of Alan's language delay was not clear at the beginning of the language intervention. However, his development at 4-years-old confirms the diagnosis of expressive aphasia which is complicated by his traumatic life history.

Alan experienced serious emotional trauma at the moment in his development when the transition from prelinguistic to linguistic communication ordinarily occurs. At 1 year of age, Alan was hospitalized for 1 month for non-accidental trauma involving injury to the left side of his head and a fractured left leg. He was released from the hospital to the foster care of a babysitter whom he knew. Alan remained in foster care from age 13 to 20 months. His foster parents, who were older and took a grandparent-like concern for him, saw Alan once he was returned to his mother's custody. They were responsible for instigating his medical workup.

Alan's failure to develop language became a serious concern at 2 years of age. His medical history suggested that there might be some organic problem. His teenage mother had toxemia of pregnancy. After 41 hours of labor, he was delivered by Caesarean section. During the first few days of his life, he had multiple seizures and was transferred to a neonatal unit. He had a history of ear infections, and tubes were placed in his ears at 27 months of age. There were two abnormal CAT scans, one at birth and one at 24 months.

In the course of determining why Alan does not speak, he was seen by neurologists, audiologists, psychologists, and speech pathologists. His hearing is within normal limits. His general functioning is superior to his language, although there is some possibility of mild retardation. The severity of his language delay has been documented on a number of standardized measures. In spite of the intensive intervention with me, sessions with speech pathologists and a year in an aphasia classroom, at 4-years-old his expressive language remains seriously delayed.

Alan's young and psychologically unstable mother has not cooperated with any type of language intervention. Although she recognizes the severity of

Alan's language delay, she is unwilling to accept sign language as an alternative to verbal communication. She has had Alan in-and-out of foster care and is trying to decide whether to relinquish him for adoption.

Theoretical Significance. Alan's case illustrates that an intact, functioning brain is necessary to the transition from prelinguistic communication to language. Alan's expressive aphasia interferes with his ability to acquire symbolic communication, and to date at 4 years of age, no amount or type of intervention has permitted him to bypass this organic limitation. Despite his persistent desire to communicate, Alan's ability to discover how differentiated linguistic forms map onto meaning and intention is severely delayed. He is unable to embed the syntactic component of language into the pragmatic/social interactional framework which he has developed.

Whether a child is credited with making the transition from prelinguistic to linguistic communication depends upon the criteria one selects for defining language. My criterion for defining the point of transition from prelinguistic communication to language is that the child begins to use a set of verbal/manual symbolic skills that involve a rule-generated and flexible system for mapping meaning into conventionalized forms. This symbolic capacity or "language" includes: (1) evidence of the ability to comprehend verbal/manual linguistic structure; (2) the acquisition of a cumulative lexicon; and (3) the ability to encode content into a sequential verbal/manual unit. A fourth criterion, which I believe is necessary to defining language in its fully human sense, is developmental potential. The child's initial symbolic capacity does in time develop into a more powerful and complex system which can express nonpresent and abstract content. To date, Alan is incapable of productive language in the sense of a powerful, generative linguistic system, although he has developed a small repertoire of words and signs.

When my observations of Alan at age four in his special education classroom are compared to my records of the language intervention, it is clear that productive language eludes him. At age four, Alan produced 25 words and signs in the course of his morning at school. Only two of the signs, "milk" and "please," were not already present in his communicative repertoire at age three when the language intervention ended. Structurally, there was one two-word combination, "go there," as Alan fitted some small pegs into a board, and there were seven instances of successive single word or word and sign constructions. All of these constructions involved words and signs which were already present at the time of the language intervention.

Example 1—Expressive Language Delay (Alan, 4;0.1. Alan is in his special education classroom. He is at the table for snack-time. T=teacher.)
A: More.
T: More what, Alan?
A: Alan points to the oranges.

T: More what, Alan? Can you say more orange?

A: Alan does not say the word "orange" but points toward himself with his left index finger to his chest.

Alan's ability to take his turn in a discourse-like sequence, as in Example 1, is one of the accomplishments of the language intervention which he retained as a compensatory strategy. Perhaps because the situation did not elicit them or perhaps because they were not retained, Alan failed to produce some of the words, signs, and combinatorial structures which were observed during the language intervention.

In order to communicate, Alan has had to rely on extending the usefulness of his prelinguistic and early transition period communicative skills long beyond their developmental limits. The willingness of his teachers to try to understand him and to bear the burden of extrapolating his meaning from the context has been essential to the success of this compensatory system. Ultimately, however, Alan's compensatory system of communication, which is appropriate to the needs of a much younger child, is doomed to failure because of its lack of power. Social interaction has permitted Alan to optimize this intact pragmatic aspect of his communicative competence. However, even the most optimal social interaction cannot offset the lack of power of this pragmatic framework as a symbolic system for mapping meanings and intentions into differentiated and structurally complex form.

Brian

Case History.   Brian was placed in the therapeutic daycare unit by court order. His case came to the attention of the court because of a specific incident of abuse in which his face was slashed with a knife in the course of a parental quarrel. However, from what can be pieced together from various sources, Brian's life-history in general was devastating. His young mother was a drug addict, and it is possible that Brian was born addicted. His mother abandoned him, although she did return periodically at which time there were violent marital arguments. His 56-year-old retarded father[2] took over the task of caring for an infant.

Insofar as anyone knows, Brian experienced extreme environmental deprivation during the first 14 months of his life. Although his father seemed to "love" him and was capable of the minimal caregiving necessary to his son's physical survival, he failed to create an experiential environment for the psychological development of his child. The experiential impoverishment of Brian's infancy involved both stimulus deprivation and social isolation.

Brian's home environment was extremely impoverished as a setting for infant

[2]The father's scores on both the TAT and WAIS reveal an impoverished cognitive ability. "His thought processes are unifocal resulting in poor abstract skills in all areas examined including those related to rudimentary social situations." (From report of father's test results.)

development and provided him with limited perceptual and cognitive stimulation. Brian lived alone with his father in a dark and cluttered 12-by-12 foot room in a boarding house. He did not even have a crib or a few toys. His only routine activities were eating and television. He was rarely taken out of this room (Margaret Troy, personal communication). In sum, Brian's home environment provided him with almost no opportunity to engage in the active exploratory interaction with people and objects which leads to the development of sensorimotor intelligence.

It is likely that the quantity and quality of Brian's social experiences were also extremely impoverished. As part of the court evaluation, Brian was assessed developmentally at 16 months of age.[3] At that time, the quality of Brian's social interaction with and attachment to his father was assessed independently by four members of the therapeutic team, including myself. Brian was observed at different times over a period of several days, and each of us submitted a separate evaluation. The following description is a summary of our impressions.

At least within the context of the daycare center, there was no evidence of attachment, mutual eye-contact, reciprocal play, or language. Brian's father cared for his son in complete silence and made no effort to interact with him. For his part, Brian was a very frightened, profoundly depressed, and socially unresponsive child. His affect was flat and avoidant, and his gaze was averted. His body was tense, and there was no sign of communication other than crying. If these impressions from the daycare center are indicative, Brian's relationship to his father must have provided him with minimal and impoverished opportunities to engage in social interaction. Although Brian and his father may have experienced one another's physical presence, it appears that they did not develop a psychological partnership in the sense of a focused and mutually gratifying interpersonal relationship.

At the time that the language intervention began, Brian was 18-months-old. He was living in a foster home with a large family in which he experienced multiple caregivers. His "official" foster mother was older and hard of hearing. She did not participate in any aspect of Brian's program at the daycare center. Brian's father, who is now deceased, did not visit him, and his drug addicted mother has disappeared.

I worked with Brian for 5 months from age 18 through 23 months. Brian's intervention was terminated due to lack of funding for my position. I continued to see him at increasingly long intervals until I felt that I could end the relationship. Brian is angry with me for breaking off the relationship, and when I saw him for follow-up observations told me "Bye. Go!"

Theoretical Significance.   Brian's case provides an opportunity to begin to define how prelinguistic communication relates to the structure and function of

---

[3]Brian was significantly delayed in all areas of development as assessed by the Bayley Scales of Infant Development. His most profound delays were in the area of gross motor and language skills.

language and to the process of language acquisition. Brian's response to environmental stimulation and the nature of his residual language delay indicate that the
structural and functional aspects of his communicative competence were differentially affected by his experientially impoverished infancy. The developmental
sequence of the language intervention implies that the maturation of a functionally intact genetic potential for symbolic communication is necessary to but
not sufficient for the process of language acquisition. The outcome to date of
Brian's development at age two-and-one half suggests that communicative competence involves separable skills which are ordinarily integrated into a single
functional system.

At the outset of the intervention, Brian was language delayed in the sense that
he had failed to develop normal prelinguistic communication. He was lacking
any but the most rudimentary interactional skills and had no functional understanding of his environment to serve as a basis for meaning. There were no signs
of language or symbolic play. Example 2 is a diagnostic description of Brian at
19 months of age. It is based on the staff's collective assessment of how he
functioned during his first month at the daycare center.

> *Example 2—Diagnostic Description* (Brian 1;7.1. 4th week of intervention)
> Problems: (1) high distractability; (2) minimal social contact; (3) poor eye
> contact—is there an actual physical problem? Brian doesn't establish eye
> contact well; (4) minimal point—more like a whole hand grasp for food or
> bottle; (5) minimal intentionality; (6) rigidity; (7) no reciprocity; (8) extreme
> passivity; (9) doesn't distinguish emotional tone; and (10) self-stim rocking.

As can be seen, Brian is emotionally disturbed to such a degree that it interferes
with his ability to establish even limited interpersonal contact.

At 19 months, Brian was within the age-range when symbolic communication
could have occurred on a purely maturational basis. Nonetheless, the increased
linguistic stimulation did not immediately trigger his genetic potential to acquire
language. Before Brian began to use meaningful referential speech, he went
through a period of prelinguistic communication in which the developmental
milestones were comparable to the normal sequence. This sequence parallels the
normal course of prelinguistic communication in terms of the definition of the
primary dyadic tasks. The basic sequence of Brian's prelinguistic communication was: (1) establishment of social contact; (2) reciprocity; (3) intentionality;
(4) internalization of social rituals; (5) internalization of functional meanings;
and (6) transition to language. There were qualitative differences in these prelinguistic processes, as compared to a mother–infant dyad, which were due to
the fact that Brian was not a baby and that his current interaction was affected by
his previous negative experience.

The structure of Brian's language proved to be a separable and hardy aspect of
his communicative competence that recovered rapidly once he received some
minimal amount of experiential and linguistic input. Within 5 months, and
despite the severity of his emotional disturbance, Brian began to develop mean-

ingful combinatorial speech. The pragmatic aspect of Brian's communicative competence was much less resilient. Brian is marginally willing to use his linguistic competence to communicate. There are day-to-day fluctuations in his willingness and/or ability to use language that seem to be associated with his ambivalent attitude toward relating to people.

At age two-and-one-half, the structural and pragmatic aspects of Brian's language are still not well integrated. Brian's lack of integration is less extreme than but similar to other case reports in which the children's knowledge of linguistic structure was separable from their pragmatic development. For example, Blank, Gessner, and Esposito (1979) describe a child whose symbolic capacity was ineffective as a means of communication because he was lacking the functional knowledge of when and how to speak. Curtiss (1977) describes a feral child, Genie, who appears to have developed certain of the structures of language but without mastery of many of the normal psychological functions of language use. Genie uses language in a restricted set of contexts and does not engage in spontaneous discourse. These examples of the failure to integrate structural and pragmatic knowledge raise the issue of how prelinguistic communication relates to the child's ability to synthesize separable aspects of language into a single unified system.

AFFECT AND THE TRANSITION PERIOD

Under ordinary circumstances, transition period children and their interactional partners have developed interpersonal expectations and set interactional routines that leave them free to concentrate on the new and developmentally appropriate task of elaborating the form of their communication. However, for Alan and Brian, there were no positive interpersonal expectations or pre-established interactional routines to serve as a framework which freed them to focus their attention on the relationship of form to content. As a consequence, the quality of the transition period was different for these abused toddlers.

Quality of the Communicative Context

Alan's and Brian's emotional disturbance influenced the contexts and the content of the activities that served as an interactional framework for language acquisition. These abused toddlers were reluctant to communicate, and it was difficult to discover activities that could be used to create a context and a content for language. Situations in which the children were engrossed in obsessive play turned out to be a productive transition period context for introducing symbolic communication into their activity.

In obsessive or compulsive play, the child engages in repetitive stereotyped activity. In contrast to a normal child's ritual play, there is an extreme inflexibility and need to maintain control over the activity. For example, a 3-year-old may spend hours every day lining up all of the toy cars into rows instead of using them as props for a pretend game of gas station.

In the language intervention with Alan and Brian, the children were willing to permit my gradual social encroachment and to allow me to establish a shared focus of interest in situations involving their obsessive play. Irrespective of whether the children were willing to respond, I began to introduce language into their idiosyncratic compulsive activities. Both children were attentive to this linguistic input and were eventually willing to talk within these child-controlled, and therefore comparatively safe, contexts of communication.

Not surprisingly, the content of the children's early language and symbolic play reflects the idiosyncratic themes of their obsessive activity. Alan's compulsive play involved the repetitive turning on and off of the hose. He produced his most structurally advanced language and learned how to pretend in this situation.

Example 3—Most Structurally Complex Sentence (Alan 2;9.4, 39th week of intervention) Immediately prior to pretending that the hose is on, Alan says: "Oh. Put duh water on."

Example 4—Learning to "Pretend" (Alan, 2;9.4–2;9.8, 39th week of intervention) 2;9.4—I demonstrated for Alan how he could pretend that the water was on. I moved my hand in a wiggly motion and made a Ssss noise. Alan imitated my model and engaged in this game . . . 2;9.5—Alan is playing alone at the faucet. Alan pretends to turn it on and makes a Ssss sound. 2;9.8—Alan remembers the word "pretend." Without any demonstration but after multiple repetitions, he responds to my word "pretend." Alan pretends the water is on and makes the sound Sssss.

In addition to the context of his compulsive play with the hose, Alan learned to say words such as "rock," "row," and "go" in social situations in which simplified language was paired with a repetitive and gratifying movement. Although Alan still remains severely handicapped by his expressive aphasia, these contexts were facilitative to his development. They maximized his limited potential to acquire symbolic communication.

Brian's obsessive play involved opening and closing doors and gates and closing me into spaces of various sizes. Brian developed some of his earliest referential language and symbolic play in this context. He learned the vocabulary to talk about open and closed doors, and he enjoyed a game of locking me up and pretending to bring me drinks of water. I responded to this theme in Brian's play as if he were working through some memory of being locked in both in a literal and an emotional sense.

I do not mean to imply that the abused children only spoke in the context of their obsessive play but rather that this context was an important and productive one for them in comparison to the types of activity which have been described as interactional frameworks for the transition period. These situations involving obsessive play are both comparable to and different from the interactional frameworks that normally serve as a context and content for the early negotiation of form. These situations are similar in that they involve ritualized activity. They are different because they are not recognized culturally defined contexts for establishing communication with a toddler. Social games such as pat-a-cake, rituals such as waving "bye-bye," labeling routines, and so on are culturally transmitted contexts of communication that are available to any competent caregiver. These conventional contexts permit children to enter into an adult-structured social world. The abused children's idiosyncratic contexts of communication were fundamentally different. These highly ritualized contexts permitted adult-entry into a child's private world.

Stable Interpersonal Expectations

An interpersonal relationship with a caregiver is one of the most important developmental continuities between the prelinguistic and linguistic period of communication. Although this relationship need not be optimal or even to a single mothering caregiver, it does need to be consistent enough for a child to develop stable and internalized interpersonal expectations. The stability and clarity of these expectations influence the child's definition of a sense of self and by extension the quality of his general interactional orientation and his motivation to communicate.

Sense of Self.   There is no need to speak unless there is some minimal degree of individuation and sense of oneself as a separate person. To bother to talk one must realize that the contents of one's mind are separate and not known to the other. One must also know that the contents of one's mind are potentially communicable. Although not in any fully developed metacognitive sense, 9-to 12-month-old infants are becoming aware of the distinction between self and other and the possibility of intersubjectivity. This is the moment in the developmental sequence of their infancy when they begin to discover their separateness in an experiential sense.

There are multiple coinciding developmental indications that infants between 9 and 12 months of age are beginning to experience themselves as separate individuals. This discovery of a sense of self is signaled developmentally by their ability to consolidate the experiences of their infancy into internalized expectations of their physical and social world. Cognitively, they are developing object permanence and means-ends intentionality. Affectively, they discriminate among people and are able to form a specific attachment or preferential relationship to a caregiver. Communicatively, they are capable of secondary intersubjectivity (Trevarthen & Hubley, 1978) or combining the experiences of their physical and social worlds into a single interactional framework and act of communication (i.e., Bates, Camaioni, & Volterra, 1975; Harding & Golinkoff, 1979). If Brian's developmental history is indicative, language acquisition does not occur until the child has defined experientially some minimal sense of self in relationship to other people.

Motivation to Communicate. The development of a stable motivation to communicate is closely related to the definition of a sense of self and to a generally positive social orientation toward people. If children's interpersonal experiences during infancy have been sufficiently consistent and satisfying, at around 9 months of age they begin to develop a stable and positive communicative attitude. This communicative attitude involves social motivation—"I want/ need to interact"—and some minimal knowledge of the function of interpersonal communication—"I can accomplish what I want/need through transaction with another person." Thus, this communicative attitude involves intentionality in the sense of recognizing the other as a potential agent of an action (i.e., Harding & Golinkoff, 1979).

Example 5, from Laura's diary, is typical of the positive communicative attitude which is normally present at the onset of the transition period.

> *Example 5—Positive Communicative Attitude* (Laura, 0;9.8) Laura is much more aware of the people in her environment. She is responsive to them within the limits of her capabilities to communicate. She smiles at us, laughs at our games, waves and "sings" with us . . . She adores pat-a-cake and will take my hands to make me repeat it a second time . . . When she wants me to hold her or to nurse her, she holds onto my knees and says "mum, mum, mum."

As can be seen, there is no doubt in Laura's mind that it is appropriate and gratifying to engage in interpersonal communication, and she anticipates a positive response (also see Cheryl, Example 11).

A positive communicative attitude influences the quality of the transition period and the optimal functioning of the child's symbolic capacity as a means for interpersonal communication. However, if Brian's and Alan's respective developmental histories are indicative, a positive motivation to communicate is neither necessary for or sufficient to the acquisition of linguistic structure.

Although Brian has developed some degree of intentionality, he has acquired the structure of language prior to the development of a stable and positive communicative attitude. In fact, the lack of a stable motivation to communicate is one of the most significant of Brian's initial and continuing developmental deficiencies. To date, it is not predictable from one moment to the next whether Brian will be socially responsive or avoidant.

> *Example 6—Unstable Motivation to Communicate* (Brian 1;8.2. 9th week of intervention) It was a very diffuse morning with Brian. He was glad to see me, worked about 5 minutes with me on language and was then not willing to sustain any interaction with me . . . Brian, 2;1.18 and 2;1.19 (follow-up

observation) There was an extreme difference between yesterday and today in the level of Brian's cognitive and linguistic performance as a consequence of his mood.

Although Brian is now capable of language in the sense of a symbolic capacity, his emotional disturbance has interfered with the development of a positive communicative attitude.

In contrast to Brian, Alan developed a stable motivation to communicate which has permitted him to optimize his restricted symbolic potential.

Example 7—Positive Motivation to Communicate (Alan 2;4.14. 15th week of intervention) What seems clear from watching Alan is that he is actually optimizing his communicative potential . . . He has a strong urge to communicate socially, and he is using what he has, namely gestures, eye-contact, and smiling.

Alan's motivation to be in social contact with people is one of the strongholds of an otherwise limited ability to communicate. Although the etiology of Alan's positive communicative attitude is ultimately unknown, it is likely that his relationships with his foster parents and various teachers were helpful to him.

Developmental Focus.   There is a subtle but significant shift in the quality of children's social interaction as they enter the transition period from prelinguistic to linguistic communication. Their interpersonal expectations, which were negotiated explicitly as the content of their interaction during infancy, are now internalized and serve as a context for a new type of content, the exchange of information. Their expectations of the interpersonal relationship have become a form of "old" or "given" information that does not have to be renegotiated each time they interact. Both the children and their caregivers are free to focus their attention on introducing a "topic" or content into this interpersonal framework. They are now ready to go onto the developmentally appropriate task of the sequential negotiation of meaning (see Golinkoff, this volume).

Unresolved emotional problems interfered with the abused toddlers' ability to make this developmental shift in the content of their interaction in a clear and definitive manner. Throughout the transition period, they would unpredictably backtrack to work through issues related to the definition of the interpersonal relationship per se. When this happened, the content of the interaction was the negotiation of the relationship. At those times, the interpersonal relationship did not function as a context for the more developmentally appropriate task of communicating on a topic. The focus of the interaction was on *whether* to communicate rather than on *what* to say.

Negative Affect as Content

Toddlers experience negative affect in response to many ordinary events in their daily lives such as separation from their mother or being prohibited from engaging in unsafe and/or inappropriate behavior. One concrete way that caregivers can assist their toddlers to cope with these negative experiences is to make the structure of the event predictable. They can use symbolic communication to teach their children to recognize and to anticipate the structure of comparable events. Caregivers can also use symbolic communication in a more abstract manner to acknowledge and/or to label the emotion which they believe their child is experiencing. I am proposing the terms "event-marker" and "affect-marker" to refer to these two qualitatively different ways of communicating about negative affect with a young child.

Event-markers.   Event-markers are any language, action or contextual cue that leads to the anticipation of the course of an event. For example, when Cheryl sees her mother picking up a purse, this action is an event-marker for her. She anticipates a situation in which her mother will leave without her. Her negative affect is aroused by her internalized expectation of the rest of the event, and she protests.

Example 8—Communication with Event-markers (Cheryl 1;0.4. M=mother. Cheryl's mother goes out every Thursday night. It is 4:30 p.m. on Thursday afternoon. Her mother picks up her purse and slings it over her shoulder. Since her mother is not near the door or moving towards it, the purse is probably Cheryl's cue.)
C: Cheryl notices the purse. She whines and cries. Tears form.
M: You can't go tonite. Dada will stay with you.

The mother's verbal response is also an event-marker. She responds to her interpretation of Cheryl's affect by defining the structure of the event as Cheryl will experience it. Irrespective of whether Cheryl understands it, her mother is trying to alleviate her child's distress by making the structure of the event predictable.

Symbolic communication in the form of event-markers is a concrete way to begin to communicate with toddlers in situations that may arouse their negative feelings. Event-marking language, such as "oh-oh," "night-night," and so on, need not be semantically or structurally complex. Moreover, the relationship among form, meaning and the situational context can be ritualized in a manner which toddlers can understand and incorporate into their own productive communicative repertoire.

Affect-markers.   Affect-markers are a more abstract and difficult form of communication than event-markers. Affect-markers are words such as "mad" or "sad" that can be used to generalize about the perception of a cross-contextual similarity in the quality of a feeling. Meaningful communication with affect-markers requires sufficient meta-awareness of feelings to identify by contrast the quality of different affects and to associate these differentiated affective constructs with specific words.

Normally, negative affect-markers are not part of children's productive communicative repertoire during the transition period. For example, beginning language learners are taught to wave and to say "bye-bye," but they are not expected to verbalize that separation from their mother makes them feel "sad" and/or "mad." The abused toddlers' unpredictable and intense emotional outbursts led to a premature attempt to teach them to substitute affect-markers for the direct expression of their negative feelings.

Example 9—Teaching a Negative Affect-marker (Brian 1;9.13. 16th week of intervention) Brian is sitting next to me at a table. Brian was able to express some of his anger toward me indirectly by using the toy cars. Brian hit me in the face with the toy cars. I stopped him and showed him how he could take the car and bang it against the table and say the word "mad" instead. Brian was able to imitate my action and word. He became intently involved with banging the car on the table and said "mah, mah" as an accompaniment to his action. After about a minute, he suddenly smiled and clapped for himself. I joined in the clapping, and he and I played a clapping game.

Example 10—A "Home Sign" for Anger (Alan 2;8.27. 32nd week of intervention) One of the caregivers is changing Alan's diaper. Apparently, he wants a bath as well. (Baths are given in this same location.) Alan gets mad and starts to hit the caregiver. I notice this and redirect his anger by showing him his sign for "mad." Alan makes the sign for "mad" and then points to the caregiver.

It was not possible to use event-markers to make the structure of these emotional episodes predictable. Instead, affect-markers were used to try to focus the children's attention on the cross-contextual similarity of their internal state and to teach them a more socially acceptable and symbolic form for expressing their negative feelings.

It was a significant developmental disadvantage to Alan and to Brian that they were taught to use affect-markers as part of their transition-period communicative repertoire. The reason for this disadvantage is that the relationship of form to meaning is not transparent from the situational context. For instance, in Example 9 how is Brian to know from the context that I am using the word "mad" to refer to his anger and not to his physical act of hitting the car on the table. To make this distinction clear to Brian, I would have to use language to explain the difference between his expression of affect—saying the word "mad" while hitting the car on the table—and his emotion—the quality of the internal state that evoked this behavior. It is not possible with transition-stage children to use language in this manner to distinguish between the perception of an internal state and the form of its expression.

WHY PRELINGUISTIC COMMUNICATION MATTERS

If their development has preceded normally, children who are entering the transition period are active and skilled nonverbal communicators. They have developed a number of nonverbal transactional skills such as taking turns (Bateson, 1979; Call, 1980), pointing (Bates, 1979; Call, 1980; Leung & Rheingold, 1981; Lock, 1980; Murphy, 1978), using actions and gestures intentionally (Bates, 1979; Bruner, 1975; Clark, 1978; Lock, 1978, 1980), filling a slot in a game or routine (Bruner, 1975; Call, 1980) and initiating and/or following a line of regard (Bruner, 1975). They know how to attract attention to themselves and/or to direct it to what they want done (Bates, Benigni, Bretherton, Camaioni, & Volterra, 1977; Bates, 1979; Harding & Golinkoff, 1979). They have some knowledge of their world in the form of meaningful internalized expectations of the people, objects and repetitive events that define their daily lives (Braunwald, 1976; Piaget, 1951/1962). In sum, transition stage children have developed a rich prelinguistic experiential and interactional framework in which to embed symbolic communication.

The following two examples from the data on Cheryl illustrate the process of embedding symbolic communication into a prelinguistic interactional framework. These two examples, both of which serve the same communicative purpose of requesting a taste of ice cream, are from the beginning and the end of the transition period. In Example 11, which is a "communicative act" (Lock, 1980) from the beginning of the transition period, the process of embedding has not yet begun. The meaning is transmitted nonverbally, and the communicative outcome is almost entirely dependent upon the listener's ability to interpret the child's intention on the basis of her knowledge of the situation.

Example 11—Prelinguistic Framework (Cheryl 0;9.6. Cheryl is sitting in her father's lap. Her mother enters the room and sits down next to them. Her mother has a dish of ice cream. Cheryl recognizes the bowl.)

Sequence of Communication	Child	Partner
C: Cheryl sees ice cream.	Notice/knowledge of ice cream in dish.	Perceives child's notice.
C: Cheryl leans toward her mother.	Use of space to establish topic.	Perceives shift in child's focus.
C: Ehhhh!	Affect/intention/attention-getting.	Interprets intention and meaning.
M: Mother gives Cheryl a taste of ice cream.		Acknowledges child's request.

As can be seen from the annotation, Cheryl and her mother play complementary and synchronized roles in the negotiation of this episode.

By the end of the transition period, Cheryl is beginning to embed differentiated, albeit still idiosyncratic, forms of communication into this prelinguistic framework.

Example 12—Embedding Language into a Prelinguistic Framework (Cheryl 1;5.24. S=Sara. From author's control observations. Cheryl is in 31 Flavors Ice Cream Store. Her neighbor, Sara has already purchased ice cream cones for herself and her two boys. Cheryl's mother is still at the counter. Sara is sitting in a chair and eating her ice cream.)

Sequence of Communication	*Child Accomplishes*
C: Cheryl stands in front of Sara at an angle parallel to the ice cream.	Selects listener/uses space to define topic as ice cream.
C: Aiy! (Cheryl's usual whiney noise)	Affect/intention/attention-getting.
C: Mama.	Defines agent/generalization of form.
C: Cheryl opens her mouth and puts her hand in fingers first almost as if her hand were an arrow.	Defines predicate "give me ice cream here" / invention of new form.
S: Sara smiles and puts the ice cream out for Cheryl to lick.	

Cheryl is now capable of the sequential encoding of meaning. She is also capable of generalizing an old form to a new context and of inventing her own communicatively clear gestural form. Her interactional partner responds in an appropriate and cooperative manner, and this transaction succeeds.

Given my interest in the relationship of social interaction to language acquisition, I watched carefully for and tried to engage the abused toddlers in transactions involving the sequential negotiation of meaning. The abused children in the therapeutic unit did not use a sequential strategy either alone or in discourse with a caregiver to encode a propositional content in a series of utterances (Ochs, Schieffelin, & Platt, 1979). I was struck by their failure to use vertical constructions (Scollon, 1973) and successive single word utterances (Bloom, 1973). Moreover, the ability to engage in discourse was a late development in both Alan's and Brian's language interventions. Nonetheless, with the exception of Alan, all of these children did acquire language. They spoke from time to time, but in general they did not embed their language into an elaborated sequential structure. (Although these are subjective impressions, I was in the therapeutic unit five mornings a week for 18 months.)

If the embedding of symbolic communication into a prelinguistic interactional framework and the sequential negotiation of meaning are not serving a special function with respect to the acquisition of the structure of language, then what is their developmental purpose? The contrast in Alan's and Brian's developmental histories provides some insight into this question. Brian, who missed out on a normal infancy and acquired his prelinguistic skills during the period of toddlerhood, is having difficulty integrating the syntactic and pragmatic aspects of his communicative competence into a single functional system. Alan, who has some type of organic difficulty in acquiring symbolic communication, has developed an adequate prelinguistic framework in response to the language intervention. Athough this framework is now finally formed, it is basically empty because he cannot embed a symbolic capacity into it. Together, Brian and Alan would make one competent speaker!

Ordinarily, transition stage children do integrate the structural and functional aspects of their language into a unitary communicative competence. Since nonverbal pragmatic skills normally develop prior to the onset of language, I am suggesting that this integration is accomplished through a process of embedding symbolic communication into a prelinguistic framework. However, if Brian's case is indicative, this process of embedding is not a developmental prerequisite to the structure of language. Rather, it is a facilitative developmental strategy for creating a functional system of communication. Although it is possible to acquire the structure of language without this facilitative developmental context, language is embedded into a qualitatively different framework in which structure and function are less richly integrated.

From this developmental perspective, the sequential negotiation of meaning is a facilitative compensatory strategy in which the child relies on his pragmatic skills to comunicate in the absence of a sufficiently developed symbolic capacity. The success of this compensatory strategy depends upon the co-participant's willingness to engage in an interpretative process of extrapolating meaning from the discourse and situational contexts. This complementary transactional process is comparable to the system of communication which Alan uses.

In sum, there is a difference between experiential input which optimizes the transition to language and that which is sufficient to trigger the onset of the transition period. If Brian's case is indicative, the developmental prerequisite to the emergence of language is some minimal experiential input that approximates the normal negotiation of an interpersonal relationship during infancy. While subject to cross-cultural variation, the quality of this relationship is constrained by the basic fact of the human infant's dependence upon his caregivers. Within this limitation, there are multiple cultural and interindividual differences in the route to a single destination (Kaye, 1979), the creation of an experiential history with other people that is sufficiently rich and stable to provide a content and a use for language.

Brian did not develop the structure of language until he achieved a certain level of psychological functioning. Although in a far from optimal manner, he backtracked developmentally to complete three basic psychological tasks of infancy. Prior to the acquisition of language, Brian developed some minimal sense of self, an ambivalent intention to communicate, and the ability to "know" or to internalize meaningful functional expectations of his physical and social world.

Children who are entering the transition period have reached a level of competence and independence during their infancy that provides a developmental context for language acquisition. The development of symbolic communication becomes in turn the prerequisite to their further psychological growth and to their future functioning as a member of their society. The children's caregivers have played and will continue to play a critical role in this process since it is their responsibility to create the matrix of experiences in which symbolic communication is embedded.

ACKNOWLEDGMENT

I would like to thank Marilou Connor, Deborah Rice–Smithson, and Margaret Troy for background information on the children and Dr. James Kent for trusting me to try my plan of intervention. I would also like to acknowledge the caregivers in the therapeutic unit, Blanche Briscoe, Ruth Bryant, Carmella Echaveste, and Jean Johnstone, as well as Richard and Ann Brislin for their diary notes on their daughter Cheryl. I would also like to thank Dr. Roberta Golinkoff for her editorial assistance in clarifying the focus of this chapter.

REFERENCES

Bates, E. *The emergence of symbols: Cognition and communication in infancy.* New York: Academic Press, 1979.

Bates, E., Benigni, L., Bretherton, I., Camaioni, L., & Volterra, V. From gesture to first word: On cognitive and social prerequisites. In M. Lewis, & L. A. Rosenblum (Eds.), *Interaction, conversation and the development of language.* New York: Wiley, 1977.

Bates, E., Camaioni, L., & Volterra, V. The acquisition of performatives prior to speech. *Merrill Palmer Quarterly,* 1975, *21,* 205–226.

Bateson, M. C. The epigenesis of conversational interaction: A personal account of research development. In M. Bullowa (Ed.), *Before speech: The beginning of interpersonal communication.* New York: Cambridge University Press, 1979.

Blank, M., Gessner, M., & Esposito, A. Language without communication: A case study. *Journal of Child Language,* 1979, *6,* 329–352.

Bloom, L. *One word at a time: The use of single word utterances before syntax.* The Hague: Mouton, 1973.

Braunwald, S. R. Mother–child communication: The function of maternal-language input. In W. von Raffler–Engle (Ed.), *Child language 1975.* Great Britain: International Linguistic Association, 1976.

Braunwald, S. R., & Brislin, R. W. The diary method updated. In E. Ochs, & B. B. Schieffelin (Eds.), *Developmental pragmatics*. New York: Academic Press, 1979.

Bronfenbrenner, U. *The ecology of human development: Experiments by nature and design.* Cambridge, Mass.: Harvard University Press, 1979.

Bruner, J. The ontogenesis of speech acts. *Journal of Child Language*, 1975, *2*, 1–19.

Call, J. D. Some prelinguistic aspects of language development. *Journal of the American Psychoanalytic Association*, 1980, *28*, 259–289.

Clark, R. A. The transition from action to gesture. In A. Lock (Ed.), *Action, gesture and symbol: The emergence of language*. London: Academic Press, 1978.

Curtiss, S. *Genie: A psycholinguistic study of a modern day 'wild child.'* New York: Academic Press, 1977.

Garvey, C. Play with language and speech. In S. Ervin–Tripp, & C. Mitchell–Kernan (Eds.), *Child discourse*. New York: Academic Press, 1977.

George, C., & Main, M. Social interactions of young abused children: Approach, avoidance, and aggression. *Child Development*, 1979, *50*, 306–318.

George, C., & Main, M. Abused children: Their rejection of peers and caregivers. In T. M. Field (Ed.), *High-risk infants and children: Adult and peer interactions*. New York: Academic Press, 1980.

Gray, H. Learning how to take an object from the mother. In A. Lock (Ed.), Action, gesture, and symbol: The emergence of language. London: Academic Press, 1978.

Harding, C., & Golinkoff, R. The origins of intentional vocalizations in prelinguistic infants. *Child Development*, 1979, *50*, 33–40.

Kaye, K. Thickening thin data: The maternal role in developing communication and language. In M. Bullowa (Ed.), *Before speech: The beginning of interpersonal communication*. New York: Cambridge University Press, 1979.

Kaye, K. Why we don't talk 'baby talk' to babies. *Journal of Child Language*, 1980, *7*, 489–507.

Leung, E., & Rheingold, H. L. Development of pointing as a social gesture. *Developmental Psychology*, 1981, *17*, 215–220.

Lock, A. (Ed.) *Action, gesture, and symbol: The emergence of language*. London: Academic Press, 1978.

Lock, A. *The guided reinvention of language*. New York: Academic Press, 1980.

Mahoney, G., & Weller, E. L. An ecological approach to language intervention. In D. Bricker (Ed.), *Language intervention with children*. San Francisco, Ca.: Jossey-Bass, 1980.

Main, M. Abusive and rejecting infants. In N. Frude (Ed.), *The understanding and prevention of child abuse: Psychological approaches*. London: Concord Press, in press.

Murphy, C. M. Pointing in the context of a shared activity. *Child Development*, 1978, *49*, 371–380.

Newson, J. The growth of shared understandings between infant and caregiver. In M. Bullowa (Ed.), *Before speech: The beginning of interpersonal communication*. New York: Cambridge University Press, 1979.

Ochs, E., Schieffelin, B. B., & Platt, M. L. Propositions across utterances and speakers. In E. Ochs, & B. B. Schieffelin (Eds.), *Developmental pragmatics*. New York: Academic Press, 1979.

Piaget, J. *Play, dreams, and imitation in childhood*. (C. Gattegno & F. M. Hodgson, Trans.) New York: Norton, 1962. (Originally published 1951.)

Richards, M. P. M. The development of psychological communication in the first year of life. In K. Connolly, & J. Bruner (Eds.), *The growth of competence*. New York: Academic Press, 1974. (a)

Richards, M. P. M. First steps in becoming social. In M. P. M. Richards (Ed.), *The integration of a child into a social world*. London: Cambridge University Press, 1974. (b)

Schaffer, R. Mothering. In J. Bruner, M. Cole, & B. Lloyd (Eds.), *The developing child*. Cambridge, Mass.: Harvard University Press, 1977.

Scollon, R. A real early stage: An unzippered condensation of a dissertation on child language. In Working papers in linguistics, University of Hawaii, 1973, vol. 5, no. 6.

Shotter, J. The development of personal powers. In M. P. M. Richards (Ed.), *The integration of a child into a social world*. London: Cambridge University Press, 1974.

Trevarthen, C., & Hubley, P. Secondary intersubjectivity: Confidence, confiding, and acts of meaning in the first year. In A. Lock (Ed.), *Action, gesture, and symbol: The emergence of language*. London: Academic Press, 1978.

Troy, M. Personal Communication, September 1981.

Zivin, G. (Ed.) *The development of self-regulation through private speech*. New York: Wiley, 1979.

15

DISCUSSION
The Preverbal Child: Lessons for Intervention Practice

Judith R. Johnston
Department of Speech and Hearing Sciences Indiana University

Speech-language pathologists, special educators, and other practitioners of language intervention increasingly rely on basic developmental research for insight into the course and mechanisms of human growth. Application of this information is at times premature, superficial, or unimaginative—children and families in need do not wait for perfect solutions. Moreover, debates continue as to the pertinance of normal models of development for atypical populations (Bricker & Carlson, 1981). Nevertheless, developmental research remains the single most powerful determinant of current intervention practice. This is particularly evident when we look at the influence of "transition period" research findings over the past 6 to 8 years.

CURRENT APPLICATIONS OF DEVELOPMENTAL RESEARCH

Three themes recur throughout the literature concerning the transition from non-verbal to verbal modes of communication, expression, and thought. First, we are reminded that social interaction provides the context and important mechanisms for language learning. Language is a vehicle for maintaining interpersonal union (Dore, this volume). Meanings are negotiated (Golinkoff, this volume) for social purposes, and success in these negotiations demands specific interactional skills such as turn taking or attention getting. Occasions for language learning as well as powerful motives for the learning task, are supplied by the business, and pleasures, of life together.

261

Secondly, the "transition period" literature affirms the essentially symbolic nature of language. This is hardly a novel claim, but the transition period child does offer new demonstrations of its meaning. Early verbal and nonverbal symbols emerge together, serve common functions, and follow similar paths of decontextualization (Bates, Benigni, Bretherton, Camaioni, & Volterra, 1979; McCune–Nicholich & Carroll, 1981; Wolf, 1981). Later developments seem to reflect differences in the structure, mode, and degree of conventionality of symbolic systems, but the early parallels are striking testimony to the psychological unity of symbolic behavior, despite our ignorance as to the cognitive processes these behaviors represent.

Finally, "transition period" research reminds us that language is necessarily viewed as a functional, communicative tool. Certain aspects of language learning (e.g., phonological development, learning of spatial prepositions) may be explained by reference to motor, perceptual, conceptual, or structural facts, but other aspects of language development (e.g., topicalization, repair strategies, indirect speech act comprehension, and use) stem directly from the need to communicate a specific message to a specific person in a unique time and space. Infant research leaves no doubt that communication, of surprising variety and effectiveness, predates linguistic expression. It is equally true that language, once available, assumes communicative dominion. To understand language learning we must understand the impelling force of both the old functions and the new forms.

Each of these research themes, in consort with other legal, fiscal, and societal expressions of the Zeitgeist, has had marked impact on language intervention practice. Attention to the social, interactional context of language acquisition has led to a deepening professional respect for parents and caretakers as agents of change (e.g., Schumaker & Sherman, 1978) and to home-based programs of the sort described by Levenstein (this volume). Descriptions of typical caretaker child interactions, both verbal and nonverbal, have been directly translated into instructional paradigms: Devices such as "topic maintenance," "expansion," "contingent queries" have entered the interventionists's repetoire of methods (e.g., Bloom & Lahey, 1978; Ruder & Smith, 1974), and prelinguistic "conversational" skills have become explicit program goals. Not incidentally, research demonstrations of the effect of caretaker interaction styles on the rate and course of language learning (see Chapman, 1981, for review) have served to validate the intervention enterprise itself.

Information concerning non-linguistic symbol use has assumed its vital role in the diagnostic assessment of young "nonverbal" children. Clinicians are frequently asked to determine the developmental status of non-speaking 2-year-olds and must decide whether the absence of productive language is symptomatic of learning disorders. Normal variation in age of onset for speech and systematic biases in the research literature make this enterprise particularly difficult. Psychometrically oriented studies of infant development such as those by Gesell,

Cattell, and Griffeths, nicely illustrate the first problem. These researchers, examining relatively large and representative samples of children, report that "age of first word" ranges from 6 to 18 months (see Darley & Winitz, 1961, for review). Given such individual differences, a 2-year-old at the one-word stage may or may not be having difficulty with language learning.

The nonrepresentative composition of many research samples likewise complicates clinical decision making. One-third of the English speaking children who participated in the Berkeley Cross-Linguistic Acquisition Project, for example, scored above the 90th percentile on a standardized language assessment measure (Johnston, unpublished data[1]).

Faced with such evidence, language clinicians increasingly rely on nonverbal data to inform their diagnostic judgements. Observations of symbolic gestures or play are added to the language evaluation in order to compare developmental levels across symbolic modes. A "nonverbal" 2-and a half-year-old with no symbolic behaviors is more clearly at risk for pervasive cognitive delay than a "nonverbal" 2-and a half-year-old who can assume the role of *Mommy* in simple pretend play routine. Likewise, a 3-year-old child with complex play narratives and a 25 word vocabulary seems more likely to experience continuing specific language deficits than a 3-year-old whose language and play behaviors are at equivalent levels. Early identification of children with developmental disorders remains a subjective clinical process, but investigations of emerging symbolic schemes have provided us with important tools for distinguishing among preverbal children.

Finally, functional perspectives on language acquisition have changed the practice of language intervention in ways almost too numerous to mention. There have been dramatic shifts in instructional focus, intervention methods, and assessment questions. Inclusion of the copula, appropriate pronominal case forms and /r/ for /l/ substitutions seems less important to the interventionist whose concern is communication; conversational repair strategies, functional diversity, constructive comprehension processes, and lexical growth, in contrast, take on new value as instructional domains with immediate communication effect. They are also, as the papers in this volume well document (Chapman, Golinkoff, Harding), domains of learning that do not necessarily require linguistic sophistication. Language clinicians from the 1970s are thus evolving as communication specialists in the 1980s.

The energy currently devoted to creating alternative communication systems for children incapable of speech is just one evidence of this broadened scope of concern, (e.g., Vanderheiden, 1978; Schiefelbusch, 1979; Shane, 1981a, 1981b; Fristoe & Lloyd, 1979). These systems range in linguistic sophistication from

---

[1]These data come from unpublished analyses prepared by the author. Conversational samples from 48 English speaking children were assessed with the Developmental Sentence Score procedure (Lee, 1974): The children ranged in age from 2;0 to 4;4.

those requiring no syntax to those requiring simple rules for lexical ordering to those allowing for full visual representations of spoken language. They utilize symbols of varying degrees of iconicity, such as pictures, line drawings, pictographs, standard orthography. Technologically, they span a continuum from clinician-constructed communication boards to sophisticated micro-processors. The ongoing proliferation of nonspeech systems bears strong witness to human ingenuity and to the motivating force of functionalism, for the one thing these systems have in common is their focus on communication. They are designed to give nonspeaking children access to a symbolic code which can be used in social interaction. McDonald (1978) summarizes the prevailing view: "We must recognize that our job is broader than just teaching the child to talk; our job is to help the child learn to communicate [p. 15]."

The new emphasis on language function has also led to re-examination of intervention methods. The most profound change can be seen in recent attempts to actually conduct language therapy in the context of dialogue, with real messages, minimally contrived outcomes, child-initiated topics and few metalinguistic intrusions (e.g., Mahoney & Weller, 1980). To appreciate this change, consider first the syntactic pattern drills typical of language intervention efforts in the 60s and early 70s. Gray and Ryan (1973, p. 32), for example, provide the following illustration of an intervention activity designed to teach the use of the copula. The clinician and Johnny, the child, are seated at a table looking at a series of pictures.

```
Adult:  The car is blue.
        Johnny, is blue.
Child:  blue.
Adult:  The boy is old. (new picture)
        Johnny, is old.
Child:  is old.
Adult:  Good. (gives token)
```

The focus of this exchange is clearly not on communication. Neither partner needs information about the pictures. They merely provide an excuse for formulating utterances.

Functionally oriented approaches to intervention are far removed from such syntactic drills. Advocates of communication-centered methods create situations which demand the use of a particular language rule and provide the child with multiple instances of this pattern while pursuing some common task. In one illustrative scenario, an 8-year-old who does not use the auxiliary BE might be asked to "spy" on events outside the window and report to his "partner," the clinician, who is crouched below the window with a pen and pad. The dialogue would unfold as follows:

Child: A man getting in car.
Adult: A man is getting in his car?
Child: Yeh. He driving away.
Adult: Oh, he is driving away. Is he speeding?
Child: No, he is going slow.
Adult: Aah, he is going slow.

The key elements in this activity are the clinician's actual need for information, the child's responsibility to provide information, and the clinician's models, expansions, and repetitions offered in the guise of acknowledgments and queries. Though not widely practiced, this approach constitutes a new and visible challenge to methods rooted in preprogrammed behavioral technology (Bricker & Carlson, 1981).

Finally, the emphasis on functional aspects of language and recent information on the growth of prelinguistic communication has raised new assessment options. As was the case for symbolic behavior, preverbal communication skills can distinguish among nonverbal 2-year-olds, helping us identify those with social and cognitive problems in addition to language delay. The child who does not show objects to gain adult attention or fails to coordinate his bids for a desired object with solicitation of adult aid (Sugarman, this volume) is clearly at greater risk for developmental delay than a child with effective prelinguistic communication schemes. The complimentary cases are equally significant. In our university clinic, we frequently meet children with remarkably effective communication despite the virtual absence of linguistic means. This clinical impression of disparity between formal and communicative competence is being corroborated by more formal studies of language-impaired and developmentally delayed persons (e.g., Abbeduto & Rosenberg, 1980; Collins & Schneider, 1979; Fey, Leonard, & Wilcox, 1981; Gallagher & Darnton, 1978; Johnston & Kamhi, 1980; Snyder, 1975; Watson, 1977). Pragmatic perspectives on language assessment allow us to recognize important social and cognitive strengths as well as to establish deficits. In the case of the nonspeaking 2-year-old, communication skills constitute one sort of evidence that a child is prepared to benefit from language intervention.

Thus far we have examined the ways in which studies of the child in transition from preverbal to verbal communication have influenced professionals engaged in language intervention. This influence has been both specific and general. Particular research findings have been transformed into methods or goals appropriate for children in the transitional phase of development, but also, the major theoretical themes which pervade the transition period literature have inspired innovations with atypical populations at all developmental levels. A more careful historical analysis might reveal that these changes and the infant research itself both reflect some shift in a larger social and intellectual climate, but the local influences would surely remain.

FUTURE APPLICATIONS OF DEVELOPMENTAL
RESEARCH

We turn next to consider several areas where the research literature suggests intervention opportunities which are as yet largely unrecognized. In describing the hypothesized mechanisms through which language is learned in the course of social transactions, researchers invoke notions of *redundancy* (e.g., Messer, this volume), *communication adjustments* (e.g., Harding, this volume; Garvey, this volume), and *affective bonding* or *relationship* (e.g., Dore, this volume). For normal children in normal learning environments these aspects of interaction may be assumed. For many atypical children, the case is different. Physical, cognitive, and social constraints reduce the likelihood that the usual facilitating conditions will occur.

Redundant messages, for example, may be of little assistance to the child with an attentional disorder who fails to notice events or is slow to interpret those that are noticed (Mackworth, Grandstaff & Pribrum, 1973; Otto, Houck, Finger, & Hart, 1973). Limitations on rate or capacity of central processing (Rosenthal, 1974) may well create competing signals out of the original complementary set. Traditional therapeutic approaches for such children advocate reduced "environmental stimulation" (e.g., Cruickshank, Bentzen, Ratzeburg, & Tannhauser, 1961), but this tactic seems somehow to have missed the point. Attention is as much the function of the organism as of the environment (e.g., Collins & Hagen, 1979; Posner & Boies, 1971). Children presented with "unimodal stimuli" (e.g., Eisenson, 1972) have no opportunity to develop the attentional strategies they lack, and redundancy is altogether precluded. A more effective approach might be one which tolerated and accommodated to deviant patterns of attention—slowing the rate of information, utilizing routine and familiar materials, intensifying the perceptual value of critical events, and following the child's own attentional flow.

As a second example, consider the phenomenon of communication failure. The papers in this volume (e.g., Golinkoff; Chapman) confirm our intuitions that infants and caretakers, like adults at conferences, do not always make their meanings clear nor quite get the message. They have communication difficulties for all the usual reasons: lapses of attention, expressive idiosyncracies, differences in conceptual or factual resources. Effective adult communicators assume responsibility for the health of a dialogue and actively maintain it by securing attention, nodding agreement, asking for clarification, and so on. These attitudes and skills must be learned, however, and this learning begins early (e.g., Bruner, this volume; Golinkoff, this volume; Harding, this volume). Very young children will persist when misunderstood, vary the form of a message when queried, seek visual assurance that they're on the right track, and construct "best guess" interpretations for partially understood messages (e.g., Chapman, this volume; Gallagher & Darnton, 1978; Garvey, this volume; Golinkoff, this volume). Such competency is the fruit of intelligent investigation of the phenomenon of miscommunication.

For some disordered populations, neither of these conditions may be met. Children may lack both the requisite intellectual energy and the experience of communication failure. Studies of effectance motivation (e.g., Harter & Zigler, 1974), for example, suggest that retarded children tend to avoid novelty, rely on familiar routines, and shy away from challenging tasks. Moreover, the typical language training programs for such children are designed to eliminate "errors" and involve virtually no true communication (e.g., Kent, 1972; Guess, Sailor, & Baer, 1974). There are as yet no comparative studies of metacommunication abilities in retarded persons, but developmental delays would seem inevitable given these organismic and environmental conditions. The problem is one which invites fundamental changes in training paradigms, and perhaps the use of explicit instruction in communication strategies analogous to that currently being used for various cognitive strategies (Hallahan, 1980).

The third intervention challenge concerns the notions of environmental responsivity and affective bonding. According to one account, infants learn the communicative potential of actions by observing their consistent effect on social objects (e.g., Garvey, this volume; Ryan, 1974; Schaffer, 1977). A set of instinctive behaviors seems to be the starting point for these action-response links (Ainsworth, 1973). Sucking, postural adjustment, vocalizing, crying, and eye contact, to name several, serve to gain necessary physical protection for the infant. These genetically predetermined schemes are the first actions to which the environment responds. They also become the mechanisms of emotional attachment since they promote proximity and mutual attention. As discussed by Dore (this volume), communication and language learning are motivated in part by a desire for interpersonal union. Some disordered children, particularly those diagnosed as autistic, seem to lack this basic motivation. They are at best ambivalent about social contact and prefer solitary activity (Wing, 1976). A second look at Ainsworth's attachment mechanisms suggests a possible source for this motivational deficit. Five of the eight behaviors she lists are mentioned as deviant in clinical accounts of autism. Parents of autistic children frequently recall that feeding was difficult; that crying was infrequent; that eye contact was actively avoided; that their infants failed to relax when held; and that their vocalizations were difficult to interpret (Wing, 1976; Rutter, 1978).

Ricks' (1975) experimental demonstration of this last point is particularly dramatic. Parents of normal infants were able to interpret vocal expressions of surprise, greeting, request, and frustration though they could not distinguish their own child's sounds from those of other infants. Parents of preverbal autistic children, in contrast, could identify as well as understand their own child's vocalizations. They could likewise understand the sounds made by retarded nonautistic children, but they could not appropriately assign meaning to the sounds made by other autistic children. It seems that autistic children produce idiosyncratic vocalizations and thus, that parents must learn to interpret these sounds before they can respond.

Following Ainsworth's and Dore's arguments, disruptions of the usual mechanisms for emotional attachment may well impede the affective growth of autistic infants, thus weakening their motivation to communicate. Such disruption may also make caretakers less consistently responsive, reducing the likelihood that autistic infants will discover the communicative potential of action. In the case of the autistic child, then, we can assume neither a normally responsive environment nor strong affective bonds. The key intervention concept here is that of functional equivalency. If looking, feeding, or crying cannot lead to proximity and pleasant mutual exchange, perhaps some other activity, like fingerplay, could. If vocalizations cannot bring consistent caretaker response, perhaps some other action, such as a contrived bell ringing, could (Watson & Hayes, 1981). Early identification and parent education are obviously crucial to such an approach. Language interventionists can usually assume that children are motivated for learning to talk, though they may balk at specific tasks. The autistic child confronts us with a profound affective disturbance, and the transition period literature provides some insight into its nature and possible consequences.

PROBLEMS IN APPLICATION: CAUSE AND CONTINUITY

The discussion thus far amply demonstrates that transition-period research has broad and beneficial implications for the language interventionist. This chapter would be incomplete, however, without two cautionary notes. First, there is the clear possibility that by stressing the importance of caretaker–child interaction for language learning, we will grant the notion of *environmental deficiency* more prominence than it deserves as an explanation for language delay. Infrequent opportunities for social exchange and generally impoverished experience can certainly lead to developmental delays in otherwise normal children. The work of Levenstein (this volume) and others (e.g., Ramey, Sparling, & Wasik, 1981) demonstrates that caretaker-centered intervention can produce long term positive changes in intellectual and school performance. The exact role of accelerated language/communication skills in this improvement is, however, unclear.

From another line of research we learn that mothers of language disordered children, in comparison to mothers of linguistically normal children, are less likely to be verbally responsive or positively involved (Wulbert, Inglis, Kriegsmann, & Mills, 1975) with their children. They exhibit a higher incidence of psychiatric disorder (Richman & Stevenson, 1977), and direct fewer topic-maintaining, intelligible utterances to their children (Newhoff, Silverman, & Millet, 1980). The explanatory significance of these facts is again, not as obvious as it first may seem. Three sorts of evidence bear on this point. First, if deficiencies in the social environment played a primary causal role in developmental language disorders, we would expect to find significant relationships between social factors and degree of impairment. In Shery's (1980) recent retrospective study of 718 language disordered children, social and emotional factors were related to school progress but did not predict severity of language delay. Secondly, the patterns of language impairment observed in some disordered groups are not those that would be predicted from an environmental deficit hypothesis. Comparing language-disordered and normal children with equivalent Mean-Length-of-Utterance (MLU), Johnston and Kamhi (1980) found evidence of special difficulty with minor syntactic forms such as auxiliaries, copulas, infinitive markers, and complemetizing particles. This finding might at first seem to implicate parameters of linguistic input, since these are exactly the sort of form which seems most open to the influence of maternal speech (Newport, Gleitman, & Gleitman, 1977). A closer look at our data revealed, however, that these syntactic difficulties stemmed from performance "errors" rather than from differences in formal knowledge. Our language disordered subjects knew those syntactic forms which were appropriate for their MLU-based stage, but produced them inconsistently. Furthermore, these children conflated fewer propositions into each utterance, but did not differ from normal children in their use of contextually sensitive forms (e.g., ellipsis, pronouns). Such linguistic profiles seem to reflect cognitively-based sentence formulation difficulties rather than social or environmental deficits. Finally, recent work on temporal resolution (e.g., Tallal & Piercy, 1978), constructive comprehension (EllisWeismer, 1981), and mental rotation (Johnston & EllisWeismer, in press) suggests that language disordered children suffer pervasive and diverse information processing deficits. These data, in conjunction with the linguistic data previously described, point to causal factors of organic rather than social origin.

The point here is not that social context is irrelevant to language delay, but rather that our models of developmental disorder and remediation must be appropriately complex. We need to incorporate organismic as well as social variables and explicitly recognize their interaction (Sameroff & Chandler, 1975). Aspects of maternal communication may impede language learning only for children who are organically predisposed to difficulty with this task. Likewise, we may be able to improve children's success in language learning by altering the typical patterns of communication addressed to them, but only within the limitations imposed by any underlying cognitive impairment. For some families, our intervention program will include efforts to "normalize" the child's social milieu. For other families, we may pursue therapeutically abnormal styles of interaction. Parents may, for example, be advised to use disproportionately high frequencies of specific words or sentence forms to simplify the child's learning task. In both cases, the literature on early caretaker–child exchange can guide our selections of learning goals and interaction strategies. We can be confident that by facilitating environmental change we are increasing the child's opportunities to learn.

But the enterprise warrants cautious prognosis and care in the message we convey to parents. By advocating changes in interaction style we may implicitly and inappropriately identify parenting as a primary causal factor in children's atypical development.

The second cautionary note is well introduced by the following clinical anecdote. J. was a 51-month-old in the transition-period. He scored within the normal range on performance IQ scales, but had only a limited single word vocabulary and a few unanalyzed verbal routines, such as "timetogo." He initiated cooperative play, but relied on pointing, tugging, and vocalization for most communiques. Explicit requests for speech were met with silence and withdrawal. J. preferred ball games to pretend play and his play symbols were limited to single conventional acts on objects (McCune-Nicholich & Carroll, 1981). There had been little change in these parameters for a year at the time J. entered our preschool-centered intervention program. J. thoroughly enjoyed the classroom where, among other things, he began to participate in teacher-initiated symbolic play activities. His language tutorials were another matter. Even though they took place just down the hall and were conducted by a familiar teacher, J. was silent and uninvolved during these sessions. He clearly disliked them. After several weeks of unhappiness, J. invented his own solution to the problem. He initiated an elaborate play scenario in which one corner of the room was his house and a distant corner was the teacher's. He would call the teacher on a play telephone and invite her over to play, "comeovermyhouse?" Immediately upon her arrival, J. would send her home.

J. had apparently discovered the communicative value of play symbols. They perfectly expressed his affective ambivalence and were effective in establishing social control. After two half-hour sessions of repeating this initial script, J. tolerated longer "visits" and allowed the teacher to initiate brief play themes. Within a month he was totally involved in play-centered language intervention activities.

As researchers, we could analyze this pivotal event according to: (1) the complexity of the play schemes; (2) their affective content and context; (3) their meaning in the larger social and physical ecology; or (4) their communicative function. From a clinical perspective, however, the event assumed significance because it was a solution to an ecological problem *and* an expression of ambivalence *and* a resumption of communication *and* an elaboration of prior play schemes. More importantly, it may well have occurred exactly because it had these several roots. What interventionists need to know is not only how to characterize the lines of social, affective, cognitive, communicative, and symbolic development that conspire to produce such growth, but also the nature of their mutual influence and the factors that promote their synthesis or coupling (Shatz, this volume). Research reported here (Dore, this volume) and elsewhere (e.g., Fisher & Watson, 1981) is just beginning to address these issues with promise of both theoretical and practical advances. We must, in the meantime, remember our ignorance.

Continuity, in the final analysis, resides within the learner. We can count on normal children to make effective use of prior learning, to create something altogether new out of old material. Interventionists frequently program the component skills and discover that the whole is no greater than the sum of its parts (Bricker & Carlson, 1981; Hogg, 1981). For us, the challenge of the transition-period is that it dramatically illustrates the normal child's integration of disparate and complex schemes. Can we help disordered children achieve the same?

REFERENCES

Abbeduto, L., & Rosenberg, S. The communicative competence of mildly retarded adults. *Applied Psycholinguistics*, 1980, *1*, 405–426.

Ainsworth, M. The development of infant–mother attachment. In B. Caldwell, & H. Ricciuti (Eds.), *Review of child development research*, Vol. 3. New York: Russell Sage Foundation, 1973.

Bates, E., Benigni, L., Bretherton, I., Camaioni, L., & Volterra, V. *The emergence of symbols: Communication and cognition in infancy.* New York: Academic Press, 1979.

Bloom, L., & Lahey, M. *Language development and language disorders.* New York: Wiley, 1978.

Bricker, D., & Carlson, L. Issues in early language intervention. In R. Schiefelbusch, & D. Bricker (Eds.), *Early language: Acquisition and intervention.* Baltimore, Md.: University Park Press, 1981.

Chapman, R. Mother–child interaction in the second year of life: Its role in language development. In R. Schiefelbusch, & D. Bricker (Eds.), *Early language: Acquisition and intervention.* Baltimore, Md.: University Park Press, 1981.

Collins, J., & Hagen, J. A constructivist account of the development of perception, attention, and memory. In G. Hale & M. Lewis (Eds.), *Attention and cognitive development.* New York: Plenum Press, 1979.

Collins, C., & Schneider, B. Revisions in the speech of normal and mentally impaired children. Paper presented to the American Speech and Hearing Association, November, 1979, Chicago, Ill.

Cruickshank, W., Bentzen, F., Ratzeburg, F., & Tannhauser, M. *A teaching method for brain-injured and hyperactive children.* Syracuse, N.Y.: Syracuse University Press, 1961.

Darley, F., & Winitz, H. Age of first word: Review of research. *Journal of Speech and Hearing Disorders*, 1961, *26*, 272–290.

Eisenson, J. *Aphasia in children.* New York: Harper & Row, 1972.

EllisWeismer, S. Constructive comprehension processes exhibited by language impaired children. Unpublished doctoral dissertation, Indiana University, 1981.

Fey, M., Leonard, L., & Wilcox, K. Speech style modifications of language-impaired children. *Journal of Speech and Hearing Research*, 1981, *46*, 91–96.

Fisher, K., & Watson, M. Explaining the Oedipus conflict. In K. Fisher (Ed.), *New directions for child development: Cognitive development, No. 12.* San Francisco, Ca.: Jossey–Bass 1981.

Fristoe, M., & Lloyd, L. Nonspeech communication. In N. Ellis (Ed.), *Handbook of mental deficiency*, 2nd Ed. Hillsdale, NJ: Lawrence Erlbaum Associates, 1979.

Gallagher, T., & Darnton, B. Conversational aspects of the speech of language-disordered children: Revision behaviors. *Journal of Speech and Hearing Research*, 1978, *21*, 118–135.

Gray, B., & Ryan, B. *A language program for the nonlanguage child.* Champaign, Ill.: Research Press, 1973.

Guess, D., Sailor, W., & Baer, D. To teach language to retarded children. In R. Schiefelbusch, & L. Lloyd (Eds.), *Language perspectives—acquisition, retardation and intervention.* Baltimore, Md.: University Park Press, 1974.

Hallahan, D. (Ed.) *Exceptional education quarterly: Teaching exceptional children to use cognitive strategies, Vol. 1:1.* Rockville, Md: Aspen Systems Corp., 1980.

Harter, S., & Zigler, E. The assessment of effectance motivation in normal and retarded children. *Developmental Psychology,* 1974, *10,* 169–180.

Hogg, J. Strategies and evaluation of early intervention. In R. Schiefelbusch, & D. Bricker (Eds.), *Early language: Acquisition and intervention.* Baltimore, Md.: University Park Press, 1981.

Johnston, J., & EllisWeismer, S. Mental rotation skills in language disordered children. *Journal of Speech and Hearing Research,* in press.

Johnston, J., & Kamhi, A. The same can be less: Syntactic and semantic aspects of the utterances of language-impaired children. *Proceedings of the first Symposium on Research in Child Language Disorders.* Department of Communicative Disorders, University of Wisconsin-Madison, 1980.

Kent, L. A language acquisition program for the retarded. In J. McLean, D. Yoder, & R. Schiefelbusch (Eds.), *Language intervention with the retarded.* Baltimore, Md.: University Park Press, 1972.

Lee, L. *Developmental sentence analysis.* Evanston, Ill.: Northwestern University Press, 1974.

Mackworth, N., Grandstaff, N., & Pribrum, K. Orientation to pictorial novelty in speech disordered children. *Neuropsychologia,* 1973, 11, 443–450.

Mahoney, G., & Weller, E. An ecological approach to language intervention. In D. Bricker (Ed.), *New directions for exceptional children: Language intervention with children, No. 2.* San Francisco, Ca.: Jossey-Bass, 1980.

McCune–Nicholich, L., & Carroll, S. Development of symbolic play: Implications for the language specialist. In J. Johnston (Ed.), *Topics in language disorders: Cognition and language in the preschool years, Vol. 2:1.* Rockville, Md: Aspen Systems Corp., 1981.

McDonald, E. Identification of children at risk. In G. Vanderheiden (Ed.), *Nonvocal communication resource book.* Baltimore, Md.: University Park Press, 1978.

Newhoff, M., Silverman, L., & Millet, A. Linguistic differences in parent's speech to normal and language disordered children. *Proceedings of the first Symposium on Research in Child Language Disorders.* Department of Communicative Disorders, University of Wisconsin-Madison, 1980.

Newport, E., Gleitman, H., & Gleitman, L. Mother, I'd rather do it myself: The contribution of selected child listener variables. In C. Snow, & C. Ferguson (Eds.), *Talking to children: Language input and acquisition.* Cambridge, Mass.: Cambridge University Press, 1977.

Otto, D., Houck, K., Finger, H., & Hart, S. Event related slow potentials in aphasic, dyslexic, and normal children during pictorial and letter matching. Proceedings of the Third International Congress of Event Related Slow Potentials of the Brain. Bristol, England, 1973.

Posner, M., & Boies, S. Components of attention. *Psychological Review,* 1971, *78,* 391–408.

Ramey, C., Sparling, J., & Wasik, B. Creating social environments to facilitate language development. In R. Schiefelbusch, & D. Bricker (Eds.), *Early language: Acquisition and intervention.* Baltimore, Md.: University Park Press, 1981.

Richman, N., & Stevenson, J. Language delay in 3-year-olds: Family and social factors. *Acta Paediatrica Belgica,* 1977, 30, 213–219.

Ricks, D. Vocal communication in preverbal normal and autistic children. In N. O'Connor (Ed.), *Language, cognitive deficits and retardation.* London: Butterworths, 1975.

Rosenthal, W. The role of perception in child language disorders: A theory based on faulty signal detection strategies. Paper presented to the American Speech and Hearing Association, month 1974.

Ruder, K., & Smith, M. Issues in language training. In R. Schiefelbusch, & L. Lloyd (Eds.),

Language perspectives—acquisition, retardation, and intervention. Baltimore, Md.: University Park Press, 1974.

Rutter, M. Diagnosis and definition. In M. Rutter, & E. Schopler (Eds.), *Autism: A reappraisal of concepts and treatment.* New York: Plennum Press, 1978.

Ryan, J. Early language development: Towards a communicational analysis. In M. Richards (Ed.), *The integration of a child into a social world.* London: Cambridge University Press, 1974.

Sameroff, A., & Chandler, M. Reproductive risk and the continuum of caretaking casualty. In F. Horowitz (Ed.), *Review of child development research, Vol. 4.* Chicago, Ill.: University of Chicago Press, 1975.

Schaffer, R. *Mothering.* Cambridge, Mass.: Harvard University Press, 1977.

Schiefelbusch, R. (Ed.), *Nonspeech language and communication: Analysis and intervention.* Baltimore, Md.: University Park Press, 1979.

Schumaker, J., & Sherman, J. Parent as intervention agent. In R. Schiefelbusch (Ed.), *Language intervention strategies.* Baltimore, Md.: University Park Press, 1978.

Shane, H. Decision making in early augmentative communication system use. In R. Schiefelbusch, & D. Bricker (Eds.), *Early language: Acquisition and intervention.* Baltimore, Md.: University Park Press, 1981. (a)

Shane, H. Working with the non-speaking person: An interview. *Asha,* 1981, *23,* 561–564. (b)

Shery, T. Correlates of language development in language disordered chidren: An archival study. Unpublished doctoral dissertation, Claremont Graduate School, 1980.

Snyder, L. Pragmatics in language disabled children: Their prelinguistic and early verbal performatives and presuppositions. Unpublished doctoral dissertation. University of Colorado, 1975.

Tallal, P., & Piercy, M. Defects of auditory perception in children with developmental dysphasia. In M. Wyke (Ed.), *Developmental dysphasia.* London: Academic Press, 1978.

Vanderheiden, G. (Ed.), *Non-vocal communication resource book.* Baltimore, Md.: University Park Press, 1978.

Watson, J., & Hayes, L. Response-contingent stimulation as a treatment for development failure in infancy. Paper presented to the Society for Research in Child Development, 1981.

Watson, L. Conversational participation by language deficient and normal children. In J. Andrews, & M. Burns (Eds.), *Selected papers in language and phonology,* Vol. II. Evanston, Il.: Institute for Continuing Education, 1977.

Wing, L. Diagnosis, clinical description, and prognosis. In L. Wing (Ed.), *Early childhood autism: Clinical, educational, and social aspects.* Oxford: Pergamon Press, 1976.

Wolf, D. Playing along: Shared meaning in pretense play. Paper presented to the Society for Research in Child Development, month 1981.

Wulbert, M., Inglis, S., Kreigsmann, E., & Mills, B. Language delay and associated mother–child interactions. *Developmental Psychology,* 1975, *11,* 61–70.

I would say
the one word period
is the transition-
s/for pre-8/ys
as it is neither one
nor the other

16

DISCUSSION OF THE VOLUME

Reconsidering the Transition from Prelinguistic to Linguistic Communication

Rochel Gelman
University of Pennsylvania

My task is to present an overview of the conference. Since the discussants have done so much already to underscore the many issues raised at the conference, I will be brief.

This was a conference on the transition period from prelinguistic to linguistic communication. As somewhat of an outsider looking in, I have several impressions. First, and perhaps foremost, I detect a serious source of miscommunication. I take the transition period from prelinguistic to linguistic communication to be that period during which a child begins to combine words and her vocabulary explodes. But, I suspect that others do not and instead take it to be that period when the infant goes from preverbal to verbal communication. What a difference! In the latter case, the child uses but one word at a time and the words she uses are few. In the former case the child talks in, what we all agree, resembles sentences and draws on an extensive vocabulary. I much prefer to restrict the phrase "linguistic communication" to the latter meaning. In being conservative, I take my cue from my colleague David Premack who points out that it is relatively easy to teach a chimpanzee a limited vocabulary; however, it is exceedingly difficult, if not impossible, to teach the same chimpanzee a grammar for generating sentences. Word use need not index linguistic prowess. Whatever the choice, it is absolutely crucial that investigators make clear which one is their's. Further, one's perspective on this conference will surely depend on which interpretation is assumed. For, from my perspective, little was said about the transition period.

Second, the assumption that prelinguistic communication skill serves as a necessary and even sufficient condition for the onset of language is being reconsidered. And one consequence of this is a returning interest in the nature of linguistic (in my sense) communication. This is good; it seemed to me, by and large, that the field of language acquisition lost sight of the need to describe language acquisition itself (cf. Bloom, this volume; Shatz, this volume). The host of interesting facts about prelinguistic communication are just that; very interesting. But it is not obvious that they bear on the problem of explaining language acquisition. Indeed, Bruner's remarks led me think that they do not. Let me expand a bit.

As Shatz (1982, in press) has indicated, much of the work on preverbal communication seems motivated by the goal to show the causal role it plays in language acquisition. We now know a great deal about early interaction rituals (e.g., Bruner, 1975); the first use of others to accomplish a goal (e.g., Bates, 1976); the onset of intentional communications (Harding, this volume); negotiations to rectify misinterpretations (Golinkoff, this volume) and so on. However, in none of this work have I been able to find an account of how these marvelous facts of infancy serve as causes of syntax. To be sure, there is something like a "syntax" of sensorimotor communications but nowhere is there a detailed account of what this might be. Bruner noted that the interactions involving giving and taking are ordered. However, he did not write the "grammar" of these or the overarching "grammar" which articulates these into coordinated preverbal communications. Without these descriptions, it is impossible to evaluate the idea that the syntax of preverbal communications foreshadows and even embodies the later use of syntax in verbal communication.

Apropos the foregoing, I have also been concerned with the absence of a theory of how the syntax of preverbal communications is translated into the syntax of language. Put differently, I have always thought that the above line of theory rested too much on metaphor and too little on the working out of this metaphor. The absence of such a line of work has led me to think that it cannot be done; I suspect that there are no translation rules which take prelinguistic accomplishments and turn them into grammatical competencies. When Bruner (this volume) said that it is impossible to do this, I was not surprised.

I do not mean to say that the work on early communication has been a waste of time. Quite the contrary. We know many wonderful things about the first two years of life that we would not have had we not studied prelinguistic communication. For example, anyone who has spent time with an infant will recognize that Golinkoff has picked up on a real phenomenon in her work on "the negotiation of meaning" and it is grand to have her account of it. I do mean to say that a more balanced allotment of research resources, one that pays more attention to the development of linguistic communication, is needed.

As an example of what I think needs researching, consider the acquisition of vocabulary. Once children begin to talk in sentences (or something resembling them) their rate of vocabulary acquisition is stupendous. Carey (1978) pointed out that a child picks up about six to 10 new words a day during the preschool period. Contrast this with the laborious efforts on the part of parents and child to get but one word learned during the prelinguistic period (Dore, this volume). These are truly remarkable facts. Why is it so hard for the child to learn words in the prelinguistic period? What is it about the onset of sentence production (and comprehension), or some correlate, that turns the matter around?

I suspect that the child who has reached a minimal stage of syntactic competence benefits from the availability of linguistic structures just as we benefit from available structures when we try to memorize facts. It is a well-known fact that the human mind has a very difficult time committing items to memory in the absence of mental organizations. Given an organization into which to slot these items, however, learning can proceed at tremendous rates (e.g., Miller, Galanter, & Pribram, 1960). My idea is that syntax provides the organization scheme that is necessary for vocabulary learning to begin to explode. One function of syntax then is to help organize the task of vocabulary learning. Of course, there also have to be parallel changes in cognitive development if the words are to be understood. Still, there can be no denying that leaps in communication skill come with the use of a rich set of vocabulary items and we need to study how this happens.

Lest I give the impression that the child who has an extended vocabulary has mastered the art of verbal communication, I must draw attention to Shatz's contribution to this volume. She, as well as Bloom and Garvey (again, this volume) remind us of the many skills the young linguistic communicator lacks or needs to develop further. My point here is simply that research on the explosion in vocabulary growth is but one area of linguistic communication skill that has been ignored and that deserves serious attention. It is good that people at this conference recognize this.

My third impression is that we have not solved the problem of when to assign intention to a baby's communication efforts. I find Schieffelen's work (this volume) particularly compelling on this point. Different cultures seem to have different definitions of the onset of language. Ours seems to be a culture which is quick to assign intentions to babies. Witness everyone's efforts to figure out why a baby is fussy. We engage in an extended guessing game, treating a baby as a guessing stimulus. A baby does X and we make a guess as to why, for example, "he's hungry" and act on this guess. Nine times out of 10 we are wrong and proceed to the next guess, for example, "he wants his blanket" and act in turn, and so on. Notice, we attribute attention when it might be sufficient to invoke notions of reinforcement. This leads me to ponder the possibility that our theories of early communication competence are too quick to assign intention. It would do well to keep in mind the possibility that simpler explanatory devices, like reinforcement contingencies, may suffice. At least, it ought to serve as an explicit alternative hypothesis which is then ruled out.

My fourth impression is that we are still too inclined to the view that mothers (or some other primary caretaker) need to engage in well coordinated, synchronized interactions with their babies for language acquisition to take place.

Commonsense alone ought to serve to mitigate this implicit belief in the Freudian theory of the role of mothers in normal development. For when else but when we train our videocameras on middle class mothers do we see carefully orchestrated interaction? (Parenthetically, if we at the conference really believed in this causal theory surely many of us would have stayed at home.) Cross-cultural work helps buttress this point. As Schieffelin's work demonstrates, we are in danger of creating a developmental account of language acquisition that is true for only middle class Anglo Saxon families. All the work on what Newport (1976) termed "motherese" should likewise give pause to those who advocate such causal accounts of language acquisition.

To be sure, there have to be and are some effects of the linguistic environment on the nature of language acquisition (see Gleitman, Newport, & Gleitman, 1982 for a recent review). But I am impressed by how difficult it is to pin down the nature of the inputs and their respective effects. I am also impressed by how gross the adjustments are to young children (e.g., Shatz, 1982)—hardly the sort of thing one expects under an assumption of exquisitely fine attention to the current competences and needs of the language learner.

There has been much talk about what the child might bring to the tasks of learning language and how to communicate. I am somewhat surprised by the absence of mention of one obvious candidate—a competence motivation which leads the child to seek out the environment which is needed to nurture the structural capacities available to the child. Piaget (1978) postulates that every scheme tends to "feed" itself, that is, to incorporate into itself external elements that are compatible with its nature. The child's schemes are thus seen as constituting the motivational source, or the motor of development. Schemes are said to actively search out the environment in their effort to "feed" or actualize themselves. The child is taken to be in control of the inputs she needs for development to proceed—inputs which are dictated by the mental structures available to the child. By such a view it is not obvious that the answer to the question of what are the required inputs will be forthcoming from studies of "motherese." In a nontrivial way the child herself is teacher and creator of learning materials. Hence, the child herself should be turned to for clues to the puzzle of how the environment contributes to language learning. Giving the child considerable control of the learning environment reduces the need for accounts that place the burden on the primary-caretaker, and hence, offers a way to deal with the kinds of problems with such theories.

Finally, on matters of continuity or not: I must underline a point that has been made by both Sugarman (this volume) and Shatz (this volume). This is that it is not necessary to observe any commonality between early stages of communication and later language acquisition. It is very possible that it is otherwise. It could be that language acquisition resembles the tadpole to frog case where what occurs at an early stage is completely transformed. Or it could be that we are dealing with a scaffolding model wherein the scaffold comes down and is thrown away as soon as the building is up. In a similar vein, it is not even necessary for a nativist to show early onset of behavior: witness the case of puberty. We need to become more sophisticated in our discussions of nature-nurture before jumping to conclusions about what is or is not brought by the child herself to the task of prelinguistic and linguistic communication (cf. Gelman, Maccoby, & Levine, 1982).

I end with a truism. I see that we have made some progress in mapping an account of how communication skill develops. Yet, we still have a long way to go—a fact which was pointed to over and over again at this conference.

ACKNOWLEDGMENTS

I thank Roberta Golinkoff and Lila Gleitman for their helpful comments on an earlier draft. Support for preparation of this commentary came from NSF grant BNS-81-40573.

REFERENCES

Bates, E. *Language and context: The acquisition of pragmatics*. N.Y.: Academic Press, 1976.

Bruner, J. S. From communication to language: a psychological perspective. *Cognition*, 1975, *3*, 1–19.

Carey, S. The child as word learner. In M. Halle, J. Bresnan, & G. A. Miller (Eds.), *Linguistic theory and psychological reality*. Cambridge, Mass.: MIT Press, 1978.

Gelman, R., Maccoby, E., & Levine, R. Complexity in development and developmental studies. In W. A. Collins (Ed.), *The concept of development. The Minnesota Symposium on Child Psychology, Vol. 15*. Hillsdale, N.J.: Lawrence Erlbaum Associates, 1982.

Gleitman, L. R., Newport, E., & Gleitman, H. The current status of the motherese hypothesis. Unpublished manuscript, University of Pennsylvania, 1982.

Miller, G. A., Galanter, E., & Pribram, K. H. *Plans and the structure of behavior*. New York: Holt, Rinehart, & Winston, 1960.

Newport, E. *Motherese: the speech of mothers to young children*. Ph.D dissertation. University of Pennsylvania, 1976.

Piaget, J. *The development of thought*. Oxford: Basil Blackwell, 1978.

Shatz, M. Learning the rules of the game: Four views of the relation between social interaction and syntax acquisition. In W. Deutsch (Ed.), *The child's construction of language*. London: Academic Press, 1982.

Shatz, M. On mechanisms of language acquisition: Can features of the communicative environment account for development? In L. Gleitman, & E. Wanner (Eds.). *Language acquisition: The state of the art*. Cambridge, Eng.: Cambridge, Univ. Press, in press.

17

DISCUSSION OF THE VOLUME
Explaining Transitions

Catherine E. Snow
Betty J. Gilbreath
Harvard Graduate School of Education

The problem which motivated and inspired the papers in this volume, and the conference on which the volume is based, is the puzzle of transition, of change, in human development. Clearly, change is the essence of what is interesting about development; if there were no transition points or discontinuities, then our theories of human development could be much simpler than they are. The notion that change is crucial in development is the essential claim of any stage theory of development. Paradoxically, though, stage theories are best at dealing with, describing, and accounting for the plateaus of nonchange, the within-stage phenomena. Stage theories do not help explain transitions except by noting that reorganization occurs between stages. The nature and the causes of change in human development are obscure to the degree that the change is important and general.

uncompromising

The problem of transitions remains as intransigent within the field of language acquisition as in other domains of human development. Years of research attention have produced increasingly detailed and useful descriptions of children's communicative abilities within different stages of development, but the nature and causes of the major transitions remain puzzling.

Growth within stages and domains, though not fully understood, seems at least comprehensible. It is an undeniably marvellous achievement for the child to move from a vocabulary of a few words to one of several hundred within a few months; from telegraphic-looking to well-formed utterances; from a limited set of syntactic structures to use of the full range within the adult language. Though impressive, however, these accomplishments are not intractably puzzling. They represent no major discontinuities. They are comprehensible, at least in theory,

∴ transition is continuous.

281

as the product of the efficient and creative application of certain identifiable principles.

discontinue here

Other points in the course of language development, however, seem to constitute real discontinuities. These developmental milestones indicate points where the child makes new discoveries and starts applying new principles. For each of these unexplained milestones, two questions remain unresolved: *how* the child makes the transition and *why* the transition occurs. For example, how and why does the child discover he can use arbitrary signals to effectively control his mother's attention and actions? How and why does the child move from using vocalizations in well-practiced, routinized sequences of naming a small set of objects or pictures to the discovery that everything has a name? How and why does the child, after struggling for months with the conflict between his need to express complex ideas and the limitations of single word utterances, suddenly break the limits and put two words together? How and why does the child move from rather limited and stereotyped two and three word utterances to fully productive use of his lexicon in multi-word combinations?

The current state of research on children's communicative development is such that the 'how' version of each of these questions is being dealt with, though it certainly is not answered for any of the phenomena. The 'why' version of each question has been almost ignored, yet it is in some ways much more interesting. Anyone who has struggled to learn a foreign language knows that it is hard work to remember all the details that make sentences correct. Anyone who has listened to a 2-year-old producing telegraphic-looking utterances knows furthermore that such details are unnecessary to effective communication. Why, then, do children make the effort to perfect their control of the language?

The only serious attempt to deal with the question 'why children learn to talk' *(1978)* comes from Dore (this volume). He proposes a motive for the child—the need to maintain interpersonal contact with the mother—as well as a motive for the mother—inducting her child into the social order. The maternal motive leads to the use of 'accountability procedures,' that can be seen as direct teaching devices. The interpersonal motives of both mother and child lead to 'nonaccountability' (which is equivalent if the maternal attitude is pro-child to play), which also contributes to learning language. Dore's paper in this volume deserves careful attention as the first serious attempt to deal with questions about *why* language acquisition occurs.

The explicit purpose of the conference held at the University of Delaware in September 1981, and of this volume of papers based on that conference, is to explore a pair of the intransigently puzzling transition points in communicative development: (1) the emergence of intentional communication; and (2) the emergence of the first words. This enterprise may have the broader theoretical relevance of generating a model for dealing with issues of continuity, transition, and reorganization throughout the course of language development. Such issues are, of course, at the center of the problems that concern all developmental theorists.

Explanations: The Kid Versus the World

The explanations that have been offered for the two transition points of interest are based on one of two factors: (1) the changes that go on inside the child's head; or (2) the nature of the social-interactive system of which the child is a member. The first explanation is usually called 'the cognition hypothesis,' and the second the 'social-interaction hypothesis.'

This dichotomy resembles another resilient dichotomy in the field of human development, heredity vs. environment. However, closer scrutiny makes clear that these two dichotomies are different. Researchers in the field of early communicative development remain remarkably unmired in the quicksand of nature-nurture arguments, which have so polarized positions on social interaction and later language acquisition. There is general agreement that heredity and environment contribute both to infants' cognitive development and to their social abilities. The critical issue is whether the transitions to intentional communication and to word use are crucially dependent on reorganizations inside the child's head or on the structure in and reorganizations of the social-interactive process.

This chapter reviews the answers offered to the question of how and why transitions occur, with special attention to the explanations presented in the other papers in this volume. In addition to identifying more clearly what the various positions are, and how they relate to one another, in the last section we present a perspective within which a synthesis of the social-interactive and the cognitive positions becomes possible.

The middle part of this chapter devotes more time to the social-interactive than the cognitive hypothesis, simply because the chapters in this volume are heavily weighted in that direction. We could have chosen to use this paper to redress the balance, and explore cognitive hypotheses more deeply. Instead, we have chosen to try to demonstrate that the distinction between cognitive and social-interactive explanations is an empty one.

The Social Interaction Hypothesis

A major theme of the papers collected here is that the transitions from prelinguistic interaction to intentional communication and from gesture to word, can be only understood if viewed within their social context. It can be demonstrated that the social context is structured in ways which could facilitate the child's discovery of new principles of communication. The existence of a facilitative social environment does not, however, constitute an argument that no transition is made. If the transition is primarily a cognitive achievement, one that occurs within the infant's head, then aspects of the social environment may facilitate and ease the transition, and the continuity achieved in the child's social communicative effectiveness may obscure the occurrence of the transition to the observer, but the transition must still be explained.

There are, as we see it, two ways in which people have used social interaction to explain (or explain away) the transitions to linguistic skills:

1. The social environment minimizes the demands on the child at each point, such that no major transition is ever necessary.

2. The social environment provides the structure that makes the transition possible. This is accomplished either by its general characteristics, or during key events such as negotiation sequences (see Golinkoff, this volume) or routines (see Bruner, this volume) from which the child can extract generally relevant principles.

The Social Environment Minimizes the Demands on the Child.   One argument proposes that studying the child's social environment illuminates the transitions by demonstrating the gradualness of the process. It is argued that any step forward the child takes in communicative skill is very small; there is, hence, no major increment in the child's communicative ability requiring a major cognitive reorganization. This might be called the 'illumination by elimination' argument. We give here two examples of the illumination-by-elimination argument, applied to the problem of *naming,* and to the problem of first *word-combinations.*

Naming.   The child's achievement of labeling presupposes the discovery of 'the referential principle,' which implies an understanding that everything has a name, similar things have the same name, and some things have specific names. This can be seen as a major step in language development. Explanations for this major transition have ranged from innateness (Dore, 1978) to seeing it as a correlate of the cognitive achievement of object permanence (Bloom, 1973; Corrigan, 1978, 1979). An alternate view, which emphasizes the gradual acquisition of naming, is available, based on data showing: (1) that labels are predictable and salient in caretaker speech (Messer, this volume); (2) that children's labeling develops from preverbal pointing (Murphy & Messer, 1977), from semi-verbal 'attention' markers (Carter, 1978), or even from the mouthing behaviors of early infancy (Piaget, 1963); (3) that highly formatted interaction situations such as book reading (Bruner, this volume; Ninio & Bruner, 1978) or ritualized naming games (McShane, 1980) contribute to the development of naming; and (4) that mothers respond to infants' points with object names (Masur, 1982; Murphy, 1978; Ninio & Bruner, 1978). Thus, it seems very possible that naming develops gradually, in complex and supportive social interaction situations. The apparent gap between nonverbal indication and true labeling narrows. Practice with *naming as a behavior* leads directly to the discovery of *naming as a principle*. The referential principle is no longer a mountain to be scaled, but a slope which the child can roll down gently.

Word Combinations.   A major question in child language research has been why it takes children so long, after they can deal with two ideas at one time, to be able to generate two words within one utterance. This decalage was a major *syntax* argument in support of the notion that syntax and semantics show distinguishable *semantics* developmental courses.

The first word combinations became somewhat less puzzling as a result of several very different observations: (1) the documentation of enormous change and growth in complexity of the semantic notions expressed by single word utterances (Bloom, 1973, Greenfield & Smith, 1976); (2) Branigan's finding (1979) that children produced two successive words with an inter-utterance pause, but single-utterance intonation contour, during the period just before they produced their first true two-word utterances; (3) the observation that children combined single word utterances with a gesture, a point, or another nonverbal indication (e.g., gaze), thus expressing a complex relationship; (4) the discovery of 'vertical constructions' or successive single-word utterances which are semantically related and express the same semantic relations as are prevalent in the first two-word utterances (Scollon, 1976); and (5) the finding that early processes of phonological simplification, which had been overcome in single-word speech, reappeared to simplify the phonological form of words in two-word utterances (deVilliers & deVilliers, 1978; Waterson, 1978).

In light of these observations, the enormous jump from one word to two words becomes a series of much more manageable steps, both in terms of meaning and in terms of speech processing (see Table 17.1). What looked to the observer in 1966 like a syntactic reorganization of the child's system appears in 1982 to be a long, gradual, laborious process during which no major reorganization occurs.

The Social Environment Provides the Structure That Makes the Transition Possible.   This volume is very rich in hypotheses about the way in which social *Bruner* interaction contributes to crucial communicative transitions. Harding discusses maternal responsiveness to specific infant signals we would identify as proto-communicative. Chapman shows the importance of adult gesture, of semantic restriction in adult speech, and of children's early induction into discourse rules. Levenstein demonstrates the effects of certain kinds of object-related and child-responsive talk. Ryan (1974), Lock (1980), McShane (1980, Ferrier (1978), Snow (1977 b), and many others have argued for the crucial role of the data-structuring provided by adult caretakers.

Messer, in his paper at the conference, gave an excellent interpretative summary of much of the literature, dividing social hypotheses into three camps:

TABLE 17.1
Steps Toward the Development of Two-Word Utterances

Meaning	Form
(a) holophrastic one-word utterances	(a) single words with sentence intonation, long inter-utterance pauses, simple phonological shapes
(b) one-word utterances expressing 'case' notions	(b) two words with long inter-word pause, single intonation contour; more complex phonological shapes
(c) combinations of one-word utterances with gesture	(c) two words with shorter inter-word pause, single intonation contour; more complex phonological shapes
(d) two-party vertical constructions	(d) two-words, no pause, single intonation contour, both words have heavy stress, simpler phonological shapes
(e) independent vertical constructions, with loosely related semantic notions expressed in successive one-word utterances	(e) two-word utterances, differentiated stress on the words, more complex phonological shapes
(f) successive one word utterances expressing semantic relations	
(g) two-word utterances expressing the same semantic relations as in (e)	

Messer :   *a methodological issue*

1. Caregivers' attribution of intention to infants' behaviors enables the infants to develop the notion of intentionality and to discover the communicative value of their own behaviors.

2. Negotiation of meaning between caregivers and infants gives infants the data necessary for learning language.

3. Caregivers' imposition of routines on children enables the child to learn their first communicative behaviors.

These three hypotheses, each suggesting a different way in which the social environment makes the crucial transitions possible, help to show how the chapters in this volume that emphasize the importance of social interaction still differ from one another.

Harding's paper discusses the importance of parental attribution of intention to the child, suggesting that the overinterpretation of child behaviors as intentional signals enables the child to discover his own intentions and his own capacity for intentionality. Similar suggestions have been made by Schaffer (1977), by Newson (1979), and by others. This hypothesis can be challenged on grounds that the parental attribution of intention is not universal, but typical only of North American/Western European mothers (see Schieffelin, this volume). How do the babies in cultures where this does not occur acquire the capacity for intentional communication? It is possible, of course, that reacting in general to infant behaviors, rather than attributing any specifically intentional interpretation to them, is the maternal behavior crucial to communicative development.

Golinkoff's recent research focuses on a subset of the cases under two, which she calls the 'negotiation of failed messages.' Golinkoff argues as follows:

> The steps taken to repair the communicative breakdown in episodes initiated by unsuccessful communicative attempts provide crucial information to the child about communication, and to the observer about the development of communication.

Bruner's paper presents a powerful case in support of the third hypothesis identified by Messer, the role of routines. The hypothesis that routines make a crucial contribution to communicative development is not new (see, for example, Bruner, 1975 a,b; Bruner & Sherwood, 1976; Haselkorn, 1981; Ninio & Bruner, 1978; Ratner & Bruner, 1978; Snow & Goldfield, 1982, in press). Before now, though, formats have been seen as just another aspect of the social environment that contributes to language, and not as its centrally important characteristic. While routines had been treated as the chocolate chips in Toll House cookies, relatively infrequent but essential and delicious, Bruner now suggests that they are more like the eggs in a chocolate souffle, contributing little to the flavor but everything to the structure of the dish.

Why do formats and routines work so effectively in *easing the transitions* from interaction to communication and from gesture or vocalization to word? Are formats magic because they are the first situations in which it becomes clear to the infant what the 'adult' or 'social' role is, and they, therefore, offer the first, best, or perhaps only, opportunity to satisfy one's needs to interact effectively by taking over the other's role? This is the explanation that has been subscribed to by Bruner, Snow, and others.

There is, however, another explanation for the magic effect of formatting on children's language growth: Perhaps formats provide the first situations within which adults understand children. Adults can actually comprehend and place the infant's behavior correctly and reliably if it occurs within the context of a format. They can, thus, respond to it appropriately, giving the infant the kind of contingent responding widely hypothesized to be crucial to language acquisition.

This view of routines is proposed by Haselkorn (1981) in her thesis. She argued that children's request behaviors are, at an early stage, quite 'incomplete,' in that most of the information the adult interactant needs to fulfill the request is not provided. The adults in her study were, nonetheless, highly effective in responding satisfactorily to request forms that occurred in, using Haselkorn's terms, 'routines' or 'formats.' Routines were previously established in the personal history of the adult–child pair and determined what should be done with a particular object (blowing up a balloon, opening a box, winding up a toy).

Formats are not object specific, but include general procedures for dealing with objects such as, "Do what you just did again," or "do what I just did," or "undo what I just did." The interaction around these routinized and formatted requests flowed quite smoothly, in Haselkorn's naturalistic data, and such request sequences showed considerable development during the 6 months of her observations.

It is entirely possible, of course, that formatted interactions work so well because they provide both these routes of facilitation—both the best opportunities for children to analyze, and learn how to act, and the best chance for adults to know what the children are doing. Mothers of 3-month-olds create an illusion of communication by inserting questions into the flow of infant behaviors, such that those behaviors can be treated as responses (Snow, 1977a). Mothers of 13-month-olds probably do the same thing to some extent, but the impression of comprehension may be somewhat less illusory, partly because 13-month-olds' behavior is organized and predictable enough that the adult can insert her questions and directives into the interaction much more artfully.

The Cognition Hypothesis

It has often been argued that too much credit is given to the role of social interaction in explaining communicative development. The fact that the social-interactive system in which the child participates is structured could perhaps explain how he or she communicates so effectively at some particular point in development (just as a groove in a pool table can explain why a ball rolls to a particular corner). However, it cannot easily explain how the child moves from stage to stage (one groove can only explain one path!).

Furthermore, whereas demonstrating the gradualness of the transitions across stages is very convincing, and helps to eliminate some of the 'magic' from our explanations of children's language acquisition, it does not help us to deal with the fact that the one-word child at 15 months has a very different cognitive organization from the 24-month-old with an MLU of 2.5. Is it perhaps the case that the gradualness of change in the child's external behavior masks rather apocalyptic internal reorganization, which we still need to explain? This presents the possibility that social interaction, rather than illuminating the transitions, provides the illusion of continuity by obfuscating the true transition points.

This possibility does not, of course, eliminate the problem of transitions, only their timing. Mothers, and sometimes even well-trained observers, mark as important events like the first word or the first two-word utterance. We argued earlier that these milestones can be viewed as the final small steps in a long history of minor achievements. At some point, though, children go beyond the need to learn all their new words from intensely involving dyadic formats, making the switch McShane (1980) describes from ritual to real naming. Similarly, children at some point go beyond the limitations of their early two-word utterances, moving from word-specific collocations to productive use of rules for word-combinations. The transitions of cognitively cataclysmic importance, out of ritual into productivity, are obscured by the folk-value attached to the earlier transitions, and by emphasis on continuity which emerges from placing so much emphasis on the social context of acquisition.

By the same logic, it is crucial when analyzing the development of routines and formats to take the analysis through to the critical transition that no one notices, beyond the obvious achievement of the child's having learned the routine to the less visible breakthrough when the routine breaks down. (Breakdowns in old routines may be the source of many of the negotiation episodes which Golinkoff reports on.) The existence of the routine provides the child and his mother with sufficient information about how to act that he can sometimes violate the routine without making his behavior incomprehensible. Violation is feasible, though, only if his mother lets him get away with it—positive nonaccountability, in Dore's terms. For example after a year during which he read one fairly complex picture book 12 times using the routine of going back again and again to the same small set of pictures, one child (see Snow & Goldfield, 1982, in press) abruptly switched to selecting previously undiscussed pictures on every single page of the book. What does such a breakdown of the routine mean about the child's developing linguistic cognitive system? Since this kind of transition has rarely been examined, we can hardly know.

The hypothesis that the important transitions in the child's communicative ability are the result of cognitive reorganizations is most closely identified with Piaget (1963), and with interpretations of Piaget's theory as applied to communication (Bates, Camaioni & Volterra, 1975; Corrigan 1978, 1979; Harding & Golinkoff, 1979; Sinclair, 1973; Sugarman, 1978). Both Harding (this volume) and Bruner (this volume) give reviews and analyses of how the cognitive hypothesis has fared.

Shatz (this volume) presents another perspective on how cognition could make the crucial contribution to communicative development, with her hypothesis that the coupling of previously independent and limited cognitive achievements results in sufficiently major reorganisation to explain the transitions.

Shatz' proposal leads almost inevitably to the question of how the original, limited cognitive steps are taken, and how the reorganizing coupling of the cognitive units occurs. What is the role of negotiation of meaning, negotiation of failed messages, adult responsiveness to minimal behaviors, or formatting in enabling the cognitive advances to be made?

Harding, Messer, Golinkoff, and Bruner all subscribe specifically in their chapters to the notion that social interaction and cognitive reorganization are both necessary to the development of communication. Harding describes how maternal responsiveness and inference of intent contribute to the development of communication, and how the cognitive achievements of means-end relationships, causality, recognition of another's agency, and tool-use contribute, without making fully clear how the social and the cognitive roots of communication relate to one another.

Messer suggests that acoustic and discourse properties of maternal utterances about objects contribute to communication by enabling the child to make the cognitive achievement of comprehending object labels. He is thus arguing that both social interaction and cognition play a crucial role in the development of communication, the first via its impact on the second.

Golinkoff argues that episodes during which mothers must and do work hard to determine what their infants want, constitute excellent occasions for the infants to make the cognitive discoveries that: (1) their intentions are important; and (2) some communicative forms work better than others.

Bruner argues for a much more complex interrelationship, in which the social-interactive framing provides training in the 'real-world' knowledge that makes the cognitive discoveries possible, and at the same time provides training in moving from prelinguistic to conventionalised ways of accomplishing one's aims. In Bruner's words, social interaction seems 'to be doing everything at once in a highly contextualized and organized fashion.'

We will argue in the next section for a more specific and more intimate set of connections between hypotheses concerning the facilitatory effects of social interaction and the reorganizing effects of cognitive development. Rather than arguing, as Harding, Messer, Golinkoff, and Bruner do, simply that both social interaction and cognitive development are prerequisite to communicative development, we argue that any specific hypothesis about the facilitatory effect of a social-interactive variable implies a hypothesis about mechanisms underlying cognitive development, and vice versa.

AN ALTERNATIVE HYPOTHESIS: SOCIAL-COGNITIVE PERSPECTIVE

The literature on the role of social interaction in language acquisition has, we feel, been somewhat confused because of the general tendency to pit social against cognitive explanations, rather than recognizing that any hypothesis about the optimal social environment implies a hypothesis about the cognitive mechanisms the child uses in language acquisition. Hypotheses about how the social environment facilitates transition do not exclude hypotheses about cognitive contributions to transition. They leave a space for cognitive hypotheses at two points: first, they recognize the existence of a transition, which is intrinsically a cognitive achievement, and second, they make an implicit claim about the nature of the child's cognitive processing mechanism, by virtue of proposing that a particular kind of information is optimally useful.

The inextricable connections between social and cognitive hypotheses will perhaps become clearer with examples. We will review some of the claims that

particular characteristics of the linguistic environment facilitate language acquisition, in order to demonstrate that they all imply hypotheses about the child's
cognitive processes.

1. Language acquisition is facilitated by short utterances which are syntactically simple and correct. This claim about linguistic input (which has been
supported empirically; see Furrow, Nelson, & Benedict, 1979), presupposes a
cognitive mechanism which cannot differentiate between correct and incorrect
utterances and which is easily overloaded by complexity. It suggests a cognitive
mechanism which will test hypotheses against clear cases more readily than
against unclear cases.

2. Language acquisition is facilitated by a linguistic environment which provides highly redundant linguistic signals, both within conversational episodes
(Snow, 1972) and across conversations (Broen, 1972). This claim presupposes
either: (1) a cognitive mechanism that operates on a probablistic basis and therefore is unlikely to make any generalization without several chances; or (2) one
that computes frequency and fails to register any form that has not achieved some
minimal frequency. The degree to which frequency of items is a crucial determinant of their acquisition has been hotly debated (Brown, 1973; Forner, 1977;
Moerk 1980, 1981; Pinker, 1981).

3. Language acquisition is facilitated by a linguistic environment which provides utterances restricted in semantic content and heavily weighted toward the
concrete and the here-and-now (Phillips, 1973). This claims presupposes a cognitive mechanism which searches for sound-meaning pairs; it operates by using
lexical and non-linguistic information to establish meanings, then assuming that
the simultaneous adult utterance expresses that meaning. Macnamara (1972) has
worked out the implications of this kind of cognitive mechanism.

4. Language acquisition is facilitated if the linguistic environment provides
correct adult utterances which express the child's simultaneous intention. This
claim associated with the literature on expansions (e.g., Cazden, 1965; Brown &
Bellugi, 1964; Nelson, Carskaddon and Bonvillian, 1973), assumes a mechanism for finding, recording, and analyzing sound-intention pairs.

5. Language acquisition is facilitated by utterances which are semantically
contingent on the child's previous utterance (Cross 1978) or behavior (Snow, de
Blauw & Dubber, 1982) and add information to that expressed by the child. This
claim presumes a mechanism which searches for sound-meaning pairs, which
switches attention from topic to topic only slowly, and which searches for more
information about the topic of its attention.

6. Language acquisition is facilitated by the occurrence of predictable events
and combinations of events with utterances (Snow & Goldfield, in press). This
claim presupposes a cognitive capacity to recognize recurrences of situations and
to remember adult utterances associated with specific events in those situations,
and a tendency to say during those events what the adult has said on previous
occurrences.

These claims, that particular aspects of the linguistic environment facilitate language learning, are all equally claims about children's cognitive capacities and limitations. Similarly, the hypotheses reviewed in the second section of this chapter concerning social facilitation of the transition into linguistic communication are all cognitive as much as social-interaction hypotheses, though the claims about cognition are usually left implicit.

Messer (this volume) and Harding (this volume) give good examples of social hypotheses which are integrated with cognitive hypotheses. Messer proposes that maternal labeling of objects with acoustically salient lexical items contributes to children's comprehension of word-meaning, and hence to language development. His argument presupposes a cognitive mechanism by virtue of which the child assumes that the salient word in the maternal utterance is a name for the simultaneously salient object. Harding suggests that maternal interpretations of infant behaviors enable the infant to make a cognitive leap to the level of appreciating his own capacity for intention. Her argument presupposes a cognitive mechanism, the workings of which are quite unclear, that somehow internalizes another's intention.

Does Social Interaction Facilitate Communicative Development?   Anyone reading through this volume is likely to be struck by how many different hypotheses were proposed concerning the ways in which social interaction facilitates the transition to intentional communication and to words. Similarly we reviewed six different hypotheses concerning the social facilitation of later language development. It seems that there are, if anything, too many social-interactive hypotheses floating around. How can one choose which among them is correct?

The correctness of any of these hypotheses remains in doubt. A serious source of question about the correctness of such claims arises because of inconsistency in results from different populations. As soon as a claim for the crucial contribution of any social variable to language development is made based on middle class North American, European, or Australian samples, results from studies of the Kipsigis (Harkness, 1977), the Gusii (LeVine, 1977), the Kaluli (Schieffelin, this volume), the Zincanteco (Brazelton, 1977), working class North Americans (Tulkin & Kagan, 1972), or some other group can be presented showing that variable to be absent.

These two facts—that many different features of the social environment can be shown to affect language acquisition, and that none of them is crucial—are, we think, intimately connected. They both relate furthermore to the fact that language is a highly buffered system which shows similar ease (though perhaps a different course) of development in widely differing social settings. For any single child in any social environment, several cognitive mechanisms are probably working simultaneously, whenever they receive the kind of linguistic information that they need from the social environment. Thus, the absence of the social features necessary to the functioning of one or another of the mechanisms in some environment would not be expected to block language acquisition—

there are several other mechanisms available and capable of working. By the same token, the demonstration that some features of the social environment facilitates language acquisition cannot be taken as evidence that it is crucial. There are undoubtedly individual (Goldfield, 1982) differences in the cognitive mechanisms available and preferred, just as there are cultural differences in the sorts of social facilitation offered.

It is clear that all normally developing children must have the ability to learn communication skills and language in many different ways. If the social environment is structured such that a particular cognitive mechanism can operate, it will. If the social environment does not allow the operation of one cognitive mechanism, then it will very likely support the operation of another one.

Resolutions

In the preface to this volume, Golinkoff and Gordon delineate a number of problems in the work on transitions to linguistic communication. The perspective presented in this chapter may help to solve some of these problems.

Briefly, the view expressed here is: (1) any claim about the desirable social environment for communicative development is equally a claim about cognitive mechanisms; (2) every child possesses a range of cognitive mechanisms which can operate in the service of learning about language and communication; and (3) different children and different social environments may exploit various subsets of the available cognitive mechanisms. *would explain long utterant a model*

This view is clearly consonant with the idea that the child is an active processor (see the Preface). It also suggests a way of understanding cross-cultural differences without requiring that every proposed social facilitator be universal. It helps us understand why the notion that children use empty syntactic frames might reappear and yet not be contradictory to the notion that children understand semantic roles; a mechanism searching for sound-meaning pairs can easily coexist with one responding to salient objects and actions. The fact that children can produce utterances that express semantic relations does not mean that all their utterances do so.

Golinkoff and Gordon are clearly right to suggest we need more information on parental belief systems to understand the nature of interaction with children. We cannot assume that parents from different classes and cultures differ only in their notions about how to promote communicative development; there is good evidence they also differ enormously on what they define as the desirable endpoint of communicative development (see, for example, LeVine, 1977, Schieffelin, this volume, Ward, 1971).

Golinkoff and Gordon's problem which motivated the conference is the most puzzling one. Why has research focused on the 10–12-month-old, and on the older, two-word utterance producer, but failed to explain much about the second year of life?

A rather unsettling possibility is that the second year of life is where the *real* transitions of interest are occurring, the ones inside the child's head that have been prepared, facilitated, smoothed over, and obfuscated by the social environment. Perhaps we have ignored the second year because explaining the changes that occur then is simply too hard for us.

REFERENCES

Bates, E., Camaioni, L., & Volterra, V. The acquisition of performatives prior to speech. *Merrill-Palmer Quarterly,* 1975, *21,* 205–226.

Bloom, L., *One word at a time.* The Hague: Mouton, 1973.

Branigan, G. Some reasons why successive single word utterances are not. *Journal of Child Language,* 1979, *6,* 443–458.

Brazelton, T. B. Implications of Infant Development among the Mayan Indians of Mexico. In P. Liederman, S. Tulkin, & A. Rosenfeld (Eds.), *Culture and infancy: Variations in the human experience.* New York: Academic Press, 1977.

Broen, P. A. The verbal environment of the language-learning child. *Monograph of American Speech and Hearing Association.* December, 1972. No. 17.

Brown, R. *A first language: The early stages.* Cambridge, Mass.: Harvard University Press, 1973.

Brown, R., & Bellugi, U. Three processes in the child's acquisition of syntax. *Harvard Educational Review,* 1964, *34,* 133–51.

Bruner, J. From communication to language: A psychological perspective. *Cognition,* 1975, *3,* 255–287. (a)

Bruner, J. The ontogenesis of speech acts. *Journal of Child Language.* 1975, *2,* 1–21. (b)

Bruner, J., & Sherwood, V. Peekaboo and the learning of rule structures. In J. Bruner, A. Jolly, & K. Sylva (Eds.) *Play: Its role in development and evolution.* Harmondsworth: Penguin, 1976.

Carter, A. From sensorimotor vocalizations to words: A case study of the evolution of attention-directing communication in the second year. In A. Lock (ed.), *Action, gesture, and symbol.* New York: Academic Press, 1978.

Cazden, C. Environmental assistance to the child's acquisition of grammar. Doctoral dissertation, Harvard University, 1965.

Corrigan, R. Language development as related to stage 6 object permanence development. *Journal of Child Language,* 1978, *5,* 173–190.

Corrigan, R. Cognitive correlates of language: Differential criteria yield differential results. *Child Development,* 1979, *50,* 617–631.

Cross, T. G. Mother's speech and its association with rate of linguistic development in young children. In N. Waterson, & C. Snow (Eds.) *The Development of Communication.* London: Wiley, 1978.

deVilliers, P., & deVilliers, J. Simplifying phonological processes in the one- and two-word stage. Paper presented at the Third Annual Boston University Conference on Language Development, October, 1978.

Dore, J. Cognition and communication in language acquisition and development. Special session paper, Third Annual Boston University Conference on Child Language Development, October, 1978.

Edwards, D. Sensorimotor intelligence and semantic relations in early child grammar. *Cognition,* 1973, *2,* 395–434.

Ferrier, L. Some observations of error in context. In N. Waterson, & C. Snow (Eds.) *The Development of Communication.* London: Wiley, 1978.

Forner, M. The mother as LAD: Interaction between order and frequency of parental input and child production. In F. Eckman, & A. Hastings (Eds.), *Studies in first and second language acquisition.* Rowley, Mass.: Newbury House, 1977.

Furrow, P. Nelson, K., & Benedict, H. Mothers' speech to children and syntactic development: Some simple relationships *Journal of Child Language,* 1979, *7,* 423–442.

Goldfield, B. Variation in child language: Form, function, and strategy. Qualifying paper. Harvard Graduate School of Education, August 1982.

Greenfield, P., & Smith, J. *The structure of communication in early language development.* New York: Academic Press, 1976.

Harding, C., & Golinkoff, R. The origins of intentional vocalisations in prelinguistic infants. *Child Development,* 1979, *50,* 33–40.

Harkness, S. Aspects of social environment and first language acquisition in rural Africa. In C. Snow, & C. Ferguson (Eds.) *Talking to children: language input and acquisition,* Cambridge, England: Cambridge University Press, 1977.

Haselkorn, S. The development of the requests of young children from nonverbal strategies to the power of language. Doctoral thesis, Harvard University, 1981.

LeVine, R. Child rearing as cultural adaptation. In P. H. Liederman, S. Tulkin, & A. Rosenfeld, (Eds.), *Culture and infancy: Variations in the human experience.* New York: Academic Press, 1977.

Lock, A. *The guided reinvention of language.* New York: Academic Press, 1980.

Macnamara, J. Cognitive basis of language learning in infants. *Psychological Review,* 1972, *79,* 1–13.

MacShane, J. *Learning to talk.* Cambridge, England: Cambridge University Press, 1980.

Masur, E. Mothers' responses to infants' object-related gestures: Influences on lexical development. *Journal of Child Language,* 1982, *9,* 23–30.

Moerk, E. Relationships between parental input frequencies and children's language acquisition: A reanalysis of Brown's data. *Journal of Child Language,* 1980, *7,* 105–118.

Moerk, E. To attend or not to attend to unwelcome reanalyses? A reply to Pinker. *Journal of Child Language,* 1981, *8,* 627–632.

Murphy, C. M. Pointing in the context of a shared activity. *Child Development,* 1978, *49,* 371–80.

Murphy, C. M., & Messer, D. Mothers, infants, and pointing: A study of a gesture. In H. Schaffer (Ed.), *Studies in mother-infant interaction.* London: Academic Press, 1977.

Nelson, N. E., Carskaddon, G., & Bonvillian, J. Syntax acquisition: Impact of experimental variation in adult verbal interaction with the child. *Child Development,* 1973, *44,* 497–504.

Newson, J. Dialogue and development. In A. Lock (Ed.) *Action, Gesture and Symbol.* London: Academic Press, 1979.

Ninio, A., & Bruner, J. The achievement and antecedents of labeling. *Journal of Child Language,* 1978, *5,* 1–15.

Phillips, J. Syntax and vocabulary of mothers' speech to young children: Age and sex comparisons. *Child Development,* 1973, *44,* 182–185.

Piaget, J. *The origins of intelligence in the child.* New York: Norton, 1963.

Pinker, S. On the acquisition of grammatical morphemes. *Journal of Child Language,* 1981, *8,* 477–484.

Ratner, N., & Bruner, J. Games, social exchange, and the acquisition of language. *Journal of Child Language,* 1978, *5,* 391–402.

Ryan, J. Early language development: Towards a communicational analysis. In M. P. M. Richards (Ed.), *The integration of a child into a social world.* Cambridge, England: Cambridge University Press, 1974.

Scollon, R. *Conversations with a 1-year-old: A case study for the developmental foundation of syntax.* Hawaii: University Press of Hawaii, 1976.

Schaffer, R. *Mothering.* Cambridge, Mass: Harvard University Press, 1977.

Sinclair, H. Language acquisition and cognitive development. In T. Moore (Ed.), *Cognitive development and the acquisition of language*. New York: Academic Press, 1973.

Snow, C. Mother's speech to children learning language. *Child Development,* 1972, *43,* 549–65.

Snow, C. The development of conversation between mothers and babies. *Journal of Child Language,* 1977, *4,* 1–22. (a)

Snow, C. Mothers speech research: From input to interaction. In C. Snow, & C. Ferguson (Eds.) *Talking to children: language input and acquisition.* Cambridge, England: Cambridge University Press, 1977. (b)

Snow, C., de Blauw, A., & Dubber, C. Are parents language teachers? In K. Borman (Ed.) *Social life of children in a changing society.* Hillsdale, N.J.: Lawrence Erlbaum Associates, 1982.

Snow, C., & Goldfield, B. Building stories: The emergence of information structures from conversation and narrative. In D. Tannen (Ed.) Georgetown University Roundtable on Language and Linguistics, 1981. *Analyzing Discourse: Text and Talk,* Georgetown University Press, Washington, D.C. 1982.

Snow, C., & Goldfield B. Turn the page please: Situation-specific language learning. *Journal of Child Language* in press.

Sugarman, S. Some organizational aspects of preverbal communication. In I. Markova (Ed.,) *The social context of language,* New York: Wiley, 1978.

Tulkin, S., & Kagan, J. Mother–child interaction in the first year of life. *Child Development,* 1972, *43,* 31–41.

Ward, M. C. *Them children: A study in language learning.* New York: Holt, Rinehart & Winston, 1971.

Waterson, N. Growth of complexity in phonological development. In N. Waterson, & C. Snow (Eds.) *The Development of Communication.* London: Wiley, 1978.

Author Index

Numbers in *italics* denote pages with complete bibliographic information.

Subject Index